Ford Ca[pri] 1300 & 1600 ohv Owners Workshop Manual

by J H Haynes
Member of the Guild of Motoring Writers
and J R S Hall

Models covered:

Capri 1300, January 1969 to February 1974
Capri 1600, January 1969 to September 1972
Covers Standard, L, XL, GT XL and GT XLR models;
manual and automatic transmission
Does not cover Capri I ohc or Capri II models

ISBN 0 85696 542 1

© Haynes Publishing Group 1971, 1978, 1979

ABCDE
FGHIJ
KL

All rights reserved. No part of this book may be reproduced or transmitted in any form or by any means, electronic or mechanical, including photocopying, recording or by any information storage or retrieval system, without permission in writing from the copyright holder.

Printed in England   (029-7D2)

Haynes

**HAYNES PUBLISHING GROUP
SPARKFORD YEOVIL SOMERSET ENGLAND**
distributed in the USA by
**HAYNES PUBLICATIONS INC
861 LAWRENCE DRIVE
NEWBURY PARK
CALIFORNIA 91320
USA**

Acknowledgements

Thanks are due to the Ford Motor Company Ltd for their assistance with the supply of technical material and for the use of certain illustrations; to Castrol Ltd who supplied details on lubrication and to the Champion Sparking Plug Company for the illustrations showing the various spark plug conditions. The bodywork repair photographs used in this manual were provided by Lloyds Industries Limited who supply 'Turtle Wax', 'Duplicolor Holts' and other Holts range products. Thanks must also go to D.H.Stead, R.T.Grainger and L.Tooze for their assistance when working on the engine and gearbox, and Lt Col F.T. Nicholson for advice on the text.

Last but not least thanks must go to all those people at Sparkford who assisted in the production of this manual, especially Alex Jones, Peter Ward and Lee Saunders.

Photographic Captions & Cross References

The book is divided into thirteen chapters. Each chapter is divided into numbered sections which are headed in **bold type** between horizontal lines. Each section consists of serially numbered paragraphs.

There are two types of illustration. (1) Figures which are numbered according to Chapter and sequence of occurrence in that chapter and having an individual caption to each figure. (2) Photographs which have a reference number in the bottom left-hand corner. All photographs apply to the chapter in which they occur so that the reference figures pinpoint the pertinent section and paragraph numbers.

Procedures, once described in the text, are not normally repeated. If it is necessary to refer to another chapter the reference will be given in chapter number and section number thus:- Chapter 1/6.

If it is considered necessary to refer to a particular paragraph in another chapter the reference is 'Chapter 1/6:5'. Cross references given without use of the word 'Chapter' apply to sections and/or paragraphs in the same chapter, e.g., 'see Section 8' means also 'in this chapter'.

When the left or right-hand side of a car is mentioned it is as if one was looking in the forward direction of travel.

Whilst every care is taken to ensure that the information in this manual is correct bearing in mind the changes in design and specification which are a continuous process, even within a model range, no liability can be accepted by the authors and publishers for any loss, damage or injury caused by any errors or omissions in the information given.

Ford Capri 1600 GT

Introduction

This manual is intended for those who wish to find out more about the Capri 1300 and 1600, which they may own, and to show them also how to carry out the maintenance and repairs necessary to keep it performing safely and economically.

The older a car gets the more attention it will need as normal wear and tear takes its toll. Thus the buyer of a cheaper, older model is faced with the need for more attention to his vehicle in order to enable it to run safely and pass the tests required by law every 12 months. As the purchase of a cheaper car is usually due to economic necessity it follows that garage bills are equally to be avoided.

This manual is the only one written which is based on the author's personal experiences. The hands in most of the photographs are those of the person who has written the book. Manufacturers' own official workshop manuals are all very well for those whose knowledge on certain basic terminology and methods is assumed. For the rest, this manual provides clear illustrations and descriptions of the order and method for the jobs to be done, step by step.

It must be assumed that a range of tools is available to the do-it-yourself owner. The accumulation of good tools is normally done over a period of time and this is the one expense that the do-it-yourself man must be prepared for. Never buy cheap tools. Be discreet in borrowing tools and do not be annoyed if someone refuses to lend them. Appreciate how much they cost if lost or damaged.

Certain jobs required specialised tools and where these are essential this manual will say so. Otherwise alternative means are given. Much of the work involved in looking after a car and carrying out repairs depends on accurate diagnosis in the first place. Where possible therefore, a methodical and progressive way of diagnosis is presented. The time that can be wasted in hopping from one possible source of trouble to another suggested at random quite often by self styled 'experts' must have been experienced by many people. It is best to say at the start therefore, 'this could be one of several things - let's get the book out'.

Contents

Chapter	Section	Page	Section	Page
	Introduction	4	Recommended Lubricants	2
	Tools & Working Facilities	6	Ordering Spare Parts	3
	Routine Maintenance	8		
	Lubrication Chart	11		
1. Engine	General Description	8	Decarbonisation	4
	Removal	9	Reassembly	6
	Dismantling	2	Replacement	4
	Examination & Renovation	2	Fault Finding Chart	5
2. Cooling System	General Description	46	Water Pump	50
	Draining, Flushing	48	Fan Belt	50
	Radiator	48	Anti-freeze Mixture	52
	Thermostat	48	Fault Finding Chart	52
3. Fuel System & Carburation	General Description	54	Fuel Tank	58
	Air Cleaners	54	Carburetters	58
	Fuel Pump	56	Exhaust System	68
	Fuel Gauge	58	Fault Finding Chart	71
4. Ignition System	General Description	74	Sparking Plugs	78
	Condenser	74	Ignition Timing	78
	Distributor	76	Fault Finding	79
5. Clutch & Actuating Mechanism	General Description	82	Clutch Inspection	84
	Clutch Pedal	84	Clutch Cable	84
	Clutch Removal	84	Clutch Release Bearing	84
	Clutch Replacement	84	Faults	86
6. Gearbox	General Description	88	Mainshaft	94
	Removal & Replacement	90	Selective Circlips	96
	Dismantling	90	Reassembly	96
	Input Shaft	94	Fault Finding Chart	101
7. Propeller Shaft & Univeral Joints	General Description	102	Two Piece Propeller Shaft	104
	One Piece Propeller Shaft	102		
8. Rear Axle	General Description	106	Half Shafts	108
	Rear Axle - Removal and Replacement	108	Differential Carrier	108
9. Braking System	General Description	111	Pedals	116
	Rear Wheel Cylinders	114	Dual Braking System	120
	Brake Master Cylinder	116	Vacuum Servo Unit	124
	Handbrake	116	Fault Finding Chart	126
10. Electrical System	General Description	129	Starter Motor	136
	Battery	130	Control Box	138
	Dynamo	131	Windscreen Wipers	142
	Alternator	134	Fault Finding Chart	155
11. Suspension - Dampers - Steering	General Description	159	Rack & Pinion Steering Gear	162
	Front Hub	160	Steering Wheel & Column	166
	Front Suspension	160	Rear Springs	166
	Torsion Bar	162	Fault Finding Chart	171
12. Bodywork & Underframe	Maintenance	171	Doors	173
	Repairs	172	Bonnet	177
	Bumpers	172	Heater	180
13. Supplement	Engine	182	Braking System	191
	Cooling System	184	Electrical System	191
	Fuel System	184	Suspension and Steering	193
	Ignition System	185	Bodywork and Underframe	194
	Automatic Transmission	186		

Index   197

Tools and Working Facilities

INTRODUCTION

A selection of good tools is a fundamental requirement for anyone contemplating the maintenance and repair of a motor vehicle. For the owner who does not possess any, their purchase will prove a considerable expense, offsetting some of the savings made by doing-it-yourself. However, provided that the tools are of good quality, they will last for many years and prove an extremely worthwhile investment.

To help the average owner to decide which tools are needed to carry out the various tasks detailed in this manual, we have compiled three lists of tools under the following headings: *Maintenance and minor repair, Repair and overhaul,* and *Special*. The newcomer to practical mechanics should start off with the *Maintenance and minor repair* tool kit and confine himself to the simpler jobs around the vehicle. Then, as his confidence and experience grows, he can undertake more difficult tasks, buying extra tools as, and when, they are needed. In this way, a *Maintenance and minor repair* tool kit can be built-up into a *Repair and overhaul* tool kit over a considerable period of time without any major cash outlays. The experienced do-it-yourselfer will have a tool kit good enough for most repair and overhaul procedures and will add tools from the *Special* category when he feels the expense is justified by the amount of use to which these tools will be put.

It is obviously not possible to cover the subject of tools fully here. For those who wish to learn more about tools and their use there is a book entitled *How to Choose and Use Car Tools* available from the publishers of this manual.

MAINTENANCE AND MINOR REPAIR TOOL KIT

The tools given in this list should be considered as a minimum requirement if routine maintenance, servicing and minor repair operations are to be undertaken. We recommend the purchase of combination spanners (ring one end, open-ended the other); although more expensive than open-ended ones, they do give the advantages of both types of spanner.

Combination spanners - 7/16, 1/2, 9/16, 5/8, 11/16, 3/4, 13/16 & 15/16 in AF
Adjustable spanner - 9 inch
Engine sump/gearbox/rear axle drain plug (where applicable)
Spark plug spanner (with rubber insert)
Spark plug gap adjustment tool
Set of feeler gauges
Brake adjuster spanner (where applicable)
Brake bleed nipple spanner
Screwdriver - 4 in long x ¼ dia (flat blade)
Screwdriver - 4 in long x ¼ dia (cross blade)
Combination pliers - 6 inch
Hacksaw, junior
Tyre pump
Tyre pressure gauge
Grease gun (where applicable)
Oil can
Fine emery cloth (1 sheet)
Wire brush (small)
Funnel (medium size)

REPAIR AND OVERHAUL TOOL KIT

These tools are virtually essential for anyone undertaking any major repairs to a motor vehicle, and are additional to those given in the *Maintenance and minor repair* list. Included in this list is a very comprehensive set of sockets. Although these are expensive they will be found invaluable as they are so versatile - particularly if various drives are included in the set. We recommend the ½ in. square-drive type, as this can be used with most proprietary torque wrenches. If you cannot afford a socket set, even bought piecemeal, then inexpensive tubular box spanners are a useful alternative.

The tools in this list will occasionally need to be supplemented by tools from the *Special* list.

Sockets (or box spanners) to cover range in previous list
Reversible ratchet drive (for use with sockets)
Extension piece, 10 inch (for use with sockets)
Universal joint (for use with sockets)
Torque wrench (for use with sockets)
'Mole' wrench - 8 inch
Ball pein hammer
Soft-faced hammer, plastic or rubber
Screwdriver - 6 in long x 5/16 in dia (flat blade)
Screwdriver - 2 in long x 5/16 square (flat blade)
Screwdriver - 1½ in long x ¼ dia (cross blade)
Screwdriver - 3 in long x 1/8 in dia (electricians)
Pliers - electricians side cutters
Pliers - needle nosed
Pliers - circlip (internal and external)
Cold chisel - ½ inch
Scriber (this can be made by grinding the end of a broken hacksaw blade)
Scraper (this can be made by flattening and sharpening one end of a piece of copper pipe)
Centre punch
Pin punch
Hacksaw
Valve grinding tool
Steel rule/straight edge
Allen keys
Selection of files
Wire brush (large)
Axle-stands
Jack (strong scissor or hydraulic type)

SPECIAL TOOLS

The tools in this list are those which not used regularly, are expensive to buy, or which need to be used in accordance with their manufacturers' instructions. Unless relatively difficult mechanical jobs are undertaken frequently, it will not be economic to buy many of these tools. Where this is the case, you could consider clubbing together with friends (or a motorists' club) to make a joint purchase, or borrowing tools against a deposit from a local garage or tool hire specialist.

The following list contains only those tools and instruments freely available to the public, and not those special tools produced by the vehicle manufacturer specifically for its dealer network. You will find occasional reference to these manufacturers special tools in the text of this manual. Generally, an alternative method of doing the job without the vehicle manufacturer's special tool is given. However,

Tools & Working Facilities

sometimes, there is no alternative to using them. Where this is the case and the relevant tool cannot be bought or borrowed you will have to entrust the work to a franchised garage.

Valve spring compressor
Piston ring compressor
Balljoint separator
Universal hub/bearing puller
Impact screwdriver
Micrometer and/or vernier gauge
Carburettor flow balancing device (where applicable)
Dial gauge
Stroboscopic timing light
Dwell angle meter/tachometer
Universal electrical multi-meter
Cylinder compression gauge
Lifting tackle
Trolley jack
Light with extension lead

BUYING TOOLS

For practically all tools a tool factor is the best source since he will have a very comprehensive range compared with the average garage or accessory shop. Having said that, accessory shops often offer excellent quality tools at discount prices, so it pays to shop around.

Remember, you don't always have to buy the most expensive items on the shelf, but it is always advisable to steer clear of the very cheap tools. There are plenty of good tools around at reasonable prices, so ask the proprietor or manager of the shop for advice before making a purchase.

CARE AND MAINTENANCE OF TOOLS

Having purchased a reasonable tool kit, it is necessary to keep the tools in a clean seviceable condition. After use, always wipe off any dirt, grease and metal particles using a clean, dry cloth, before putting the tools away. Never leave them lying around after thay have been used. A simple tool rack on the garage or workshop wall, for items such as screwdrivers and pliers is a good idea. Store all normal spanners and sockets in a metal box. Any measuring instruments gauges, meters, etc, must be carefully stored where they cannot be damaged or become rusty.

Take a little care when tools are used. Hammer heads inevitably become marked and screwdrivers lose the keen edge on their blades from time-to-time. A little timely attention with emery cloth or a file will soon resore items like this to a good seviceable finish.

WORKING FACILITIES

Not to be forgotten when discussing tools, is the workshop itself. If anything more than routine maintenance is to be carried out, some form of suitable working area becomes essential.

It is appreciated that many an owner mechanic is forced by circumstances to remove an engine or similar item, without the benefit of a garage or workshop. Having done this, any repairs should always be done under cover of a roof.

Wherever possible, any dismantling should be done on a clean flat workbench or table at a suitable working height.

Any workbench needs a vice: one with a jaw opening of 4 in (100 mm) is suitable for most jobs. As mentioned previously, some clean dry storage space is also required for tools, as well as the lubricants, cleaning fluids, touch-up paints and so on which become necessary.

Another item which may be required, and which has a much more general usage, is an electric drill with a chuck capacity of at least 5/16 in (8 mm). This, together with a good range of twist drills, is virtually essential for fitting accessories such as wing mirrors and reversing lights.

Last, but not least, always keep a supply of old newspapers and clean, lint-free rags available, and try to keep any working area as clean as possible.

SPANNER JAW GAP COMPARISON TABLE

Jaw gap (in)	Spanner size
0.250	¼ in AF
0.275	7 mm AF
0.312	5/16 in AF
0.315	8 mm AF
0.340	11/32 in AF; 1/8 in Whitworth
0.354	9 mm AF
0.375	3/8 in AF
0.393	10 mm AF
0.433	11 mm AF
0.437	7/16 in AF
0.445	3/16 in Whitworth; ¼ in BSF
0.472	12 mm AF
0.500	½ in AF
0.512	13 mm AF
0.525	¼ in Whitworth; 5/16 in BSF
0.551	14 mm AF
0.562	9/16 in AF
0.590	15 mm AF
0.600	5/16 in Whitworth; 3/8 in BSF
0.625	5/8 in AF
0.629	16 mm AF
0.669	17 mm AF
0.687	11/16 in AF
0.708	18 mm AF
0.710	3/8 in Whitworth; 7/16 in BSF
0.748	19 mm AF
0.750	¾ in AF
0.812	13/16 in AF
0.820	7/16 in Whitworth; ½ in BSF
0.866	22 mm AF
0.875	7/8 in AF
0.920	½ in Whitworth; 9/16 in BSF
0.937	15/16 in AF
0.944	24 mm AF
1.000	1 in AF
1.010	9/16 in Whitworth; 5/8 in BSF
1.023	26 mm AF
1.062	1 1/16 in AF; 27 mm AF
1.100	5/8 in Whitworth; 11/16 in BSF
1.125	1 1/8 in AF
1.181	30 mm AF
1.200	11/16 in Whitworth; ¾ in BSF
1.250	1¼ in AF
1.259	32 mm AF
1.300	¾ in Whitworth; 7/8 in BSF
1.312	1 5/16 in AF
1.390	13/16 in Whitworth; 15/16 in BSF
1.417	36 mm AF
1.437	1 7/16 in AF
1.480	7/8 in Whitworth; 1 in BSF
1.500	1½ in AF
1.574	40 mm AF; 15/16 in Whitworth
1.614	41 mm AF
1.625	15/8 in AF
1.670	1 in Whitworth; 1 1/8 in BSF
1.687	1 11/16 in AF
1.811	46 mm AF
1.812	1 13/16 in AF
1.860	1 1/8 in Whitworth; 1¼ in BSF
1.875	1 7/8 in AF
1.968	50 mm AF
2.000	2 in AF
2.050	1¼ in Whitworth; 1 3/8 in BSF
2.165	55 mm AF
2.362	60 mm AF

Routine Maintenance

Maintenance should be regarded as essential for ensuring safety and desirable for the purpose of obtaining economy and performance from the car. By far the largest element of the maintenance routine is visual examination. Each chapter of the manual gives details of the routine maintenance requirements. In the summary given here the safety items are shown in **bold type**. These **must** be attended to regularly in the interests of preventing accidents and possible loss of life.

Neglect of other items results in unreliability, overall increased running costs and more rapid depreciation of the value of the car.

500 miles

EVERY 500 MILES (or weekly)

ENGINE
  Check the oil level in the sump and top up as required.
  Check the radiator coolant level and top up as required.
  Check the battery electrolyte level and top up as required.

STEERING
  Check the tyre pressures.
  Examine tyres for wear or damage.
  Is the steering still smooth and accurate?

BRAKES
  Check the hydraulic fluid reservoir level. If a significant drop is apparent examine the system for leaks immediately.
  Is there any reduction in braking efficiency?
  Try an emergency stop. Is adjustment necessary?

LIGHTS
  Do all bulbs work at the front and rear?
  Are the headlight beams correctly aligned?

Routine Maintenance

6,000 miles

EVERY 6,000 MILES (or every six months if 6,000 miles are not exceeded) or if indications are that safety items in particular are not performing correctly.

ENGINE
Drain the sump of oil when hot, renew the oil filter element and refill the sump with fresh oil.
Check the valve clearances and adjust as necessary.
Check the distributor contact breaker points and adjust as necessary.
Check the tension of the fan belt.
Clean the fuel pump filter.
Check the sparking plug electrode gaps.
Lubricate the distributor.
Lubricate the generator rear end bush.

CLUTCH
Check the clutch cable adjustment and adjust as required.

STEERING
Is there free play between the steering wheel and road wheels?
Examine all steering linkage rods, joints and bushes for signs of wear or damage.
Check the front wheel hub bearings and adjust if necessary.
Check the oil level in the steering box and top up as required.

BRAKES
Examine the disc pads and drum shoes to determine the amount of friction material remaining. Renew as necessary.
Examine all hydraulic pipes, cylinders and unions for signs of chafing, corrosion, dents or any other form of deterioration or leaks.

SUSPENSION
Examine all bolts and shackles securing the suspension units and springs and tighten as necessary.
Check for play in the rubber bushes.

12,000 miles

EVERY 12,000 MILES (or annually if 12,000 miles are not exceeded) or if indications are that safety items in particular are not performing correctly.

ENGINE
Fit new distributor contact breaker points.
Fit new sparking plugs.
Fit a new carburetter air cleaner element.
Flush out the cooling system.

GEARBOX
Check the oil level and top up as required.

REAR AXLE
Check the oil level and top up as required.

STEERING
Remove front wheel hub bearings, flush, inspect and repack with grease.

BODYFRAME
Examine for rust where suspension is attached.

Checking fan belt tension

clutch cable adjustment

Air filter element

Routine Maintenance

36,000 miles

GEARBOX
Drain and replenish the oil.

REAR AXLE
Drain and replenish the oil.

Additionally the following items should be attended to as time can be spared:—

CLEANING
Examination of components requires that they be cleaned. The same applies to the body of the car, inside and out, in order that deterioration due to rust or unknown damage may be detected. Certain parts of the bodyframe, if rusted badly, can result in the vehicle being declared unsafe and it will not pass the annual test for roadworthiness.

EXHAUST SYSTEM
An exhaust system must be leakproof, and the noise level below a certain minimum. Excessive leaks may cause carbon monoxide fumes to enter the passenger compartment. Excessive noise constitutes a public nuisance. Both these faults may cause the vehicle to be kept off the road. Repair or replace defective sections when symptoms are apparent.

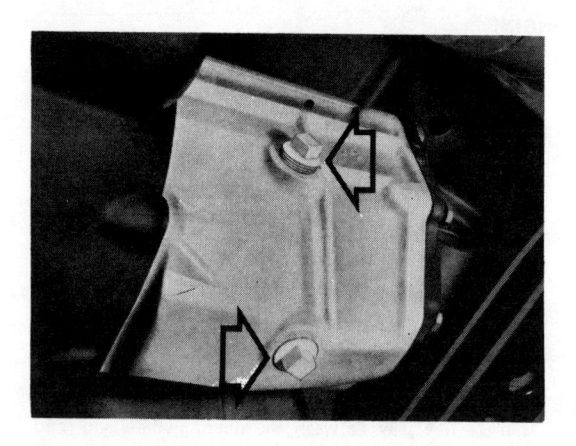

Gearbox drain and filler plugs

LUBRICATION CHART

EXPLANATION OF SYMBOLS

● **CASTROL GTX**
An ultra high performance motor oil approved for use in the engine in summer and winter.

◯ **CASTROL HYPOY LIGHT GEAR OIL**
A powerful, extreme pressure lubricant recommended for the transmission and steering gear.

◯ **CASTROL HYPOY GEAR OIL**
A powerful, extreme-pressure gear oil essential for the lubrication of the hypoid rear axle.

▢ **CASTROL LM GREASE**
Recommended for the wheel bearings. May also be used for chassis lubrication.

WEEKLY

●

ENGINE
Check oil level, and if necessary refill to correct level with **Castrol GTX**.

EVERY 6,000 MILES
Including Weekly service

●

ENGINE
After the first 3,000 miles, and thereafter every 6,000 miles, drain off the old oil while warm, clean and replace drain plug, change complete filter unit. Refill with fresh **Castrol GTX**.

NOTE:—Owners are advised that more frequent sump-draining periods are desirable if the operation of the car involves:—

(1) *Frequent stop/start driving.
(2) *Operation during cold weather, especially when appreciable engine idling is involved.
(3) *When much driving is done under dusty conditions.

*When such conditions are experienced, consult your authorised dealer regarding **Ford Midway Service**.

SUMP CAPACITY:—

1300
1300 GT } all in-line engines
1600   } 7.184 pints including
1600 GT } filter and oilways

◯

GEARBOX.
At the first 3,000 miles, drain the gearbox while warm and refill with **Castrol Hypoy Light Gear Oil**. No further draining of this unit is required and it is only necessary to check and top up the level if required every 6,000 miles. Use **Castrol Hypoy Light Gear Oil**.
Capacity—1.97 pts.

OVERSEAS
Castrol Hypoy Light Gear Oil is recommended for all climatic conditions.

EVERY 6,000 MILES

◯

REAR AXLE
At the first 3,000 miles, thereafter every 6,000 miles, check the oil level and top up if necessary to the correct level with **Castrol Hypoy Gear Oil**.
Capacity: 2 pints.

V.4. models only:
Rear axle capacity: 1.9 pints.

OVERSEAS
Air temperature below 23°C
Castrol Hypoy Light Gear Oil.

EVERY 24,000 MILES

▢

FRONT WHEEL BEARINGS.
After the first 27,000, thereafter every 24,000 miles, repack and adjust the front wheel bearings. Use **Castrol LM Grease**.

11

Recommended Lubricants

COMPONENT	TYPE OF LUBRICANT OR FLUID	CASTROL PRODUCT
ENGINE	Multigrade engine oil	Castrol GTX
GEARBOX	S.A.E. 80 E.P	Castrol Hypoy Light
REAR AXLE	S.A.E. 90 E.P	Castrol Hypoy
STEERING BOX	S.A.E. 90 E.P	Castrol Hypoy
FRONT WHEEL BEARINGS	Medium grade multi-purpose grease	Castrol L.M. grease
DISTRIBUTOR, STARTER & GENERATOR BUSHES	Engine or light oil	Castrol GTX
DISTRIBUTOR CONTACT BREAKER CAM & BATTERY	Petroleum jelly	
UPPER CYLINDER LUBRICANT		'Castrollo'
HYDRAULIC PISTONS	Rubber grease	Castrol rubber grease
BRAKE MASTER CYLINDER FLUID RESERVOIR	Hydraulic fluid	Castrol Girling brake fluid

Additionally Castrol 'Everyman' oil can be used to lubricate door, boot and bonnet hinges, locks and pivots etc.

Ordering Spare Parts

Buy genuine Fo Mo Co spare parts from a Ford dealer direct, or through a local garage. If you go to an authorised dealer the correctly fitting genuine parts can usually be supplied from stock which, of course, is a greatly added convenience.

Always have details of the car's serial number available when obtaining parts. If you can take along the part to be renewed as well it is helpful. Modifications are a continuing and unpublicized process in car manufacture, apart from all the variations of model types. If a storeman says he cannot guarantee that the part he supplies is correct, because the engine number is not known, he is perfectly justified. Variations can occur from month to month.

The vehicle identification plate is mounted on the right hand mudguard apron inside the engine compartment. It is not a bad idea to write down the details in your diary or pocket book.

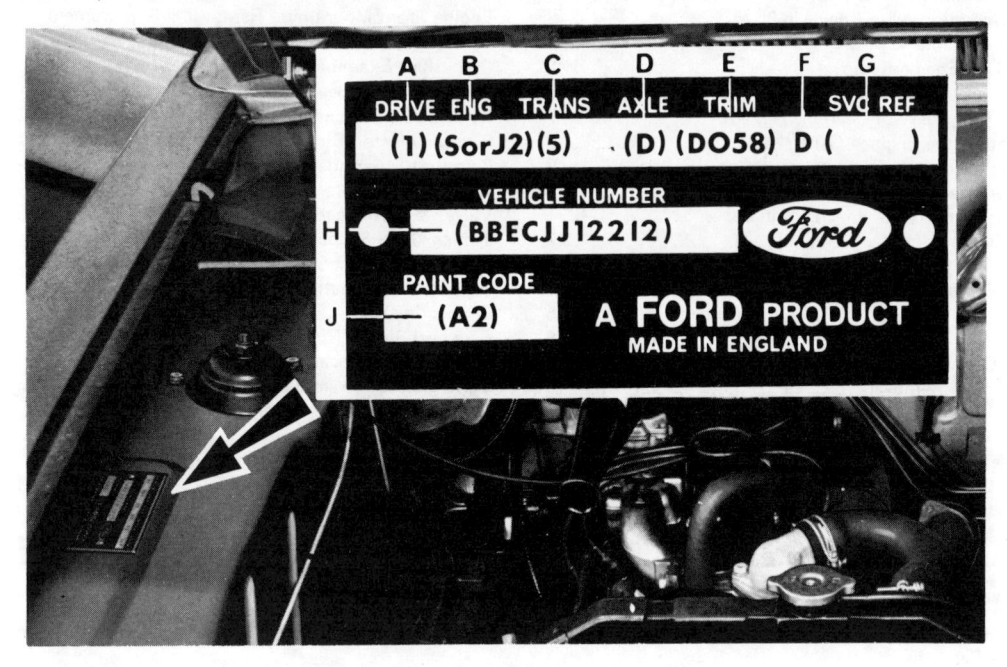

	A	B	C	D	E	F	G
	DRIVE	ENG	TRANS	AXLE	TRIM		SVC REF
	(1)	(S or J2)	(5)	(D)	(DO58)	D	( )

VEHICLE NUMBER
H — (BBECJJ12212)   Ford

PAINT CODE
J — (A2)

A FORD PRODUCT
MADE IN ENGLAND

A:—DRIVE	1. Right-hand drive		2. Left-hand drive
B:—ENGINE	S or J2	1,300 c.c. High Compression	
	T or J1	1,300 c.c. Low Compression	
	U or L2	1,600 c.c. High Compression	
	W or L1	1,600 c.c. Low Compression	
	R or J3	1,300 c.c. G.T.	
	X or L3	1,600 c.c. G.T.	
C:—TRANSMISSION	5	Floor change manual	
	7	Floor mounted automatic	
D:—REAR AXLE	A.	3.545 to 1	B. 3.777 to 1
	C.	3.900 to 1	D. 4.125 to 1
	E.	4.444 to 1	
E:—TRIM	This code consists of a letter and three numbers (DO58) and indicates the colour and type of material used within the car.		
F:—BODY	D.	DeLuxe	
	G.	G.T.	
G:—S.V.C.	This denotes the date of manufacture of the car if the vehicle is shipped un-assembled from one factory to another for assembly.		
H:—VEHICLE NUMBER	A code, which is explained at the front of every parts list denoting country and plant of manufacture, body style, year and month of manufacture and serial number.		
PAINT CODE	Indicates the colour and type of original paint.		

Chapter 1/Engine

Contents

General Description ... 1	Oil Filter - Removal & Replacement ... 24
Routine Maintenance ... 2	Oil Pump Overhaul ... 25
Major Operations with Engine in Place ... 3	Engine Front Mountings - Removal & Replacement ... 26
Major Operations with Engine Removed... 4	Examination & Renovation - General.. ... 27
Methods of Engine Removal ... 5	Crankshaft Examination & Renovation ... 28
Engine Removal Without Gearbox.. ... 6	Big End & Main Bearings - Examination & Renovation ... 29
Engine Removal With Gearbox.. ... 7	Cylinder Bores - Examination & Renovation ... 30
Dismantling the Engine - General ... 8	Pistons & Piston Rings - Examination & Renovation ... 31
Removing Ancillary Engine Components.. ... 9	Camshaft & Camshaft Bearings - Examination & Renovation ... 32
Cylinder Head Removal - Engine on Bench ... 10	Valves & Valve Seats - Examination & Renovation.. ... 33
Cylinder Head Removal - Engine in Car ... 11	Timing Gears & Chain - Examination & Renovation ... 34
Valve Removal ... 12	Rockers & Rocker Shaft - Examination & Renovation ... 35
Dismantling the Rocker Assembly... 13	Tappets - Examination & Renovation.. ... 36
Timing Cover, Gear Wheel & Chain Removal ... 14	Connecting Rods - Examination & Renovation... ... 37
Camshaft Removal ... 15	Flywheel Starter Ring - Examination & Renovation ... 38
Sump Removal ... 16	Cylinder Head Decarbonisation ... 39
Piston, Connecting Rod & Big End Removal ... 17	Valve Guides - Examination & Renovation ... 40
Gudgeon Pin Removal ... 18	Engine Reassembly - General ... 41
Piston Ring Removal 19	Assembling the Engine ... 42
Flywheel Removal ... 20	Final Assembly ... 43
Main Bearing & Crankshaft Removal ... 21	Engine Replacement - General... ... 44
Timing Chain Tensioner... ... 22	Engine Replacement Without Gearbox ... 45
Lubrication & Crankcase Ventilation Systems - Description ... 23	Engine Replacement With Gearbox ... 46

Specifications - Engine Specifications & Data - 1298 c.c.

Engine - General

Type ...	4 cylinder in line pushrod operated O.H.V.
Bore ...	3.1881 in. (80.978 mm)
Stroke ...	2.480 in. (62.99 mm)
Cubic Capacity.. ...	1,298 c.c. (79.18 cu.in.)
Compression ratio - High C... ...	9.0 to 1
Low C... ...	8.0 to 1
G.T. ...	9.2 to 1
Compression pressure - High C and G.T ...	168 lb/sq.in. (11.81 kg/sq.cm) at 360 r.p.m.
Low C... ...	157 lb/sq.in. (11.04 kg/sq.cm) at 360 r.p.m.
Maximum B.H.P. High C... ...	58 (nett) at 5,000 r.p.m.
Low C	53.5 (nett) at 5,000 r.p.m.
G.T. ...	71.0 (nett) at 6,000 r.p.m.
Maximum torque- High C.. ...	71.5 lb/ft. (9.88 kg.m) at 2,500 r.p.m.
Low C	68 lb/ft. (9.45 kg.m) at 2,500 r.p.m.
G.T. ...	70.0 lb/ft. (9.66 kg.m) at 4,300 r.p.m.
Engine idle speed - Optimum	580 r.p.m. to 620 r.p.m.
G.T. ...	680 r.p.m. to 720 r.p.m.
Location of No.1 cylinder ...	Next to radiator
Firing order ...	1, 2, 4, 3
Engine mounting ...	3 - one each side of engine, one under gearbox extension

Camshaft & Camshaft Bearings

Camshaft drive.. ...	Single roller chain from crankshaft
Camshaft bearings. ...	3 steel back white metal replaceable bushes
Bearing oversize available ...	.020 in. (.513 mm) oversize on old. Standard i/d.
Camshaft journal diameter ...	1.5597 in. to 1.5605 in. (39.617 to 39.637 mm)
Bearing internal diameter ...	1.5615 in. to 1.5620 in. (39.662 to 39.675 mm)
Diametrical bearing clearance ...	.001 to .0023 in. (.025 to .058 mm)
End float ...	.0025 to .0075 in. (.064 to .191 mm)
Thrust plate thickness ...	.176 to .178 in. (4.47 to 4.52 mm)
Maximum cam lift - Inlet ...	.2108 in. (5.350 mm)
Exhaust	.2176 in. (5.523 mm)
G.T - Inlet ...	.2309 in. (5.865 mm)
Exhaust ...	.2321 in. (5.905 mm)

Chapter 1/Engine

Cam heel to toe dimension - Inlet ... 1.3308 in. (33.802 mm)
                                    Exhaust ... 1.3176 in. (33.467 mm)
                 G.T - Inlet ... 1.3109 in. (33.277 mm)
                                    Exhaust ... 1.3121 in. (33.327 mm)

Connecting Rods & Big & Little End Bearings

Connecting rod - Type	'H' Section steel forging
Length between centres	4.132 to 4.135 in. (104.98 to 105.03 mm)
End-float on crankpin	.004 to .010 in. (.10 to .25 mm)
Big end bearings - Type	Shell
Big end bearings - Material	Steel backed copper/lead, lead/bronze or aluminium/tin
Big end bore	2.0825 to 2.0830 in. (52.896 to 52.908 mm)
Bearing liner wall thickness	.0719 to .07225 in. (1.8269 to 1.8347 mm)
Undersize bearings available	-.002, -.010, -.020, -.030, -.040 in. (-.05, -.25, -.51, -.76, -1.02 mm)
Small end bush - Type	Steel backed bronze
Small end bush internal diameter	Graded
Grade - White	.8121 to .8122 in. (20.627 to 20.630 mm)
- Red	.8122 to .8123 in. (20.630 to 20.632 mm)
- Yellow	.8123 to .8124 in. (20.632 to 20.635 mm)
- Blue	.8124 to .8125 in. (20.635 to 20.638 mm)

Crankshaft & Main Bearings

Number of bearings	5
Main bearing journal diameter - Blue	2.1253 to 2.1257 in. (53.983 to 53.993 mm)
Red	2.1257 to 2.1261 in. (53.993 to 54.003 mm)
Green	2.1153 to 2.1157 in. (53.729 to 53.739 mm)
Yellow	2.1157 to 2.1161 in. (53.739 to 53.749 mm)
Regrind diameters - .010 in. (.25 mm)	2.1152 to 2.1157 in. (53.726 to 53.739 mm)
.020 in. (.51 mm)	2.1055 to 2.1060 in. (53.480 to 53.492 mm)
.030 in. (.76 mm)	2.0955 to 2.0960 in. (53.226 to 53.238 mm)
Main journal length - Front	1.219 to 1.239 in. (30.95 to 31.47 mm)
Centre	1.247 to 1.249 in. (31.67 to 31.73 mm)
Rear	1.308 to 1.318 in. (33.22 to 33.48 mm)
Intermediates	1.273 to 1.283 in. (32.33 to 32.59 mm)
Crankshaft end thrust	Taken by thrust washers at centre main bearing
Crankshaft end float	.003 to .011 in. (.08 to .28 mm)
Main bearing material	Steel backed white metal liners
G.T.	Steel backed copper/lead or lead/bronze liners
Undersize bearings available	-.002, -.010, -.020, -.030, -.040 in. (-.05, -.25, -.51, -.76, -1.02 mm)
Crank throw	1.238 to 1.242 in. (31.44 to 31.54 mm)

Cylinder Block

Type	Cylinder cast integral with top half of crankcase
Water jackets	Full length
Height, sump face to head face	7.224 to 7.229 in. (183.49 to 183.62 mm)
Cylinder liners available	Standard and .020 in. (.51 mm) o/s on O.D.
Bore for cylinder liners	3.3115 to 3.3125 in. (84.112 to 84.138 mm) Standard

Cylinder Head

Type	Cast iron with vertical valves
Port arrangement	Separate inlet and exhaust ports on opposite sides
Number of ports - Inlet	4
Exhaust	4

Flywheel

Run-out (maximum)	.005 in. (.13 mm)

Gudgeon Pin

Type	Fully floating retained by end circlips
Material	Machined seamless steel tubing
Length	2.80 to 2.81 in. (71.1 to 71.4 mm)
Fit in piston	.0001 to .0003 in. (.003 to .008 mm) Selective
Fit in small end bush	.0001 to .0003 in. (.003 to .008 mm) Selective

Lubrication System

Type	Pressure and splash wet sump
Oil filter	Full flow with replaceable element
Oil filter capacity	2/3 pint (.8 U.S. pint, .38 litres)
Sump capacity (with filter)	7.2 pints (8.6 U.S. pints, 4.09 litres)

15

Chapter 1/Engine

Oil pump type...	Eccentric rotor
Capacity...	2 gallon per min. (2.4 US galls, 9.085 litres) at 2,000 r.p.m.
Pump body bore diameter...	.500 to .501 in. (12.70 to 12.73 mm)
Drive shaft diameter...	.498 to .4985 in. (12.65 to 12.66 mm)
Drive shaft to body clearance...	.0015 to .003 in. (.038 to .076 mm)
Inner and outer rotor clearance...	.006 in. (.15 mm) maximum
Outer rotor and housing clearance...	.010 in. (.13 mm) maximum
Inner and outer rotor end float...	.005 in. (.13 mm) maximum
Oil pressure	35 to 40 lb/sq.in. (2.46 to 2.81 kg/sq.cm)

Pistons

Type...	Solid skirt with thermal slots
Material...	Aluminium alloy, tin plated
Clearance in bore...	.0019 to .0025 in. (.048 to .064 mm)
Number of rings...	3. Two compression, one oil control
Width of ring grooves:	
Compression...	.0796 to .0816 in. (2.022 to 2.073 mm)
Oil control...	.1568 to .1598 in. (3.983 to 4.059 mm)
Gudgeon pin bore...	Graded
Grade - 10...	.8120 to .8121 in. (20.625 to 20.627 mm)
- One spot...	.8117 to .8118 in. (20.617 to 20.620 mm)
- Two spot...	.8118 to .8119 in. (20.620 to 20.622 mm)
- Three spot...	.8119 to .8120 in. (20.622 to 20.625 mm)
Piston oversizes available...	.0025, .015, .030 in. (.064, .38, .76 mm)
Combustion bowl depth:	
High C...	.540 to .548 in. (13.72 to 13.92 mm)
Low C...	.640 to .648 in. (16.25 to 16.46 mm)
G.T...	.531 to .539 in. (13.50 to 13.70 mm)

Piston Rings

Top compression ring...	Tapered cast iron, chromium plated
Lower compression ring...	Cast iron, stepped on lower face
Top ring width...	.077 to .078 in. (1.96 to 1.98 mm)
Lower ring width...	.077 to .078 in. (1.96 to 1.98 mm)
Top ring fitted gap...	.009 to .014 in. (.23 to .36 mm)
Lower ring fitted gap...	.009 to .014 in. (.23 to .36 mm)
Groove clearance...	.0016 to .0036 in. (.041 to .091 mm)
Oil control ring...	'Micro-land' cast iron slotted scraper
Oil control ring - width...	.155 to .156 in. (3.94 to 3.96 mm)
Oil control ring - fitted gap...	.009 to .014 in. (.23 to .36 mm)
Groove clearance...	.0018 to .0038 in. (.046 to .097 mm)

Tappets

Type...	Barrel with flared base
Stem diameter...	.4360 to .4365 in. (11.072 to 11.085 mm)
Length...	1.85 in. (47.0 mm)

Rocker Gear

Rocker shaft diameter...	.623 to .624 in. (15.83 to 15.85 mm)
Rocker bore...	.625 to .6265 in. (15.88 to 15.913 mm)
Shaft clearance in rocker...	.001 to .0035 in. (.03 to .089 mm)
Rocker arm ratio...	1.54 to 1

Valves

Head diameter - Inlet...	1.405 to 1.415 in. (35.69 to 35.94 mm)
Exhaust...	1.240 to 1.250 in. (31.50 to 31.75 mm)
Valve seat angle...	44° 30' to 45° inlet and exhaust
Valve seat width — Inlet...	1/16 in (1.59 mm)
— Exhaust...	5/64 in (1.98 mm)
Valve face angle...	45° to 45° 15'
Stem diameter - Inlet...	.3095 to .3105 in. (7.861 to 7.887 mm)
Exhaust...	.3086 to .3096 in. (7.838 to 7.864 mm)
Stem to guide clearance - Inlet...	.0008 to .0030 in. (.020 to .080 mm)
Exhaust...	.0017 to .0039 in. (.043 to .099 mm)
Oversize stems available...	.003 in. (.08 mm) and .015 in. (.38 mm)
Valve lift - Inlet...	.315 in. (8.00 mm)
Exhaust...	.319 in. (8.10 mm)
G.T. - Inlet...	.342 in. (8.69 mm)
- Exhaust...	.337 in. (8.56 mm)

Chapter 1/Engine

Valve stem to rocker arm clearance (cold)
- Inlet ... .008 to .010 in. (.20 to .25 mm)
- Exhaust ... .018 to .020 in. (.46 to .51 mm)

G.T.
- Inlet ... .011 to .013 in. (.28 to .33 mm)
- Exhaust ... .021 to .023 in. (.53 to .58 mm)

Valve Timing
Inlet valve - Opens ... 17° B.T.D.C.
- Closes ... 51° A.B.D.C.
Exhaust valve - Opens ... 51° B.B.D.C.
- Closes ... 17° A.T.D.C.
G.T. Inlet valve - Opens ... 27° B.T.D.C.
- Closes ... 65° A.B.D.C.
Exhaust valve - Opens ... 65° B.B.D.C.
- Closes ... 27° A.T.D.C.

Valve Guides
Type ... Machined in cylinder head, guide bushes available
Bore for guide bushes .. ... .4383 to .4391 in. (11.133 to 11.153 mm)
Valve guide inside diameter ... .3113 to .3125 in. (7.907 to 7.938 mm)

Valve Springs
Type ... Single valve springs
Free length ... 1.48 in. (37.6 mm)
Fitted length (valve closed) ... 1.263 in. (32.08 mm)
Load at fitted length ... 44 to 49 lb. (19.96 to 22.23 kg)
Total number of coils 6

Torque Wrench Settings
Big end bolts ... 30 to 35 lb/ft. (4.15 to 4.84 kg.m)
Camshaft sprocket ... 12 to 15 lb/ft. (1.66 to 2.07 kg.m)
Camshaft thrust plate .. ... 2.5 to 3.5 lb/ft. (.35 to .48 kg.m)
Crankshaft pulley ... 24 to 28 lb/ft. (3.32 to 3.87 kg.m)
Cylinder head bolts ... 65 to 70 lb/ft. (8.98 to 9.67 kg.m)
Engine front cover ... 5 to 7 lb/ft. (.69 to .97 kg.m)
Flywheel securing bolts ... 50 to 54 lb/ft. (6.91 to 7.50 kg.m)
Main bearing bolts ... 65 to 70 lb/ft. (8.98 to 9.67 kg.m)
Manifold bolts and nuts ... 15 to 18 lb/ft. (2.07 to 2.49 kg.m)
Oil filter centre bolt ... 12 to 15 lb/ft. (1.66 to 2.07 kg.m)
Oil pump ... 12 to 15 lb/ft. (1.66 to 2.07 kg.m)
Rear oil seal retainer ... 12 to 15 lb/ft. (1.66 to 2.07 kg.m)
Rocker cover ... 2.5 to 3.5 lb/ft. (.35 to .48 kg.m)
Rocker shaft ... 17 to 22 lb/ft. (2.35 to 3.04 kg.m)
Sump ... 6 to 8 lb/ft. (.83 to 1.11 kg.m)
Sump drain plug ... 20 to 25 lb/ft. (2.76 to 3.46 kg.m)
Tappet adjusting screw locknut .. ... 8 to 12 lb/ft. (1.11 to 1.66 kg.m)

Engine Specifications & Data - 1599 c.c.

The engine specification is identical to the 1298 c.c. type except for the differences listed below.

Engine - General
Stroke ... 3.056 in. (77.62 mm)
Cubic capacity .. ... 1,599 c.c. (97.51 cu.in.)
Compression ratio - 1600 G.T ... 9.0 to 1
Compression pressure - High C & G.T ... 188 lb/sq.in. (13.22 kg/sq.cm) at 300 r.p.m.
Low C ... 170 lb/sq.in. (11.95 kg/sq.cm) at 300 r.p.m.
Maximum B.H.P. - High C ... 71 (nett) at 5,000 r.p.m.
Low C ... 69.5 (nett) at 5,000 r.p.m.
G.T ... 88 (nett) at 5,400 r.p.m.
Maximum Torque - High C ... 91.5 lb/ft. (12.64 kg.m) at 2,500 r.p.m.
Low C ... 87 lb/ft. (12.10 kg.m) at 2,500 r.p.m.
G.T ... 96 lb/ft. (13.27 kg.m) at 3,600 r.p.m.

Connecting Rods & Big & Little End Bearings
Length between centres ... 4.926 to 4.929 in. (125.15 to 125.20 mm)

Chapter 1/Engine

Crankshaft & Main Bearings
Crank throw ... ... 1.526 to 1.530 in. (38.76 to 38.86 mm)

Cylinder Block
Height, sump face to head face... ... ... 8.326 to 8.331 in. (211.48 to 211.61 mm)

Pistons
Clearance in bore ... ... .0013 to .0019 in. (.033 to .048 mm)
Combustion bowl depth - High C and G.T ... ... .496 to .504 in. (12.60 to 12.80 mm)
                     - Low C ... ... .599 to .607 in. (15.22 to 15.42 mm)

Valves
Head diameter - Inlet.. ... ... 1.497 to 1.507 in. (38.02 to 38.28 mm)
               - Exhaust.. ... ... 1.240 to 1.250 in. (31.50 to 31.75 mm)

1. General Description

The engine fitted may be one of two units, either of 1298 c.c. or 1599 c.c. Tuned versions of both engines are available in the G.T. models.

The bore on all engines is identical, the variations in capacity being achieved by different crankshaft strokes. All units are identical in design and differ only in the size of some of the components used, e.g. the crankshaft block, connecting rods and pistons.

Two valves per cylinder are mounted vertically in the cast iron cylinder head and run in integral valve guides. They are operated by rocker arms, pushrods and tappets from the camshaft which is located at the base of the cylinder bores in the right-hand side of the engine. The correct valve stem to rocker arm pad clearance can be obtained by the adjusting screws in the ends of the rocker arms.

A crossflow cylinder head is used with four inlet ports on the right-hand side and four exhaust ports on the left. High or low compression ratios may be used.

The cylinder block and the upper half of the crankcase are cast together. The height of the block varies depending on the stroke of the crankshaft fitted. The open half of the crankcase is closed by a pressed steel sump.

The pistons are made from anodised aluminium alloy with solid skirts. Two compression rings and a slotted oil control ring are fitted. The gudgeon pin is retained in the little end of the connecting rod by circlips. The combustion chamber is machined in the piston crown and a different piston is used for each engine capacity and compression ratio. The connecting rod bearings are all steel backed and may be of copper/lead, lead/bronze, or aluminium/tin.

At the front of the engine a single chain drives the camshaft via the camshaft and crankshaft chain wheels which are enclosed in a pressed steel cover.

The chain is tensioned automatically by a snail cam which bears against a pivoted tensioner arm. This presses against the non driving side of the chain so avoiding any lash or rattle.

The camshaft is supported by three renewable bearings located directly in the cylinder block. Endfloat is controlled by a plate bolted to the front of the cylinder block and positioned between the front bearing journal and the chain wheel flange. G.T. models are fitted with a camshaft with higher lift and more overlap than normal.

The statically and dynamically balanced cast iron crankshaft is supported by five renewable thinwall shell main bearings which are in turn supported by substantial webs which form part of the crankcase. Crankshaft endfloat is controlled by semi-circular thrust washers located on each side of the centre main bearings. The main bearings fitted are of the white metal type except on the G.T. when they are of copper/lead or lead/bronze.

The centrifugal water pump and radiator cooling fan are driven, together with the dynamo, from the crankshaft pulley wheel by a rubber/fabric belt. The distributor is mounted towards the front of the right-hand side of the cylinder block and advances and retards the ignition timing by mechanical and vacuum means. The distributor is driven at half crankshaft speed from a skew gear on the camshaft.

The oil pump is mounted externally on the right-hand side of the engine under the distributor and is driven by a short shaft from the same skew gear on the camshaft as for the distributor and is of the eccentric bi-rotor type.

Bolted to the flange on the end of the crankshaft is the flywheel to which is bolted in turn the clutch. Attached to the rear of the engine is the gearbox bellhousing.

2. Routine Maintenance

1. Once a week or daily if experience dictates this necessary remove the dipstick, wipe it, replace it and remove it again to check the engine oil level which should be at the 'FULL' mark. Top up if the oil level is at the 'FILL' mark with one of the recommended lubricants on page 10. On no account allow the oil level to drop into the very bottom portion of the dipstick marked 'DANGER'. The amount of oil needed to bring the level up from the 'FILL' to the 'FULL' marks is 1½ pints. Do not overfill as the oil will only be wasted.
2. Every 6,000 miles run the engine till it is hot; place a container with a capacity of at least 7 pints under the sump drain plug; undo and remove the drain plug; and allow at least 10 minutes for all the oil to drain. While the oil is draining renew the filter element as described in Section 24.
3. Clean the drain plug, ensure the washer is in place, and return the plug to the sump, tightening the plug firmly. Refill the sump with 5.72 pints of the recommended grade of oil (see page 10 for details).
4. In very hot or dusty conditions, or in cold weather with much slow stop/start driving, with much use of the choke, it is beneficial to change the engine oil every 3,000 miles.
5. Every 6,000 miles the following operations should also be made:—

a) Adjust the fan belt tension as described in Chapter 2, Section 10.
b) Check and adjust the valve to rocker arm clearances as described in Section 42.
c) Clean the crankcase emission valve (if fitted).
d) Check the tightness of the dynamo or alternator securing bolts and the exhaust manifold to downpipe bolts.
e) Carefully examine the engine for oil or water leaks and if any are found renew the faulty gasket or oil seal.

Chapter 1/Engine

3. Major Operations With Engine in Place

The following major operations can be carried out to the engine with it in place in the bodyframe:—
1. Removal and replacement of the cylinder head assembly.
2. Removal and replacement of the timing chain and gears.
3. Removal and replacement of the engine front mountings.
4. Removal and replacement of the engine/gearbox rear mounting.

4. Major Operations With Engine Removed

The following major operations can be carried out with engine out of the bodyframe and on the bench or floor:—
1. Removal and replacement of the main bearings.
2. Removal and replacement of the crankshaft.
3. Removal and replacement of the flywheel.
4. Removal and replacement of the crankshaft rear bearing oil seal.
5. Removal and replacement of the camshaft.
6. Removal and replacement of sump.
7. Removal and replacement of big end bearings.
8. Removal and replacement of pistons and connecting rods.
9. Removal and replacement of oil pump.

5. Method of Engine Removal

The engine complete with gearbox can be lifted as a unit from the engine compartment. Alternatively the engine and gearbox can be split at the front of the bellhousing, a stand or jack placed under the gearbox to provide additional support, and the engine lifted out. The easiest method of engine removal is to remove the engine leaving the gearbox in place in the car. If the engine and gearbox are removed as a unit they have to be lifted out at a very steep angle which can be difficult.

6. Engine Removal Without Gearbox

1. A do-it-yourself owner should be able to remove the engine from the car in about 3 hours. It is essential to have a good hoist. If an inspection pit is not available, two support stands will also be required. In the later stages, when the engine is being separated from the gearbox and lifted, the assistance of another person is most useful to help guide the engine and prevent it from swaying about and possibly causing damage.
2. Disconnect the battery by removing the battery leads (photo).
3. Undo the bolts securing the battery clamp (photo) and remove the clamp from the battery tray.
4. Remove the battery from the car (photo) and put it in a safe place such as the boot.
5. Undo the nuts (two each side) on the bonnet hinges with the bonnet propped up on its stay (photo). Care must be taken not to allow the bonnet to slide back when the nuts are loosened as this could easily chip the paint in front of the windscreen.
6. Carefully remove the bolts which are inter-connected (photo). This is best done with a piece of rag between the bonnet edge and the paintwork as shown.
7. With an assistant, lift the bonnet from the car and place it out of harms way (photo).
8. Undo the five cross-head screws holding the metal deflector plate in place in front of the radiator (photo).
9. Lift the deflector plate from the car (photo). This item must be removed as it could easily get in the way when the engine is lifted from the car.
10 Obtain two suitable receptacles to collect the engine oil and cooling water. Rather than use the washing up bowls from the kitchen, it is better to find an empty gallon oil can and cut one side out to use as a container for the oil. If the coolant is to be kept because of anti-freeze a 2 gallon container will be required.
11 In the interests of cleanliness or if it is wished to retain the coolant it is necessary to remove the fibre-board deflector from under the radiator.
12 Undo the two cross-head screws from either side of the deflector adjacent to the anti-roll bar front mounting points (photo).
13 Then pull the deflector off its spring clips to the bodywork, two at the front, one at the rear and remove it from the car (photo).
14 Remove the radiator cap and undo the drain tap in the base of the radiator (photo) having first placed a suitable container under it to collect the coolant.
15 To ensure all the coolant leaves the block the drain plug on the left side of the block should also be opened after the radiator is empty. Unless there are blockages in the cooling system it will be found that very little coolant will drain out. Undo the sump plug and allow the oil to drain for at least ten minutes, then replace the plug.
16 Undo the clip on the top radiator hose at the thermostat housing (photo A), then pull the hose off (photo B).
17 Undo the clip on the bottom radiator hose where it enters the water pump (photo A) then pull the hose off (photo B).
18 Undo the four bolts (two either side) which hold the radiator to the front bodywork (photo).
19 Then lift the radiator clear of the engine compartment, complete with its top and bottom hoses (photo).
20 Unscrew the clip on the longer heater hose where it enters the water pump and pull the hose off (photo).
21 Disconnect the shorter heater hose at the inlet manifold by the same method (photo).
22 If a servo is fitted undo the clip on the vacuum pipe at the inlet manifold (photo A) and pull the pipe off (photo B).
23 Pull the wire off the oil pressure sender unit next to the distributor (photo).
24 Pull the wire off the water temperature sender unit which is located on the exhaust manifold side of the thermostat housing (photo).
25 Remove the three bolts retaining the air cleaner stays to the engine, one on the inlet manifold (photo A), one next to the accelerator linkage bracket (photo B) and the other on the exhaust side of the rocker cover (photo C).
26 Pull the air cleaner assembly off the top of the carburetter and lift it from the car (photo).
27 Take off the accelerator linkage return spring as shown (photo) noting the correct method of fitting for replacement purposes.
28 Undo and remove the two bolts securing the accelerator linkage bracket (photo).
29 At the very end of the accelerator cable prise open the spring clip with a screwdriver (photo A) and separate the ball joint from the cable end (photo B).
30 Undo the choke outer cable clamping screw adjacent to the carburetter intake (photo) noting how much of the outer cable protrudes beyond the clamp to ensure that it is replaced in the same position on reassembly.
31 Then release the inner cable from the choke linkage on the carburetter by slackening off the cross-head screw (photo). Tuck both the accelerator and choke cables out of harms way.
32 Pull off the flexible pipe from the petrol tank to the

6.2　6.3　6.4　6.5　6.6　6.7　6.8　6.9　6.12　6.13　6.14　6.16a　6.16b　6.17a　6.17b　6.18　6.19　6.20

6.21 6.22a 6.22b
6.23 6.24 6.25a
6.25b 6.25c 6.26
6.27 6.28 6.29a
6.29b 6.30 6.31

21

Chapter 1/Engine

petrol pump where it enters the pump. As the tank is higher than the pump it will be found that petrol will flow from the pipe and thereby cause a considerable fire risk. It is therefore, necessary to block off the flow and it was found that an ordinary pencil proved ideal for this job (photo). Tuck the pipe out of harms way.

33 On some models the coil may be attached to the engine assembly. In this case unless damage to the wiring is possible it will not be necessary to disconnect it from the distributor, but the (+) positive terminal must be pulled off at the 'Lucar' connector.

34 On the particular model worked on, the coil was mounted on the right-hand side panel, so it was necessary to remove the HT lead from the distributor (photo A) and the LT (−) lead from the coil (photo B).

35 Pull off the two wires leading to the rear of the generator (or alternator if fitted) noting their correct positioning for reassembly (photo).

36 Remove the single wire to the starter motor by undoing the nut (photo). Replace the nut and washers on the stud for safe keeping.

37 Disconnect the earthing strap on the front left-hand side of the engine (just below the water temperature sender unit) by removing the bolt (photo).

38 As it will now be necessary to work under the car, raise the front on a jack and place chassis stands under the front crossmember.

39 Disconnect the exhaust downpipe from the manifold by undoing the two brass nuts (photo).

40 Working under the car, pull the rubber boot off the bellhousing where the clutch mechanism enters the bellhousing on the right-hand side.

41 Undo the locknut on the clutch cable and slacken off the sleeved adjusting nut until the pedal in the car is about one inch from the floor.

42 Now pull the cable towards the rear of the car and slide the ball end of the cable out of its slot in the clutch release mechanism.

43 Moving to the other side of the car remove the three bolts which hold the starter motor to the bellhousing and carefully lift out the starter motor. If a pre-engaged type of starter motor is fitted there will be only two retaining bolts.

44 The bracing plate between the engine and the bellhousing must now be disconnected by removing the two bolts where it is attached to the bellhousing.

45 The lifting tackle should now be moved into position above the engine. The author found it convenient to undo the front right-hand inlet manifold bolt (photo A) and the rear left-hand exhaust manifold bolt (photo B) and attach a chain, as shown to these points, thereby ensuring even weight distribution of the engine when lifting commenced.

46 If a suitable chain is not readily available a stout rope slung round the engine will do the job just as well, but care must be taken to ensure it does not damage any of the ancillary components when it is taut.

47 Now remove the single lower engine mounting bolts from both the front mounting points as shown (photo).

48 Undo and remove the lower bellhousing bolts noting that some are longer than others and their correct positioning.

49 Take the weight off the gearbox, by placing a jack under it, and also take the strain on the engine lifting tackle.

50 Remove the remaining bellhousing bolts. It may be necessary to remove the dipstick tube to get at the bolt behind it, but this can easily be done by simply pulling it from the engine.

51 Lift the engine about two inches so that it is clear of the front engine mounting points. Photo shows how much the stud protrudes below the rubber mounting.

52 Ensure that the jack under the gearbox is raised an appropriate amount to suitably support the gearbox. The engine must be pulled forward to disengage it from the splined end of the gearbox input shaft. This may call for two people and a certain amount of sideways rocking to disengage it completely. It will be free when the gap between the engine and the bellhousing is about 3 in. (75 mm).

53 Once the engine is free from the gearbox input shaft it can now be gently lifted upwards (photo).

54 If your lifting tackle is static it will be necessary to lower the car off its chassis stands and push it from under the engine. It is unwise to hurry the lifting operations as damage to components can easily occur unless the engine is watched carefully all the way out.

7. Engine Removal With Gearbox

1. Proceed exactly as outlined in Section 6 up as far as paragraph 47 inclusive, but ignore paragraph 44 as the bracing plate can be removed with the engine and gearbox out of the car.

2. Unscrew the gearbox drain plug and allow the oil to drain out. Then replace the drain plug.

3. From inside the car completely remove the gearchange remote control assembly as detailed in Chapter 6, Section 3.

4. Support the gearbox with a jack in the vicinity of the oil drain plug.

5. Remove the centre bolt which locates the gearbox extension into the rear support member. Then making sure the gearbox support jack is firmly in position remove the four bolts attaching the crossmember to the body frame. Remove the crossmember.

6. On some models there is a support bracket running from the gearbox to the exhaust system. This should be removed by removing the retaining bolt.

7. The speedometer cable is held into the gearbox by a circular spring clip. This should be removed and the cable withdrawn and tucked out of harms way.

8. Remove the front engine mounting bolts as described in Section 6, paragraph 47.

9. With the jack under the gearbox still in position start lifting and at the same time, once the front mountings are clear, move the engine forwards until the propeller shaft is nearly ready to come out of the gearbox extension. Do not let the propeller shaft drop to the ground but support it until clear and then lower it and rest it on a suitable block.

10 Due to the fact that the gearbox is attached, the engine will have to be lifted out at a much steeper angle than for removing the engine on its own. As the weight is now more towards the rear it will be fairly easy to achieve this angle.

11 Continue to raise the engine and move it forwards at the necessary angle. At this stage the forward edge of the bellhousing is likely to catch against the front crossmember and the tail end of the gearbox will need raising until the whole unit is forward and clear of it.

12 Finally the whole unit will rise clear and if the maximum height of the lifting tackle has been reached, it will be necessary to swing the unit so that the tail end can be lifted clear whilst the hoist is moved away or the car pushed clear.

13 The whole unit should be lowered to the ground (or bench) as soon as possible and the gearbox may then be separated from the engine.

8. Dismantling The Engine — General

1. It is best to mount the engine on a dismantling stand

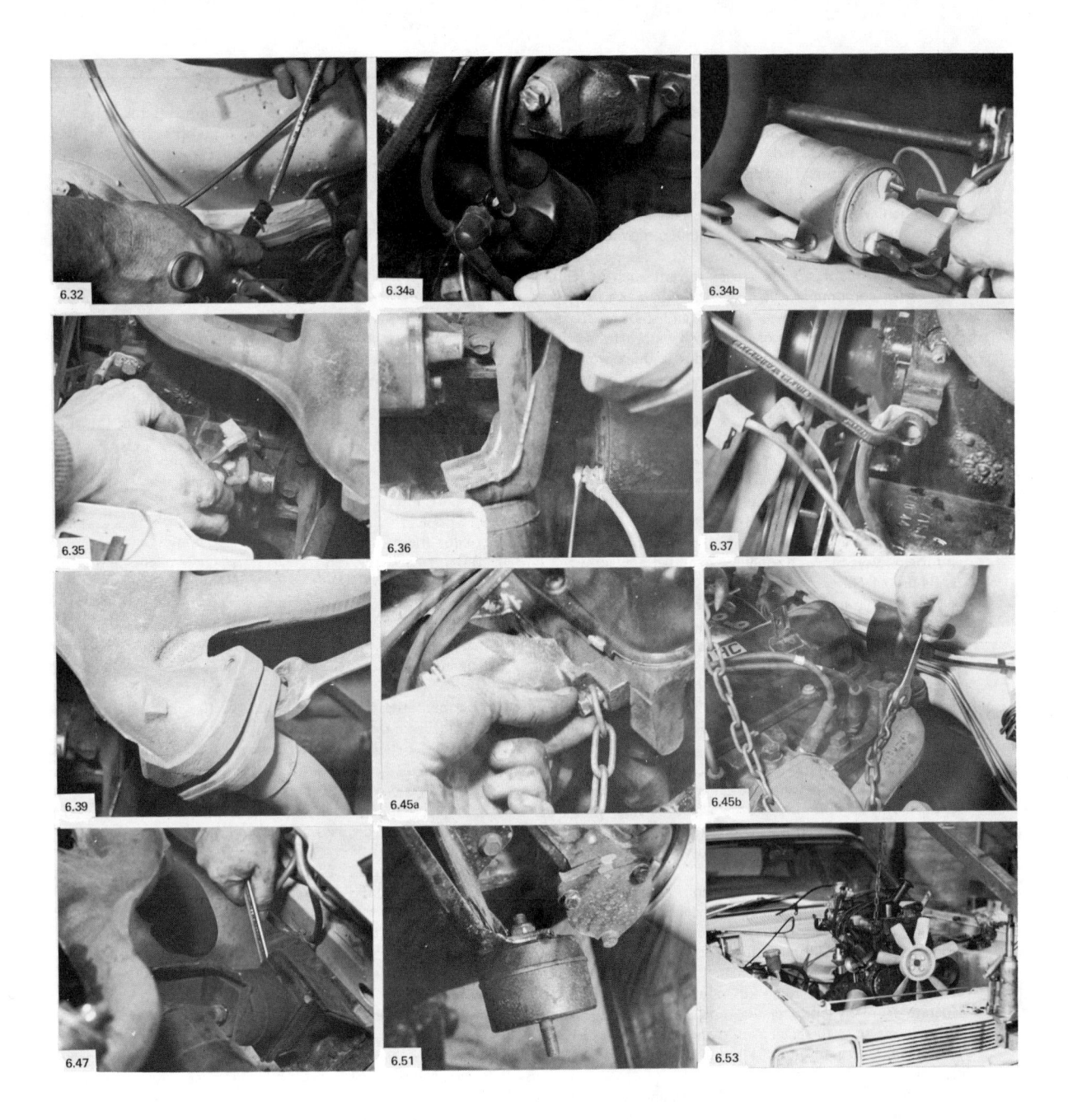

6.32 6.34a 6.34b
6.35 6.36 6.37
6.39 6.45a 6.45b
6.47 6.51 6.53

23

Chapter 1/Engine

but if one is not available, then stand the engine on a strong bench so as to be at a comfortable working height. Failing this, the engine can be stripped down on the floor.

2. During the dismantling process the greatest care should be taken to keep the exposed parts free from dirt. As an aid to achieving this, it is a sound scheme to thoroughly clean down the outside of the engine, removing all traces of oil and congealed dirt.

3. Use paraffin or a good grease solvent such as 'Gunk'. The latter compound will make the job much easier, as, after the solvent has been applied and allowed to stand for a time, a vigorous jet of water will wash off the solvent and all the grease and filth. If the dirt is thick and deeply embedded, work the solvent into it with a stiff paint brush.

4. Finally wipe down the exterior of the engine with a rag and only then, when it is quite clean should the dismantling process begin. As the engine is stripped, clean each part in a bath of paraffin or petrol.

5. Never immerse parts with oilways in paraffin, eg the crankshaft, but to clean wipe down carefully with a petrol dampened rag. Oilways can be cleaned out with pipe cleaners. If an air line is present all parts can be blown dry and the oilways blown through as an added precaution.

6. Re-use of old engine gaskets is a false economy and can give rise to oil and water leaks, if nothing worse. To avoid the possibility of trouble after the engine has been re-assembled ALWAYS use new gaskets throughout.

7. Do not throw the old gaskets away as it sometimes happens that an immediate replacement cannot be found and the old gasket is then very useful as a template. Hang up the old gaskets as they are removed on a suitable hook or nail.

8. To strip the engine it is best to work from the top down. The sump provides a firm base on which the engine can be supported in an upright position. When the stage where the sump must be removed is reached, the engine can be turned on its side and all other work carried out with it in this position.

9. Wherever possible, replace nuts, bolts and washers finger-tight from wherever they were removed. This helps avoid later loss and muddle. If they cannot be replaced then lay them out in such a fashion that it is clear from where they came.

10 If the engine was removed in unit with the gearbox, separate them by undoing the nuts and bolts which hold the bellhousing to the engine endplate.

11 Also undo the three bolts holding the starter motor in place and lift off the motor.

12 Carefully pull the gearbox and bellhousing off the engine to separate them.

9. Removing Ancillary Engine Components

1. Before basic engine dismantling begins the engine should be stripped of all its ancillary components. These items should also be removed if a factory exchange reconditioned unit is being purchased. The items comprise:—

> Dynamo and dynamo brackets.
> Water pump and thermostat housing.
> Distributor and sparking plugs.
> Inlet and exhaust manifold and carburetters.
> Fuel pump and fuel pipes.
> Oil filter and dipstick.
> Oil filler cap.
> Clutch assembly.
> Engine mountings.
> Oil pressure sender unit/pressure gauge adaptor (G.T. models).
> Oil separator unit (positive ventilation systems only).
> Alternator and alternator brackets (if fitted).

2. Without exception all these items can be removed with the engine in the car if it is merely an individual item which requires attention. (It is necessary to remove the gearbox if the clutch is to be renewed with the engine ('in situ').

3. Remove the dynamo after undoing the nuts and bolts which secure it in place. Remove the dynamo securing straps. Do the same for an alternator if fitted.

4. Remove the distributor by disconnecting the vacuum pipe, unscrew the single bolt at the clamp plate and lift out the distributor.

5. Remove the oil filter assembly by unscrewing it.

6. Unscrew the two bolts securing the fuel pump.

7. Unscrew the oil pressure gauge unit or the oil pressure sender unit depending on model.

8. Remove the inlet and exhaust manifolds together with the carburetter by undoing the bolts and nuts which hold the units in place.

9. Unbolt the securing bolts of the water elbow and lift out the thermostat.

10 Bend back the tab lockwashers where fitted and undo the bolts which hold the water pump and engine mountings in place.

11 Undo the bolts which hold the clutch cover flange to the flywheel a third of a turn each in a diagonal sequence repeating until the clutch and driven plate can be lifted off.

12 Loosen the clamp which secures the rubber tube from the oil separator unit to the inlet manifold and pull off the tube (where a positive ventilation system is fitted). Remove the oil separator located on the fuel pump mounting pad by carefully prising it off.

13 The engine is now stripped of ancillary components and ready for major dismantling to begin.

10. Cylinder Head Removal — Engine on Bench

1. Undo the four screw headed bolts and flat washers which hold the flange of the rocker cover to the cylinder head and lift off the rocker cover and gasket.

2. Unscrew the four rocker shaft pedestal bolts evenly and remove together with their washers.

3. Lift off the rocker assembly as one unit.

4. Remove the pushrods, keeping them in the relative order in which they were removed. The easiest way to do this is to push them through a sheet of thick paper or thin card in the correct sequence.

5. Undo the cylinder head bolts half a turn at a time in the reverse order shown in Fig.1.2. When all the bolts are no longer under tension they may be screwed off the cylinder head one at a time.

6. The cylinder head can now be removed by lifting upwards. If the head is jammed, try to rock it to break the seal. Under no circumstances try to prise it apart from the block with a screwdriver or cold chisel as damage may be done to the faces of the head or block. If the head will not readily free, turn the engine over by the flywheel as the compression in the cylinders will often break the cylinder head joint. If this fails to work, strike the head sharply with a plastic headed hammer, or with a wooden hammer, or with a metal hammer with an interposed piece of wood to cushion the blows. Under no circumstances hit the head directly with a metal hammer as this may cause the iron casting to fracture. Several sharp taps with the hammer at the same time pulling upwards should free the head. Lift the head off and place on one side.

7. Do not lay the cylinder head face downwards unless the

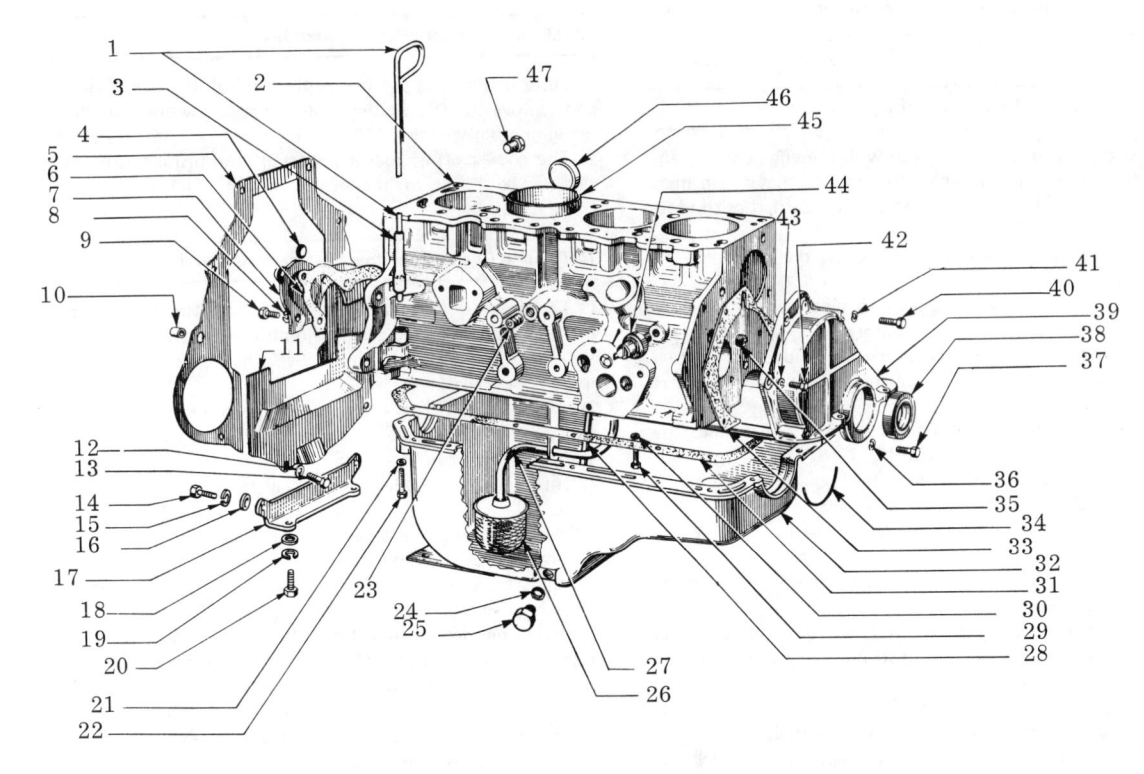

Fig.1.1. EXPLODED VIEW OF THE STATIC ENGINE COMPONENTS

1. Dipstick
2. Cylinder block
3. Dipstick tube
4. Plug
5. Engine endplate
6. Gasket
7. Camshaft end cover
8. Locking washer
9. Bolt
10. Dowel
11. Engine end plate
12. Washer
13. Bolt
14. Bolt
15. Locking washer
16. Washer
17. Angle bracket
18. Washer
19. Locking washer
20. Bolt
21. Washer
22. Bolt
23. Plug
24. Sealing ring
25. Sump plug
26. Oil pump pick-up filter
27. Oil pump pick-up tube
29. Sump bolt
30. Washer
31. Gasket
32. Sump
33. Gasket
34. Seal
35. Plug
36. Locking washer
37. Bolt
38. Oil seal
39. Timing chain cover
40. Bolt
41. Locking washer
42. Bolt
43. Locking washer
44. Low oil pressure warning switch
45. Cylinder sleeve
46. Welch plug
47. Plug

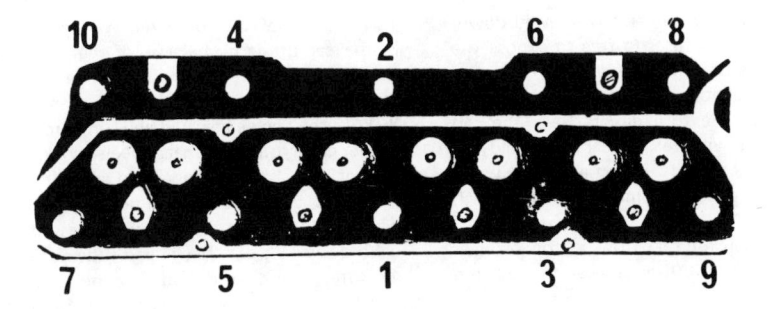

Fig.1.2. Cylinder head bolts tightening and loosening sequence

Chapter 1/Engine

plugs have been removed as they protrude and can be easily damaged.

11. Cylinder Head Removal — Engine in Car

To remove the cylinder head with the engine still in the car the following additional procedure to that above must be followed. This procedure should be carried out before that listed in Section 10.
1. Disconnect the battery by removing the lead from the negative terminal.
2. Drain half the water (approx. 5 pints) by undoing the drain plug at the base of the radiator.
3. Take off the carburetter air cleaner and undo the two bolts which hold the thermostat housing in place. Remove the thermostat.
4. Undo the clips which hold the heater hoses and the vacuum hose to the inlet manifold.
5. Undo the bolts which hold the exhaust manifold to the exhaust pipe and on the G.T. engine undo the nuts bolts and washers which hold the exhaust manifold to the cylinder head.
6. Pull the cable away from the temperature gauge sender unit.
7. Also free from the carburetter, the throttle cable and linkage, the petrol pipe, the distributor vacuum pipe and the choke cable (where fitted).
8. On models other than G.T. unclip from the rocker cover the carburetter ventilation pipe (if fitted).
9. Pull the leads off the sparking plugs and flip back the clips which hold the distributor cover in place. Place the cover and leads to one side.
10 The procedure is now the same as for removing the cylinder head when on the bench. One tip worth noting is that should the cylinder head refuse to free easily, the battery can be reconnected up, and the engine turned over on the solenoid switch. Under no circumstances turn the ignition on and ensure the fuel inlet pipe is disconnected from the mechanical fuel pump.

12. Valve Removal

1. The valves can be removed from the cylinder head by the following method. Compress each spring in turn with a valve spring compressor until the two halves of the collets can be removed. Release the compressor and remove the spring and spring retainer.
2. If, when the valve spring compressor is screwed down, the valve spring retaining cap refuses to free to expose the split collet, do not continue to screw down on the compressor as there is a likelihood of damaging it.
3. Gently tap the top of the tool directly over the cap with a light hammer. This will free the cap. To avoid the compressor jumping off the valve spring retaining cap when it is tapped, hold the compressor firmly in position with one hand.
4. Slide the rubber oil control seal off the top of each inlet valve stem and then drop out each valve through the combustion chamber.
5. It is essential that the valves are kept in their correct sequence unless they are so badly worn that they are to be renewed. If they are going to be kept and used again, place them in a sheet of card having eight holes numbered 1 to 8 corresponding with the relative positions the valves were in when fitted. Also keep the valve springs, washers etc., in the correct order. Make No.1 hole the one at the front of the cylinder head.

13. Dismantling the Rocker Assembly

1. Pull out the split pin from either end of the rocker shaft and remove the flat washer, crimped spring washer and the remaining flat washer.
2. The rocker arms, rocker pedestals, and distance springs can now be slid off the end of the shaft.

14. Timing Cover, Gearwheel & Chain Removal

1. The timing cover, gear wheels, and chain can be removed with the engine in the car providing the radiator, fan, and water pump are first removed. See Chapter 2, Sections 6 and 8 for details.
2. Undo the bolt from the centre of the crankshaft fan belt pulley wheel noting there may be a spring as well as a flat washer under the bolt's head.
3. The crankshaft pulley wheel may pull off quite easily. If not place two large screwdrivers behind the wheel at 180° to each other, and carefully lever off the wheel. It is preferable to use a proper pulley extractor if this is available, but large screwdrivers or tyre levers are quite suitable, providing care is taken not to damage the pulley flange.
4. Undo the bolts which hold the timing cover in place noting that four sump bolts must also be removed before the cover can be taken off.
5. Check the chain for wear by measuring how much it can be depressed. More than ½ in. means a new chain must be fitted on reassembly.
6. With the timing cover off, take off the oil thrower. NOTE that the concave side faces outwards.
7. With a drift or screwdriver tap back the tabs on the lockwasher under the two camshaft gearwheel retaining bolts and undo the bolts.
8. To remove the camshaft and crankshaft timing wheels complete with chain, ease each wheel forward a little at a time levering behind each gear wheel in turn with two large screwdrivers at 180° to each other. If the gearwheels are locked solid then it will be necessary to use a proper gearwheel and pulley extractor, and if one is available this should be used anyway in preference to screwdrivers. With both gearwheels safely off, remove the woodruff key from the crankshaft with a pair of pliers and place it in a jam jar for safe keeping.

15. Camshaft Removal

1. The camshaft cannot be removed with the engine in place in the car primarily because of the restriction imposed by the inverted umbrella shaped tappets which can only be removed downwards, i.e. towards the camshaft.
2. With the engine inverted and sump, rocker gear, pushrods, timing cover, oil pump, gearwheels and timing chain removed take off the chain tensioner and arm.
3. Knock back the lockwasher tabs from the two bolts which hold the horseshoe shaped camshaft retainer in place behind the camshaft flange and slide out the retainer.
4. Rotate the camshaft so that the tappets are fully home and then withdraw the camshaft from the block. Take great care that the cam lobe peaks do not damage the camshaft bearings as the shaft is pulled forward.

16. Sump Removal

1. With the engine out of the car, first of all drain the oil by removing the sump plug if this has not already been

Fig.1.3. VIEW OF THE CYLINDER HEAD COMPONENTS

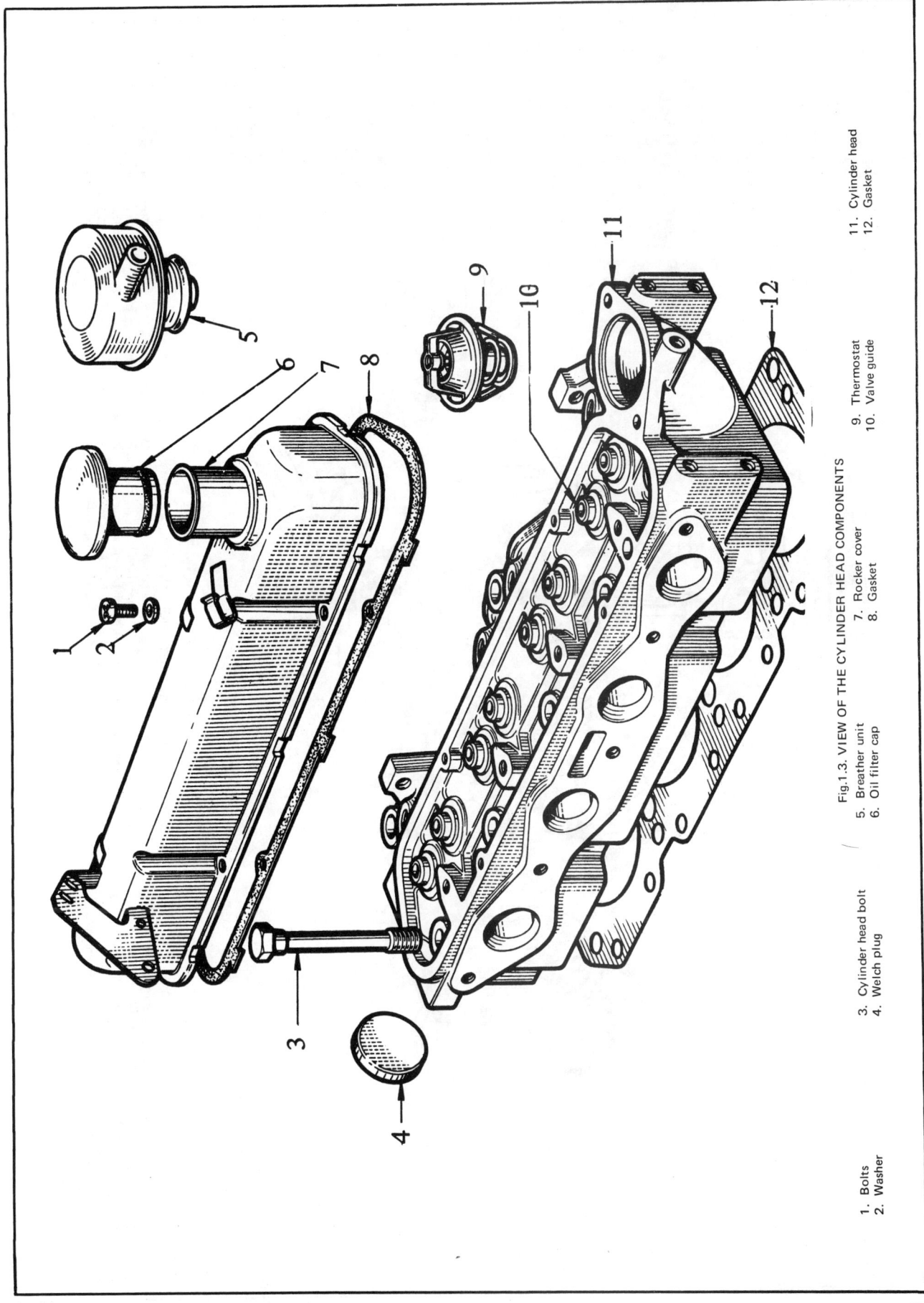

1. Bolts
2. Washer
3. Cylinder head bolt
4. Welch plug
5. Breather unit
6. Oil filter cap
7. Rocker cover
8. Gasket
9. Thermostat
10. Valve guide
11. Cylinder head
12. Gasket

27

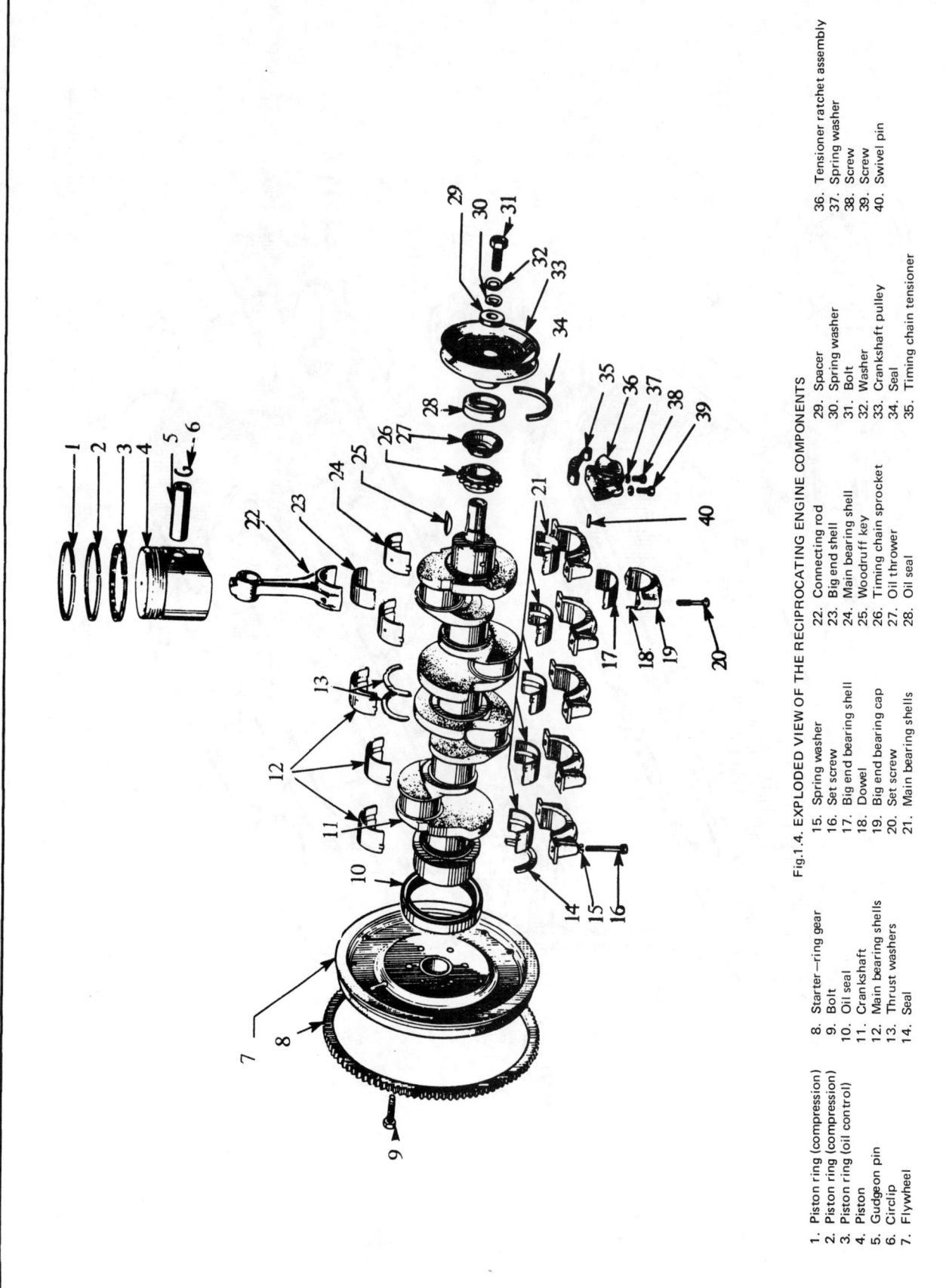

Fig.1.4. EXPLODED VIEW OF THE RECIPROCATING ENGINE COMPONENTS

1. Piston ring (compression)
2. Piston ring (compression)
3. Piston ring (oil control)
4. Piston
5. Gudgeon pin
6. Circlip
7. Flywheel
8. Starter—ring gear
9. Bolt
10. Oil seal
11. Crankshaft
12. Main bearing shells
13. Thrust washers
14. Seal
15. Spring washer
16. Set screw
17. Big end bearing shell
18. Dowel
19. Big end bearing cap
20. Set screw
21. Main bearing shells
22. Connecting rod
23. Big end shell
24. Main bearing shell
25. Woodruff key
26. Timing chain sprocket
27. Oil thrower
28. Oil seal
29. Spacer
30. Spring washer
31. Bolt
32. Washer
33. Crankshaft pulley
34. Seal
35. Timing chain tensioner
36. Tensioner ratchet assembly
37. Spring washer
38. Screw
39. Screw
40. Swivel pin

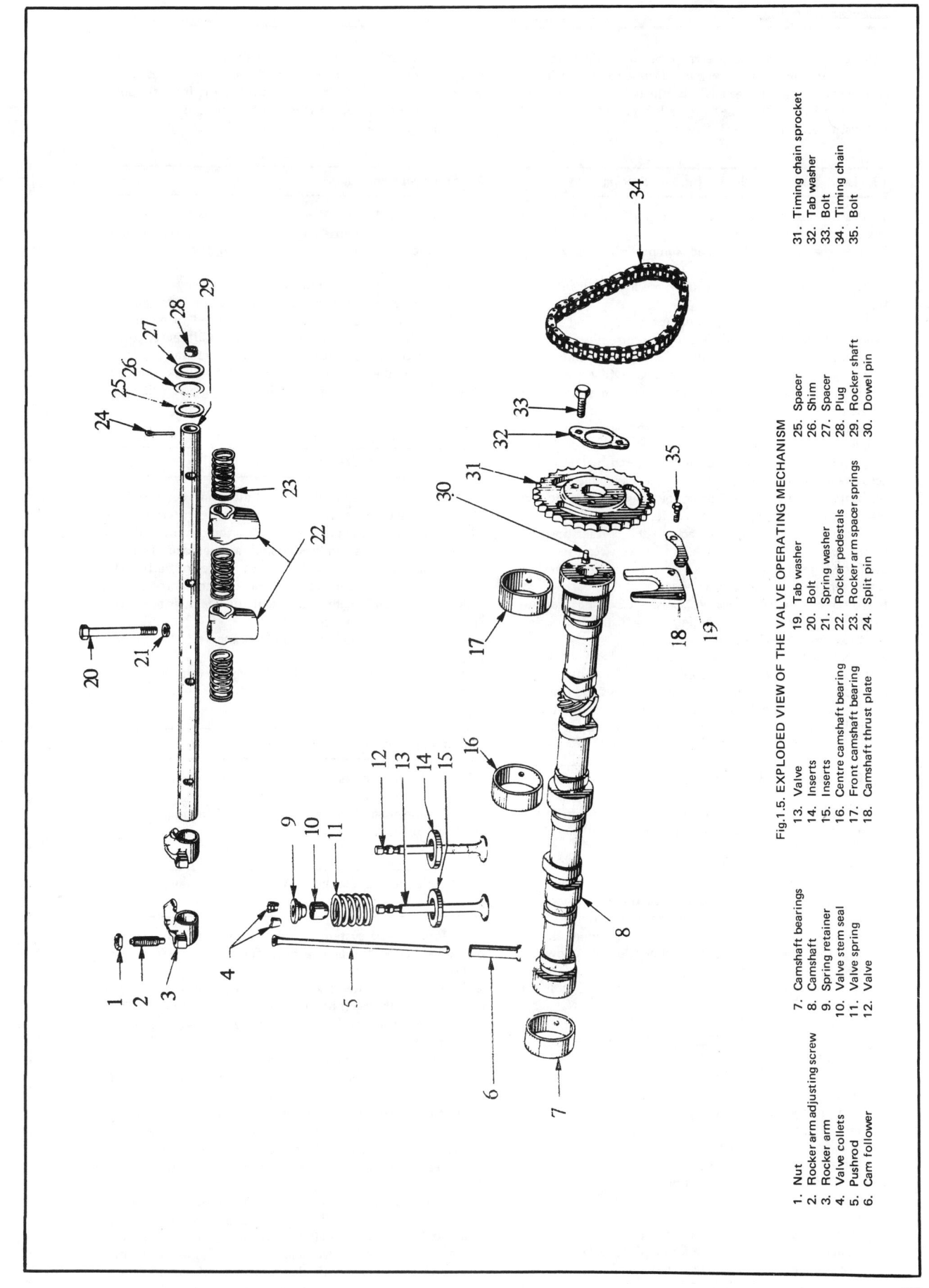

Fig.1.5. EXPLODED VIEW OF THE VALVE OPERATING MECHANISM

1. Nut
2. Rocker arm adjusting screw
3. Rocker arm
4. Valve collets
5. Pushrod
6. Cam follower
7. Camshaft bearings
8. Camshaft
9. Spring retainer
10. Valve stem seal
11. Valve spring
12. Valve
13. Valve
14. Inserts
15. Inserts
16. Centre camshaft bearing
17. Front camshaft bearing
18. Camshaft thrust plate
19. Tab washer
20. Bolt
21. Spring washer
22. Rocker pedestals
23. Rocker arm spacer springs
24. Split pin
25. Spacer
26. Shim
27. Spacer
28. Plug
29. Rocker shaft
30. Dowel pin
31. Timing chain sprocket
32. Tab washer
33. Bolt
34. Timing chain
35. Bolt

29

Chapter 1/Engine

done, then invert the engine and remove the sump bolts.
2. The sump may be stuck quite firmly to the engine if sealing compound has been used on the gasket. It is in order to lever it off in this case. The gasket should be removed and discarded in any case.

17. Piston, Connecting Rod & Big End Bearing Removal

1. The pistons and connecting rods can be removed with the engine on the bench.
2. With the cylinder head and sump removed undo the big end retaining bolts.
3. The connecting rods and pistons are lifted out from the top of the cylinder block.
4. Remove the big end caps one at a time, taking care to keep them in the right order and the correct way round. Also ensure that the shell bearings are kept with their correct connecting rods and caps unless they are to be renewed. Normally, the numbers 1 to 4 are stamped on adjacent sides of the big end caps and connecting rods, indiacting which cap fits on which rod and which way round the cap fits. If no numbers or lines can be found then with a sharp screwdriver or file scratch mating marks across the joint from the rod to the cap. One line for connecting rod No.1, two for connecting rod No.2 and so on. This will ensure there is no confusion later as it is most important that the caps go back in the correct position on the connecting rods from which they were removed.
5. If the big end caps are difficult to remove they may be gently tapped with a soft hammer.
6. To remove the shell bearings, press the bearing opposite the groove in both the connecting rod, and the connecting rod caps and the bearings will slide out easily.
7. Withdraw the pistons and connecting rods upwards and ensure they are kept in the correct order for replacement in the same bore. Refit the connecting rod caps and bearings to the rods, if the bearings do not require renewal, to minimise the risk of getting the caps and rods muddled.

18. Gudgeon Pin — Removal

1. To remove the gudgeon pin to free the piston from the connecting rod remove one of the circlips at either end of the pin with a pair of circlip pliers.
2. Press out the pin from the rod and piston with your finger.
3. If the pin shows reluctance to move, then on no account force it out, as this could damage the piston. Immerse the piston in a pan of boiling water for three minutes. On removal the expansion of the aluminium should allow the gudgeon pin to slide out easily.
4. Make sure the pins are kept with the same piston for ease of refitting.

19. Piston Ring Removal

1. To remove the piston rings, slide them carefully over the top of the piston, taking care not to scratch the aluminium alloy. Never slide them off the bottom of the piston skirt. It is very easy to break the iron piston rings if they are pulled off roughly so this operation should be done with extreme caution. It is helpful to make use of an old hacksaw blade, or better still, an old .020 in. feeler gauge.
2. Lift one end of the piston ring to be removed out of its groove and insert the end of the feeler gauge under it.
3. Turn the feeler gauge slowly round the piston and as the ring comes out of its groove apply slight upward pressure so that it rests on the land above. It can then be eased off the piston with the feeler gauge stopping it from slipping into any empty groove if it is any but the top piston ring that is being removed.

20. Flywheel Removal

1. Remove the clutch as described in Chapter 5.
2. No lock tabs are fitted under the six bolts which hold the flywheel to the flywheel flange on the rear of the crankshaft.
3. Unscrew the bolts and remove them.
4. Lift the flywheel away from the crankshaft flange.
NOTE: Some difficulty may be experienced in removing the bolts by the rotation of the crankshaft every time pressure is put on the spanner. To lock the crankshaft in position while the bolts are removed, wedge a block of wood between the crankshaft and the side of the block inside the crankcase.

21. Main Bearing & Crankshaft Removal

1. With the engine out of the car and the timing gears, sump, flywheel, connecting rods and pistons removed, undo evenly the ten bolts retaining the five main bearing caps in place.
2. Lift out the bolts and lock washers and remove the main bearing caps together with the bottom halves of each shell bearing. Take great care to keep the caps the correct way round and in their right order, and the shells in the right caps, Mark No.1 cap as such.
3. Remove the semi-circular thrust washers fitted to the centre main bearing.
4. Remove the crankshaft by lifting it out from the crankcase.

22. Timing Chain Tensioner — Removal

1. Undo the two bolts and washers which hold the timing chain tensioner in place. Lift off the tensioner.
2. Pull the timing chain tensioner arm off its hinge pin on the front of the block.

23. Lubrication & Crankcase Ventilation Systems — Description

1. A forced feed system of lubrication is fitted with oil circulated round the engine by a pump draining from the sump below the block.
2. The full flow filter and oil pump assembly is mounted externally on the right-hand side of the cylinder block. The pump is driven by means of a short shaft and skew gear off the camshaft.
3. Oil reaches the pump via a tube pressed into the cylinder block sump face. Initial filtration is provided by a spring loaded gauze on the end of the tube. Drillings in the block carry the oil under pressure to the main and big end bearings. Oil at a reduced pressure is fed to the valve and rocker gear and the timing chain and gearwheels.
4. An eccentric bi-rotor type of oil pump is fitted to all models.
5. A semi-closed positive ventilation system is fitted. A breather valve in the oil filler cap allows air to enter as required. Crankcase fumes travel out through an oil separator and emission control valve, and then via a connecting tube back into the inlet manifold. In this way the majority of

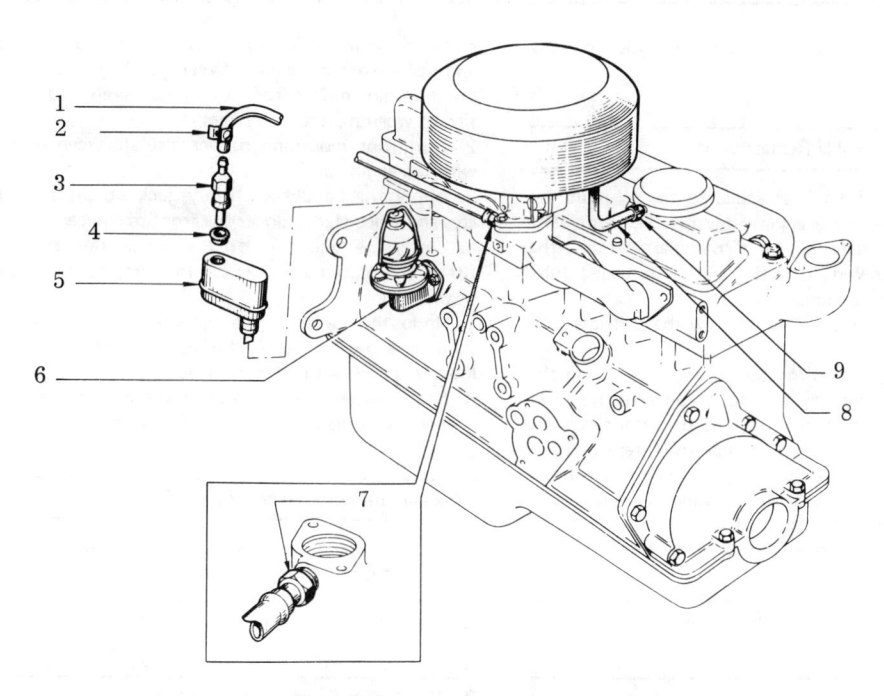

Fig.1.6. EXPLODED VIEW OF CRANKCASE EMISSION CONTROL SYSTEM

1. Hose
2. Clip
3. Union
4. Grommet
5. Oil separator
6. Fuel pump assembly
7. Adaptor elbow
8. Hose
9. Clip

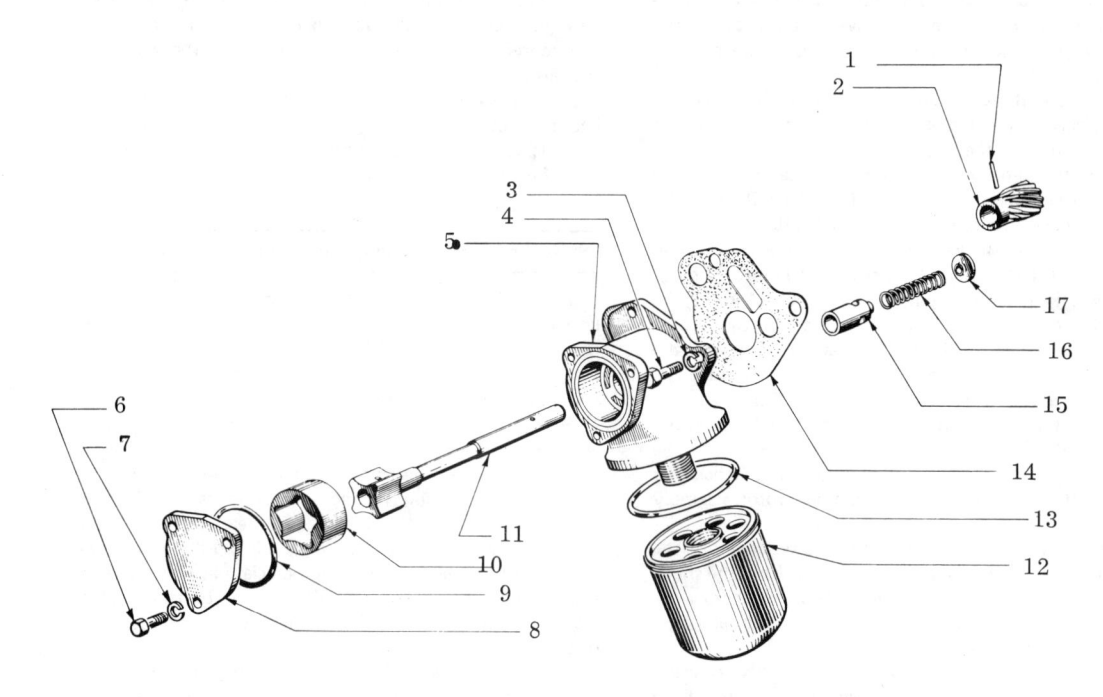

Fig.1.7. EXPLODED VIEW OF OIL PUMP & FILTER

1. Pin
2. Pinion
3. Spring washer
4. Bolt
5. Pump body
6. Bolt
7. Spring washer
8. Cover
9. Sealing ring
10. Outer rotor
11. Inner rotor
12. Filter
13. Sealing ring
14. Gasket
15. Plunger
16. Spring
17. Retainer

31

Chapter 1/Engine

crankcase fumes are burnt during the combustion process in the cylinder.

24. Oil Filter — Removal & Replacement

1. The full flow oil filter is attached to the oil pump on the right-hand side of the engine towards the front. The element comes in the form of a disposable cartridge, the whole cartridge screwing directly onto a threaded tube protruding from the oil pump.
2. To remove the filter, simply unscrew the cartridge and throw it away.
3. A rubber sealing ring is located in a groove round the head of the filter cartridge and forms an effective leak-proof joint between the pump body and the filter cartridge. A new sealing ring is supplied with each new filter cartridge.
4. Before fitting a new filter cartridge thoroughly clean the pump face and ensure that the new sealing ring is correctly located in its groove in the filter cartridge.
5. Lightly oil the sealing ring then screw the filter cartridge onto its thread until tight.
6. Run the engine for a few minutes and check for leaks the area where the filter cartridge and oil pump join.

25. Oil Pump Overhaul

1. If the oil pump is worn it is best to purchase an exchange reconditioned unit as a good oil pump is at the very heart of long engine life. Generally speaking an exchange or overhauled pump should be fitted at a major engine reconditioning. If it is wished to overhaul the oil pump, detach the pump and filter unit from the cylinder block, and remove the filter body and element.
2. Remove the three bolts and lockwashers securing the end plate and remove the plate. Lift away the 'O' ring from the sealing groove in the body.
3. On eccentric bi-rotor pumps check the clearance between the inner and outer rotors (B in Fig.1.8.) with a feeler blade. The clearance should not exceed 0.006 inch (0.15 mm). The clearance between the outer rotor and the pump body (C in Fig.1.8) should not exceed 0.010 in. (0.25 mm).
4. The endfloat of the pump can be checked in the following manner:- Lay a straight edge across the face of the pump in order to check the clearance between the faces of the rotors and the bottom of the straight edge. This clearance should not exceed 0.005 in. If the clearance is excessive the face of the pump body can be carefully lapped on a flat surface.
5. Replacement rotors are supplied only as a matched pair so that, if the clearance is excessive, a new rotor assembly must be fitted.
6. When it is necessary to renew the rotors, drive out the pin securing the skew gear and pull the gear from the shaft. Remove the inner rotor and drive shaft and withdraw the outer rotor. Install the outer rotor with the chamfered end towards the pump body.
7. Fit the inner rotor and drive shaft assembly, position the skew gear and install the pin. Tap over each end of the pin to prevent it loosening in service. Position a new 'O' ring in the groove in the pump body, fit the end plate in position and secure with the four bolts and lockwashers.
8. Refit the oil pump assembly together with a new gasket and secure in place with three bolts and lockwashers.

26. Engine Front Mountings — Removal & Replacement

1. With time the bonded rubber insulators, one on each of the front mountings, will perish causing undue vibration and noise from the engine. Severe juddering when reversing or when moving off from rest is also likely and is a further sign of worn mounting rubbers.
2. The front mounting rubber insulators can be changed with the engine in the car.
3. Apply the handbrake firmly, jack up the front of the car, and place stands under the front of the car.
4. Lower the jack, take off the engine sump shield where fitted, and place the jack under the sump to take the weight of the engine.
5. Undo the lower engine mounting nut on either side, then raise the engine on the jack until the threads of the lower studs clear the slots in which they lie.
6. Now remove the top nuts from either side, remove the rubber insulators and replace with new ones.

27. Examination & Renovation — General

With the engine stripped down and all parts thoroughly cleaned, it is now time to examine everything for wear. The following items should be checked and where necessary renewed or renovated as described in the following sections.

28. Crankshaft Examination & Renovation

1. Examine the crankpin and main journal surfaces for signs of scoring or scratches. Check the ovality of the crankpins at different positions with a micrometer. If more than 0.001 inch out of round, the crankpins will have to be reground. They will also have to be reground if there are any scores or scratches present. Also check the journals in the same fashion.
2. If it is necessary to regrind the crankshaft and fit new bearings your local Ford garage or engineering works will be able to decide how much metal to grind off and the size of new bearing shells.

29. Big End & Main Bearings—Examination & Renovation

Big end bearing failure is accompanied by a noisy knocking from the crankcase, and a slight drop in oil pressure. Main bearing failure is accompanied by vibration which can be quite severe as the engine speed rises and falls and a drop in oil pressure.

Bearings which have not broken up, but are badly worn give rise to low oil pressure and some vibration. Inspect the big ends, main bearings, and thrust washer for signs of general wear, scoring, pitting and scratches. The bearings should be matt grey in colour. With lead-indium bearings should a trace of copper colour be noticed the bearings are badly worn as the lead bearing material has worn away to expose the indium underlay. Renew the bearings if they are in this condition or if there is any sign of scoring or pitting.

The undersizes available are designed to correspond with the regrind sizes, i.e. -.010 inch bearings are correct for a crankshaft reground -.010 inch undersize. The bearings are in fact, slightly more than the stated undersize as running clearances have been allowed for during their manufacture.

Very long engine life can be achieved by changing big end bearings at intervals of 30,000 miles and main bearings at intervals of 50,000 miles, irrespective of bearing wear. Normally, crankshaft wear is infinitesimal and a change of bearings will ensure mileages of between 80,000 to 100,000 miles before crankshaft regrinding becomes necessary.

Chapter 1/Engine

Crankshafts normally have to be reground because of scoring due to bearing failure.

30. Cylinder Bores — Examination & Renovation

1. The cylinder bores must be examined for taper, ovality, scoring and scratches. Start by carefully examining the top of the cylinder bores. If they are at all worn a very slight ridge will be found on the thrust side. This marks the top of the piston ring travel. The owner will have a good indication of the bore wear prior to dismantling the engine, or removing the cylinder head. Excessive oil consumption accompanied by blue smoke from the exhaust is a sure sign of worn cylinder bores and piston rings.

2. Measure the bore diameter just under the ridge with a micrometer and compare it with the diameter at the bottom of the bore, which is not subject to wear. If the difference between the two measurements is more than .006 inch then it will be necessary to fit special pistons and rings or to have the cylinders rebored and fit oversize pistons. If no micrometer is available remove the rings from a piston and place the piston in each bore in turn about ¾ inch below the top of the bore. If an 0.010 feeler gauge can be slid between the piston and the cylinder wall on the thrust side of the bore then remedial action must be taken. Oversize pistons are available in the following sizes:—

+.0025 inch (.064 mm) +.015 inch (.38 mm)
+.030 inch (.762 mm)

3. These are accurately machined to just below these measurements so as to provide correct running clearances in bores bored out to the exact oversize dimensions.

4. If the bores are slightly worn, but not so badly worn as to justify reboring them, then special oil control rings and pistons can be fitted which will restore compression and stop the engine burning oil. Several different types are available and the manufacturers instructions concerning their fitting must be followed closely.

5. If new pistons are being fitted and the bores have not been reground, it is essential to slightly roughen the hard glaze on the sides of the bores with fine glass paper so the new piston rings will have a chance to bed in properly.

31. Pistons & Piston Rings—Examination & Renovation

1. If the old pistons are to be refitted, carefully remove the piston rings and then thoroughly clean them. Take particular care to clean out the piston ring grooves. At the same time do not scratch the aluminium in any way. If new rings are to be fitted to the old pistons then the top ring should be stepped so as to clear the ridge left above the previous top ring. If a normal but oversize new ring is fitted, it will hit the ridge and break, because the new ring will not have worn in the same way as the old, which will have worn in unison with the ridge.

2. Before fitting the rings on the pistons each should be inserted approximately 2 inch down the cylinder bore and the gap measured with a feeler gauge. This should be between .009 inch and .014 inch. It is essential that the gap should be measured at the bottom of the ring travel, as if it is measured at the top of a worn bore and gives a perfect fit, it could easily seize at the bottom. If the ring gap is too small rub down the ends of the ring with a very fine file until the gap, when fitted, is correct. To keep the rings square in the bore for measurement line each up in turn by inserting an old piston in the bore upside down, and use the piston to push the ring down about 2 inches. Remove the piston and measure the piston ring gap.

3. When fitting new pistons and rings to a rebored engine the piston ring gap can be measured at the top of the bore as the bore will not now taper (photo). It is unnecessary to measure the side clearance in the piston ring grooves with the rings fitted as the groove dimensions are accurately machined during manufacture. When fitting new oil control rings to old pistons it may be necessary to have the grooves widened by machining to accept the new wider rings. In this instance the manufacturers representative will make this quite clear and will supply the address to which the pistons must be sent for machining.

32. Camshaft & Camshaft Bearings — Examination & Renovation

1. Carefully examine the camshaft bearings for wear. If the bearings are obviously worn or pitted then they must be renewed. This is an operation for your local Ford dealer or the local engineering works as it demands the use of specialised equipment. The bearings are removed with a special drift after which new bearings are pressed in, care being taken to ensure the oil holes in the bearings line up with those in the block.

2. The camshaft itself should show no signs of wear. If scoring on the cams is noticed, the only permanently satisfactory cure is to fit a new camshaft. A temporary cure can be effected by removing the score marks by very gentle rubbing down with fine emery cloth. This latter course is likely to break through the case hardening if the score marks are of any depth.

3. Examine the skew gear for wear, chipped teeth or other damage.

4. Carefully examine the camshaft thrust plate. Excessive wear will be visually self evident and will require the fitting of a new plate.

33. Valves & Valve Seats — Examination & Renovation

1. Examine the heads of the valves for pitting and burning, especially the heads of the exhaust valves. The valve seatings should be examined at the same time. If the pitting on valve and seat is very slight the marks can be removed by grinding the seats and valves together with coarse, and then fine, valve grinding paste.

2. Where bad pitting has occured to the valve seats it will be necessary to recut them and fit new valves. If the valve seats are so worn that they cannot be recut, then it will be necessary to fit new valve seat inserts. These latter two jobs should be entrusted to the local Ford agent or engineering works. In practice it is very seldom that the seats are so badly worn that they require renewal. Normally, it is the valve that is too badly worn for replacement, and the owner can easily purchase a new set of valves and match them to the seats by valve grinding.

3. Valve grinding is carried out as follows:—

Smear a trace of coarse carborundum paste on the seat face and apply a suction grinder tool to the valve head. With a semi-rotary motion, grind the valve head to its seat, lifting the valve occasionally (photo) to redistribute the grinding paste. When a dull matt even surface finish is produced on both the valve seat and the valve, then wipe off the paste and repeat the process with fine carborundum paste, lifting and turning the valve to redistribute the paste as before. A light spring placed under the valve head will greatly ease this operation. When a smooth unbroken ring of light grey matt finish is produced, on both valve and valve seat faces, the grinding operation is completed.

4. Scrape away all carbon from the valve head and the

Chapter 1/Engine

valve stem. Carefully clean away every trace of grinding compound, taking great care to leave none in the ports or in the valve guides. Clean the valves and valve seats with a paraffin soaked rag then with a clean rag, and finally, if an air line is available, blow the valves, valve guides and valve ports clean.

34. Timing Gears & Chain — Examination & Renovation

1. Examine the teeth on both the crankshaft gear wheel and the camshaft gear wheel for wear. Each tooth forms an inverted 'V' with the gear wheel periphery, and if worn the side of each tooth under tension will be slightly concave in shape when compared with the other side of the tooth, i.e. one side of the inverted 'V' will be concave when compared with the other. If any sign of wear is present the gear wheels must be renewed.
2. Examine the links of the chain for side slackness and renew the chain if any slackness is noticeable when compared with a new chain. It is a sensible precaution to renew the chain at about 30,000 miles and at a less mileage if the engine is stripped down for a major overhaul. The actual rollers on a very badly worn chain may be slightly grooved.

35. Rockers & Rocker Shaft — Examintion & Renovation

Thoroughly clean the rocker shaft and then check the shaft for straightness by rolling it on the bench. It is most unlikely that it will deviate from normal, but, if it does, then a judicious attempt must be made to straighten it. If this is not successful purchase a new shaft. The surface of the shaft should be free from any worn ridges caused by the rocker arms. If any wear is present, renew the shaft.

Check the rocker arms for wear of the rocker bushes, for wear at the rocker arm face which bears on the valve stem, and for wear of the adjusting ball ended screws. Wear in the rocker arm bush can be checked by gripping the rocker arm tip and holding the rocker arm in place on the shaft, noting if there is any lateral rocker arm shake. If shake is present, and the arm is very loose on the shaft, a new bush or rocker arm must be fitted.

Check the tip of the rocker arm where it bears on the valve head for cracking or serious wear on the case hardening. If none is present re-use the rocker arm. Check the lower half of the ball on the end of the rocker arm adjusting screw. Check the pushrods for straightness by rolling them on the bench. Renew any that are bent.

36. Tappets — Examination & Renovation

Examine the bearing surface of the mushroom tappets which lie on the camshaft. Any indentation in this surface or any cracks indicate serious wear and the tappets should be renewed. Thoroughly clean them out, removing all traces of sludge. It is most unlikely that the sides of the tappets will prove worn, but, if they are a very loose fit in their bores and can readily be rocked, they should be exchanged for new units. It is very unusual to find any wear in the tappets, and any wear is likely to occur only at very high mileages.

37. Connecting Rods — Examination & Renovation

1. Examine the mating faces of the big end caps to see if they have ever been filed in a mistaken attempt to take up wear. If so the offending rods must be renewed.
2. Insert the gudgeon pin into the little end of the connecting rod. It should go in fairly easily, but if any slackness is present then take the rod to your local FORD dealer or engineering works and exchange it for a rod of identical weight.

38. Flywheel Starter Ring — Examination & Renovation

1. If the teeth on the flywheel starter ring are badly worn, or if some are missing then it will be necessary to remove the ring and fit a new one.
2. The number of teeth on the ring varies depending on the type of starter motor fitted. With the more usual inertia type starter (3 bolt fixing) the ring gear has 100 teeth. With the pre-engaged starter (2 bolt fixing) the ring gear has 132 teeth.
3. Various weights of flywheel are fitted to the Capri according to the model and whether a pre-engaged starter motor is being used. The correct part number is always stamped on the flywheel and should be quoted when ordering a new unit or starter ring.
4. To remove a starter ring either split it with a cold chisel after making a cut with a hacksaw blade between two teeth, or heat the ring, and use a soft headed hammer (not steel) to knock the ring off, striking it evenly and alternately, at equally spaced points. Take great care not to damage the flywheel during this process.
5. Clean and polish with emery cloth four evenly spaced areas on the outside face of the new starter ring.
6. Heat the ring evenly with an oxyacetylene flame until the polished portions turn dark blue. Hold the ring at this temperature for five minutes and then quickly fit it to the flywheel so the chamfered portion of the teeth faces the gearbox side of the flywheel.
7. The ring should be tapped gently down onto its register and left to cool naturally when the contraction of the metal on cooling will ensure that it is a secure and permanent fit. Great care must be taken not to overheat the ring, indicated by it turning light metallic blue, as if this happens the temper of the ring will be lost.
8. It does not matter which way round the 132 toothed ring is fitted as it has no chamfers on its teeth. This also makes for quick identification between the two rings.

39. Cylinder Head — Decarbonisation

1. This can be carried out with the engine either in or out of the car. With the cylinder head off carefully remove with a wire brush mounted in an electric drill (photo) and blunt scraper, all traces of carbon deposits from the combustion spaces and the ports. The valve head stems and valve guides should also be freed from any carbon deposits. Wash the combustion spaces and ports down with petrol and scrape the cylinder head surface free of any foreign matter with the side of a steel rule, or a similar article.
2. Clean the pistons and top of the cylinder bores. If the pistons are still in the block then it is essential that great care is taken to ensure that no carbon gets into the cylinder bores as this could scratch the cylinder walls or cause damage to the piston and rings. To ensure this does not happen, first turn the crankshaft so that two of the pistons are at the top of their bores. Stuff rag into the other two bores or seal them off with paper and masking tape. The waterways should also be covered with small pieces of masking tape to prevent particles of carbon entering the cooling system and damaging the water pump.
3. There are two schools of thought as to how much

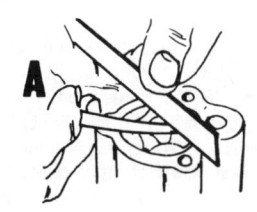

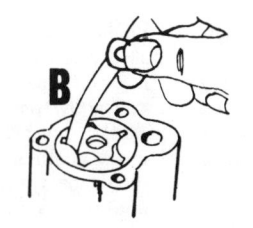

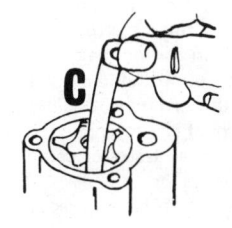

Fig.1.8. MEASURING THE OIL PUMP CLEARANCES
(A) Measuring rotor endfloat. (B) Measuring clearance between inner and outer rotors. (C) Measuring clearance between outer rotor and pump body

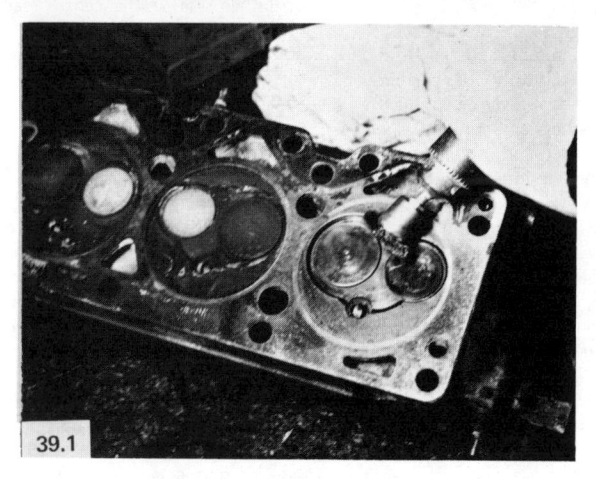

Chapter 1/Engine

carbon should be removed from the piston crown. One school recommends that a ring of carbon should be left round the edge of the piston and on the cylinder bore wall as an aid to low oil consumption. Although this is probably true for early engines with worn bores, on later engines the thought of the second school can be applied; which is that for effective decarbonisation all traces of carbon should be removed.

4. If all traces of carbon are to be removed, press a little grease into the gap between the cylinder walls and the two pistons which are to be worked on. With a blunt scraper carefully scrape away the carbon from the piston crown, taking great care not to scratch the aluminium. Also scrape away the carbon from the surrounding lip of the cylinder wall. When all carbon has been removed, scrape away the grease which will now be contaminated with carbon particles, taking care not to press any into the bores. To assist prevention of carbon build-up the piston crown can be polished with a metal polish such as Brasso. Remove the rags or masking tape from the other two cylinders and turn the crankshaft so that the two pistons which were at the bottom are now at the top. Place rag or masking tape in the cylinders which have been decarbonised and proceed as just described.

5. If a ring of carbon is going to be left round the piston then this can be helped by inserting an old piston ring into the top of the bore to rest on the piston and ensure that the carbon is not accidentally removed. Check that there are no particles of carbon in the cylinder bores. Decarbonising is now complete.

40. Valve Guides — Examination & Renovation

1. Examine the valve guides internally for scoring and other signs of wear. If a new vlave is a very loose fit in a guide and there is a trace of lateral rocking then new guides will have to be fitted.
2. The fitting of new guides is a job which should be done by your local FORD dealer or local engineering works.

41. Engine Reassembly — General

1. To ensure maximum life with minimum trouble from a rebuilt engine, not only must everything be correctly assembled, but everything must be spotlessly clean, all the oilways must be clear, locking washers and spring washers must always be fitted where indicated and all bearing and other working surfaces must be thoroughly lubricated during assembly.
2. Before assembly begins renew any bolts or studs the threads of which are in any way damaged, and whenever possible use new spring washers.
3. Apart from your normal tools, a supply of clean rag, an oil can filled with engine oil (an empty plastic detergent bottle thoroughly cleaned and washed out, will invariably do just as well), a new supply of assorted spring washers, a set of new gaskets, and a torque spanner, should be collected together.

42. Assembling the Engine

1. Thoroughly clean the block and ensure all traces of old gaskets etc., are removed.
2. Fit a new rear main oil seal bearing retainer gasket to the rear end of the cylinder block (photo).
3. Then fit the rear main oil seal bearing retainer housing (photo). Note that on some engines the housing is not split as the semi-circular one shown here. Where a fully circular retainer housing is fitted, the oil seal is also circular and is simply prised out when removed, a new one being pressed in with the aid of a flat block of wood.
4. Lightly tighten the four retaining bolts with spring washers under their heads noting that the two bolts arrowed in the photo are dowelled to ensure correct alignment and should be tightened first. Do not fully tighten the bolts until the crankshaft is in place and securely torqued down to ensure proper centralisation of the housing on the flywheel mounting flange.
5. On models with the split oil seal turn the block upside down and fit the crankshaft rear bearing oil seal (photo).
6. Position the upper halves of the shell bearings in their correct positions so that the tabs of the shells engage in the machined keyways in the sides of the bearing locations, (photo).
7. Oil the main bearing shells after they have been fitted in position (photo).
8. Thoroughly clean out the oilways in the crankshaft with the aid of a thin wire brush or pipe cleaners (photo).
9. To check for the possibility of an error in the grinding of the crankshaft journal (presuming the crankshaft has been reground) smear engineers blue evenly over each big end journal in turn (photo) with the crankshaft end flange held firmly in position in a vice.
10 With new shell bearings fitted to the connecting rods fit the correct rod to each journal in turn (photo) fully tightening down the securing bolts.
11 Spin the rod on the crankshaft a few times and then remove the big end cap. A fine unbroken layer of engineers blue should cover the whole of the journal. If the blue is much darker on one side than the other or if the blue has disappeared from a certain area (ignore the very edges of the journal) then something is wrong and the journal will have to be checked with a micrometer.
12 The main journals should also be checked in similar fashion with the crankshaft in the crankcase. On completion of these tests remove all traces of the engineers blue.
13 The crankshaft can now be lowered carefully into place. (photo).
14 Fit new end float thrust washers. These locate in recesses on either side of the centre main bearing in the cylinder block and must be fitted with the oil grooves facing the crankshaft flange. With the crankshaft in position check for float which should be between 0.003 and 0.011 inch (0.076 to 0.279 mm). If the end float is incorrect remove the thrust washers and select suitable washers to give the correct end float (photo).
15 Place the lower halves of the main bearing shells in their caps making sure that the locking tabs fit into the machined grooves. Refit the main bearing caps ensuring that they are the correct way round and that the correct cap is on the correct journal. The two front caps are marked 'F' (photo), the centre cap 'CENTRE' and the two rear caps 'R'. Tighten the cap bolts to a torque of 65 to 70 lbs/ft. Spin the crankshaft to make certain it is turning freely.
16 Check that the piston ring grooves and oilways are thoroughly clean and unblocked. Piston rings must always be fitted over the head of the piston and never from the bottom. The easiest method to use when fitting rings is to wrap a .020 feeler gauge round the top of the piston and place the rings one at a time, starting with the bottom oil control ring, over the feeler gauge.
17 The feeler gauge, complete with ring, can then be slid down the piston over the other piston ring grooves until the correct groove is reached. The piston ring is then slid gently off the feeler gauge into the groove.
18 An alternative method is to fit the rings by holding them slightly open with the thumbs and both of your index

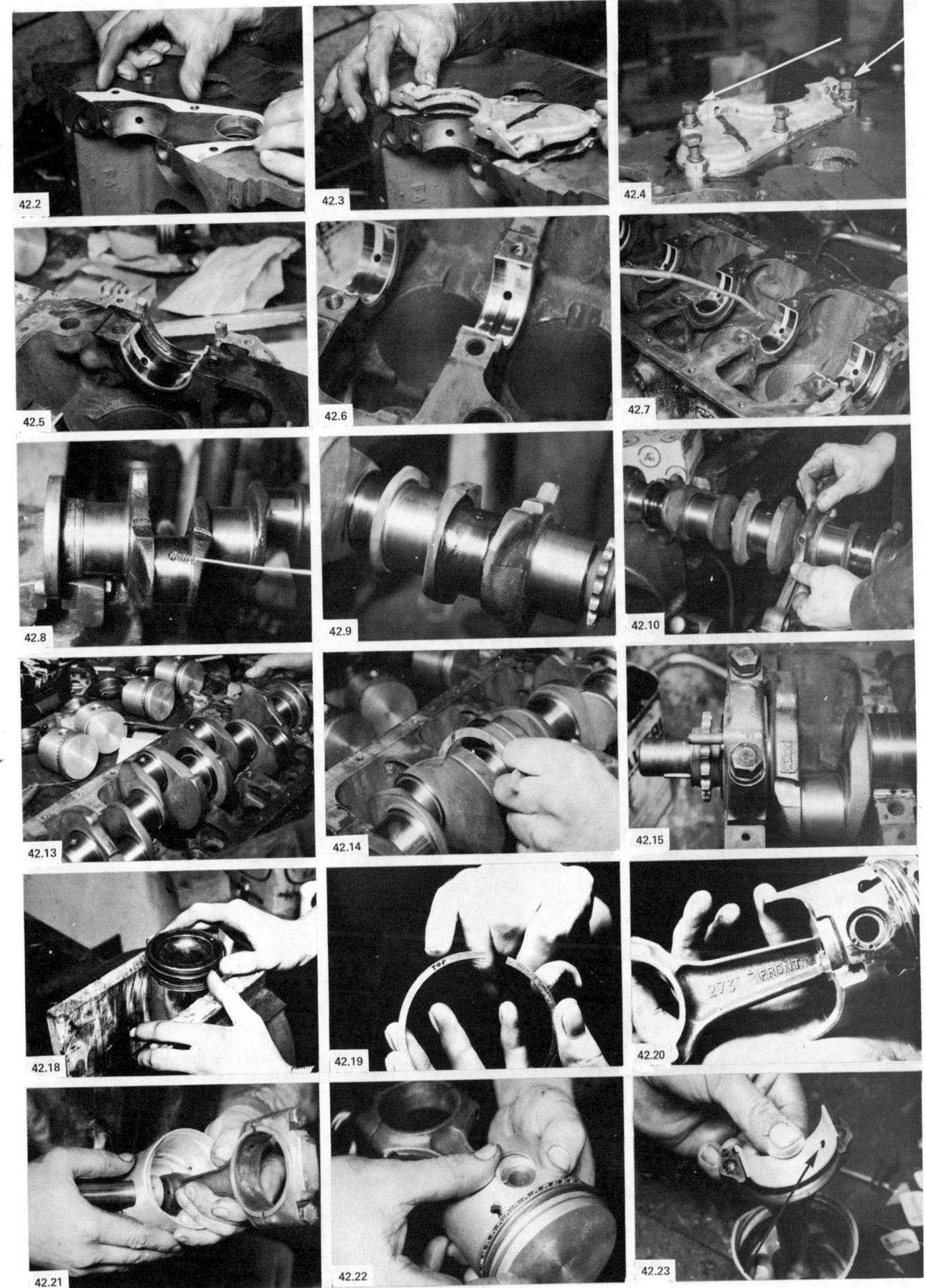

42.2 42.3 42.4
42.5 42.6 42.7
42.8 42.9 42.10
42.13 42.14 42.15
42.18 42.19 42.20
42.21 42.22 42.23

37

fingers (photo). This method requires a steady hand and great care as it is easy to open the ring too much and break it.

19 When assembling the rings, note that the compression rings are marked 'top', (photo) and that the upper ring is chromium plated. The ring gaps should be spaced equally round the piston.

20 If the same pistons are being used, then they must be mated to the same connecting rod with the same gudgeon pin. If new pistons are being fitted it does not matter which connecting rod they are used with. Note that the word FRONT is stamped on one side of each of the rods. (photo). On reassembly the side marked 'FRONT' must be towards the front of the engine.

21 Fit a gudgeon pin circlip in position at one end of the gudgeon pin hole in the piston and fit the piston to the connecting rod by sliding in the gudgeon pin (photo). The arrow on the crown of each piston must be on the same side as the word 'FRONT' on the connecting rod.

22 Fit the second circlip in position (photo). Repeat this procedure for the remaining three pistons and connecting rods.

23 Fit the connecting rod in position and check that the oil hole (arrowed in photo) in the upper half of each bearing aligns with the oil squirt hole in the connecting rod.

24 With a wad of clean rag wipe the cylinder bores clean, and then oil them generously. The pistons complete with connecting rods, are fitted to their bores from above, (photo). As each piston is inserted into its bore ensure that it is the correct piston/connecting rod assembly for that particular bore and that the connecting rod is the right way round, and that the front of the piston is towards the front of the bore, i.e. towards the front of the engine.

25 The piston will only slide into the bore as far as the oil control ring. It is then necessary to compress the piston rings in a clamp (photo).

26 Gently tap the piston into the cylinder bore with a wooden or plastic hammer (photo). If a proper piston ring clamp is not available then a suitable jubilee clip does the job very well.

27 Note that the directional arrow is on the side of the piston (photo).

28 Fit the shell bearings to the big end caps so the tongue on the back of each bearing lies in the machined recess, (photo).

29 Generously oil the crankshaft connecting rod journals and then replace each big end cap on the same connecting rod from which it was removed. Fit the locking plates under the head of the big end bolts, tap the caps right home on the dowels and then tighten the bolts to a torque of 30 to 35 lbs/ft. Lock the bolts in position by knocking up the tabs on the locking washers (photo).

30 The semi rebuilt engine will now look like this (photo), and is ready for the cam followers and cam to be fitted.

31 Fit the eight cam followers into the same holes in the block from which each was removed (photo). The cam followers can only be fitted with the block upside down.

32 Fit the woodruff key in its slot on the front of the crankshaft and then press the timing sprocket into place so the timing mark faces forward. Oil the camshaft shell bearings and insert the camshaft into the block (which should still be upside down). (photo).

33 Make sure the camshaft turns freely and then fit the thrust plate behind the camshaft flange as shown (photo). Measure the endfloat with a feeler gauge - it should be between 0.0025 and 0.0075 inch. If this is not so then renew the plate.

34 Fit the two camshaft flange bolts into their joint washer and screw down the bolts securely (photo).

35 Turn up the tab (arrowed in photo) under the head of each bolt to lock it in place.

36 When refitting the timing chain round the gearwheels and to the engine, the two timing lines (arrowed in photo) must be adjacent to each other on an imaginary line passing through each gearwheel centre.

37 With the timing marks correctly aligned turn the camshaft until the protruding dowel locates in the hole (arrowed in photo) in the camshaft sprocket wheel.

38 Tighten the two retaining bolts and bend up the tabs on the lockwasher (photo).

39 Fit the oil slinger to the nose of the crankshaft, concave side facing outwards. The cut-out (arrowed in photo) locates over the woodruff key.

40 Then slide the timing chain tensioner arm over its hinge pin on the front of the block (photo).

41 Turn the tensioner back from its free position so it will apply pressure to the tensioner arm and replace the tensioner on the block sump flange (photo).

42 Bolt the tensioner to the block using spring washers under the heads of the two bolts (arrowed in photo).

43 Remove the front oil seal from the timing chain cover and with the aid of a vice carefully press a new seal into position (photo). Lightly lubricate the face of the seal which will bear against the crankshaft.

44 Using jointing compound fit a new gasket in place. (photo).

45 Fit the timing chain cover replacing and tightening the two dowel bolts first. These fit in the holes nearest the sump flange and serve to align the timing cover correctly. Ensure spring washers are used and then tighten the bolts evenly.

46 Refit the tube or oil breather device to its recess in the top of the petrol pump housing on the block tapping it gently into place (photo). Replace the oil pump suction pipe using a new tab washer and position the gauze head so it clears the crankshaft throw and the oil return pipe, (where fitted). Tighten the nut and bend back the tab of the lockwasher.

47 Clean the flanges of the sump and fit new gaskets in place. Fit a new oil seal to the flange at the rear of the crankcase and at the front (photo).

48 Replace the flywheel and tighten down the six securing bolts to a torque of 50 to 54 lb/ft. Carefully replace the sump (photo) taking care not to dislodge the gaskets.

49 Finally lower the sump into place (photo) and replace the bolts holding the sump in place.

50 The engine can now be turned over so it is the right way up. Coat the oil pump flanges with jointing compound (photo).

51 Fit a new gasket in place on the oil pump (photo).

52 Position the oil pump against the block ensuring the skew gear teeth on the drive shaft mate with those on the camshaft (photo).

53 Replace the three securing bolts and spring washers and tighten them down evenly (photo).

54 Moving to the front of the engine align the slot in the crankshaft pulley wheel with the key on the crankshaft and gently tap the pulley wheel home (photo).

55 Secure the pulley wheel by fitting the large flat washer, the spring washer and then the bolt which should be tightened securely (photo).

56 The next step is to thoroughly clean the faces of the block and cylinder head. Then fit a new cylinder head gasket (photo).

57 With the cylinder head on its side lubricate the valve stems and refit the valves to their correct guides (photo). The valves should previously have been ground in. (See Section 33).

58 Then fit the valve stem umbrella oil seals open ends down (photo).

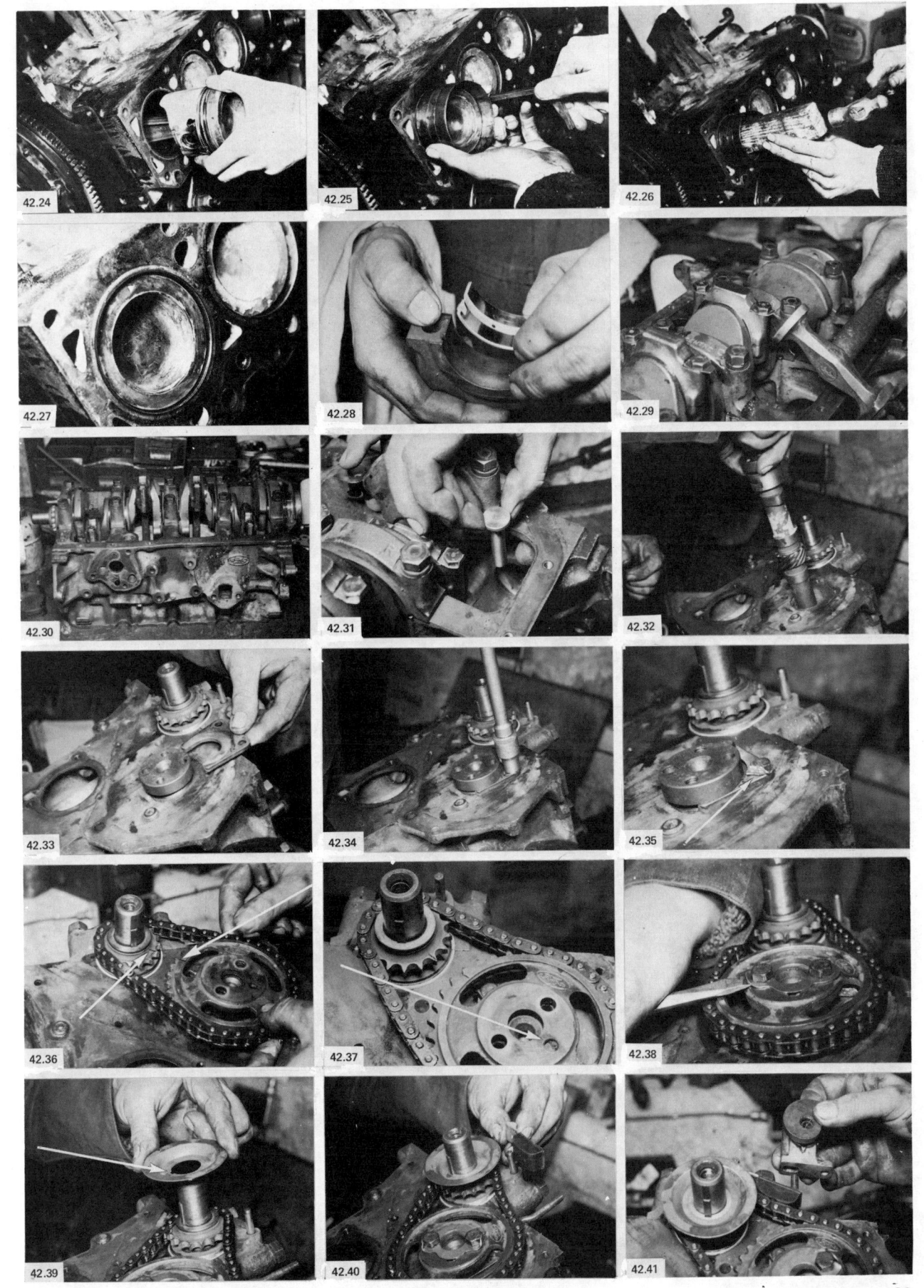

42.24 42.25 42.26
42.27 42.28 42.29
42.30 42.31 42.32
42.33 42.34 42.35
42.36 42.37 42.38
42.39 42.40 42.41

39

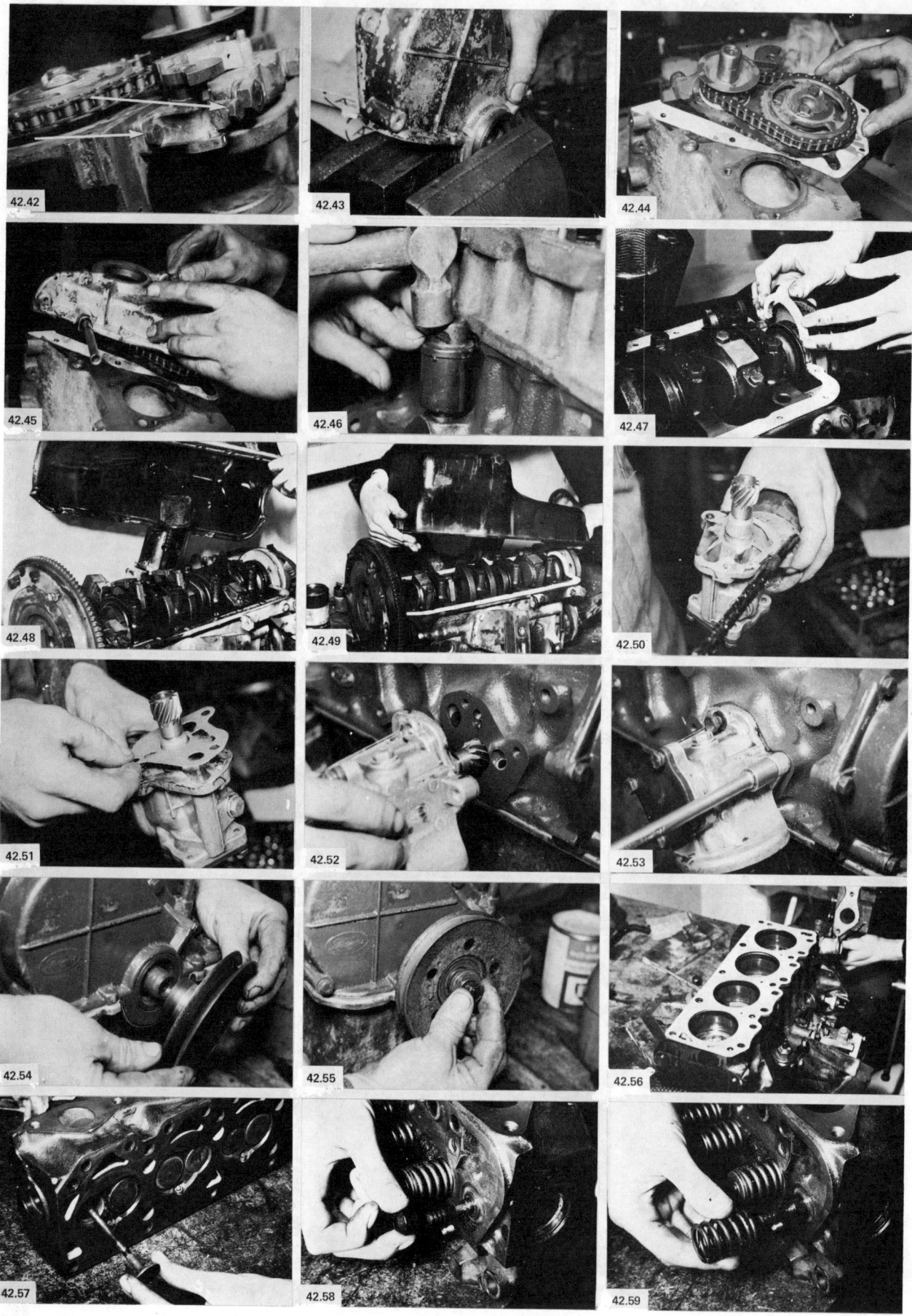

42.42
42.43
42.44
42.45
42.46
42.47
42.48
42.49
42.50
42.51
42.52
42.53
42.54
42.55
42.56
42.57
42.58
42.59

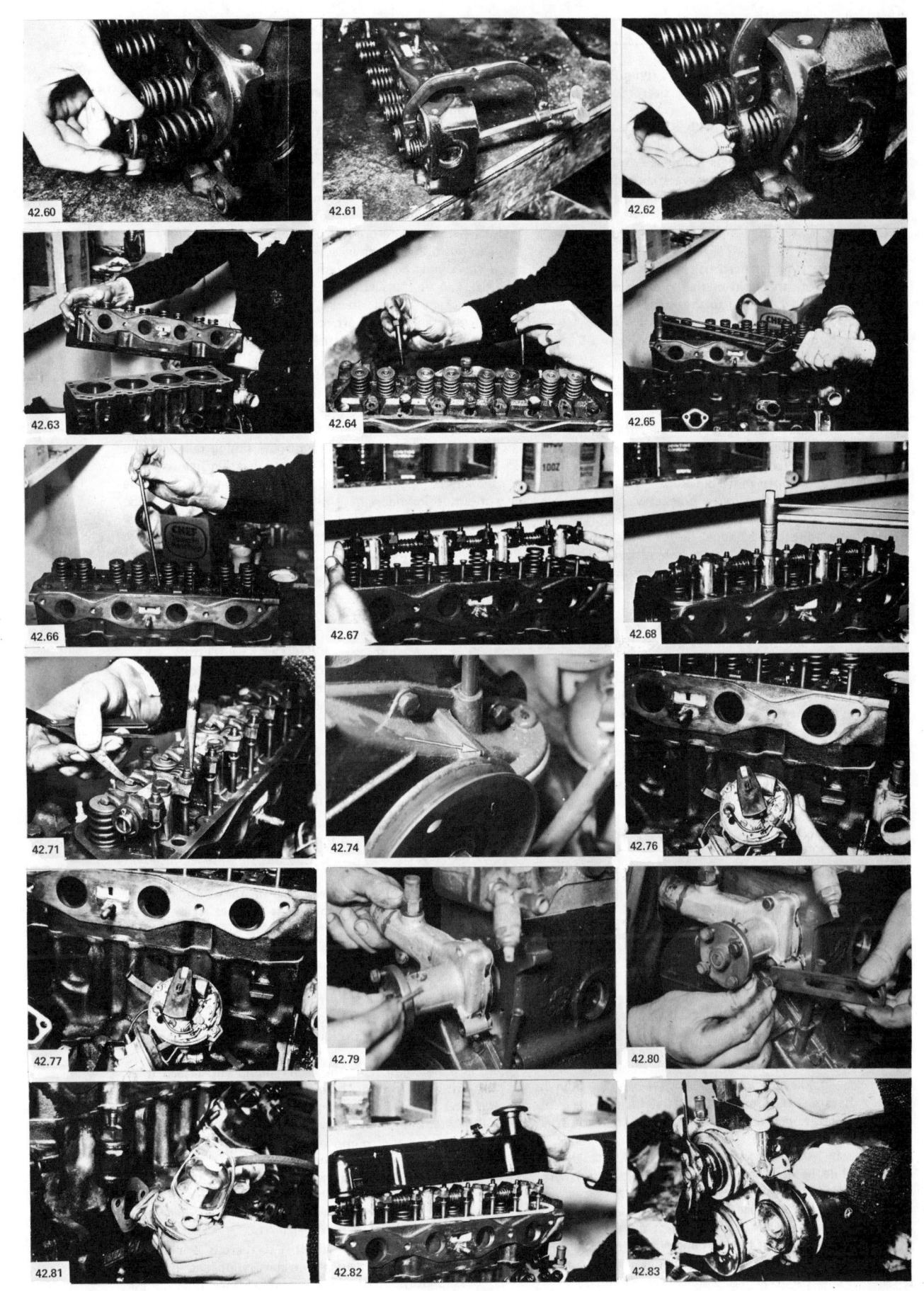

42.60 42.61 42.62
42.63 42.64 42.65
42.66 42.67 42.68
42.71 42.74 42.76
42.77 42.79 42.80
42.81 42.82 42.83

41

Chapter 1/Engine

59 Next slide the valve spring into place (photo).
60 Slide the valve spring retainer over the valve stem (photo).
61 Compress the valve spring with a compressor as shown in the photograph.
62 Then refit the split collets (photo). A trace of grease will help to hold them to the valve stem recess until the spring compressor is slackened off and the collets are wedged in place by the spring.
63 Carefully lower the cylinder head onto the block (photo).
64 Replace the cylinder head bolts and screw them down finger tight. Note that two of the bolts are of a different length and should be fitted to the holes indicated in the photograph.
65 With a torque wrench, tighten the bolts to 65 to 70 lbs/ft. (photo) in the order shown in Fig.1.2.
66 Fit the pushrods into the same holes in the block from which they were removed. Make sure the pushrods seat properly in the cam followers (photo).
67 Reassemble the rocker gear into the rocker shaft and fit the shaft to the cylinder head (photo). Ensure that the oil holes are clear and that the cut-outs for the securing bolts lie facing the holes in the brackets.
68 Tighten down the four rocker bracket washers and bolts to a torque of 17–22 lbs/ft. (photo).
69 The valve adjustments should be made with the engine cold. The importance of correct rocker arm/valve stem clearances cannot be overstressed as they vitally affect the performance of the engine. If the clearances are set too open, the efficiency of the engine is reduced as the valves open late and close earlier than was intended. If, on the other hand the clearances are set too close there is a danger that the stems will expand upon heating and not allow the valves to close properly which will cause burning of the valve head and seat and possible warping. If the engine is in the car, access to the rockers is by removing the four holding down screws from the rocker cover, and then lifting the rocker cover and gasket away.
70 It is important that the clearance is set when the tappet of the valve being adjusted is on the heel of the cam, (i.e. opposite the peak). This can be ensured by carrying out the adjustments in the following order (which also avoids turning the crankshaft more than necessary):—

Valve fully open	Check & Adjust	Clearance	G.T.
Valve No.8.	Valve No.1.	0.018 in.	0.021 in.
Valve No.6.	Valve No.3.	0.008 in.	0.011 in.
Valve No.4.	Valve No.5.	0.018 in.	0.021 in.
Valve No.7.	Valve No.2.	0.008 in.	0.011 in.
Valve No.1.	Valve No.8.	0.018 in.	0.021 in.
Valve No.3.	Valve No.6.	0.008 in.	0.011 in.
Valve No.5.	Valve No.4.	0.018 in.	0.021 in.
Valve No.2.	Valve No.7.	0.008 in.	0.011 in.

71 The correct feeler gauge clearances between the valve stem and rocker arm pad with the engine cold is on non-G.T. models 0.008 inch for the inlet valves and 0.018 inch for the exhausts. On G.T. models it is 0.011 inch on the inlet valves and 0.021 inch on the exhausts. Working from the front of the engine (No.1 valve) the correct clearance is obtained by slackening the hexagon locknut with a spanner while holding the ball pin against rotation with a screwdriver. Then, still pressing down with the screwdriver, insert a feeler gauge in the gap between the valve stem head and the rocker arm and adjust the ball pin until the feeler gauge will just move in and out without nipping. (photo). Then, still holding the ball pin in the correct position, tighten the locknut. An alternative method is to set the gaps with the engine running, and although this may be faster it is no more reliable.

72 Do not refit the rocker cover before replacing the distributor and setting the ignition timing. It is important to set the distributor drive correctly as otherwise the ignition timing will be totally incorrect. It is possible to set the distributor drive in apparently the right position, but, in fact, 180° out, by omitting to select the correct cylinder which must not only be at T.D.C. but must also be on its firing stroke with both valves closed. The distributor drive should therefore not be fitted until the cylinder head is in position and the valves can be observed. Alternatively if the timing cover has not been replaced, the distributor drive can be replaced when the lines on the timing wheels are adjacent to each other.
73 Rotate the crankshaft so that No.1 piston is at T.D.C. and on its firing stroke (the lines in the timing gears will be adjacent to each other). When No.1 piston is at T.D.C. both valves will be closed and both rocker arms will 'rock' slightly because of the stem to arm pad clearance.
74 Note the two timing marks on the timing case (arrowed in photo) and the notch on the crankshaft wheel periphery. When the cut-out is in line with the timing mark on the left this indicates 10° B.T.D.C. and when in line with the one on the right 6° B.T.D.C. Set the crankshaft so the cut-out is in the right position of initial advance which varies depending on the model and is detailed below:—

1300 c.c. G.T.	10° BTDC	Using 97 octane fuel
1600 c.c. G.T.	8° BTDC	Ditto
1300 c.c. High compress.	10° BTDC	Ditto
1600 c.c. High compress.	10° BTDC	Ditto
1300 c.c. Low compress.	10° BTDC	Using 89 octane fuel
1600 c.c. Low compress.	10° BTDC	Ditto
1300 c.c. High compress.	6° BTDC	Using 94 octane fuel
1600 c.c. High compress.	6° BTDC	Ditto
1300 c.c. Low compress.	4° BTDC	Using 86 octane fuel
1600 c.c. Low compress.	4° BTDC	Ditto

75 Hold the distributor in place so the vacuum unit is towards the rear of the engine and at an angle of about 30° to the block. Do not yet engage the distributor drive gear with the skew gear on the camshaft.
76 Turn the rotor arm so that it points towards No.2 inlet port (photo).
77 Push the distributor shaft into its bore and note as the distributor drive gear and skew gear on the camshaft mate, that the rotor arm turns so that it assumes a position of approximately 90° to the engine (photo). Fit the bolt and washer which holds the distributor clamp plate to the block.
78 Loosen the clamp on the base of the distributor and slightly turn the distributor body until the points just start to open while holding the rotor arm against the direction of rotation so no lost motion is present. Tighten the clamp. For a full description of how to do this accurately see Chapter 4/10.
79 Fit a new gasket to the water pump and attach it to the front of the cylinder block (photo).
80 Note that the dynamo support strap fits under the head of the lower bolt on the water pump as shown, (photo).
81 Replace the fuel pump using a new gasket and tighten up the two securing bolts (photo).
82 Fit the thermostat and thermostat gasket to the cylinder head and then replace the thermostat outlet pipe. Replace the sparking plugs and refit the rocker cover using a new gasket (photo).
83 Refit the dynamo and adjust it so there is ½ inch play in the fan belt between the water pump and dynamo pulleys (photo). Refit the vacuum advance pipe to the distributor and refit the sender units.

Fig.1.9. View of the ignition timing marks

43

Chapter 1/Engine

43. Final Assembly

1. Reconnect the ancillary components to the engine in the reverse order to which they were removed.
2. It should be noted that in all cases it is best to reassemble the engine as far as possible before refitting it to the car. This means that the inlet and exhaust manifolds (photo), carburetter, dynamo, water thermostat, oil filter, distributor and engine mounting brackets, should all be in position. Ensure that the oil filter is filled with engine oil, as otherwise there will be a delay in the oil reaching the bearings while the oil filter refills.

44. Engine Replacement — General

1. Although the engine can be replaced with one man and a suitable winch, it is easier if two are present. One to lower the engine into the engine compartment and the other to guide the engine into position and to ensure it does not foul anything.
2. At this stage one or two tips may come in useful. Ensure all the loose leads, cables, etc., are tucked out of the way. If not it is easy to trap one and so cause much additional work after the engine is replaced. Smear grease on the tip of the gearbox input shaft before fitting the gearbox.
3. Always fit a new fan belt and new cooling hoses and jubilee clips as this will help eliminate the possibility of failure while on the road. An exchange rebuilt carburetter also helps!
4. Two pairs of hands are better than one when refitting the bonnet. Do not tighten the bonnet securing bolts fully until it is ascertained that the bonnet is on straight.

45. Engine Replacement Without Gearbox

1. Position a sling around the engine and support its weight on suitable lifting tackle. If using a fixed hoist raise the engine and then roll the car under it. Place a jack under the gearbox.
2. Lower the engine into the engine compartment ensuring that nothing is fouling. Line up the engine and gearbox raising the height of the gearbox if necessary with the jack until the splines on the gearbox input shaft mate with the splined grooves in the clutch disc centre.
3. To line up the mounting bracket holes it may be necessary to move the engine about slightly and this will be found to be much easier if the lifting slings are still in position and taking most of the weight.
4. Replace the bolts and washers - one on each side - which hold the engine mountings to the bodyframe.
5. Do up those engine to clutch housing bolts which are accessible from above. Remove the slings from the engine, and jack up the front of the car securely so it can be worked on from underneath.
6. Working underneath the car, replace the bracing bracket on the bellhousing, and all the lower clutch housing bolts. Do up the bolts holding the clutch housing to the rear of the engine.
7. Refit the starter motor, replace the three retaining bolts, and the starter cable which is held in place with a nut and washer.
8. Replace the engine breather pipe on the clutch housing, (where fitted) and reconnect the fuel lines.
9. Reconnect the high tension lead to the distributor centre terminal and the low tension lead to the terminal on the side of the coil. Refit the ignition distributor cap and connect the H.T. leads to the plugs (if not already done).
10 Reconnect the exhaust downpipe to the exhaust manifold; and secure the throttle linkage and choke control to the carburetter.
11 Replace the temperature gauge sender unit lead.
12 Replace the radiator and reconnect the top and bottom hoses and the heater hoses (on models fitted with a heater unit).
13 Replace the engine splash shield (where fitted); the air cleaner; the bonnet; and reconnect the two leads to the rear of the dynamo.
14 Reconnect the battery.
15 Reconnect the clutch cable to the clutch release mechanism and replace the rubber boot. Adjust the clutch.
16 Check that the drain taps are closed and refill the cooling system with water and the engine with the correct grade of oil. Start the engine and carefully check for oil or water leaks. There should be no oil or water leaks if the engine has been reassembled carefully, all nuts and bolts tightened down correctly, and new gaskets and joints used throughout.

46. Engine Replacement With Gearbox

1. Position a sling or rope round the engine/gearbox unit and support its weight on suitable lifting tackle. If using a fixed hoist, raise the power unit and roll the car underneath so the power unit will easily drop into the engine compartment.
2. Lower the assembly into position moving the car forward at the same time. When the engine is three-quarters in it will help to place a trolley jack under the gearbox.
3. Line up the splined end of the propeller shaft and the gearbox extension and mate the two together. This may require a certain amount of rocking to and fro to get the splines into the correct position.
4. Lower the engine onto its front mountings and fit the retaining bolts.
5. Place a jack under the rear of the engine and raise it enough to fit the rear mounting under the gearbox extension.
6. Refit the gear lever and gaiter, replace the exhaust system bracing bracket on the gearbox, replace the clutch cable and adjust as necessary. Replace the speedometer cable and then proceed as in Section 45, paragraphs 7 to 16 inclusive having first refilled the gearbox with the correct oil.

Fault Finding Chart — Engine

Symptom	Reason/s	Remedy
Engine will not turn over when starter switch is operated	Flat battery. Bad battery connections. Bad connections at solenoid switch and/or starter motor.	Check that battery is fully charged and that all connections are clean and tight.
	Starter motor jammed.	Turn the square headed end of the starter motor shaft with a spanner to free it. Where a pre-engaged starter is fitted rock the car back and forth with a gear engaged. If this does not free pinion remove starter.
	Defective solenoid.	Bridge the main terminals of the solenoid switch with a piece of heavy duty cable in order to operate the starter.
	Starter motor defective.	Remove and overhaul starter motor.
Engine turns over normally but fails to fire and run	No spark at plugs.	Check ignition system according to procedures given in Chapter 4.
	No fuel reaching engine.	Check fuel system according to procedures given in Chapter 3.
	Too much fuel reaching the engine (flooding).	Check the fuel system as above.
Engine starts but runs unevenly and misfires	Ignition and/or fuel system faults	Check the ignition and fuel systems as though the engine had failed start.
	Incorrect valve clearances.	Check and reset clearances.
	Burnt out valves. Blown cylinder head gasket.	Remove cylinder head and examine and overhaul as necessary.
	Worn out piston rings. Worn cylinder bores.	Remove cylinder head and examine pistons and cylinder bores. Overhaul as necessary.
Lack of power	Ignition and/or fuel system faults.	Check the ignition and fuel systems for correct ignition timing and carburetter settings.
	Incorrect valve clearances	Check and reset the clearances.
	Burnt out valves. Blown cylinder head gasket.	Remove cylinder head and examine and overhaul as necessary.
	Worn out piston rings. Worn cylinder bores.	Remove cylinder head and examine pistons and cylinder bores. Overhaul as necessary.
Excessive oil consumption	Oil leaks from crankshaft rear oil seal, timing cover gasket and oil seal, rocker cover gasket, oil filter gasket, sump gasket, sump plug washer.	Identify source of leak and renew seal as appropriate.
	Worn piston rings or cylinder bores resulting in oil being burnt by engine. Smoky exhaust is an indication.	Fit new rings or rebore cylinders and fit new pistons, depending on degree of wear.
	Worn valve guides and/or defective valve stem seals. Smoke blowing out from the rocker cover vents is an indication.	Remove cylinder heads and recondition valve stem bores and valves and seals as necessary.
Excessive mechanical noise from engine	Wrong valve to rocker clearances.	Adjust valve clearances.
	Worn crankshaft bearings. Worn cylinders (piston slap).	Inspect and overhaul where necessary.
	Slack or worn timing chain and sprockets.	Adjust chain and/or inspect all timing mechanism.

NOTE: When investigating starting and uneven running faults do not be tempted into snap diagnosis. Start from the beginning of the check procedure and follow it through. It will take less time in the long run. Poor performance from an engine in terms of power and economy is not normally diagnosed quickly. In any event the ignition and fuel systems must be checked first before assuming any further investigation needs to be made.

Chapter 2/Cooling System

Contents

General Description	1	Water Pump - Removal & Replacement	8
Routine Maintenance	2	Water Pump - Dismantling & Reassembly	9
Cooling System - Draining	3	Fan Belt - Adjustment	10
Cooling System - Flushing	4	Fan Belt - Removal & Replacement	11
Cooling System - Filling	5	Temperature Gauge - Fault Finding	12
Radiator - Removal, Inspection, Cleaning & Replacement	6	Temperature Gauge & Sender Unit - Removal & Replacement	13
Thermostat - Removal, Testing & Replacement	7	Anti-Freeze Mixture	14

Specifications

Type of system	Pressurised pump impellor and fan assisted
Thermostat - Type	Wax
Thermostat - Location	In cylinder head
Starts to open	85° to 89°C (185° to 192°F)
Fully open	99° to 102°C (210° to 216°F)
Radiator pressure cap opens	13 lb/sq.in. (.91 kg/cm^2)
Fan - Type - Standard	8 blades 12 inch
- Heavy duty	10 blades 12 inch
Width of fan belt	.38 inch (9.7 mm)
Outside length of fan belt	29 inch (740 mm)
Tension of fan belt	½ inch (12.8 mm) free play between dynamo and water pump pulley wheel
Water pump drive	Belt from crankshaft pulley
Coolant capacity - 1300 - without heater	8.82 pints (10.58 US pints, 5.03 litres)
- with heater	10.20 pints (12.24 US pints, 5.81 litres)
- 1600 - without heater	10.07 pints (12.08 US pints, 5.74 litres)
- with heater	11.45 pints (13.74 US pints, 6.53 litres)
Radiator - Type	Corrugated high efficiency fin
Core height - 1300 c.c.	11.0 inch (279 mm)
- 1600 c.c. and G.T.	12.0 inch (305 mm)
Width	17.26 inch (438.4 mm)
Fins per inch - 1300 c.c	10
- 1600 c.c. and G.T	12

Torque Wrench Settings

Water pump nuts	5 to 7 lb/ft. (.69 to .97 kg.m)
Thermostat housing	12 to 15 lb/ft. (1.66 to 2.07 kg.m)
Fan blade	5 to 7 lb/ft. (.69 to .97 kg.m)

1. General Description

The engine cooling water is circulated by a thermo-syphon, water pump assisted system, and the whole system is pressurised. This is both to prevent the loss of water down the overflow pipe with the radiator cap in position and to prevent premature boiling in adverse conditions. The radiator cap is pressurised to 13 lb/sq.in. This has the effect of considerably increasing the boiling point of the coolant. If the water temperature goes above this increased boiling point the extra pressure in the system forces the internal part of the cap off its seat, thus exposing the overflow pipe down which the steam from the boiling water escapes thereby relieving the pressure. It is therefore, important to check that the radiator cap is in good condition and that the spring behind the sealing washer has not weakened. Most garages have a special machine in which radiator caps can be tested. The cooling system comprises the radiator, top and bottom water hoses, heater hoses, the impeller water pump, (mounted on the front of the engine, it carries the fan blades, and is driven by the fan belt), the thermostat and the two drain taps. The inlet manifold is water heated.

The system functions in the following fashion. Cold water in the bottom of the radiator circulates up the lower radiator hose to the water pump where it is pushed round the water passages in the cylinder block, helping to keep the cylinder bores and pistons cool.

The water then travels up into the cylinder head and circulates round the combustion spaces and valve seats absorbing more heat, and then, when the engine is at its

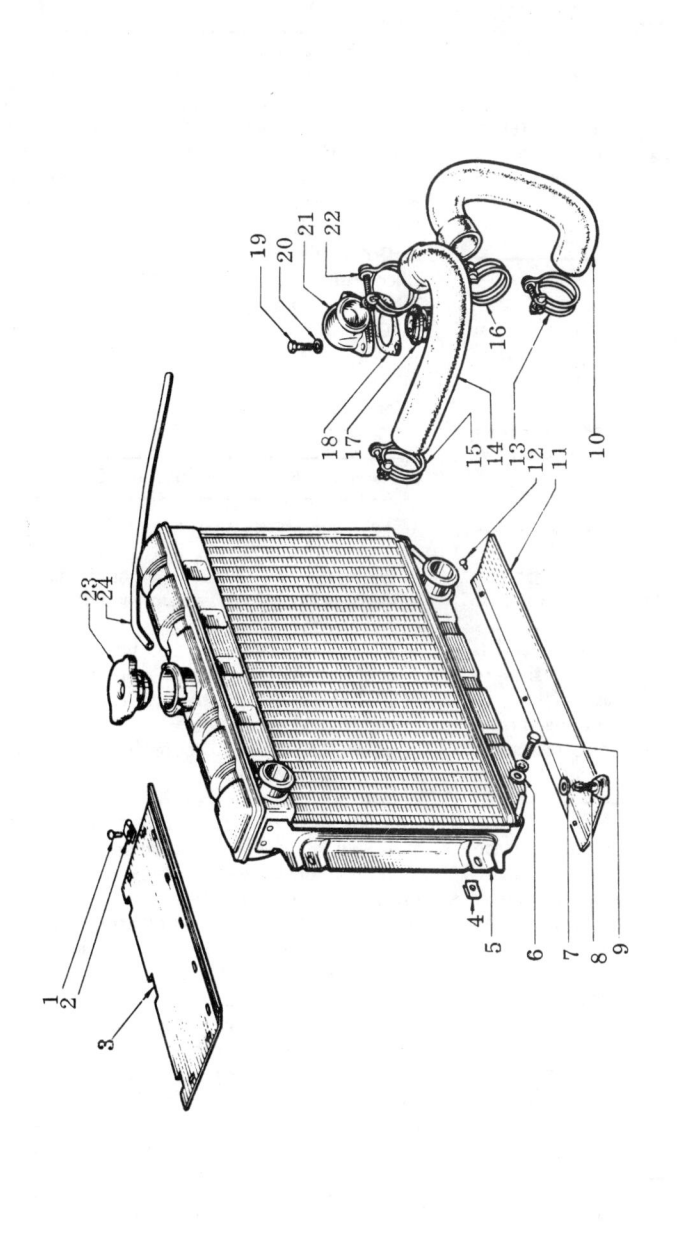

Fig.2.1. EXPLODED VIEW OF THE RADIATOR & HOSES

1. Stud
2. Clip
3. Deflector plate
4. Clip
5. Radiator
6. Washer
7. Washer
8. Drain tap
9. Bolt
10. Bottom hose
11. Deflector
12. Stud
13. Clip
14. Top hose
15. Clip
16. Clip
17. Thermostat
18. Gasket
19. Bolt
20. Washer
21. Outlet elbow
22. Clip
23. Radiator cap
24. Overflow pipe

Chapter 2/Cooling System

proper operating temperature, travels out of the cylinder head, past the open thermostat into the upper radiator hose and so into the radiator header tank.

The water travels down the radiator where it is rapidly cooled by the in-rush of cold air through the radiator core, which is created by both the fan and the motion of the car. The water, now cold, reaches the bottom of the radiator, when the cycle is repeated.

When the engine is cold the thermostat (which is a valve which opens and closes according to the temperature of the water) maintains the circulation of the same water in the engine.

Only when the correct minimum operating temperature has been reached, as shown in the specification, does the thermostat begin to open, allowing water to return to the radiator.

2. Routine Maintenance

1. Check the level of the coolant in the radiator at least once a week or more frequently if high mileages are being done, and top up with soft water (rain water is excellent) as required.
2. Once every 6,000 miles check the fan belt for wear and correct tension and renew or adjust the belt as necessary. (See Sections 10 and 11 for details).

3. Cooling System - Draining

1. With the car on level ground drain the system as follows:
2. If the engine is cold, remove the filler cap from the radiator by turning the cap anti-clockwise. If the engine is hot having just been run, then turn the filler cap very slightly until the pressure in the system has had time to disperse. Use a rag over the cap to protect your hand from escaping steam. If, with the engine very hot, the cap is released suddenly, the drop in pressure can result in the water boiling. With the pressure released the cap can be removed.
3. If anti-freeze is in the radiator drain it into a clean bucket or bowl for re-use.
4. Remove the two drain plugs and ensure that the heater control is in the hot position. The radiator plug is removed by hand, by unscrewing the wing nut, but the cylinder block plug must be removed with the aid of a spanner. The drain plugs are located at the bottom of the radiator and at the rear on the left-hand side of the block.
5. When the water has finished running, probe the drain tap orifices with a short piece of wire to dislodge any particles of rust or sediment which may be blocking the taps and preventing all the water draining out.

4. Cooling System - Flushing

1. With time the cooling system will gradually lose its efficiency as the radiator becomes choked with rust scales, deposits from the water and other sediment. To clean the system out, remove the radiator cap and the drain plugs and leave a hose running in the radiator cap orifice for ten to fifteen minutes.
2. Then close the drain taps and refill with water and a proprietary cleansing compound. Run the engine for ten to fifteen minutes and then drain it and flush out thoroughly for a further ten minutes. All sediment and sludge should now have been removed.
3. In very bad cases the radiator should be reverse flushed.

This can be done with the radiator in position. The cylinder block plug is closed and a hose placed over the open radiator drain plug. Water, under pressure, is then forced up through the radiator and out of the header tank filler orifice.
4. The hose is then removed and placed in the filler orifice and the radiator washed out in the usual fashion.

5. Cooling System - Filling

1. Close the two drain taps.
2. Fill the system slowly to ensure that no air locks develop. If a heater is fitted, check that the valve to the heater unit is open, otherwise an air lock may form in the heater. The best type of water to use in the cooling system is rain water, so use this whenever possible.
3. Do not fill the system higher than within ½ inch of the filler orifice. Overfilling will merely result in wastage, which is especially to be avoided when anti-freeze is in use.
4. Only use anti-freeze mixture with an ethylene glycol base.
5. Replace the filler cap and turn it firmly clockwise to lock it in position.

6. Radiator - Removal, Inspection, Cleaning & Replacement

1. To remove the radiator, first drain the cooling system as described in Section 3.
2. Undo the wire clips which hold the top and bottom radiator hoses on the radiator and then pull off the two hoses.
3. Undo and remove the two bolts and washers on either side of the radiator which hold it in place. It may be helpful to remove the battery to give better access to the top left-hand bolt.
4. Having removed the bolts lift the radiator out of the engine compartment.
5. With the radiator out of the car any leaks can be soldered up or repaired with a substance such as 'cataloy'. Clean out the inside of the radiator by flushing as detailed in the section before last. When the radiator is out of the car it is advantageous to turn it upside down for reverse flushing. Clean the exterior of the radiator by hosing down the radiator matrix with a strong jet of water to clear away road dirt, dead flies etc.
6. Inspect the radiator hoses for cracks, internal or external perishing, and damage caused by over-tightening of the securing clips. Replace the hoses as necessary. Examine the radiator hose securing clips and renew them if they are rusted or distorted. The drain taps should be renewed if leaking, but ensure the leak is not because of a faulty washer behind the tap. If the tap is suspected try a new washer to see if this clears the trouble first.
7. Replacement is a straightforward reversal of the removal procedure.

7. Thermostat - Removal, Testing & Replacement

1. To remove the thermostat partially drain the cooling system (4 pints is enough) then loosen the wire clip retaining the top radiator hose to the outlet elbow and pull the hose off the elbow.
2. Undo the two bolts holding the elbow to the cylinder head and remove the elbow and gasket (photo).
3. The thermostat can now be lifted out (photo). Occasionally it will be found that the thermostat has to be gently

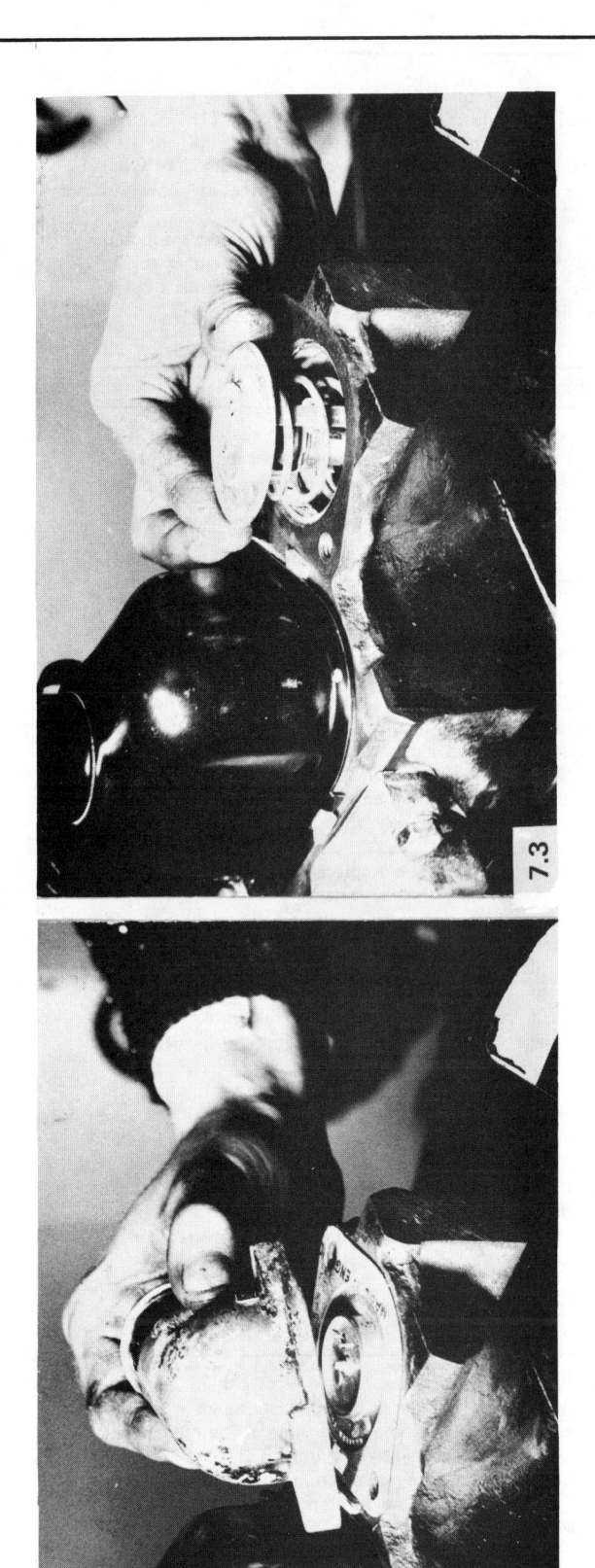

Fig.2.3. View of the dynamo adjustment bolts and the correct fan belt tension

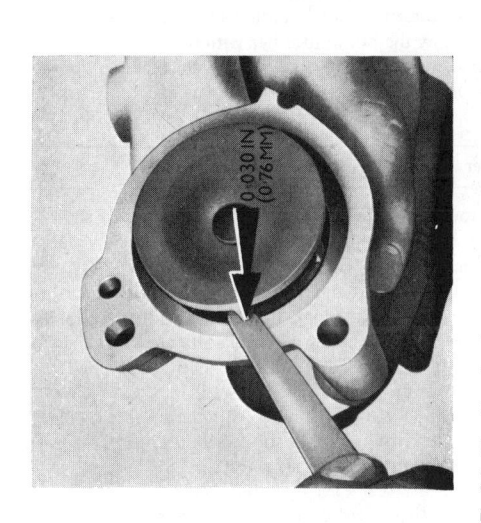

Fig.2.2. Checking the clearance between the impeller blades and the pump body

49

Chapter 2/Cooling System

levered out with a screwdriver due to corrosion. If this operation damages the thermostat in any way always replace it with a new unit.

4. Test the thermostat for correct functioning by dangling it by a length of string in a saucepan of cold water together with a thermometer.

5. Heat the water and note when the thermostat begins to open. This temperature is stamped on the flange of the thermostat, and is also given in the specifications.

6. Discard the thermostat if it opens too early. Continue heating the water until the thermostat is fully open. Then let it cool down naturally. If the thermostat will not open fully in boiling water, or does not close down as the water cools, then it must be exchanged for a new one.

7. If the thermostat is stuck open when cold this will be apparent when removing it from the housing.

8. Replacing the thermostat is a reversal of the removal procedure. Remember to use a new gasket between the elbow and the cylinder head. If any pitting or corrosion is apparent it is advisable to apply a layer of sealing compound such as 'Hermetite' to the metal surfaces before reassembly. If the elbow is badly eaten away it must be replaced with a new unit.

8. Water Pump - Removal & Replacement

1. Drain the cooling system as described in Section 3, then loosen the spring clip on the bottom radiator hose at the pump inlet and pull off the hose. Also undo the clip on the small heater hose if fitted and pull off the hose.

2. All numbers used in this section and section 9 refer to Fig.2.4. Loosen the dynamo securing bolts and swing the dynamo in towards the cylinder block. This frees the fan belt (13) which can now be removed.

3. Undo the four bolts and washers (11,12) which hold the fan (10) and the pulley wheel (14) in place.

4. Remove the fan (10) and the pulley wheel (14) and then undo the three bolts holding the water pump in place and withdraw the pump together with its gasket.

5. Replacement is a reversal of the above procedure but always remember to use a new gasket.

9. Water Pump - Dismantling & Reassembly

1. Remove the hub (15) from the water pump shaft (3) either by judicious levering or by using a suitable hub puller such as Ford Tools CPT.8000 and P.8000–4.

2. Carefully pull out the bearing retainer wire (7) and then with the aid of two blocks (a small mandrel and a large vice, if the proper tools are not available) press out the shaft and bearing assembly (3) together with the impeller (1) and seal from the water pump body (5).

3. The impeller vane is removed from the spindle by careful tapping or levering or preferably to ensure no damage and for ease of operation, with an extractor.

4. Remove the seal (19) and the slinger (18) by splitting the latter with the aid of a sharp cold chisel.

5. The repair kit available comprises a new shaft and bearing assembly, a slinger, seal, bush, clip and gasket.

6. To reassemble the water pump, press the shaft and bearing assembly (3) into the housing with the short end of the shaft to the front, until the groove in the shaft is in line with the groove in the housing. The bearing retainer wire (7) can then be inserted.

7. Press the pulley hub (15) on to the front end of the shaft (3) until the end of the shaft is half an inch from the outer face of the hub.

8. Fit the new slinger bush (18) with the flanged end first on to the rear of the shaft (3) and refit the pump seal (19) with the thrust face towards the impeller (1).

9. Press the impeller (1) onto the shaft (3) until a clearance of 0.030 inch (0.76 mm) is obtained between the impeller blades and the housing face as shown in Fig.2.2.

10 It is important to check at this stage that the pump turns freely and smoothly before replacement onto the block as detailed in Section 8. After replacement check carefully for leaks.

10. Fan Belt - Adjustment

1. The fan belt tension is correct when there is ½ inch of lateral movement at the mid point position of the belt between the dynamo pulley wheel and the water pump pulley wheel.

2. To adjust the fan belt, slacken the dynamo securing bolts as indicated in Fig.2.3. and move the dynamo either in or out until the correct tension is obtained. It is easier if the dynamo securing bolts are only slackened slightly so it requires some force to move the dynamo. In this way the tension of the belt can be arrived at more quickly than by making frequent adjustments.

3. If difficulty is experienced in moving the dynamo away from the engine, a long spanner or screwdriver placed behind the dynamo and resting against the cylinder block serves as a very good lever and can be held in this position while the dynamo securing bolts are tightened down.

11. Fan Belt - Removal & Replacement

1. If the fan belt is worn or has stretched unduly it should be replaced. The most usual reason for replacement is that the belt has broken in service. It is therefore recommended that a spare belt is always carried. Replacement is a reversal of the removal sequence, but as replacement due to breakage is the most usual operation, it is described below.

2. To remove the belt loosen the dynamo securing bolts and push the dynamo in towards the engine.

3. Slip the old belt over the crankshaft, dynamo and water pump pulley wheels and lift it off over the fan blades.

4. Put on a new belt in the same way and adjust it as described in the previous section. NOTE After fitting a new belt it will require adjustment due to its initial stretch after about 250 miles.

12. Temperature Gauge - Fault Finding

1. If the temperature gauge fails to work either the gauge, the sender unit, the wiring or the connections are at fault.

2. It is not possible to repair the gauge or the sender unit and they must be replaced by new units if at fault.

3. First check the wiring connections and if sound, check the wiring for breaks using an ohmmeter. The sender unit and gauge should be tested by substitution.

13. Temperature Gauge & Sender Unit - Removal & Replacement

1. For details of how to remove and replace the temperature gauge see Chapter 10, Section 45.

2. To remove the sender unit, disconnect the wire leading into the unit as its connector and undo the unit with a spanner. The unit is located in the cylinder head just below

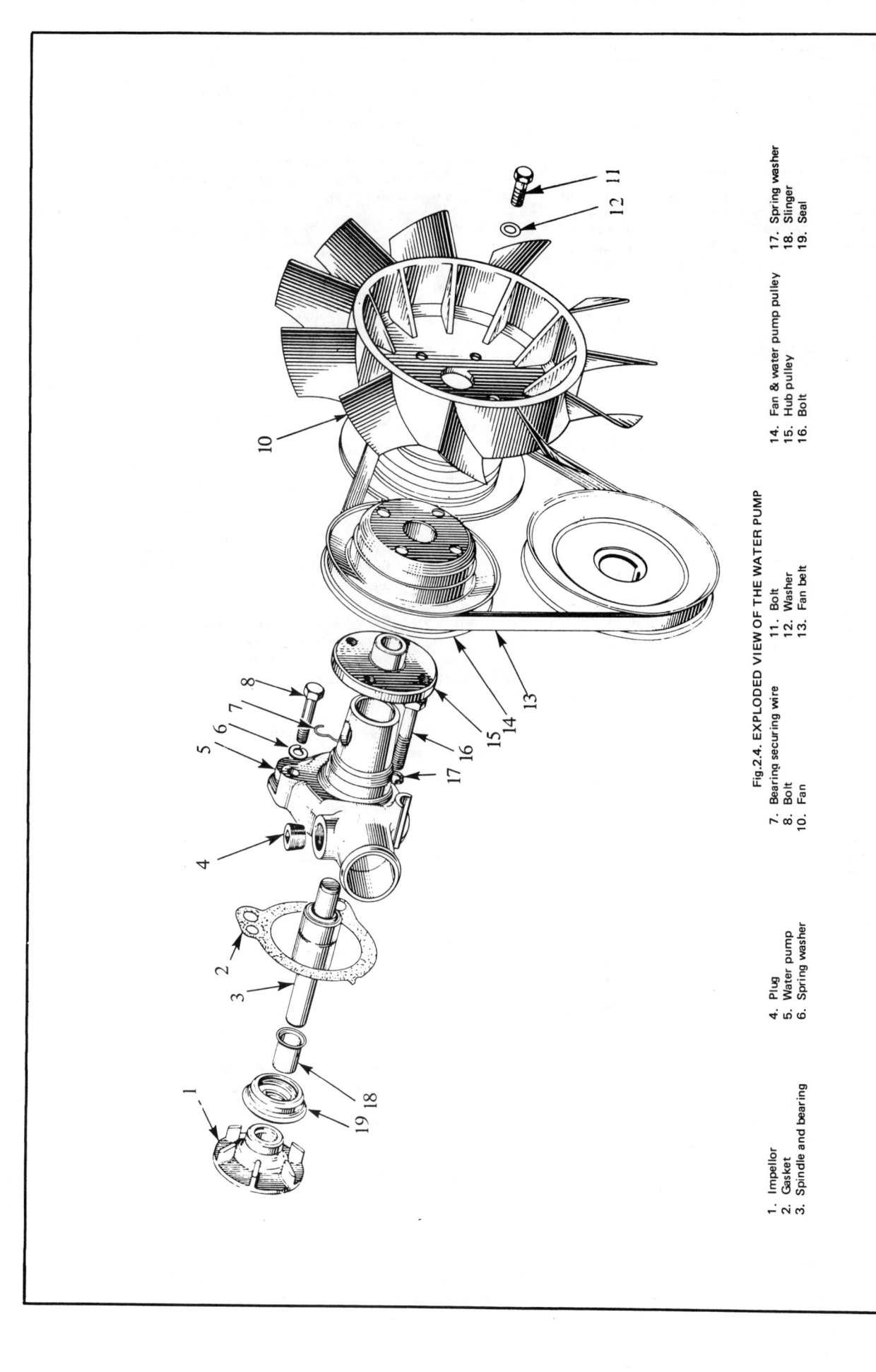

Fig.2.4. EXPLODED VIEW OF THE WATER PUMP

1. Impellor	4. Plug	7. Bearing securing wire	11. Bolt	14. Fan & water pump pulley	17. Spring washer
2. Gasket	5. Water pump	8. Bolt	12. Washer	15. Hub pulley	18. Slinger
3. Spindle and bearing	6. Spring washer	10. Fan	13. Fan belt	16. Bolt	19. Seal

51

Chapter 2/Cooling System

the water outlet elbow on the left side. Replacement is a reversal of the above procedure.

14. Anti-Freeze Mixture

1. In circumstances where it is likely that the temperature will drop to below freezing it is essential that some of the water is drained and an adequate amount of ethylene glycol anti-freeze such as Fords Long Life Anti-freeze Ford Part No.M97B18-C or Bluecol is added to the cooling system.
2. If either of the above anti-freezes are not available at the time any anti-freeze which conforms with specification BS3151 or BS3152 can be used. Never use an anti-freeze with an alcohol base as evaporation is too high.
3. Either of the above mentioned anti-freezes can be left in the cooling system for up to two years, but after six months it is advisable to have the specific gravity of the coolant checked at your local garage, and thereafter once every three months.
4. Below are the amounts of anti-freeze by percentage volume which should be added to ensure adequate protection down to the temperature given.

Amount of A.F.	Protection To
50%	-37°C (-34°F)
40%	-25°C (-13°F)
30%	-16°C (+3°F)
25%	-13°C (+9°F)
20%	-9°C (+15°F)
15%	-7°C (+20°F)
10%	-4°C (+25°F)

Fault Finding Chart — Cooling System

Symptom	Reason/s	Remedy
Loss of coolant	Leak in system	Examine all hoses, hose connections, drain taps and the radiator and heater for signs of leakage when the engine is cold, then when hot and under pressure. Tighten clips, renew hoses and repair radiator.
	Defective radiator pressure cap.	Examine cap for defective seal or spring and renew if necessary.
	Overheating causing rapid evaporation due to excessive pressure in system forcing vapour past radiator cap.	Check reasons for overheating.
	Blown cylinder head gasket causing excess pressure in cooling system forcing coolant past radiator cap overflow.	Remove cylinder head for examination
	Cracked block or head due to freezing.	Strip engine and examine. Repair as required.
Overheating	Insufficient coolant in system.	Top up.
	Water pump not turning properly due to slack fan belt.	Tighten fan belt.
	Kinked or collapsed water hoses causing restriction to circulation of coolant.	Renew hose as required.
	Faulty thermostat (not opening properly).	Fit new thermostat.
	Engine out of tune.	Check ignition setting and carburetter adjustments.
	Blocked radiator either internally or externally.	Flush out cooling system and clean out cooling fins.
	Cylinder head gaskets blown forcing coolant out of system.	Remove head and renew gasket.
	New engine not run-in.	Adjust engine speed until run-in.
Engine running too cool	Missing or faulty thermostat.	Fit new thermostat.

Chapter 3/Fuel System and Carburation

Contents

General Description ...	1
Air Cleaners - Removal, Replacement & Servicing ...	2
Fuel Pump - Routine Servicing...	3
Carburetter - Routine Servicing..	4
A.C. Fuel Pump - Description ...	5
A.C. Fuel Pump - Removal & Replacement ...	6
A.C. Fuel Pump - Testing ...	7
A.C. Fuel Pump - Dismantling ...	8
A.C. Fuel Pump - Examination & Reassembly ...	9
Fuel Tank - Removal & Replacement ..	10
Fuel Gauge Sender Unit - Removal & Replacement ...	11
Fuel Tank Cleaning ...	12
Carburetters - General Description.. ...	13
Ford Single Choke Carburetter - Removal & Replacement ...	14
Weber Twin Choke Carburetter - Removal & Replacement ...	15
Carburetters - Dismantling & Reassembly - General ...	16
Ford Single Choke Carburetter - Dismantling & Reassembly ...	17
Ford Carburetter - Fuel Level Setting... ...	18
Ford Carburetter - Accelerator Pump Adjustment ...	19
Ford Carburetter - Idling Adjustment... ...	20
Ford Carburetter - Choke & Fast Idling Adjustment ...	21
Ford Carburetter - Automatic Choke Adjustment ...	22
Weber 32-DFE & 32-DFM-2 Carburetter - Dismantling & Reassembly ...	23
Weber Carburetters - Fuel Level Setting ...	24
Weber Carburetters - Slow Running Adjustment.. ...	25
Weber Carburetters - Choke Adjustment ...	26
Exhaust System - Description, Removal & Replacement	27
Fuel System - Fault Finding... ...	28
Lack of Fuel at Engine ...	29
Weak Mixture ...	30
Rich Mixture ...	31
Fuel Gauge & Sender Unit - Fault Finding ...	32

Specifications

Fuel Pump
Type...	Mechanical driven from eccentric on camshaft
Delivery pressure ...	3½ to 5 lb/sq.in. (.25 to .35 kg/cm^2)
Inlet vacuum ...	8.5 in. (21.60 cm) Hg.
Fuel tank capacity	10.5 gallons (12.7 U.S. gals. 48.0 litres)

Carburetters

	1300 c.c.	1600 c.c.
Type...	Ford single choke downdraught	
Starting device ..	Semi automatic or fully automatic choke	
Identification Number:-		
Manual choke ...	C7AH - B	C9CH - E
Automatic choke ...	Not fitted	C9CH - F
Idling speed ...	580 to 620 r.p.m.	
Fast idle - manual...	1300 to 1500 r.p.m.	900 to 1100 r.p.m.
- auto - standard ...	—	1850 to 2050 r.p.m.
- auto - cold climate ...	—	2200 to 2400 r.p.m.
Float setting - up ...	1.15 to 1.17 inch. (28.5 to 28.9 mm)	
- down ...	1.41 to 1.43 inch. (35.1 to 35.5 mm)	
Choke plate pull down - manual ...	.14 to .16 inch	.16 to .18 inch
- automatic ...	—	.13 to .15 inch
Accelerator pump stroke.. ...	.135 to .145 inch (3.43 to 3.68 mm)	.135 to .145 inch (3.43 to 3.68 mm)
Throttle barrel diameter...	34 mm	36 mm
Venturi diameter ...	25 mm	28 mm
Main jet - manual choke ...	1.32 mm	1.50 mm
- auto choke...	—	1.47 mm
High speed bleed ...	1.50 mm	1.50 mm
Idling jet ...	.60 mm	.65 mm
Idling air bleed - manual choke (1st) ...	1.00 mm	1.05 mm
(2nd) ...	.65 mm	.60 mm
- auto choke (1st) ...	—	1.05 mm
(2nd)...	—	.60 mm

53

Chapter 3/Fuel System & Carburation

Idle channel restrictor - manual choke	1.15 mm	1.35 mm
- auto choke	–	1.35 mm
Power jet - manual choke	.75 mm	.90 mm
- auto choke	–	.90 mm
Pump jet	.45 mm	.55 mm
Pump spring	RED	RED
Vacuum piston link hole	Inner	Inner
Thermostatic spring slot	Centre	Centre

Weber Carburetter

	1300 G.T.		1600 G.T.	
Type	Dual barrel, twin choke downdraught			
Identification number	32-DFE		32 DFM-2	
	Primary	Secondary	Primary	Secondary
Venturi diameter	23	24	26	27
Auxiliary venturi	4.5	4.5	4.5.	4.5
Main jet	125	115	150	155
Air correction jet	135	160	140	160
Emulsion tube type	F6	F6	F6	F6
Slow running petrol jet	50	45	50	45
Slow running air jet (bush)	185	100	180	70
Upper progression hole	70 to 120		70 to 120	
Lower progression hole	110 to 120		100 to 120	
Slow running volume control port	85	100	70	120
Full load enrichment jet	–	85	–	100
Full load air bleed	–	100	–	100
Full load mixture jet	–	100	–	110
Accelerator pump jet	60		65	
Accelerator pump back bleed	40		40	
Needle valve	2.0 mm		2.0 mm	
Float level	7 to 7.5 mm		6.25 to 6.75 mm	
Fast idle setting	15 to 15.5 mm		14.25 to 14.75 mm	
Choke plate pull down	5 mm		5 mm	
Choke plate opening	7.5 to 8.5 mm. with lever backed off 10 mm.			
Idling speed	680 to 720 r.p.m.			
Fast idle speed	2000 r.p.m.		2500 r.p.m.	

Air Cleaner

Type ... Replaceable paper element

Torque Wrench Settings

Fuel pump	12 to 15 lb/ft. (1.66 to 2.07 kg.m)
1300 and 1600 air cleaner	3 to 5 lb/ft. (.42 to .69 kg.m)
G.T. air cleaner	2.5 to 3 lb/ft. (.35 to .42 kg.m)
G.T. air cleaner cover	5 to 7 lb/ft. (.69 to .97 kg.m)

1. General Description

1. The fuel system of all saloon models consists of a nine gallon fuel tank, a mechanically operated fuel pump, a single venturi downdraught Ford carburetter (G.T. models use a Weber twin choke downdraught carburetter) and the necessary fuel lines between the tank and the pump, and the pump and the carburetter.

2. Air Cleaners - Removal, Replacement & Servicing

1. A paper element type of air cleaner is fitted to all Capri models.
2. The air cleaner should be serviced at intervals of 6,000 miles and the paper element renewed at intervals of 18,000 miles.
3. On all models, except G.T. cars fitted with Weber carburetters, undo the single bolt in the centre of the air cleaner lid, unclip the throttle cable and remove the lid, element and air cleaner body.
4. Thoroughly clean the interior of the air cleaner lid and body then gently brush out the dust from the folds of the air cleaner element. Every 18,000 miles, or earlier if the element becomes torn renew the paper filter.
5. The air cleaner lid on G.T. models is retained by two nuts in the dished section of the lid. The paper element is serviced in the same way as in paragraph 4 above.
6. To remove the body of the air cleaner from the Weber carburetter, turn back the locking tabs and undo and remove the four nuts, tabs, plain and rubber washers from the bottom of the body. Then unclip the dipstick tube extension and the throttle cable and where fitted the support stay bolt. The air cleaner can then be lifted off complete with gasket and tubular inserts. On replacement fit the tubular inserts over the studs and then a new gasket. Offer up and correctly position the air cleaner body on the carburetter and fit the rubber and plain washers, lock tab and nuts. Tighten the nuts and turn up the tabs on the lock washers. Reclip the dipstick tube extension and throttle cable and where fitted do up the support stay bolt. Centralise the element on its seat, and refit the top cover with the arrow towards the air cleaner spout and the front of the car.
7. Replacement of the standard single bolt fixing type of air cleaner is a reversal of the removal procedure. Ensure that the spout faces towards the front of the car and that the arrow on the lid towards the spout.

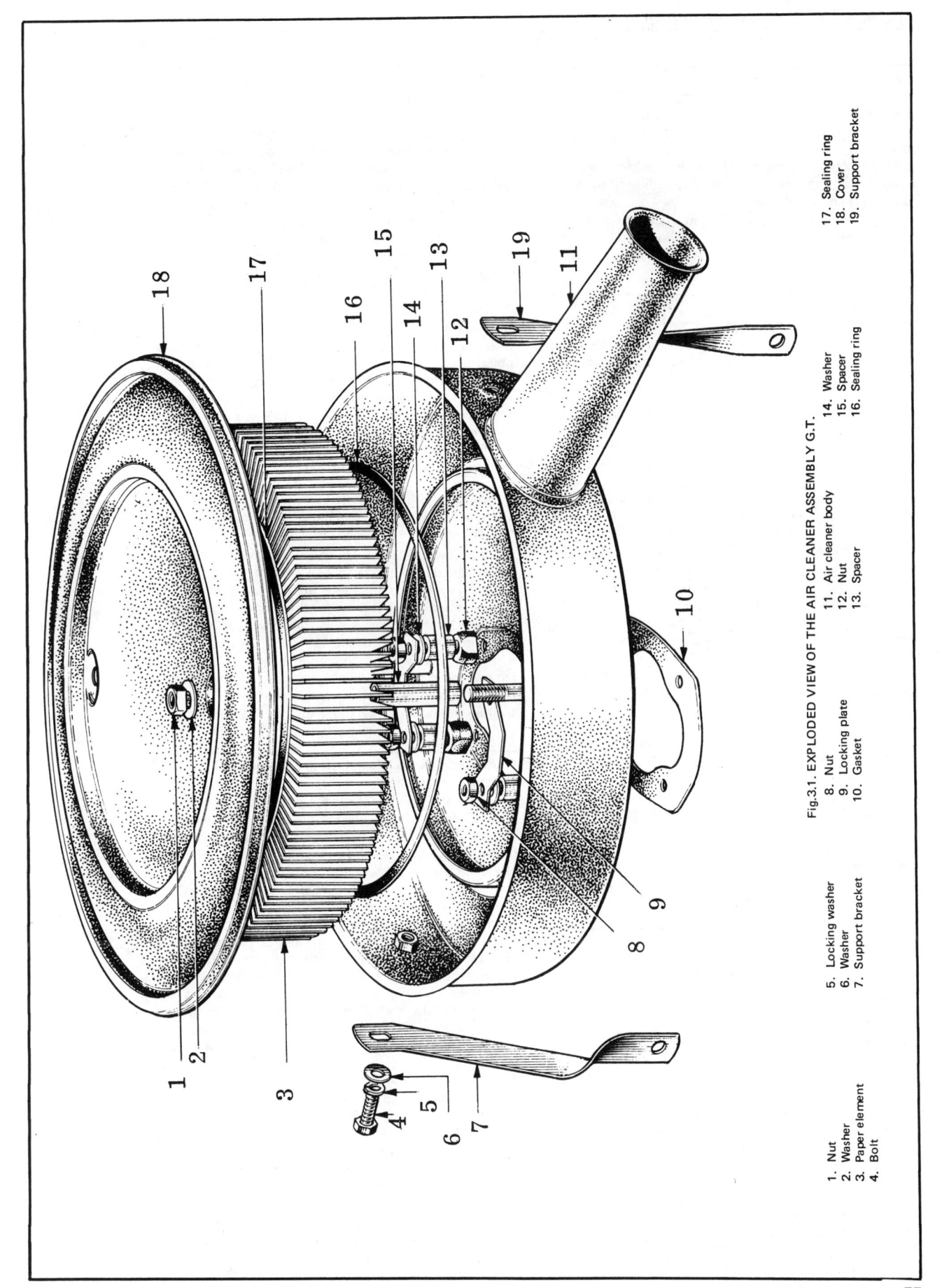

Fig.3.1. EXPLODED VIEW OF THE AIR CLEANER ASSEMBLY G.T.

1. Nut
2. Washer
3. Paper element
4. Bolt
5. Locking washer
6. Washer
7. Support bracket
8. Nut
9. Locking plate
10. Gasket
11. Air cleaner body
12. Nut
13. Spacer
14. Washer
15. Spacer
16. Sealing ring
17. Sealing ring
18. Cover
19. Support bracket

Chapter 3/Fuel System & Carburation

3. Fuel Pump - Routine Servicing

1. At intervals of 6,000 miles unscrew the clamp nut on top of the fuel pump, pull aside the clamp and remove the glass bowl.
2. Thoroughly clean the glass bowl inside and out, and use a paintbrush and petrol to clean any sediment from the pump body and filter screen.
3. Ensure that the gasket which seats under the glass bowl is not pitted or split, refit the glass bowl, pull over the retaining clamp and tighten down the clamp nut.

4. Carburetter - Routine Servicing

1. At intervals of 6,000 miles, check the carburetter idling mixture setting and adjust as necessary as described in Section 21.

5. A.C. Fuel Pump - Description

1. The mechanically operated A.C. fuel pump is actuated through a spring loaded rocker arm. One arm of the rocker (20) bears against an eccentric on the camshaft and the other arm (21) operates a diaphragm pull rod. NOTE All references in brackets should be co-related with Fig.3.2.
2. As the engine camshaft rotates, the eccentric moves the pivoted rocker arm outwards which in turn pulls the diaphragm pull rod and the diaphragm (15) down against the pressure of the diaphragm spring (5).
3. This creates sufficient vacuum in the pump chamber to draw in fuel from the tank through the fuel filter gauze (13), and non-return valve (4A).
4. The rocker arm is held in constant contact with the eccentric by an anti-rattle spring (16), and as the engine camshaft continues to rotate the eccentric allows the rocker arm to move inwards. The diaphragm spring (5) is thus free to push the diaphragm (15) upwards forcing the fuel in the pump chamber out to the carburetter through the non-return outlet valve (4B).
5. When the float chamber in the carburetter is full, the float chamber needle valve will close so preventing further flow from the fuel pump.
6. The pressure in the delivery line will hold the diaphragm downwards against the pressure of the diaphragm spring, and it will remain in this position until the needle valve in the float chamber opens to admit more petrol.

6. A.C. Fuel Pump - Removal & Replacement

1. Remove the fuel inlet and outlet pipes by unscrewing the union nuts. On some models it is easier to undo the securing clips which hold the flexible pipes to the metal pipes which emerge from the pump.
2. Undo the two bolts which hold the pump in place and then lift the pump together with the gasket away from the crankcase (photo).
3. Replacement of the pump is a reversal of the above process. Remember to use a new crankcase to fuel pump gasket to ensure no oil leaks, ensure that both faces of the flange are perfectly clean, and check that the rocker arm lies on top of the camshaft eccentric and not underneath it.

7. A.C. Fuel Pump Testing

Presuming that the fuel lines and unions are in good condition and that there are no leaks anywhere, check the performance of the fuel pump in the following manner. Disconnect the fuel pipe at the carburetter inlet union, and the high tension lead to the coil, and with a suitable container or a large rag in position to catch the ejected fuel, turn the engine over on the starter motor solenoid. A good spurt of petrol should emerge from the end of the pipe every second revolution.

8. A.C. Fuel Pump Dismantling

1. Unscrew the finger nut on top of the bowl and push the clamp aside. Lift off the glass cover.
2. Remove the cork sealing washer and the fine mesh filter gauze.
3. If the condition of the diaphragm is suspect or for any other reason it is wished to dismantle the pump fully, proceed as follows:- Mark the upper and lower flanges of the pump that are adjacent to the flange on the diaphragm and to each other. Unscrew the five screws and spring washers which hold the two halves of the pump body together. Separate the two halves with great care, ensuring that the diaphragm does not stick to either of the two flanges.
4. Carefully prise the valves out of their six point staking and remove them from the upper body with their sealing gaskets.
5. Press down and rotate the diaphragm a quarter of a turn (in either direction) to release the pull rod from the operating lever, and lift away the diaphragm and pull rod (which is securely fixed to the diaphragm and cannot be removed from it). Remove the diaphragm spring and the metal and fibre washer underneath it.
6. If it is necessary to dismantle the rocker arm assembly, remove the retaining circlips and washer from the rocker arm pivot rod and slide out the rod which will then free the rocker arm, operating rod, and anti-rattle spring.

9. A.C. Fuel Pump - Examination & Reassembly

1. Check the condition of the glass bowl cover sealing washer, and if it is hardened or broken it must be replaced. The diaphragm should be checked similarly and replaced if faulty. Clean the pump thoroughly and agitate the valves in paraffin to clean them out. This will also improve the contact between the valve seat and the valve. It is unlikely that the pump body will be damaged, but check for fractures and cracks.
2. To reassemble the pump, proceed as follows:- Replace the rocker arm assembly comprising the operating link, rocker arm, anti-rattle spring and washer in their relative positions in the pump body. Align the holes in the operating link, rocker arm, and washers with the holes in the body and insert the pivot pin.
3. Refit the circlips to the grooves in each end of the pivot pin.
4. Fit the small valve sealing gaskets into their locations in the upper body. Replace the valves in the upper body and carefully stake them into place.
5. The valves will only seat properly when in their correct locations and the right way up.
6. Clean out the pump chamber to remove any bits due to the staking of the valves.
7. Position the fibre and steel washer in that order in the base of the pump and place the diaphragm spring over them.
8. Replace the diaphragm and pull rod assembly with the pull rod downwards and the small tab on the diaphragm

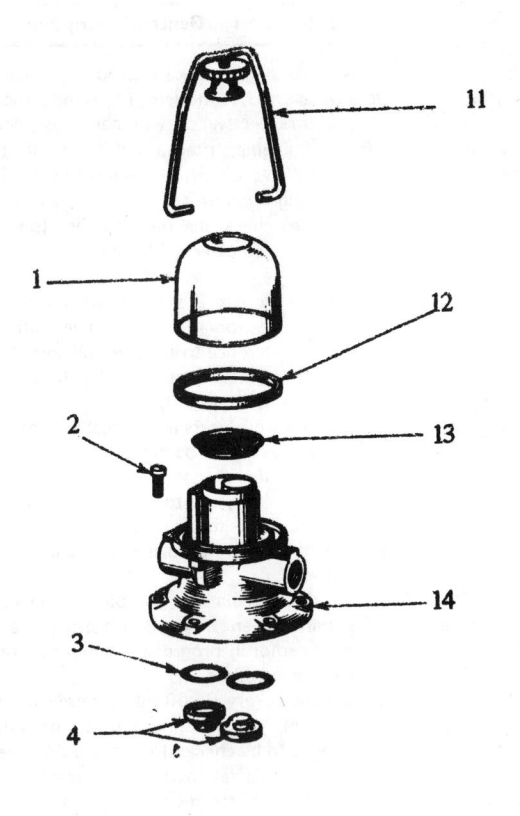

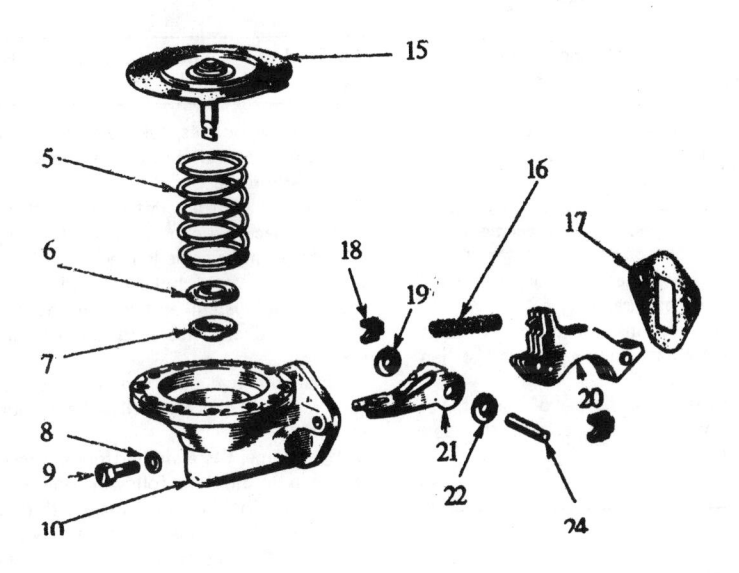

Fig.3.2. EXPLODED VIEW OF THE A.C. TYPE FUEL PUMP

1. Glass dome
2. Screw
3. Valve gasket
4. Inlet & outlet valves
5. Diaphragm return spring
6. Spring seats
7. Spring seats
8. Spring washer
9. Bolt
10. Lower pump body
11. Dome retaining clamp
12. Dome to body sealing ring
13. Filter element
14. Upper pump body
15. Diaphragm
16. Actuating arm return spring
17. Gasket
18. Actuating arm swivel pin retaining plates
19. Shim
20. Primary actuating arm
21. Secondary actuating arm
22. Shim
24. Actuating arm swivel pin

Chapter 3/Fuel System & Carburation

adjacent to the centre of the flange and rocker arm.

9. With the body of the pump held so that the rocker arm is facing away from one, press down the diaphragm, turning it a quarter of a turn to the left at the same time. This engages the slot on the pull rod with the operating lever. The small tab on the diaphragm should now be at an angle of 90° to the rocker arm and the diaphragm should be firmly located.

10 Move the rocker arm until the diaphragm is level with the body flanges and hold the arm in this position. Re-assemble the two halves of the pump, ensuring that the previously made marks on the flanges are adjacent to each other.

11 Insert the five screws and lockwashers and tighten them down finger tight.

12 Move the rocker arm up and down several times to centralise the diaphragm, and then with the arm released, tighten the screws securely in a diagonal sequence.

13 Replace the gauze filter in position and fit a new glass dome seal. Refit the glass dome to the pump body, pull over the clamp and tighten down the finger nut.

10. Fuel Tank - Removal & Replacement

1. Disconnect the battery, then remove all the petrol from the tank by either syphoning or disconnecting the fuel line under the car and allowing the contents to drain into a suitable container.

2. From under the filler cap, remove the three screws which hold the filler pipe in place.

3. Remove the flexible pipe from between the filler pipe and the fuel tank by loosening off the wire clips. Lift the filler pipe from the car.

4. Undo and remove the two nuts and bolts securing the fuel tank to the rear bulkhead and withdraw the tank a few inches into the boot.

5. Disconnect the wire from the fuel gauge sender unit at its snap connector and undo the fuel pipe at its union on the floor of the boot.

6. The fuel tank can now be lifted out of the car. Replacement is a direct reversal of the above procedure.

11. Fuel Gauge Sender Unit - Removal & Replacement

1. Remove the fuel tank a few inches into the boot of the car as described in Section 10, paragraphs 1 to 4.

2. With a cold chisel carefully unscrew the sender unit retainer ring and then remove the sender unit and sealing ring from the tank.

3. Replacement is a straightforward reversal of the removal sequence. Always fit a new seal to the recess in the tank to ensure no leaks develop.

12. Fuel Tank Cleaning

1. With time it is likely that sediment will collect in the bottom of the fuel tank. Condensation, resulting in rust and other impurities, will usually be found in the fuel tank of any car more than three or four years old.

2. When the tank is removed it should be vigorously flushed out and turned upside down, and if facilities are available, steam cleaned.

3. Never weld or bring a naked light close to an empty fuel tank unless it has been steamed out for at least two hours, or washed internally with boiling water and detergent several times. If using the latter method, finally fill the tank with boiling water and detergent and allow to stand for at least three hours.

13. Carburetters - General Description

1. A Ford single choke downdraught carburetter is fitted to all except G.T. models. The same basic Ford carburetter is used irrespective of whether it is fitted to a 1300 or 1600 c.c. engine. Internally different sized jets and chokes cater for the variations in engine capacity. If ever purchasing an exchange carburetter, as they all look identical it is essential to check the part number (see specifications) to ensure a carburetter with the correct jets and choke is obtained.

2. Certain models are fitted with the same carburetter, but with an automatic choke. The addition of this device makes no difference to the internal layout of the unit.

3. The carburetter fitted to the 1300 G.T. is the Weber 32-DFE whilst the 1600 G.T. fits a Weber 32 DFM-2. These two carburetters are basically identical. The variations in jet sizes etc, can be found in the specifications at the beginning of this chapter.

4. Small auxiliary venturi tubes are located at the top of each barrel and these discharge fuel into the narrowest parts of the larger venturis which are located further down the barrels.

5. The throttle plate in one barrel opens before that in the other barrel to ensure good performance at high revolutions as well as smooth progression when the throttle is operated at low engine speeds.

6. At about every 6,000 miles these carburetters should be checked for slow running, and at the same time the float level needs to be checked to ensure that the correct amount of fuel is being retained. At the same time the float bowl is cleaned of any sediment which may have collected.

14. Ford Single Choke Carburetter - Removal & Replacement

1. Open the bonnet, take off the air cleaner as described in Section 2, and disconnect the vacuum and fuel pipes at the carburetter.

2. Free the throttle shaft from the throttle lever by sliding back the securing clip and undo the screw which holds the end of the choke cable in place.

3. If an automatic choke is fitted drain about 5 pints from the cooling system and loosen the clips which hold the automatic choke hoses to the carburetter. Pull off the hoses.

4. Undo the two nuts and spring washers which hold the carburetter in place and lift the carburetter off the inlet manifold.

5. Replacement is a straightforward reversal of the removal sequence but note the following points:-

a) Remove the old inlet manifold to carburetter gasket, clean the mating flanges and fit a new gasket in place.

b) Ensure that the choke knob is in the off position before connecting the inner choke cable at the carburetter. After connection ensure that the choke opens and closes fully with a very slight amount of slack in the cable when the choke control is pushed right in.

15. Weber Twin Choke Carburetter - Removal & Replacement

1. The Weber carburetter is removed and replaced in exactly the same way as the single choke carburetter (See Section 14), but note the following points:-

Chapter 3/Fuel System & Carburation

2. The carburetter is retained to the inlet manifold by four nuts.

3. When refitting the air cleaner first fit a rubber gasket to the top of the carburetter. Then fit the air cleaner body placing a rubber insulator round each mounting stud and a sleeve through each insulator. Place a flat washer and then double type tab washers over the studs and tighten down the securing nuts. Turn up the tab washers to lock the nuts in position.

16. Carburetters - Dismantling & Reassembly - General

1. With time the component parts of the Ford or Weber carburetter will wear and petrol consumption will increase. The diameter of drillings and jets may alter, and air and fuel leaks may develop round spindles and other moving parts. Because of the high degree of precision involved, in the authors opinion it is best to purchase an exchange rebuilt carburetter. This is one of the few instances where it is better to take the latter course rather than to rebuild the component oneself.

2. It may be necessary to partially dismantle the carburetter to clear a blocked jet or to renew the accelerator pump diaphragm. The accelerator pump itself may need attention and gaskets may need renewal. Providing care is taken there is no reason why the carburetter may not be completely reconditioned at home, but ensure a full repair kit can be obtained before you strip the carburetter down. NEVER poke out jets with wire or similar to clean them but blow them out with compressed air or air from a car tyre pump.

17. Ford Single Choke Carburetter - Dismantling & Reassembly

1. The instructions in this section apply to all non G.T. models including cars with an external automatic choke. All numerical references are to Fig.3.3., unless otherwise stated.

2. Undo the six screws and washers (33) which hold the carburetter top (35) to the main body (43).

3. Lift off the top (35) from the main body (43) at the same time unlatching the choke control rod (12). Ensure that the gasket (39) comes off with the top cover (35). On cars fitted with an automatic choke undo the screw which holds the fast idle cam and rod assembly to the lower body.

4. From the top cover pull out the float pivot pin (41) and remove the float (42). The needle valve and body (38) can then be unscrewed and the gasket (36) removed.

5. Only on cars fitted with an automatic choke, undo the screw which holds the choke piston lever. Then take off the lever, the link, the choke control lever and finally the piston from the inner housing. Undo the two screws holding the inner housing to the carburetter, remove the housing and gasket, the choke housing lever, shaft assembly, choke control rod, and the Teflon bush.

6. On all models remove the accelerator pump discharge ball valve (14) and weight (13).

7. If it is wished to remove the choke plate (4) first cut the heads off the retaining pins (50) which hold the air cleaner retainer bracket in place (1). Next undo the grub screws (6) which hold the plate to the spindle (5) and pull out the plate.

8. Carefully smooth away the burrs from around the choke plate screw holes on the spindle and pull out the choke spindle at the same time sliding the choke control lever (2) and spring (3) off.

9. The main jet (40) can now be unscrewed from the top cover (35).

10 Undo the screw which holds the pump control lever (25) to the throttle spindle (20) and detach it from the pump actuating lever with spring and washer.

11 The four screws and split washers (31) which hold the accelerator pump cover (47) in place can now be undone and the cover, operating arm (49), diaphragm (46), and return spring (45) removed.

12 Undo the cheese head pivot screw (19) and remove the fast idle cam (17) and the return spring (16).

13 Undo the two grub screws (21) which hold the choke plate (22) in position on the spindle (20), and remove the plate.

14 Carefully file down any burrs round the grub screw holes on the spindle and slide the spindle out of the main body. Undo the idling mixture adjustment needle (27) and spring (26), and the throttle stop screw (24) and spring (23).

15 Reassembly commences by refitting the throttle stop screw (24) and spring (23), and the idling mixture adjustment needle (27) and spring (26). Screw in the latter so it just seats and then back off one turn.

16 Slide the choke spindle (5) into place on the top cover (35) after ensuring the spring (3) and choke control lever (2) are in position.

17 Refit the choke plate (4) so the small rectangular stamping on the plate faces upwards and is adjacent to the spindle (5) when the plate is in the closed position. Tighten down the two grub screws (6) which hold the plate in place.

18 Refit the air cleaner retaining bracket (1) and tap in two new retaining pins.

19 Screw the main jet (40) into position and then replace the needle valve housing (38). Fit a new gasket on the top cover (35) and then refit the needle, sharp end upwards, to the valve housing.

20 Replace the float (42) securing it in position with the pin (41). Check the float and fuel level setting as described in Section 18.

21 Position the return spring (16) on the bearing abutment on the lower body (43), and refit the choke lever (17) retaining it in place by its pivot screw (19). On automatic choke carburetters only fit the piston, piston lever and link in the inner position to the inner housing. Refit the choke thermostat lever and then screw it into the inner housing. Next position the choke control rod in the choke lever and with the vacuum gasket in place refit the inner housing with the two screws. Finally ensure when the outer housing assembly is fitted to the inner housing that the index marks align, the gasket is in place, and the three securing screws are tightened down evenly.

22 Carefully replace the accelerator pump discharge ball valve (14) and weight (13). Slide one end of the choke control lever into the pull down stop and the other end into the fast idle cam, and with a new gasket (39) positioned between the upper cover (35) and lower body (43) and with the choke plate closed, fit the two halves together and retain with five of the six screws. Note that the sixth screw (A) holds the choke cable bracket in place.

23 Slide the throttle spindle (20) into the main body and refit the throttle plate (22) so the two recessed indentations in the plate are adjacent to the recesses of the screw heads when the throttle plate is closed. Ensure the throttle plate is fully centralised.

24 Fit the accelerator pump diaphragm (46) to the pump cover (47), replace the return spring (45) larger diameter against the carburetter body and secure the assembly in place by means of the four screws and lockwashers (31).

25 The spring (30) and pushrod (28) are then connected

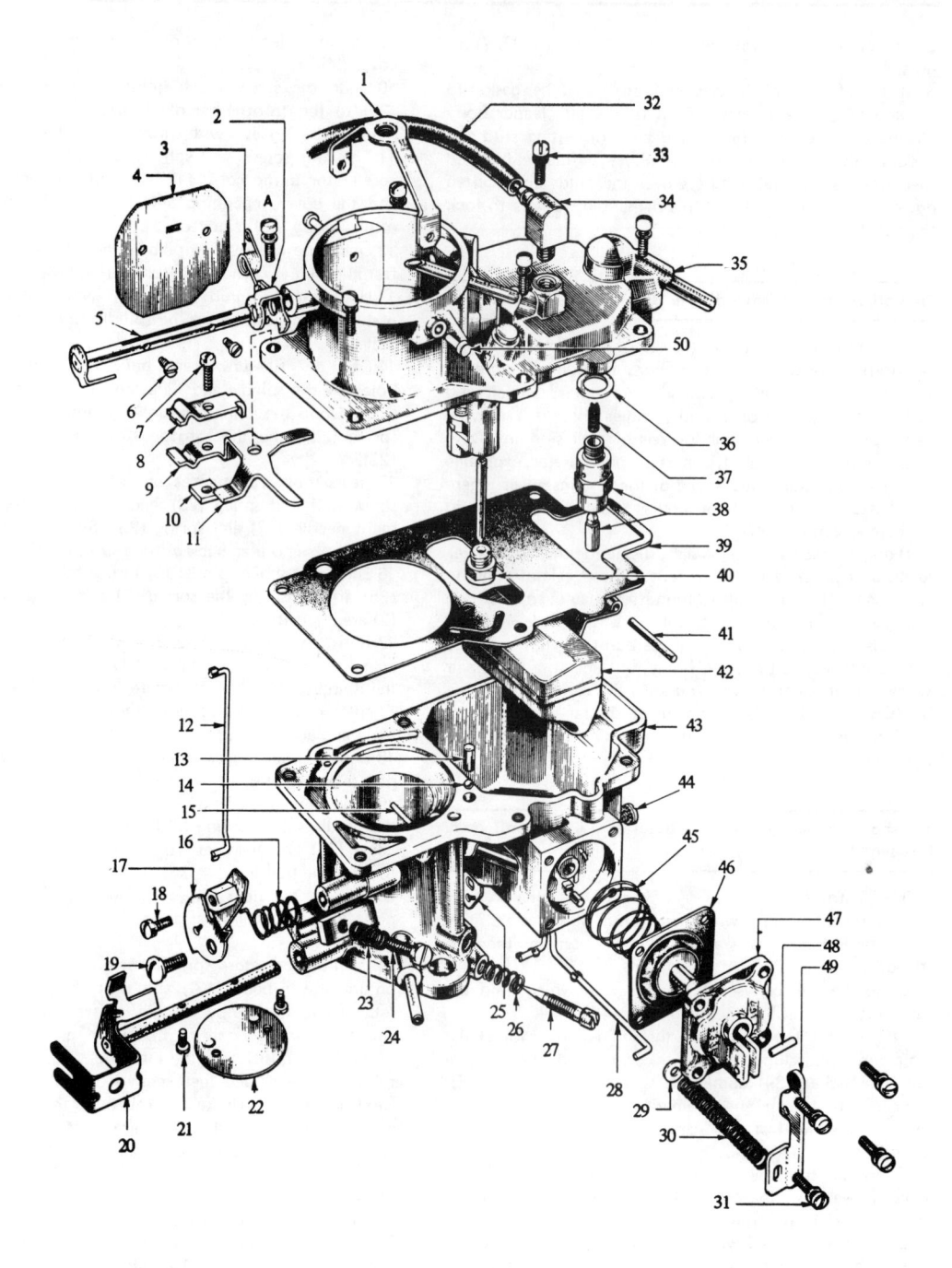

Fig.3.3. EXPLODED VIEW OF CARBURETTER WITH MANUAL CHOKE—EXCEPT G.T.

1. Air cleaner retaining bracket
2. Choke control lever
3. Spring
4. Choke plate
5. Choke spindle
6. Plate to spindle retaining screws
7. Screw
8. Cable clamp—top
9. Cable clamp—bottom
10. Nut
11. Bracket
12. Choke control rod
13. Pump discharge ball weight
14. Discharge ball valve
16. Spring
17. Fast idle cam
18. Screw
19. Screw
20. Throttle lever & spindle assembly
21. Plate retaining screws
22. Throttle plate
23. Spring
24. Throttle stop screw
25. Pump control lever
26. Spring
27. Idling mixture adjustment needle
28. Accelerator pump link to lever rod
29. Washer
30. Spring
31. Screw
32. Overflow pipe
33. Screw
34. Adaptor
35. Carburetter top cover
36. Washer
37. Filter
38. Needle valve
39. Gasket
40. Main metering jet
41. Float pivot pin
42. Float
43. Carburetter body
44. Screw
45. Diaphragm return spring
46. Accelerator pump diaphragm
47. Accelerator pump cover
48. Actuating lever pivot pin
49. Actuating lever
50. Air cleaner bracket retaining pin

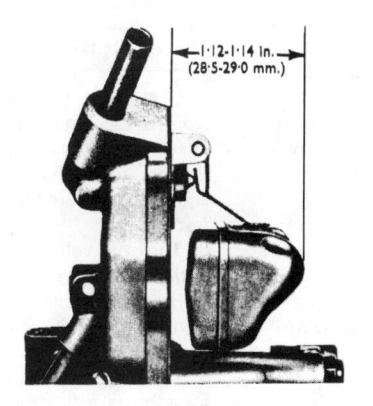

Fig.3.4. Float setting closed - Ford carburetter

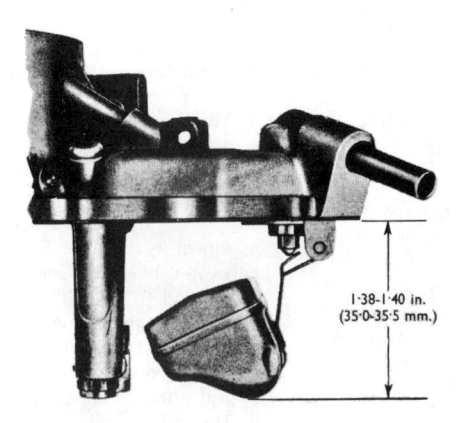

Fig.3.5. Float setting fully open - Ford carburetter

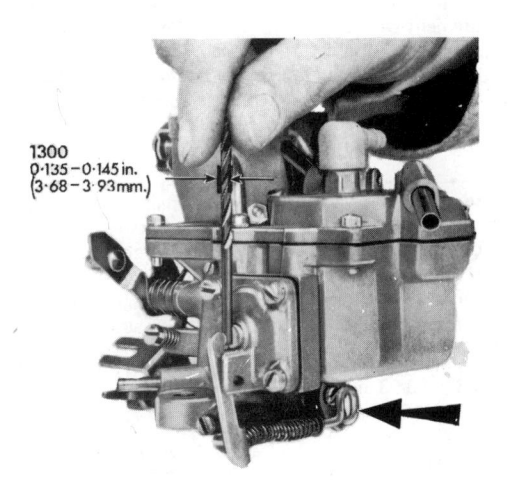

Fig.3.6. Accelerator pump stroke adjustment on the manual choke 1300 c.c. engine

Chapter 3/Fuel System & Carburation

to the accelerator pump lever (49) and the gooseneck end of the pushrod attached to the throttle arm. The arm is secured to the throttle spindle end with a screw and lock washer.

26 This now completes the reassembly operations, but the fast idle setting, accelerator pump stroke, and choke plate pull down must be checked and adjusted as required. (See Sections 19 to 21).

18. Ford Carburetter - Fuel Level Setting

1. Since the height of the float is important in the maintenance of a correct flow of fuel, the correct height is determined by measurement and by bending the tab which rests on the end of the needle valve. If the height of the float is incorrect there will either be fuel starvation symptoms or fuel will leak from the joint of the float chamber. All numbers in brackets refer to Fig.3.3.
2. To check the float first remove the air cleaner as described in Section 2.
3. Undo the choke cable clamp screw (7) and the six screws and washers (33) which hold the carburetter top cover (35) in place.
4. Remove the cover (35) taking care that the gasket (39) does not stick to the main carburetter body (43) and at the same time unlatch the choke link rod (12).
5. The float (42) can now be examined. Shake it to ensure there is no fuel in it and if it has been punctured discard immediately. Check too that the float arm is not bent or damaged.
6. To check the fuel level setting turn the cover (35) upside down so that the float closes the needle valve by its own weight. This corresponds to its true position in the float chamber when the needle valve is closed and no more fuel can enter the chamber.
7. Measure the distance from the normal base of the float to the mating surface of the gasket which should be between 1.12 and 1.14 inch (28.5 to 29.0 mm) as shown in Fig.3.4. If this measurement is not correct then bend the tab which rests on the fuel inlet needle valve as required until the correct measurement is obtained. Turn the cover the right way up and take the same measurement with the float in the fully open position. The measurement should now be between 1.38 and 1.40 inch (35.0 to 35.5 mm), as shown in Fig.3.5. Bend the other tab (the hinge tab) as required.

19. Ford Carburetter - Accelerator Pump Adjustment

1. Under normal conditions the accelerator pump requires no adjustment. If it is wished to check the accelerator pump action first slacken the throttle stop screw (24 in Fig.3.3. so the throttle plate is completely closed.
2. Press in the diaphragm plunger fully, and check that there is then a 0.135 to 0.145 inch (3.68 to 3.93 mm) clearance on 1300 c.c. engines and on 1600 c.c. engines with automatic choke. The clearance on 1600 c.c. manual choke engines should be 0.105 to 0.115 inch (2.67 to 2.92 mm). This clearance is measured between the operating lever and the plunger. The clearance is most easily checked by using a suitably sized drill. (Fig.3.6).
3. To shorten the stroke open the gooseneck of the pump pushrod, and to lengthen the stroke, close the gooseneck.
4. If poor acceleration can be tolerated for maximum economy disconnect the operating lever to the accelerator pump entirely.

20. Ford Carburetter - Idling Adjustment

1. If available the idling adjustment is best made with the aid of a vacuum gauge. Disconnect the blanking plug on the inlet manifold and connect a suitable adaptor and gauge.
2. Ensure the engine is at its normal operating temperature and then turn in the throttle stop screw (24) to obtain a fast idle.
3. Turn the volume control screw (27) in either direction until a maximum reading is obtained on the gauge.
4. Re-adjust the idling speed as required and continue these adjustments until the maximum vacuum reading is obtained with the engine running smoothly at about 600 r.p.m.
5. To adjust the slow running without a vacuum gauge turn the throttle stop screw (24) clockwise so the engine is running at a fast idle, then turn the volume control screw (27) in either direction until the engine just fires evenly. Continue the adjustments until the engine will run as slowly as possible, but smoothly, with regular firing and no hint of stalling. (Fig.3.7).

21. Ford Carburetter - Choke & Fast Idling Adjustment

1. To check the choke control first take off the air cleaner as described in Section 2, and then rotate the choke lever until it is against its stop.
2. Depress the choke plate and check the gap between the edge of the plate and the side of the carburetter air intake as shown in Fig.3.8. The gap is correct when it measures between 0.14 to 0.16 inch (3.6 to 4.1 mm) for the 1300 c.c. engine and 0.16 to 0.18 inch (4.06 to 4.57 mm) for the 1600 c.c. engine using the shank of a drill of the correct size as a measuring instrument.
3. If the gap is incorrect bend the tab on the choke spindle until the drill will just fit.
4. The fast idle check and any necessary adjustment should only be made after the choke has been checked and adjusted.
5. If the engine is cold run it until it reaches its normal operating temperature and then allow it to idle naturally.
6. Hold the choke plate in the fully open vertical position and turn the choke lever until it is stopped by the choke linkage. With the choke lever in this position the engine speed should rise to about 1,000 r.p.m. as the fast idle cam will have opened the throttle flap very slightly.
7. Check how much radial movement is needed on the throttle lever to obtain this result and then stop the engine.
8. With a pair of mole grips clamp the throttle lever fully open on the stop portion of the casting boss and bend down the tab to decrease, or up to increase, the fast idle speed.
9. Remove the grips and check again if necessary repeating the operation until the fast idling is correct. It may also be necessary to adjust the slow idling speed and recheck the choke. (Fig.3.9.).

22. Ford Carburetter - Automatic Choke Adjustment

1. The automatic choke (see Fig 3.10) fitted to certain models is mounted on the side of the Ford single choke carburetter. The choke works by means of a water actuated bi-metallic spring (15) which turns the choke spindle (2) which in turn opens and closes the choke plate (3).
2. The slow running fuel level, and accelerator pump adjustments are identical to those made for the non-automatic carburetter (see Sections 18, 19 and 20) with one

Fig.3.7. Slow running adjustment screws - Ford carburetter

0.14 - 0.16 in.
(3.6 - 4.1 mm.)

Fig.3.8. Choke plate pull down adjustment for 1300 c.c. engines

Fig.3.9. Fast idle adjustment - Ford carburetter

Chapter 3/Fuel System & Carburation

exception. The gap between the operating lever and plunger when checking accelerator pump operation should be 0.135 to 0.145 inch (3.43 to 3.68 mm) on 1600 engines. The gap on 1300 c.c. models is the same as on non-automatic Ford carburetters.

3. To adjust the choke, take off the outer choke housing (14) and open the throttle plate (26).

4. The piston should now be held in the fully depressed position and the choke plate (3) closed manually until further movement is prevented by the linkage. The bottom edge of the choke plate (3) mounted with a 5/32nd inch (4.0 mm) drill should now be 0.130 to 0.150 inch (3.30 to 3.81 mm) from the side of the carburetter. (Fig.3.12).

5. If the clearance needs to be adjusted bend the extension part of the choke thermostat lever which rests against the choke piston lever until the correct measurement is obtained.

6. The fast idle should only be checked after the choke adjustment has been made.

7. Hold the choke in the full down position and note that the fast idle tab of the throttle lever should be in the first high speed step in the fast idle cam. The engine speed should be 1,850 to 2,050 r.p.m. in temperate climates or 2,200 to 2,400 r.p.m. in cold climates. Should the tab be incorrectly positioned in relation to the high speed step in the cam, with a pair of pliers increase or decrease the existing bend on the fast idle cam rod. To obtain the correct engine speed, bend the throttle lever fast idle tab.

23. Weber 32-DFE & 32 DFM-2 Carburetter - Dismantling & Reassembly

1. All numbers in brackets in this section refer to Fig.3.11. Undo the plug (4) and take out the gauze petrol filter (3). Free the choke actuating arm (22) and its lower end by removing the split pin (27) and nylon washer.

2. Undo the screws and spring washers (2) which hold the top cover (24) in place and lift off the cover and the gasket (25).

3. Pull out the pin (29) which retains the float (5) in place, lift out the needle valve (28) and unscrew the needle valve housing (28) from the top cover. Remove the small washer (26).

4. On the side of the carburetter, undo the four screws and washers (13) which hold the accelerator pump cover (14) in place. Remove the cover (14), diaphragm (15) and the diaphragm return spring (16).

5. If the accelerator pump lever is badly worn, drive out the pivot pin from the plain end.

6. Pull out the split pin (21) which holds the upper end of the choke actuating arm (22) to the choke spindle (20), undo the choke plate retaining grub screws (19); and pull out the choke plates (18). The choke spindle (20) can now be removed from the side of the carburetter.

7. Unscrew from the bottom of the float chamber the primary (8) and secondary (6) main jets.

8. With a screwdriver undo the accelerator pump discharge valve (31) from the middle of the carburetter and take off the pump discharge nozzle (33) and the gasket (34).

9. Directly behind the discharge nozzle orifice lie the two air correction jets (30) and their emulsion tubes (32). Unscrew the air correction jet (30), turn the carburetter upside down and shake out the emulsion tubes (32).

10 From either side of the carburetter (only one side is shown) unscrew the two idling jet holders (36) and the idling jets (35). From the bottom of the carburetter undo and remove the volume control screw (39) and the spring (40).

11 Take off from between the carburetter body and the secondary throttle lever the return spring.

12 Turn back the lock tab (65) on the primary throttle shaft (10) unscrew the nut (67) and pull off the throttle control lever (64), bush (63), secondary throttle control lever, and the other components.

13 Then disconnect the fast idle connecting rod (47), and remove the bush, washers and fast idle lever.

14 With all the levers, springs and bushes removed from the throttle spindles (9,10) undo the grub screws (12) which hold the butterfly valves (11) to the spindles, remove the valves (11) and slide the spindles out of the carburetter.

15 Finally undo the retaining screw and take off the choke operating lever, spring and washer.

16 Reassembly commences with refitting the cleaned gauze filter (3) to the top cover (24), and securing the filter in place with the large brass plug (4).

17 Slide the choke spindle (20) into its bore in the top cover (24) so the lever on the spindle lies adjacent to the secondary choke. Replace the choke plates (18) ensuring that the smaller portion faces the rear and that when closed the plate chamfers are parallel to the sides of the air intake. Centralise and secure with grub screws (19). Peen over the ends of the screws to ensure no possibility of their working loose.

18 The dust seal (23) can now be fitted to the top cover flange and the choke rod (22) passed through the seal and the flange and connected by means of the split pin (21) to the choke spindle (20).

19 Fit the choke relay lever (53) and washer (54) to the spindle on the carburetter body and retain in place with the split pin (37).

20 Now assemble the fast idle rod (47) and the toggle spring to the choke control lever (42) and fit the return spring (41) around the carburetter body pivot boss, so the straight ends rests in the location hole.

21 Place the choke control lever (42) on the pivot boss, and fix the toggle spring to the relay lever (53). Make sure that the relay lever toggle spring arm lies against the cam portion of the choke control lever (42) and that the fast idle rod lies between the two throttle spindle bosses. The screw (46) flat and spring washers which secure the lever (42) in place should now be refitted.

22 The end of the return spring should be hooked under the fast idle rod bracket.

23 Slide the primary (10) and secondary (9) throttle spindles into the carburetter, turning the spindles until the slots are parallel with the choke bore and the threaded holes face inwards. Slide the butterfly valves into the slots so the faces marked '78°' are facing outwards with the numbers below the spindles. Ensure that the valves are centralised and then retain them in place with the grub screws (12). Peen over the threaded ends of the screws to ensure they will not loosen.

24 To the secondary throttle spindle (9) fit the throttle lever (44) so the abutment rests against the stop. Replace the plain and spring washer (48,49) and do up the retaining nut (50).

25 Close the secondary throttle and then check with a feeler gauge the clearance between the carburetter barrel at its widest point and the butterfly valve. Adjust the stop to give a clearance of 0.0015 inch (0.038 mm).

26 Fit the slotted washer (55), return spring (56), and idling adjustment lever (58) to the primary throttle spindle (10) wrapping the hooked end of the spring around the lower arm of the idling adjustment lever, the other straight end resting on top of the flange between the two chokes.

27 Slide the plain washer (60), fast idle lever (61), wave washer (62), and bush (63) onto the primary throttle spindle (10). Fit the fast idle rod (47) to the fast idle lever

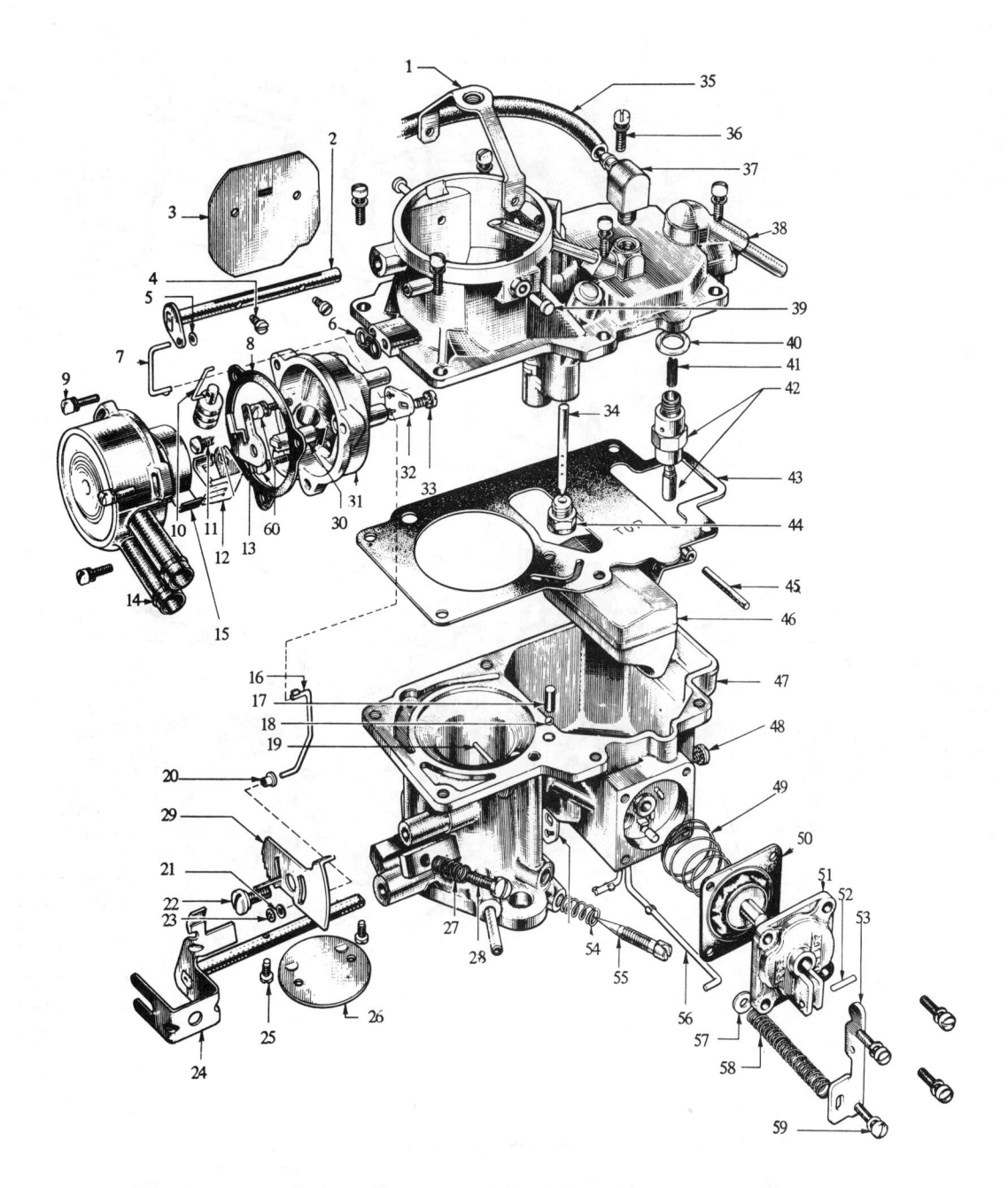

Fig.3.10. EXPLODED VIEW OF CARBURETTER WITH AUTOMATIC CHOKE—EXCEPT G.T.

1. Air filter	17. Pump discharge ball weight	34. Main metering jet tube	49. Diaphragm return spring
2. Choke spindle	18. Pump discharge ball	35. Overflow pipe	50. Diaphragm
3. Choke plate	20. Bush	36. Screw	51. Accelerator pump cover
4. Plate retaining screw	21. Washer	37. Adaptor	52. Lever pivot pin
5. Clip	22. Screw	38. Carburetter horn assembly	53. Accelerator pump actuating lever
6. Gasket	23. Shakeproof washer	39. Air filter bracket retaining pin	54. Spring
7. Choke control rod	24. Throttle lever and spindle assembly	40. Washer	55. Idling mixture adjustment screw
8. Gasket	25. Plate retaining screw	41. Filter	56. Pump to lever rod
9. Screw	26. Throttle plate	42. Needle valve assembly	57. Spring retaining washer
10. Automatic)	27. Spring	43. Gasket	58. Spring
11. choke)	28. Throttle stop screw	44. Main metering jet	59. Screw
12. assembly)	30. Spindle	45. Float pivot spindle	60. Screw
13.)	31. Auto-choke housing	46. Float	
14. Auto-choke housing cover	32. Bracket	47. Carburetter body	
15. Bi-metallic spring	33. Screw	48. Screw	
16. Fast idler cam rod			

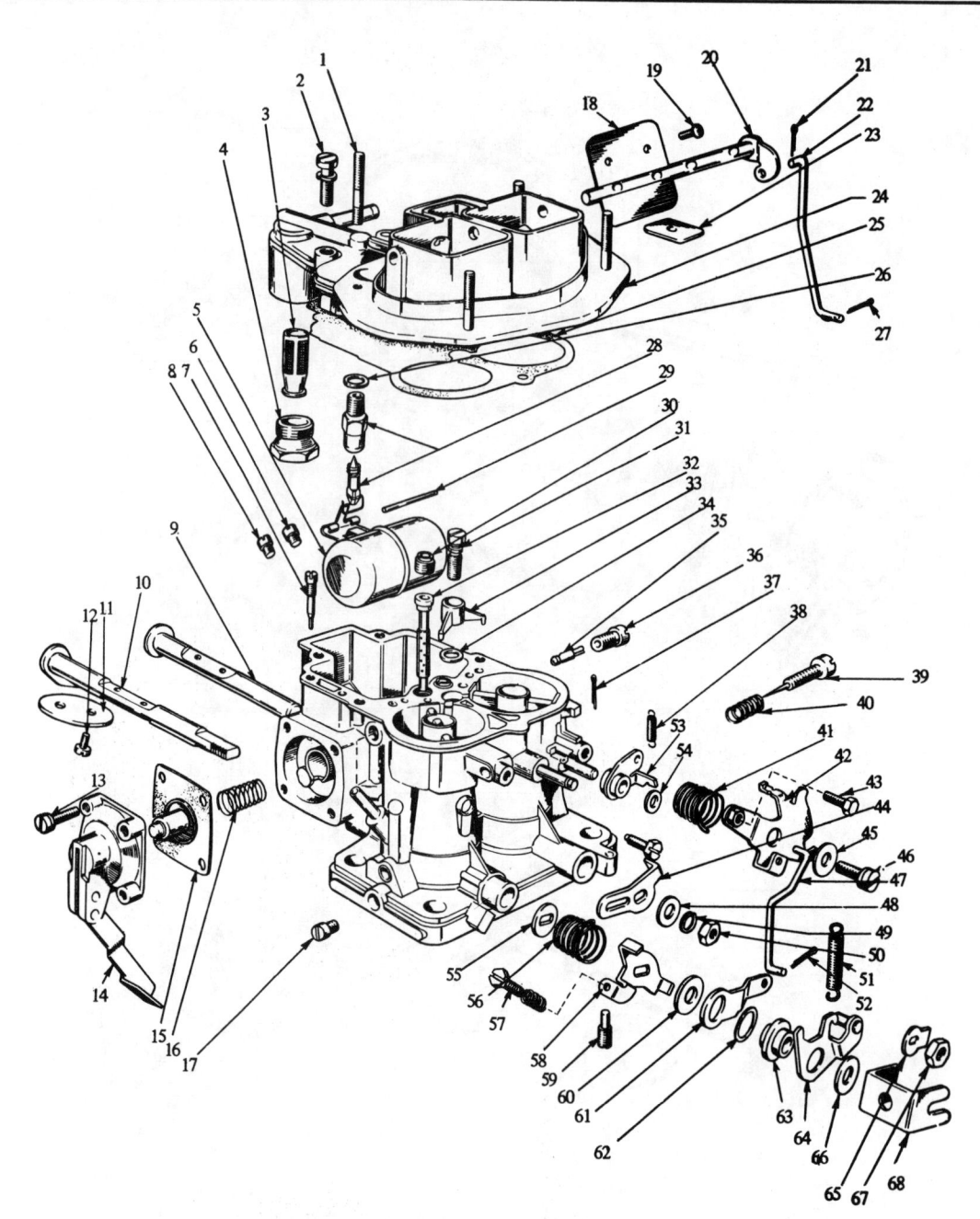

Fig.3.11. EXPLODED VIEW OF THE WEBER 32DFE & 32DFM-2 CARBURETTER FITTED TO G.T. MODELS

1. Stud
2. Screw
3. Gauze filter element
4. Plug
5. Float
6. Main metering jet
7. Accelerator pump blanking needle
8. Main metering jet
9. Spindle
10. Spindle
11. Throttle plate or butterfly valve
12. Screw
13. Screw
14. Accelerator pump cover
15. Diaphragm
16. Diaphragm return spring
17. Plug
18. Choke spindle plate
19. Plate retaining screw
20. Choke spindle
21. Split pin
22. Choke actuating arm
23. Dust seal
24. Carburetter top cover
25. Gasket
26. Washer
27. Split pin
28. Needle valve
29. Float pivot spindle
30. Starting air adjusting jet
31. Accelerator pump discharge valve
32. Starting jet
33. Pump discharge nozzle
34. Gasket
35. Secondary idling jet
36. Idling jet holder
37. Split pin
38. Spring
39. Volume control screw
40. Spring
41. Spring
42. Choke control lever
43. Bolt
44. Throttle stop lever
45. Washer
46. Screw
47. Fast idle rod
48. Washer
49. Spring washer
50. Nut
51. Spring
52. Split pin
53. Choke relay lever
54. Nylon washer
55. Slotted washer
56. Spring
57. Idling adjustment lever screw
58. Idling adjustment lever
59. Adjuster
60. Spacer
61. Choke/throttle interconnecting fast idle lever
62. Washer
63. Bush
64. Throttle control lever
65. Tab washer
66. Washer
67. Nut
68. Throttle lever assembly

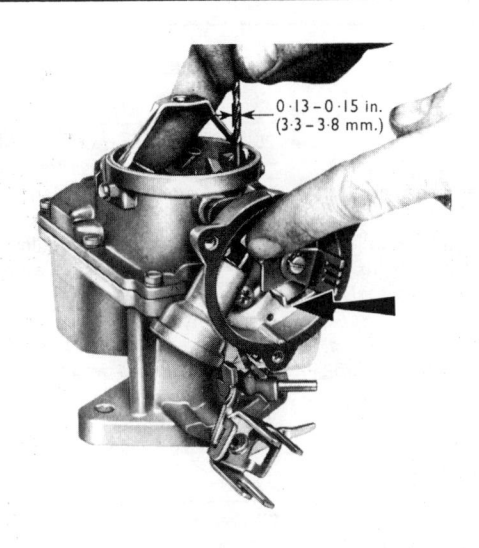

Fig.3.12. Choke plate pull-down adjustment - Ford automatic choke

Fig.3.13. Weber carburetters float and fuel level setting

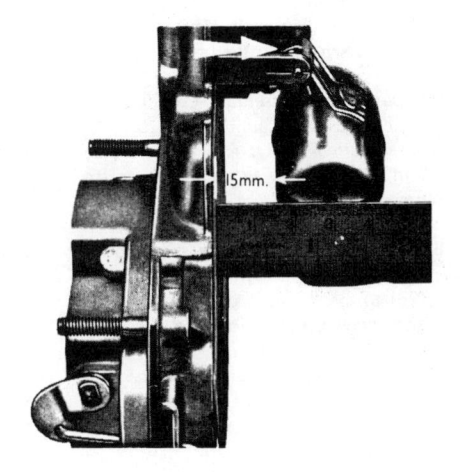

Fig.3.14. Weber carburetters float stroke dimension

Fig.3.15. Weber carburetters slow running adjustment screws

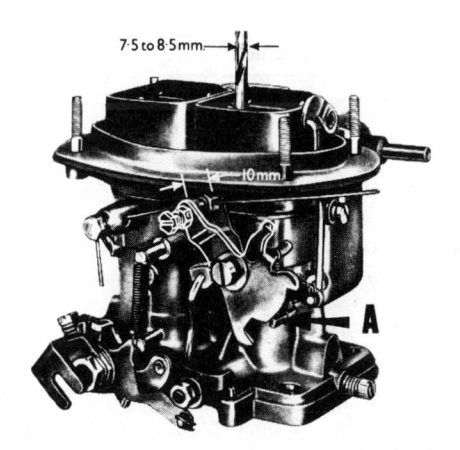

Fig.3.16. Weber carburetters choke plate opening adjustment

67

Chapter 3/Fuel System & Carburation

(61), securing the split pin (52).

28 The throttle relay lever (64) can now be fitted to the bush (63) so the peg on the relay lever fits into the slot in the secondary throttle lever (44).

29 Now fit the plain washer (66) throttle lever (68) and the tab washer (65) and tighten down the retaining nut (67). Turn up the tab on the lockwasher.

30 Fit the secondary idling jet (35) '45' to the secondary idling holder (36), and the primary idling jet '50' to its idling holder, and screw the holders one into each side of the float chamber.

31 The main primary (8) '125' on 1300 G.T., '150' on 1600 G.T., and main secondary (6) '115' on 1300 G.T.'155' on 1600 G.T., jets can now be screwed into their recesses in the float chamber.

32 Slide the emulsion tubes into their wells and screw down the primary (32) '135' on 1300 G.T,, '160' on 1600 G.T., and secondary, '160' on 1300 G.T., '140' on 1600 G.T., air correction jets.

33 Fit a new accelerator pump discharge jet washer (34) to the carburetter, position the jet (33) and secure with the discharge valve (31).

34 Slide the accelerator pump spring (16) into the recess in the carburetter and place the diaphragm (15) against the pump cover (14) so the plunger lies in the operating lever recess.

35 Fit the accelerator pump cover assembly (14) in place so the operating lever engages the cam. Now insert and tighten down the four securing screws and washers (13) at the same time pulling the lever away from the cam to the limit of the diaphragm travel.

36 Fully screw in the volume control screw (39) and then undo it 1½ turns. Screw in a further half turn the throttle stop screw when it just contacts the throttle top lever.

37 Fit a new gasket (26) to the threaded end of the needle valve housing (28) and screw the housing into the float chamber cover (24).

38 Place a new gasket (25) on the underside of the carburetter top cover, fit the needle valve to the housing, and then replace the float (5) and pivot pin (29). Check the fuel level setting as described in Section 24.

38 Bring together the top cover and the main carburetter body at the same time connecting the relay lever (53) to the choke plate operating rod (22). Evenly tighten down the securing screws and spring washers. Reassembly is now complete.

24. Weber Carburetters - Fuel Level Setting

1. Since the height of the float is important in the maintenance of a correct flow of fuel, the correct height is obtained by measurement and adjustment. This is particularly the case if fuel is leaking from the joint of the float chamber.

2. First carefully remove the cover which contains the float and the flow control valve. Hold the cover vertically so that the float hangs down, and it will be seen that a tab, hooked to the needle control valve is in light contact with the ball, and this should be perpendicular.

3. The distance between the float and the cover at this stage should be 7 mm. as shown in Fig.3.13.

4. If this measurement is not correct, then the tabs should be carefully bent at the float end until the distance is obtained.

5. Since the stroke of the float is 8 mm. it follows that when the needle valve is at its extreme as seen in Fig.3.14 then the distance should be 15 mm.

6. From time to time it may be necessary to replace the sealing washers, and when any part is renewed, then this float adjustment is essential.

25. Weber Carburetters - Slow Running Adjustment

1. Slow running adjustment is best performed with the aid of a vacuum gauge as described in Section 20. Should a vacuum gauge not be available then turn the throttle stop screw so the engine when warm runs at a fast idle.

2. Turn the volume control screw in or out until the engine runs really smoothly and fires evenly. While this is being done, adjust the throttle stop screw until the correct idling speed is obtained which on G.T. engines is about 680 to 720 r.p.m. (Fig.3.15).

3. Do not try and set the idling speed too slow and if necessary check the ignition timing.

26. Weber Carburetters - Choke Adjustment

1. If the choke is not working correctly the choke plate pull down and the choke plate opening must be checked.

2. Close the choke and hold the choke lever against its stop. The choke plates should now be opened against the resistance of the toggle spring. The distance between the bottom edge of the plates and the side of the inside choke wall should be 5 mm. checked with a correctly sized drill. If necessary bend the choke lever stop until the gap is correct.

3. To verify the choke plate opening from the fully closed position move the lever back 10 mm. which can be most easily measured along the line of the choke cable. The distance between the bottom edge of the plates and the inside choke wall should be 7.5 to 8.5 mm. checked with a drill of this size.

4. If the gap is incorrect bend the tag marked 'A' in Fig. 3.16. in towards the cam to increase the opening, and away from it to decrease it. NOTE: Bend the tag a very small amount at a time as a very small difference to the tag position will make a considerable difference to the position of the chokes.

27. Exhaust System - Description, Removal & Replacement

1. Exhaust systems do not normally last for more than two or three years. Provision has therefore been made for easy removal and replacement of the exhaust system components on the Capri.

2. The exhaust system is divided into two main parts. The front part comprises the exhaust downpipe, a small expansion chamber and a silencer with a further pipe leading from it to the rear section which consists of a further silencer and a tail pipe. It is possible to split the system just forward of the rear silencer.

3. Running down the left-hand side of the car the system is supported by a stay just forward of the gearbox rear mounting plate and from these to the rear of the car by 'O' rings suspended from brackets on the underframe.

4. Before trying to remove a leaking or badly rusted exhaust system squirt 'Plus Gas' or a similar de-rusting and lubricating agent over:-

a) The clamp bolts just in front of the rear silencer securing the pipe from the front silencer to the rear silencer.

b) The bolts securing the stay clamp to the downpipe just forward of the gearbox rear mounting plate.

c) The nuts/studs which secure the exhaust manifold to exhaust downpipe.

5. Then chock the front wheels, jack up the rear of the

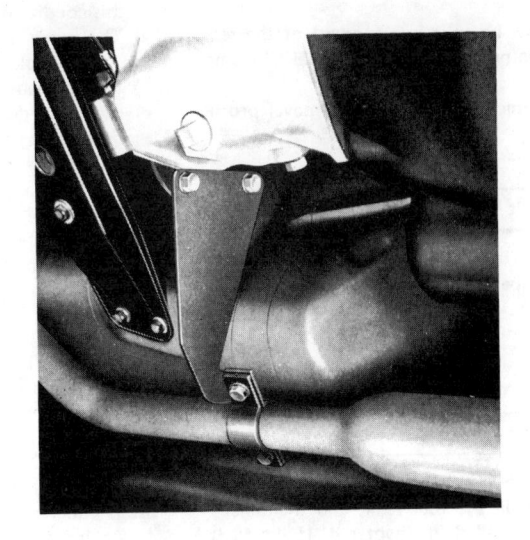

Fig.3.17. Exhaust system front support stay

Fig.3.18. The 'O' rings supporting the tail pipe and rear silencer

Chapter 3/Fuel System & Carburation

car and fit stands for safety. Undo the bolts on the stay clamp and remove the clamp.

6. Undo the nuts on the clamp which secures the exhaust downpipe to the exhaust manifold. Unhook the two sets of 'O' rings holding the remainder of the system in place.

7. Lower the system to the ground and remove it from under the car.

8. The system can now be split just forward of the rear silencer by undoing the nuts on the ends of the 'U' clamp bolt.

9. Replacement is a direct reversal of the removal procedure.

28. Fuel System - Fault Finding

There are three main types of fault the fuel system is prone to, and they may be summarised as follows:-
a) Lack of fuel at engine.
b) Weak mixture.
c) Rich mixture.

29. Lack of Fuel at Engine

1. If it is not possible to start the engine, first positively check that there is fuel in the fuel tank, and then check the ignition system as detailed in Chapter 4. If the fault is not in the ignition system then disconnect the fuel inlet pipe from the carburetter and turn the engine over by the starter relay switch.

2. If petrol squirts from the end of the inlet pipe, reconnect the pipe and check that the fuel is getting to the float chamber. This is done by unscrewing the bolts from the top of the float chamber, and lifting the cover just enough to see inside.

3. If fuel is there then it is likely that there is a blockage in the starting jet, which should be removed and cleaned.

4. No fuel in the float chamber, is caused either by a blockage in the pipe between the pump and float chamber or a sticking float chamber valve. Alternatively on the twin choke G.T. carburetter the gauze filter at the top of the float chamber may be blocked. Remove the securing nut and check that the filter is clean. Washing in petrol will clean it.

5. If it is decided that it is the float chamber valve that is sticking, remove the fuel inlet pipe, and lift the cover, complete with valve and floats, away.

6. Remove the valve spindle and valve and thoroughly wash them in petrol. Petrol gum may be present on the valve or valve spindle and this is usually the cause of a sticking valve. Replace the valve in the needle valve assembly, ensure that it is moving freely, and then reassemble the float chamber. It is important that the same washer be placed under the needle valve assembly as this determines the height of the floats and therefore the level of petrol in the chamber.

7. Reconnect the fuel pipe and refit the air cleaner.

8. If no petrol squirts from the end of the pipe leading to the carburetter then disconnect the pipe leading to the inlet side of the fuel pump. If fuel runs out of the pipe then there is a fault in the fuel pump, and the pump should be checked as has already been detailed.

9. No fuel flowing from the tank when it is known that there is fuel in the tank indicates a blocked pipe line. The line to the tank should be blown out. It is unlikely that the fuel tank vent would become blocked, but this could be a reason for the reluctance of the fuel to flow. To test for this, blow into the tank down the fill orifice. There should be no build up of pressure in the fuel tank, as the excess pressure should be carried away down the vent pipe.

30. Weak Mixture

1. If the fuel/air mixture is weak there are six main clues to this condition:-
a) The engine will be difficult to start and will need much use of the choke, stalling easily if the choke is pushed in.
b) The engine will overheat easily.
c) If the sparking plugs are examined (as detailed in the section on engine tuning), they will have a light grey/white deposit on the insulator nose.
d) The fuel consumption may be light.
e) There will be a noticeable lack of power.
f) During acceleration and on the over-run there will be a certain amount of spitting back through the carburetter.

2. As the carburetters are of the fixed jet type, these faults are invariably due to circumstances outside the carburetter. The only usual fault likely in the carburetter is that one or more of the jets may be partially blocked. If the car will not start easily but runs well at speed, then it is likely that the starting jet is blocked, whereas if the engine starts easily but will not rev, then it is likely that the main jets are blocked.

3. If the level of petrol in the float chamber is low this is usually due to a sticking valve or incorrectly set floats.

4. Air leaks either in the fuel lines, or in the induction system should also be checked for. Also check the distributor vacuum pipe connection as a leak in this is directly felt in the inlet manifold.

5. The fuel pump may be at fault as has already been detailed.

31. Rich Mixture

1. If the fuel/air mixture is rich there are also six main clues to this condition:-
a) If the sparking plugs are examined they will be found to have a black sooty deposit on the insulator nose.
b) The fuel consumption will be heavy.
c) The exhaust will give off a heavy black smoke, especially when accelerating.
d) The interior deposits on the exhaust pipe will be dry, black and sooty (if they are wet, black and sooty this indicates worn bores, and much oil being burnt).
e) There will be a noticeable lack of power.
f) There will be a certain amount of back-firing through the exhaust system.

2. The faults in this case are usually in the carburetter and the most usual is that the level of petrol in the float chamber is too high. This is due either to dirt behind the needle valve, or a leaking float which will not close the valve properly, or a sticking needle.

3. With a very high mileage (or because someone has tried to clean the jets out with wire), it may be that the jets have become enlarged.

4. If the air correction jets are restricted in any way the mixture will tend to become very rich.

5. Occasionally it is found that the choke control is sticking or has been maladjusted.

6. Again, occasionally the fuel pump pressure may be excessive so forcing the needle valve open slightly until a higher level of petrol is reached in the float chamber.

32. Fuel Gauge & Sender Unit - Fault Finding

1. If the fuel gauge fails to give a reading with the ignition

Chaper 3/Fuel System & Carburation

on or reads 'FULL' all the time, then a check must be made to see if the fault is in the gauge, sender unit, or wire in between.

2. Turn the ignition on and disconnect the wire from the fuel tank sender unit. Check that the fuel gauge needle is on the empty mark. To check if the fuel gauge is in order now earth the fuel tank sender unit wire. This should send the needle to the full mark.

3. If the fuel gauge is in order check the wiring for leaks or loose connections. If none can be found, then the sender unit will be at fault and must be replaced.

4. Should both the fuel gauge, and where fitted the temperature gauge fail to work, or if they both give unusually high readings, then a check must be made of the instrument voltage regulator which is positioned behind the speedometer.

Fault Finding Chart — Fuel System & Carburation

Symptom	Reason/s	Remedy
Carburation and ignition faults	Air cleaner choked and dirty giving rich mixture.	Remove, clean and replace air cleaner.
	Fuel leaking from carburetter(s), fuel pumps, or fuel lines.	Check for and eliminate all fuel leaks. Tighten fuel line union nuts.
	Float chamber flooding.	Check and adjust float level.
	Generally worn carburetter(s)	Remove, overhaul and replace.
	Distributor condenser faulty	Remove, and fit new unit.
	Balance weights or vacuum advance mechanism in distributor faulty	Remove, and overhaul distributor.
Incorrect adjustment	Carburetter(s) incorrectly adjusted mixture too rich.	Tune and adjust carburetter(s).
	Idling speed too high.	Adjust idling speed.
	Contact breaker gap incorrect.	Check and reset gap.
	Valve clearances incorrect.	Check rocker arm to valve stem clearances and adjust as necessary.
	Incorrectly set sparking plugs.	Remove, clean and regap.
	Tyres under-inflated	Check tyre pressures and inflate if necessary.
	Wrong sparking plugs fitted.	Remove and replace with correct units.
	Brakes dragging.	Check and adjust brakes.
Dirt in system	Petrol tank air vent restricted.	Remove petrol cap and clean out air vent.
	Partially clogged filters in pump and carburetter(s).	Remove and clean filters.
	Dirt lodged in float chamber needle housing.	Remove and clean out float chamber and needle valve assembly.
	Incorrectly seating valves in fuel pump	Remove, dismantle, and clean out fuel pump.
Fuel pump faults	Fuel pump diaphragm leaking or damaged.	Remove, and overhaul fuel pump.
	Gasket in fuel pump damaged.	Remove, and overhaul fuel pump.
	Fuel pump valves sticking due to petrol gumming.	Remove, and thoroughly clean fuel pump.
Air leaks.	Too little fuel in fuel tank (Prevalent when climbing steep hills).	Refill fuel tank.
	Union joints on pipe connections loose.	Tighten joints and check for air leaks.
	Split in fuel pipe on suction side of fuel pump.	Examine, locate, and repair.
	Inlet manifold to block or inlet manifold to carburetter(s) gasket leaking.	Test by pouring oil along joints — bubbles indicate leak. Renew gasket as appropriate.

Chapter 4/Ignition System

Contents

General Description ... 1	Distributor Reassembly ... 9
Contact Breaker Adjustment ... 2	Refitting Distributor ... 10
Removing & Replacing Contact Breaker Points... 3	Sparking Plugs & Leads ... 11
Condenser Removal, Testing & Replacement ... 4	Ignition Timing.. ... 12
Distributor Lubrication ... 5	Ignition System - Fault Finding.. ... 13
Distributor Removal ... 6	Ignition System - Fault Symptoms... ... 14
Distributor Dismantling... 7	Fault Diagnosis - Engine Fails to Start.. ... 15
Distributor Inspection & Repair ... 8	Fault Diagnosis - Engine Misfires ... 16

Specifications

Sparking Plugs... Autolite A.G.22A
   Size ... 14 mm.
   Plug gap .. .023 in. (.58 mm)

Coil
   Type ... Oil filled low voltage
   Resistance at 20°C (68°F)
      Primary ... 3.1 to 3.5 ohms
      Secondary ... 4,750 to 5,750 ohms
   Output ... 30 k.v.

Distributor... Ford
   Contact points gap setting ... .025 in. (.64 mm)
   Rotation of rotor ... Anti-clockwise
   Automatic advance ... Mechanical and vacuum
   Condenser capacity ... .21 to .25 microfarad
   Contact breaker spring tension... 17 to 21 oz. (481.9 to 567.0 gms)
   Identification Numbers:-
      1300 c.c. H.C ... C8AH - A
      1300 c.c. L.C ... C8AH - B
      1300 c.c. G.T ... C8AH - C
      1600 c.c. H.C ... C8BH - A
      1600 c.c. L.C ... C8BH - B
      1600 c.c. G.T ... C8BH - C
   Identification Colour:-
      H.C.. ... Red
      L.C.. ... Green
      G.T.. ... Blue

Initial Advance Timing
   1300 G.T ... 10° B.T.D.C. On 97 octane fuel
   1600 G.T ... 8° B.T.D.C. On 97 octane fuel
   1300 c.c. High C ... 10° B.T.D.C. On 97 octane fuel
   1600 c.c. High C ... 10° B.T.D.C. On 97 octane fuel
   1300 c.c. Low C ... 10° B.T.D.C. Using 89 octane fuel
   1600 c.c. Low C ... 10° B.T.D.C. Using 89 octane fuel
   1300 c.c. High C ... 6° B.T.D.C. Using 94 octane fuel
   1600 c.c. High C ... 6° B.T.D.C. Using 94 octane fuel
   1300 c.c. Low C ... 4° B.T.D.C. Using 86 octane fuel
   1600 c.c. Low C ... 4° B.T.D.C. Using 86 octane fuel
   Dwell angle ... 38° to 40°

Torque Wrench Setting
   Sparking plugs ... 24 to 28 lb/ft. (3.32 to 3.87 kg.m)

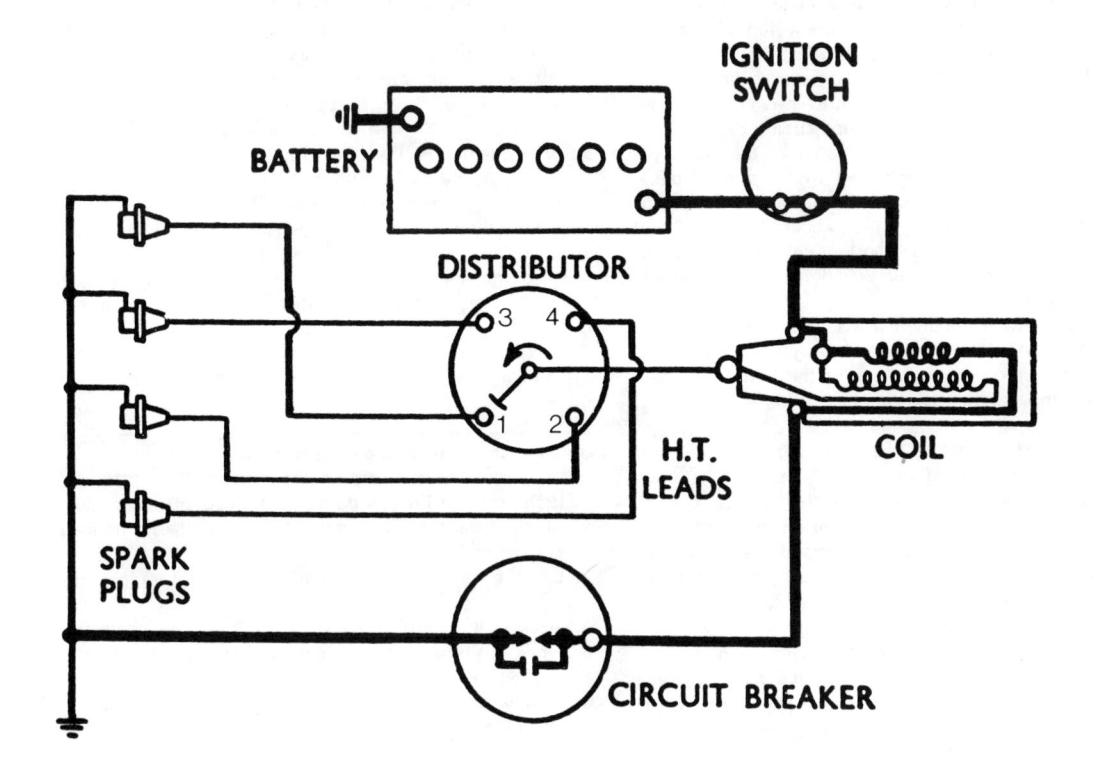

Fig.4.1. Diagram of the ignition circuit. Primary circuit (low tension) is indicated by the heavier lines

Chapter 4/Ignition System

1. General Description

In order that the engine can run correctly it is necessary for an electrical spark to ignite the fuel/air mixture in the combustion chamber at exactly the right moment in relation to engine speed and load. The ignition system is based on feeding low tension voltage from the battery to the coil where it is converted to high tension voltage. The high tension voltage is powerful enough to jump the sparking plug gap in the cylinders many times a second under high compression pressures, providing that the system is in good condition and that all adjustments are correct.

The ignition system is divided into two circuits. The low tension circuit and the high tension circuit.

The low tension (sometimes known as the primary) circuit consists of the battery, lead to the control box, lead to the ignition switch, lead from the ignition switch to the low tension or primary coil windings (terminal SW), and the lead from the low tension coil windings (coil terminal CB) to the contact breaker points and condenser in the distributor.

The high tension circuit consists of the high tension or secondary coil windings, the heavy ignition lead from the centre of the coil to the centre of the distributor cap, the rotor arm, and the sparking plug leads and sparking plugs.

The system functions in the following manner. Low tension voltage is changed in the coil into high tension voltage by the opening and closing of the contact breaker points in the low tension circuit. High tension voltage is then fed via the carbon brush in the centre of the distributor cap to the rotor arm of the distributor cap, and each time it comes in line with one of the four metal segments in the cap, which are connected to the sparking plug leads, the opening and closing of the contact breaker points causes the high tension voltage to build up, jump the gap from the rotor arm to the appropriate metal segment and so via the sparking plug lead to the sparking plug, where it finally jumps the spark plug gap before going to earth.

The ignition is advanced and retarded automatically, to ensure the spark occurs at just the right instant for the particular load at the prevailing engine speed.

The ignition advance is controlled both mechanically and by a vacuum operated system. The mechanical governor comprises two lead weights, which move out from the distributor shaft as the engine speed rises due to centrifugal force. As they move outwards they rotate the cam relative to the distributor shaft, and so advance the spark. The weights are held in position by two light springs and it is the tension of the springs which is largely responsible for correct spark advancement.

The vacuum control consists of a diaphragm, one side of which is connected via a small bore tube to the carburetter, and the other side to the contact breaker plate. Depression in the inlet manifold and carburetter, which varies with engine speed and throttle opening, causes the diaphragm to move, so moving the contact breaker plate, and advancing or retarding the spark. A fine degree of control is achieved by a spring in the vacuum assembly.

2. Contact Breaker Adjustment

1. To adjust the contact breaker points to the correct gap, first pull off the two clips securing the distributor cap to the distributor body, and lift away the cap. Clean the cap inside and out with a dry cloth. It is unlikely that the four segments will be badly burned or scored, but if they are the cap will have to be renewed.
2. Inspect the carbon brush contact located in the top of the cap - see that it is unbroken and stands proud of the plastic surface.
3. Check the contact spring on the top of the rotor arm. It must be clean and have adequate tension to ensure good contact.
4. Gently prise the contact breaker points open to examine the condition of their faces. If they are rough, pitted, or dirty, it will be necessary to remove them for resurfacing, or for replacement points to be fitted.
5. Presuming the points are satisfactory, or that they have been cleaned and replaced, measure the gap between the points by turning the engine over until the heel of the breaker arm is on the highest point of the cam. (photo).
6. A .025 in. (.64 mm) feeler gauge should now just fit between the points (See Fig.4.2).
7. If the gap varies from this amount, slacken the contact plate securing screw (see photo).
8. Adjust the contact gap by inserting a screwdriver in the notched hole, (see photo) in the breaker plate. Turn clockwise to increase and anti-clockwise to decrease the gap. When the gap is correct, tighten the securing screw and check the gap again.
9. Make sure the rotor is in position, replace the distributor cap and clip the spring blade retainers into position.

3. Removing & Replacing Contact Breaker Points

1. If the contact breaker points are burned, pitted or badly worn, they must be removed and either replaced, or their faces must be filed smooth.
2. Lift off the rotor arm by pulling it straight up from the spindle.
3. Slacken the self-tapping screw holding the condenser and low tension leads to the contact breaker and slide out the forked ends of the leads.
4. Remove the points by taking out the two retaining screws and lifting off the points assembly.
5. Replacing the points assembly is a reversal of the removal procedure. Take care not to trap the wires between the points and the breaker plate. (Fig.4.3).
6. When the points are replaced the gap should be set as described in the previous section.
7. Finally replace the rotor arm and then the distributor cap.

NOTE: Should the contact points be badly worn, a new set should be fitted. As an emergency measure clean the faces with fine emery paper folded over a thin steel ruler. It is necessary to completely remove the built-up deposits, but not necessary to rub the pitted point right down to the stage where all the pitting has disappeared. When the surfaces are flat a feeler gauge can be used and the gap set as above.

4. Condenser Removal, Testing & Replacement

1. The purpose of the condenser, (sometimes known as a capacitor) is to ensure that when the contact breaker points open there is no sparking across them which would waste voltage and cause wear.
2. The condenser is fitted in parallel with the contact breaker points. If it develops a short circuit, it will cause ignition failure as the points will be prevented from interrupting the low tension circuit.
3. If the engine becomes very difficult to start or begins to miss after several miles running and the breaker points show signs of excessive burning, then the condition of the condenser must be suspect. A further test can be made by separating the points by hand with the ignition switched

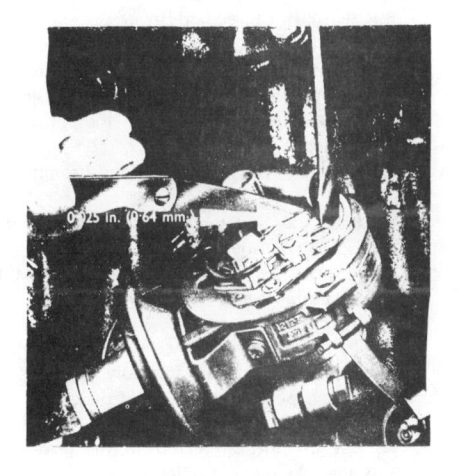

Fig.4.2. Adjusting contact breaker points

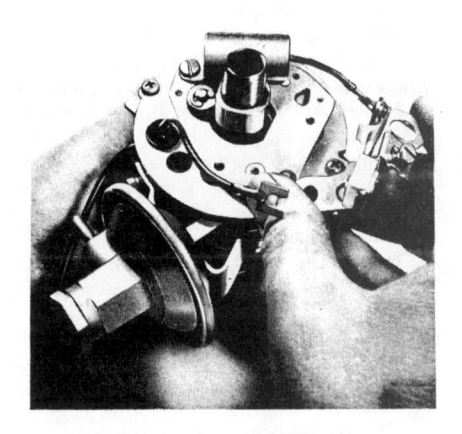

Fig.4.3. Fitting the contact breaker assembly

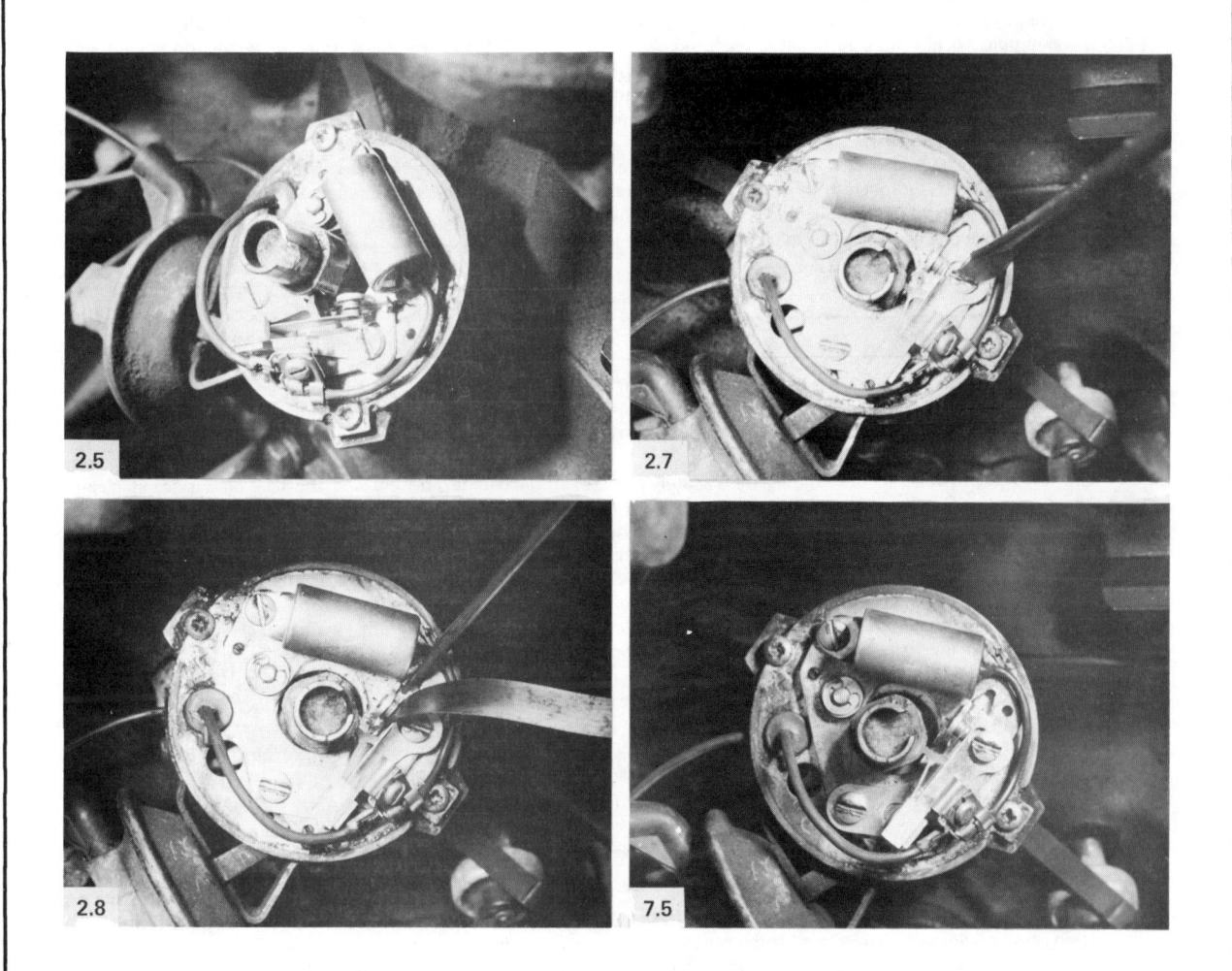

2.5

2.7

2.8

7.5

75

Chapter 4/Ignition System

on. If this is accompanied by a flash it is indicative that the condenser has failed.

4. Without special test equipment the only sure way to diagnose condenser trouble is to replace a suspected unit with a new one and note if there is any improvement.

5. To remove the condenser from the distributor take off the distributor cap and rotor arm. Slacken the self-tapping screw holding the condenser lead and low tension lead to the points, and slide out the fork on the condenser lead. Undo the condenser retaining screw and remove the condenser from the breaker plate.

6. To refit the condenser, simply reverse the order of removal. Take care that the condenser lead is clear of the moving part of the points assembly.

5. Distributor Lubrication

1. It is important that the distributor cam is lubricated with petroleum jelly at the specified mileages, and that the breaker arm, governor weights, and cam spindle, are lubricated with engine oil once every 6,000 miles.

2. Great care should be taken not to use too much lubricant, as any excess that finds its way onto the contact breaker points could cause burning and misfiring.

3. To gain access to the cam spindle, lift away the rotor arm. Drop no more than two drops of engine oil onto the felt pad. This will run down the spindle when the engine is hot and lubricate the bearings.

4. To lubricate the automatic timing control allow a few drops of oil to pass through the hole in the contact breaker base plate through which the four sided cam emerges. Apply not more than one drop of oil to the pivot post and remove any excess.

6. Distributor Removal

1. To remove the distributor from the engine, pull off the four leads from the sparking plugs.

2. Disconnect the high tension and low tension leads from the distributor.

3. Pull off the rubber union holding the vacuum pipe to the distributor vacuum advance housing.

4. Remove the distributor body clamp bolt which holds the distributor clamp plate to the engine and lift out the distributor. BUT SEE NOTE BELOW BEFORE REMOVAL. NOTE: If it is not wished to disturb the timing under no circumstances should the body clamp pinch bolt be loosened. For the same reason the precise direction in which the rotor arm points should be noted before it is removed. This enables the drive gear to be settled on the same tooth when the distributor is refitted. While the distributor is removed care must be taken not to turn the engine. If these precautions are observed there will be no need to retime the ignition.

7. Distributor Dismantling

1. With the distributor on the bench, pull off the two spring clips retaining the cover and lift the cover off.
2. Pull the rotor arm off the distributor cam shaft.
3. Remove the points from the breaker plate as detailed in Section 3.
4. Undo the condenser retaining screw and take off the condenser.
5. Next prise off the small circlip from the vacuum unit pivot post. (photo).
6. Take out the two screws holding the breaker plate to the distributor body and lift away.

7. Take off the circlip flat washer and wave washer from the pivot post. Separate the two plates by bringing the holding down screw through the keyhole slot in the lower plate. Be careful not to lose the spring now left on the pivot post.

8. Pull the low tension wire and grommet from the lower plate.

9. Undo the two screws holding the vacuum unit to the body. Take off the unit.

10 To dismantle the vacuum unit, unscrew the bolt on the end of the unit and withdraw the vacuum spring, stop, and shims. (Fig.4.4).

11 The mechanical advance is next removed but first make a careful note of the assembly particularly which spring fits which post and the position of the advance springs. Then remove the advance springs.

12 Prise off the circlips from the governor weight pivot pins and take out the weights.

13 Dismantle the shaft by taking out the felt pad in the top of the spindle. Expand the exposed circlip and take it out.

14 Now mark which slot in the mechanical advance plate is occupied by the advance stop which stands up from the action plate, and lift off the cam spindle.

15 It is only necessary to remove the lower shaft and action plate if it is excessively worn. If this is the case, with a small punch drive out the gear retaining pin and remove the gear with the two washers located above it.

16 Withdraw the shaft from the distributor body and take off the two washers from below the action plate. The distributor is now completely dismantled.

8. Distributor Inspection & Repair

1. Check the points as described in Section 3. Check the distributor cap for signs of tracking, indicated by a thin black line between the segments. Replace the cap if any signs of tracking are found.

2. If the metal portion of the rotor arm is badly burned or loose, renew the arm. If only slightly burned clean the end with a fine file. Check that the contact spring has adequate pressure and the bearing surface is clean and in good condition.

3. Check that the carbon brush in the distributor cap is unbroken and stands proud of its holder.

4. Examine the fly weights and pivots for wear and the advance springs for slackness. They can best be checked by comparing with new parts. If they are slack they must be renewed.

5. Check the points assembly for fit on the breaker plate, and the cam follower for wear.

6. Examine the fit of the lower shaft in the distributor body. If this is excessively worn it will be necessary to fit a new assembly.

9. Distributor Reassembly

1. Reassembly is a straightforward reversal of the dismantling process, but there are several points which must be noted.

2. Lubricate with S.A.E.20 engine oil the balance weights and other parts of the mechanical advance mechanism, the distributor shaft, and the portion of the shaft on which the cam bears, during assembly. Do not oil excessively but ensure these parts are adequately lubricated.

3. When fitting the lower shaft, first replace the thrust washers below the action plate before inserting into the distributor body. Next fit the wave washer and thrust

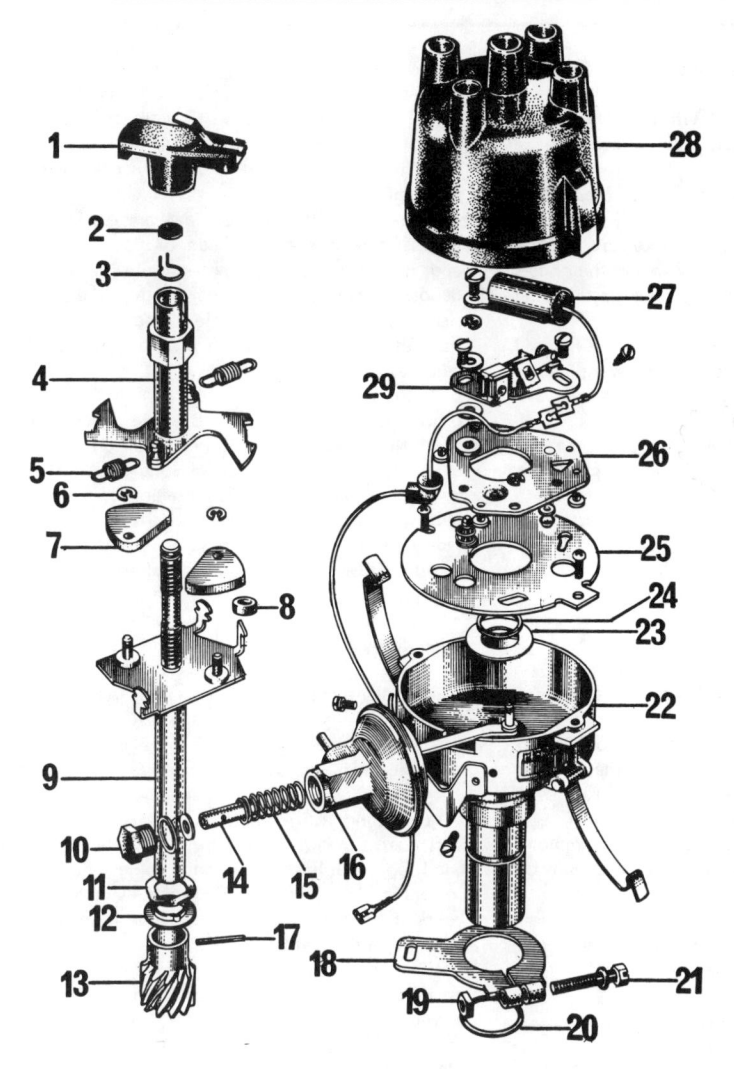

Fig.4.4. EXPLODED VIEW OF THE AUTOLITE DISTRIBUTOR

1. Rotor arm
2. Oil pad
3. Spring clip
4. Mechanical advance and cam assembly
5. Flyweight tension spring
6. Circlip
7. Flyweight
8. Stop
9. Action plate & main shaft
10. Shim retaining bolt
11. Wave washer
12. Thrust washer
13. Skew gear
14. Stop
15. Spring
16. Vacuum advance retard unit
17. Skew gear retaining pin
18. Clamp plate
19. Nut
20. 'O' ring oil seal
21. Bolt and washer
22. Distributor body
23. Washer
24. Washer
25. Lower C.B. plate
26. Upper contact breaker plate
27. Capacitor
28. Distributor cap
29. Contact breaker assembly

Fig.4.5. Breaker plate and vacuum unit assembly

77

Chapter 4/Ignition System

washer at the lower end and replace the drive gear. Secure it with a new pin.
4. Assemble the upper and lower shaft with the advance stop in the correct slot (the one which was marked) in the mechanical advance plate.
5. After assembling the advance weights and springs, check that they move freely without binding.
6. Before assembling the breaker plates make sure that the three nylon bearing studs are properly located in their holes in the upper breaker plate, and that the small earth spring is fitted on the pivot post.
7. As you refit the upper breaker plate pass the holding down spindle through the keyhole slot in the lower plate.
8. Hold the upper plate in position by refitting the wave washer, flat washer and large circlip.
9. When all is assembled, remember to set the contact breaker gap to .025 inch (0.64 mm) as described in Section 2.8.
10 If a new gear or shaft is being fitted it is necessary to drill a new pin hole. Proceed this way.
12 Make a .015 inch (0.38 mm) forked shim to slide over the drive shaft (Fig.4.6).
12 Assemble the shaft, wave washer, thrust washer, shim and gear wheel in position in the distributor body.
13 Hold the assembly in a large clamp such as a vice or carpenters clamp using only sufficient pressure to take up all end play.
14 There is a pilot hole in a new gear wheel for drilling the new hole. Set this pilot hole at 90° to the existing hole in an old shaft if the old one is being reused. Drill a 1/8th inch (3.18 mm) hole through both gear and shaft.
15 Fit a new pin in the hole. Release the clamp and remove the shim. The shaft will now have the correct amount of clearance.
16 When fitting an existing gear wheel still in good condition to a new shaft drill a new pin hole through the gear wheel at 90° to the existing hole. Secure with a new pin.

10. Refitting Distributor

1. If a new shaft or gear wheel has not been fitted, i.e. the original parts are still being used, it will not be necessary to retime the ignition.
2. Insert the distributor with the vacuum advance assembly to the rear and the mounting plate against the engine block.
3. Notice that the rotor arm rotates as the gears mesh. The rotor arm must settle in exactly the same direction that it was in before the distributor was removed. To do this lift out the assembly far enough to rotate the shaft one tooth at a time lowering it home to check the direction of the rotor arm. When it points in the desired direction with the assembly fully home, fit the distributor clamp plate bolt.
4. With the distributor assembly fitted reconnect the low tension lead from the side of the distributor to the CB terminal on the coil. Reconnect the H.T. lead between the centre of the distributor cover and the centre of the coil, and refit the rubber union of the vacuum pipe which runs from the induction manifold to the side of the vacuum advance unit.

11. Sparking Plugs & Leads

1. The correct functioning of the sparking plugs are vital for the correct running and efficiency of the engine.
2. At intervals of 6,000 miles the plugs should be removed, examined, cleaned, and if worn excessively, replaced. The condition of the sparking plugs will also tell much about the overall condition of the engine.
3. If the insulator nose of the sparking plug is clean and white, with no deposits, this is indicative of a weak mixture, or too hot a plug. (A hot plug transfers heat away from the electrode slowly - a cold plug transfers it away quickly.)
4. The plugs fitted as standard are AUTOLITE as listed in Specifications at the head of this chapter. If the tip and insulator nose is covered with hard black looking deposits, then this is indicative that the mixture is too rich. Should the plug be black and oily, then it is likely that the engine is fairly worn, as well as the mixture being too rich.
5. If the insulator nose is covered with light tan to greyish brown deposits, then the mixture is correct and it is likely that the engine is in good condition.
6. If there are any traces of long brown tapering stains on the outside of the white portion of the plug, then the plug will have to be renewed, as this shows that there is a faulty joint between the plug body and the insulator, and compression is being allowed to leak away.
7. Plugs should be cleaned by a sand blasting machine, which will free them from carbon more thoroughly than cleaning by hand. The machine will also test the condition of the plugs under compression. Any plug that fails to spark at the recommended pressure should be renewed.
8. The sparking plug gap is of considerable importance, as, if it is too large or too small, the size of the spark and its efficiency will be seriously impaired. The sparking plug gap should be set to the figure given in Specifications at the beginning of this chapter.
9. To set it, measure the gap with a feeler gauge, and then bend open, or close, the outer plug electrode until the correct gap is achieved. The centre electrode should never be bent as this may crack the insulation and cause plug failure if nothing worse.
10 When replacing the plugs, remember to use new plug washers, and replace the leads from the distributor in the correct firing order, which is 1,2,4,3, No.1. cylinder being the one nearest the radiator. No.1 lead from the distributor runs from the 1.o'clock position when looking down on the distributor cap. 2,3 and 4 are anti-clockwise from No.1.
11 The plug leads require no routine attention other than being kept clean and wiped over regularly.
At intervals of 6,000 miles, however, pull the leads off the plugs and distributor one at a time and make sure no water has found its way onto the connections. Remove any corrosion from the brass ends, wipe the collars on top of the distributor, and refit the leads.

12. Ignition Timing

1. When a new gear or shaft has been fitted or the engine has been rotated, or if a new assembly is being fitted it will be necessary to retime the ignition. Carry it out this way:-
2. Look up the initial advance for the particular model in the Specifications at the beginning of this chapter.
3. Turn the engine until No.1 piston is coming up to T.D.C. on the compression stroke. This can be checked by removing No.1 sparking plug and feeling the pressure being developed in the cylinder, or by removing the rocker cover and noting when the valves in No.4 cylinder are rocking, i.e. the inlet valve just opening and exhaust valve just closing. If this check is not made it is all too easy to set the timing 180° out, as both No.1 and 4 cylinders come up to T.D.C. at the same time, but only one is on the firing stroke. The engine can most easily be turned by engaging top gear and edging the car along.

Chapter 4/Ignition System

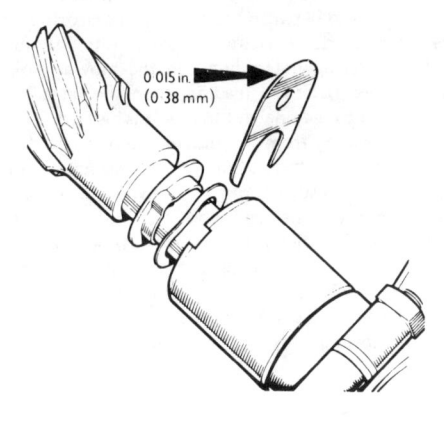

Fig.4.6. Setting distributor shaft endfloat

Fig.4.7. Ignition timing marks

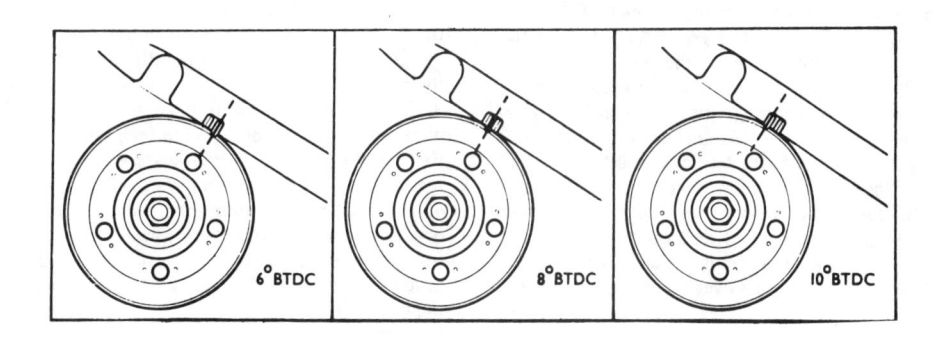

Fig.4.8. Diagrams showing the different degrees of ignition timing possible

4. Continue turning the engine until the appropriate timing mark on the timing cover is in line with the notch on the crankshaft pulley (arrowed). This setting must be correct for the initial advance for the engine which has already been looked up. (Fig.4.7).

5. Now with the vacuum advance unit pointing to the rear of the car insert the distributor assembly so that the rotor points to No.2 inlet port on crossflow engines. The rotor will rotate slightly as the gear drops into mesh.

6. Fit the clamp plate retaining bolt to hold the assembly to the engine block and tighten it.

7. Slacken the distributor clamp pinch bolt.

8. Gently turn the distributor body until the contact breaker points are just opening when the rotor is pointing at the contact in the distributor cap which is connected to No.1 sparking plug. A convenient way is to put a mark on the outside of the distributor body in line with the terminal on cover, so that it shows when the cover is removed.

9. If this position cannot easily be reached, check that the drive gear has meshed on the correct tooth by lifting out the distributor once more. If necessary rotate the drive shaft one tooth and try again.

10. Tighten the distributor body clamp enough to hold the distributor, but do not overtighten.

11 Set in this way the timing should be correct, but small adjustments may be made by slackening the distributor clamp bolt once more and rotating the distributor body clockwise to advance and anti-clockwise to retard.

12 The setting of a distributor including the amount of vacuum and mechanical advance can only be accurately carried out on an electronic tester. Alterations to the vacuum advance shims or tension on the mechanical advance unit springs will change the characteristics of the unit.

13 Since the ignition timing setting enables the firing point to be correctly related to the grade of fuel used, the fullest advantage of a change of grade from that recommended for the engine will only be attained by re-adjustment of the ignition setting.

13. Ignition System Fault Finding

By far the majority of breakdown and running troubles are caused by faults in the ignition system either in the low tension or high tension circuits.

Chapter 4/Ignition System

14. Ignition System Fault Symptoms

There are two main symptoms indicating ignition faults. Either the engine will not start or fire, or the engine is difficult to start and misfires. If it is a regular misfire, i.e. the engine is only running on two or three cylinders the fault is almost sure to be in the secondary, or high tension circuit. If the misfiring is intermittent, the fault could be in either the high or low tension circuits. If the car stops suddenly, or will not start at all, it is likely that the fault is in the low tension circuit. Loss of power and overheating, apart from faulty carburation settings, are normally due to faults in the distributor or incorrect ignition timing.

15. Fault Diagnosis - Engine Fails to Start

1. If the engine fails to start and the car was running normally when it was last used, first check there is fuel in the petrol tank. If the engine turns over normally on the starter motor and the battery is evidently well charged then the fault may be in either the high or low tension circuits. First check the H.T. circuit. NOTE: If the battery is known to be fully charged; the ignition light comes on, and the starter motor fails to turn the engine CHECK THE TIGHTNESS OF THE LEADS ON THE BATTERY TERMINALS and also the secureness of the earth lead to its CONNECTION TO THE BODY. It is quite common for the leads to have worked loose, even if they look and feel secure. If one of the battery terminal posts gets very hot when trying to work the starter motor this is a sure indication of a faulty connection to that terminal.
2. One of the commonest reasons for bad starting is wet or damp sparking plug leads and distributor. Remove the distributor cap. If condensation is visible internally dry the cap with a rag and also wipe over the leads. Replace the cap.
3. If the engine still fails to start, check that current is reaching the plugs, by disconnecting each plug lead in turn at the sparking plug end, and hold the end of the cable about 3/16th inch away from the cylinder block. Spin the engine on the starter motor.
4. Sparking between the end of the cable and the block should be fairly strong with a regular blue spark. (Hold the lead with rubber to avoid electric shocks). If current is reaching the plugs, then remove them and clean and regap them to 0.023 inch. The engine should now start.
5. If there is no spark at the plug leads take off the H.T. lead from the centre of the distributor cap and hold it to the block as before. Spin the engine on the starter once more. A rapid succession of blue sparks between the end of the lead and the block indicate that the coil is in order and that the distributor cap is cracked the rotor arm faulty or the carbon brush in the top of the distributor cap is not making good contact with the spring on the rotor arm. Possibly the points are in bad condition. Clean and reset them as described in this chapter, Section 2:5 to 9.
6. If there are no sparks from the end of the lead from the coil check the connections at the coil end of the lead. If it is in order start checking the low tension circuit.
7. Use a 12v voltmeter or a 12v bulb and two lengths of wire. With the ignition switch on and the points open, test between the low tension wire to the coil (it is marked S.W. or +) and earth. No reading indicates a break in the supply from the ignition switch. Check the connections at the switch to see if any are loose. Refit them and the engine should run. A reading shows a faulty coil or condenser or broken lead between the coil and the distributor.
8. Take the condenser wire off the points assembly and with the points open test between the moving point and earth. If there is now a reading, then the fault is in the condenser. Fit a new one and the fault is cleared.
9. With no reading from the moving point to earth, take a reading between earth and the CB or - terminal of the coil. A reading here shows a broken wire which will need to be replaced between the coil and distributor. No reading confirms that the coil has failed and must be replaced, after which the engine will run once more. Remember to refit the condenser wire to the points assembly. For these tests it is sufficient to separate the points with a piece of dry paper while testing with the points open.

16. Fault Diagnosis - Engine Misfires

1. If the engine misfires regularly, run it at a fast idling speed. Pull off each of the plug caps in turn and listen to the note of the engine. Hold the plug cap in a dry cloth or with a rubber glove as additional protection against a shock from the H.T. supply.
2. No difference in engine running will be noticed when the lead from the defective circuit is removed. Removing the lead from one of the good cylinders will accentuate the misfire.
3. Remove the plug lead from the end of the defective plug and hold it about 3/16th inch away from the block. Restart the engine. If the sparking is fairly strong and regular the fault must lie in the sparking plug.
4. The plug may be loose, the insulation may be cracked, or the points may have burnt away giving too wide a gap for the spark to jump. Worse still, one of the points may have broken off. Either renew the plug, or clean it, reset the gap, and then test it.
5. If there is no spark at the end of the plug lead, or if it is weak and intermittent, check the ignition lead from the distributor to the plug. If the insulation is cracked or perished, renew the lead. Check the connections at the distributor cap.
6. If there is still no spark, examine the distributor cap carefully for tracking. This can be recognised by a very thin black line running between two or more electrodes, or between an electrode and some other part of the distributor. These lines are paths which now conduct electricity across the cap thus letting it run to earth. The only answer it a new distributor cap.
7. Apart from the ignition timing being incorrect, other causes of misfiring have already been dealt with under the section dealing with the failure of the engine to start. To recap - these are that:-
a) The coil may be faulty giving an intermittent misfire.
b) There may be a damaged wire or loose connection in the low tension circuit.
c) The condenser may be short circuiting.
d) Thre may be a mechanical fault in the distributor (Broken driving spindle or contact breaker spring).
8. If the ignition timing is too far retarded, it should be noted that the engine will tend to overheat, and there will be a quite noticeable drop in power. If the engine is overheating and the power is down, and the ignition timing is correct, then the carburetter should be checked, as it is likely that this is where the fault lies.

Measuring plug gap. A feeler gauge of the correct size (see ignition system specifications) should have a slight 'drag' when slid between the electrodes. Adjust gap if necessary

Adjusting plug gap. The plug gap is adjusted by bending the earth electrode inwards, or outwards, as necessary until the correct clearance is obtained. Note the use of the correct tool

Normal. Grey-brown deposits, lightly coated core nose. Gap increasing by around 0.001 in (0.025 mm) per 1000 miles (1600 km). Plugs ideally suited to engine, and engine in good condition

Carbon fouling. Dry, black, sooty deposits. Will cause weak spark and eventually misfire. Fault: over-rich fuel mixture. Check: carburettor mixture settings, float level and jet sizes; choke operation and cleanliness of air filter. Plugs can be re-used after cleaning

Oil fouling. Wet, oily deposits. Will cause weak spark and eventually misfire. Fault: worn bores/piston rings or valve guides; sometimes occurs (temporarily) during running-in period. Plugs can be re-used after thorough cleaning

Overheating. Electrodes have glazed appearance, core nose very white – few deposits. Fault: plug overheating. Check: plug value, ignition timing, fuel octane rating (too low) and fuel mixture (too weak). Discard plugs and cure fault immediately

Electrode damage. Electrodes burned away; core nose has burned, glazed appearance. Fault: pre-ignition. Check: as for 'Overheating' but may be more severe. Discard plugs and remedy fault before piston or valve damage occurs

Split core nose (may appear initially as a crack). Damage is self-evident, but cracks will only show after cleaning. Fault: pre-ignition or wrong gap-setting technique. Check: ignition timing, cooling system, fuel octane rating (too low) and fuel mixture (too weak). Discard plugs, rectify fault immediately

Chapter 5/Clutch and Actuating Mechanism

Contents

General Description ... 1	Clutch Cable - Removal & Replacement ... 8
Routine Maintenance 2	Clutch Release Bearing - Removal & Replacement ... 9
Clutch Pedal - Removal & Replacement ... 3	Clutch Faults ... 10
Clutch Removal ... 4	Clutch Squeal - Diagnosis & Cure ... 11
Clutch Replacement ... 5	Clutch Slip - Diagnosis & Cure ... 12
Clutch Dismantling & Replacement ... 6	Clutch Spin - Diagnosis & Cure ... 13
Clutch Inspection ... 7	Clutch Judder - Diagnosis & Cure ... 14

Specifications

Clutch type ..	Single dry plate diaphragm spring
Actuation ...	Cable
Number of damper springs ...	6
Lining outside diameter ...	7.5 inch (19.05 cm)
Lining inside diameter ...	5.36 inch (136.1 mm)
Total friction area ..	43.2 sq/in. (279.4 sq.cm)

Torque Wrench Settings

Clutch to flywheel bolts ...	12 to 15 lb/ft. (1.66 to 2.07 kg.m)
Bellhousing to gearbox ...	40 to 45 lb/ft. (5.53 to 6.22 kg.m)

1. General Description

1. All models are fitted with a 7½ inch (19.05 cm) single dry plate diaphragm spring clutch. G.T. models have a slightly stronger diaphragm spring than other models. The unit comprises a steel cover which is dowelled and bolted to the rear face of the flywheel, and contains the pressure plate, diaphragm spring and fulcrum rings.
2. The clutch disc is free to slide along the splined first motion shaft and is held in position between the flywheel and the pressure plate by the pressure of the pressure plate spring. Friction lining material is riveted to the clutch disc and it has a spring cushioned hub to absorb transmission shocks and to help ensure a smooth take-off.
3. The circular diaphragm spring is mounted on shoulder pins and held in place in the cover by two fulcrum rings. The spring is also held to the pressure plate by three spring steel clips which are riveted in position.
4. The clutch is actuated by a cable controlled by the clutch pedal. The clutch release mechanism consists of a release fork and bearing which are in permanent contact with the release fingers on the pressure plate. There should therefore never be any free play at the release fork. Wear of the friction material in the clutch is adjusted out by means of a cable adjuster at the lower end of the cable where it passes through the bellhousing.
5. Depressing the clutch pedal actuates the clutch release arm by means of the cable.
6. The release arm pushes the release bearing forwards to bear against the release fingers, so moving the centre of the diaphragm spring inwards. The spring is sandwiched between two annular rings which act as fulcrum points. As the centre of the spring is pushed in the outside of the spring is pushed out, so moving the pressure plate backwards and disengaging the pressure plate from the clutch disc.
7. When the clutch pedal is released the diaphragm spring forces the pressure plate into contact with the high friction linings on the clutch disc and at the same time pushes the clutch disc a fraction of an inch forwards on its splines so engaging the clutch disc with the flywheel. The clutch disc is now firmly sandwiched between the pressure plate and the flywheel so the drive is taken up.

2. Routine Maintenance & Clutch Adjustment

1. Every 6,000 miles adjust the clutch cable to compensate for wear in the linings.
2. The clutch should be adjusted until there is a clearance of 0.138 to 0.144 inch (3.5 to 3.7 mm) between the adjusting nut and its abutment on the bellhousing as indicated in Fig.5.1. When correctly adjusted there should be 0.50 to 0.75 inch (12.7 to 19.1 mm) free play at the clutch pedal.
3. To obtain the correct adjustment, slacken off the locknut (B in Fig.5.1.) and get an assistant to pull the clutch pedal onto its stop, then move the adjusting nut 'A' until the correct clearance has been obtained as mentioned in paragraph 2, above.
4. Hold the adjusting nut 'A' steady to prevent it moving and retighten the locknut 'B' then recheck the clearance and also the pedal free movement.
5. When fitting a new friction plate it will be found that the cable will need fairly extensive adjustment particularly if the old friction plate was well worn.

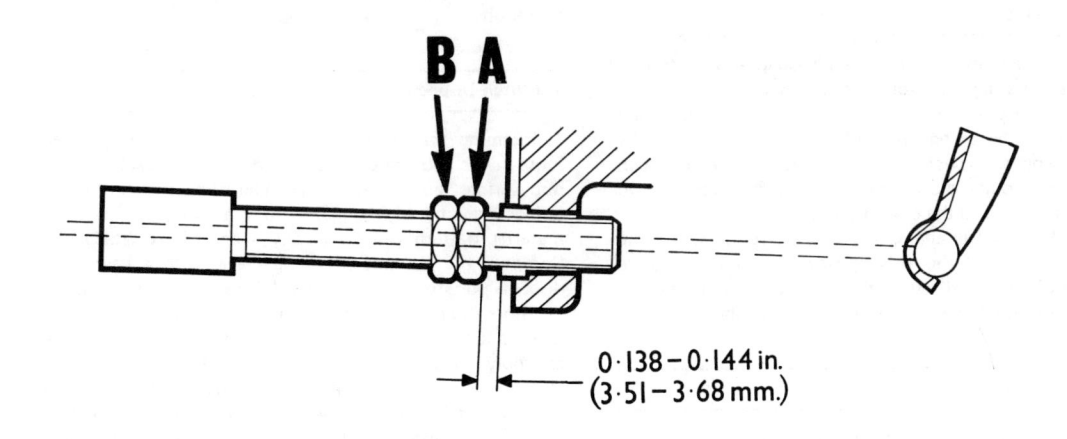

Fig.5.1. VIEW OF THE CORRECT CLUTCH CABLE ADJUST-
MENT CLEARANCE

A Adjusting nut   B Locknut

Chapter 5/Clutch & Actuating Mechanism

3. Clutch Pedal - Removal & Replacement

1. The clutch pedal is removed and replaced in exactly the same way as the brake pedal.
2. A full description of how to remove and replace the brake pedal can be found in Chapter 9/11.

4. Clutch Removal

1. Remove the gearbox as described in Chapter 6, Section 3.
2. Scribe a mating line from the clutch cover to the flywheel to ensure identical positioning on replacement and then remove the clutch assembly by unscrewing the six bolts holding the cover to the rear face of the flywheel. Unscrew the bolts diagonally half a turn at a time to prevent distortion to the cover flange.
3. With all the bolts and spring washers removed lift the clutch assembly off the locating dowels. The driven plate or clutch disc may fall out at this stage as it is not attached to either the clutch cover assembly or the flywheel.

5. Clutch Replacement

1. It is important that no oil or grease gets on the clutch disc friction linings, or the pressure plate and flywheel faces. It is advisable to replace the clutch with clean hands and to wipe down the pressure plate and flywheel faces with a clean dry rag before assembly begins.
2. Place the clutch disc against the flywheel, ensuring that it is the correct way round. The flywheel side of the clutch disc is clearly marked near the centre. If the disc is fitted the wrong way round, it will be quite impossible to operate the clutch.
3. Replace the clutch cover assembly loosely on the dowels. Replace the six bolts and spring washers and tighten them finger tight so that the clutch disc is gripped but can still be moved.
4. The clutch disc must now be centralised so that when the engine and gearbox are mated, the gearbox input shaft splines will pass through the splines in the centre of the driven plate hub.
5. Centralisation can be carried out quite easily by inserting a round bar or long screwdriver through the hole in the centre of the clutch, so that the end of the bar rests in the small hole in the end of the crankshaft containing the input shaft bearing bush. Ideally an old Ford input shaft should be used.
6. Using the input shaft bearing bush as a fulcrum, moving the bar sideways or up and down will move the clutch disc in whichever direction is necessary to achieve centralisation.
7. Centralisation is easily judged by removing the bar and viewing the driven plate hub in relation to the hole in the centre of the clutch cover plate diaphragm spring. When the hub appears exactly in the centre of the hole all is correct (photo). Alternatively the input shaft will fit the bush and centre of the clutch hub exactly obviating the need for visual alignment.
8. Tighten the clutch bolts firmly in a diagonal sequence to ensure that the cover plate is pulled down evenly and without distortion of the flange. Finally tighten the bolts down to a torque of 15 lb/ft. (photo).

6. Clutch Dismantling & Replacement

1. It is not practical to dismantle the pressure plate assembly and the term 'clutch dismantling and replacement' is the term usually used for simply fitting a new clutch friction plate.
2. If a new clutch disc is being fitted it is a false economy not to renew the release bearing at the same time. This will preclude having to replace it at a later date when wear on the clutch linings is still very small.
3. If the pressure plate assembly requires renewal (see Section 7.3 and 4) an exchange unit must be purchased. This will have been accurately set up and balanced to very fine limits.

7. Clutch Inspection

1. Examine the clutch disc friction linings for wear and loose rivets and the disc for rim distortion, cracks, broken hub springs, and worn splines. The surface of the friction linings may be highly glazed, but as long as the clutch material pattern can be clearly seen this is satisfactory. Compare the amount of lining wear with a new clutch disc at the stores in your local garage, and if the linings are more than three quarters worn replace the disc.
2. It is always best to renew the clutch driven plate as an assembly to preclude further trouble, but, if it is wished to merely renew the linings, the rivets should be drilled out and not knocked out with a punch. The manufacturers do not advise that only the linings are renewed and personal experience dictates that it is far more satisfactory to renew the driven plate complete than to try and economise by only fitting new friction linings.
3. Check the machined faces of the flywheel and the pressure plate. If either are grooved they should either be machined until smooth, or renewed.
4. If the pressure plate is cracked or split it is essential that an exchange unit is fitted, also if the pressure of the diaphragm spring is suspect.
5. Check the release bearing for smoothness of operation. There should be no harshness and no slackness in it. It should spin reasonably freely bearing in mind it has been pre-packed with grease.

8. Clutch Cable - Removal & Replacement

1. Place chocks behind the rear wheels, jack up the front of the car, and place stands under the front crossmember.
2. Loosen the locknut on the cable adjuster on the bellhousing and slacken off the adjuster.
3. Spring off the clip (A in Fig.5.2.) from the top of the clutch pedal, push out the pivot pin (B) and pull the cable into the engine compartment.
4. Under the car, pull the rubber gaiter clear of the release arm and push the cable towards the gearbox and then out sideways through the slot in the outer end of the arm (See Fig.5.3).
5. Replacement is a straightforward reversal of the removal sequence. Ensure the pivot pin is lubricated.

9. Clutch Release Bearing - Removal & Replacement

1. With the gearbox and engine separated to provide access to the clutch, attention can be given to the release bearing located in the bellhousing, over the input shaft.
2. The release bearing is a relatively inexpensive but important component and unless it is nearly new it is a mistake not to replace it during an overhaul of the clutch.
3. To remove the release bearing first pull off the release arm rubber gaiter.
4. The release arm and bearing assembly can then be

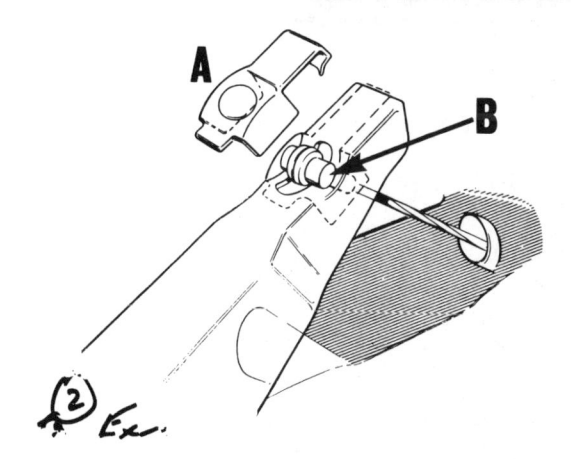

Fig.5.2. Diagram shows clutch cable attachment to the clutch pedal

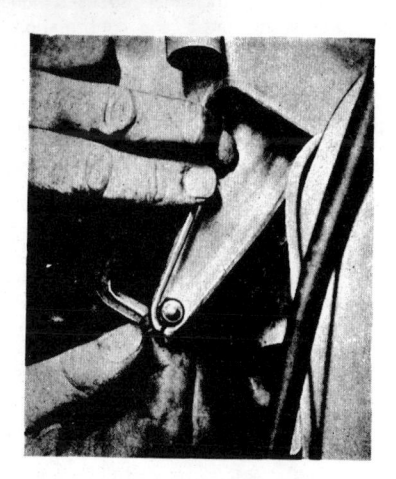

Fig.5.3. Removing the clutch cable from the clutch release fork

85

Chapter 5/Clutch & Actuating Mechanism

withdrawn from the clutch housing.

5. To free the bearing from the release arm simply unhook it, and then with the aid of two blocks of wood and a vice press off the release bearing from its hub.

6. Replacement is a straightforward reversal of these instructions.

10. Clutch Faults

There are four main faults to which the clutch and release mechanism are prone. They may occur by themselves or in conjunction with any of the other faults. They are clutch squeal, slip, spin and judder.

11. Clutch Squeal - Diagnosis & Cure

1. If on taking up the drive or when changing gear, the clutch squeals, this is a sure indication of a badly worn clutch release bearing.

2. As well as regular wear due to normal use, wear of the clutch release bearing is much accentuated if the clutch is ridden, or held down for long periods in gear, with the engine running. To minimise wear of this component the car should always be taken out of gear at traffic lights and for similar hold-ups.

3. The clutch release bearing is not an expensive item, but difficult to get at.

12. Clutch Slip - Diagnosis & Cure

1. Clutch slip is a self evident condition which occurs when the clutch friction plate is badly worn, oil or grease have got onto the flywheel or pressure plate faces, or the pressure plate itself is faulty.

2. The reason for clutch slip is that, due to one of the faults listed above, there is either insufficient pressure from the pressure plate, or insufficient friction from the friction plate to ensure solid drive.

3. If small amounts of oil get onto the clutch, they will be burnt off under the heat of clutch engagement, and in the process, gradually darkening the linings. Excessive oil on the clutch will burn off leaving a carbon deposit which can cause quite bad slip, or fierceness, spin and judder.

4. If clutch slip is suspected, and confirmation of this condition is required, there are several tests which can be made.

5. With the engine in second or third gear and pulling lightly up a moderate incline, sudden depression of the accelerator pedal may cause the engine to increase its speed without any increase in road speed. Easing off on the accelerator will then give a definite drop in engine speed without the car slowing.

6. In extreme cases of clutch slip the engine will race under normal acceleration conditions.

7. If slip is due to oil or grease on the linings a temporary cure can sometimes be effected by squirting carbon tetrachloride into the clutch. The permanent cure is, of course, to renew the clutch driven plate and trace and rectify the oil leak.

13. Clutch Spin - Diagnosis & Cure

1. Clutch spin is a condition which occurs when the release arm travel is excessive, there is an obstruction in the clutch either on the primary gear splines, or in the operating lever itself, or the oil may have partially burnt off the clutch linings and have left a resinous deposit which is causing the clutch disc to stick to the pressure plate or flywheel.

2. The reason for clutch spin is that due to any, or a combination of, the faults just listed, the clutch pressure plate is not completely freeing from the centre plate even with the clutch pedal fully depressed.

3. If clutch spin is suspected, the condition can be confirmed by extreme difficulty in engaging first gear from rest, difficulty in changing gear, and very sudden take-up of the clutch drive at the fully depressed end of the clutch pedal travel as the clutch is released.

4. Check that the clutch cable is correctly adjusted and if in order then the fault lies internally in the clutch. It will then be necessary to remove the clutch for examination, and to check the gearbox input shaft.

14. Clutch Judder - Diagnosis & Cure

1. Clutch judder is a self evident condition which occurs when the gearbox or engine mountings are loose or too flexible, when there is oil on the faces of the clutch friction plate, or when the clutch pressure plate has been incorrectly adjusted during assembly.

2. The reason for clutch judder is that due to one of the faults just listed, the clutch pressure plate is not freeing smoothly from the friction disc, and is snatching.

3. Clutch judder normally occurs when the clutch pedal is released in first or reverse gears, and the whole car shudders as it moves backwards or forwards.

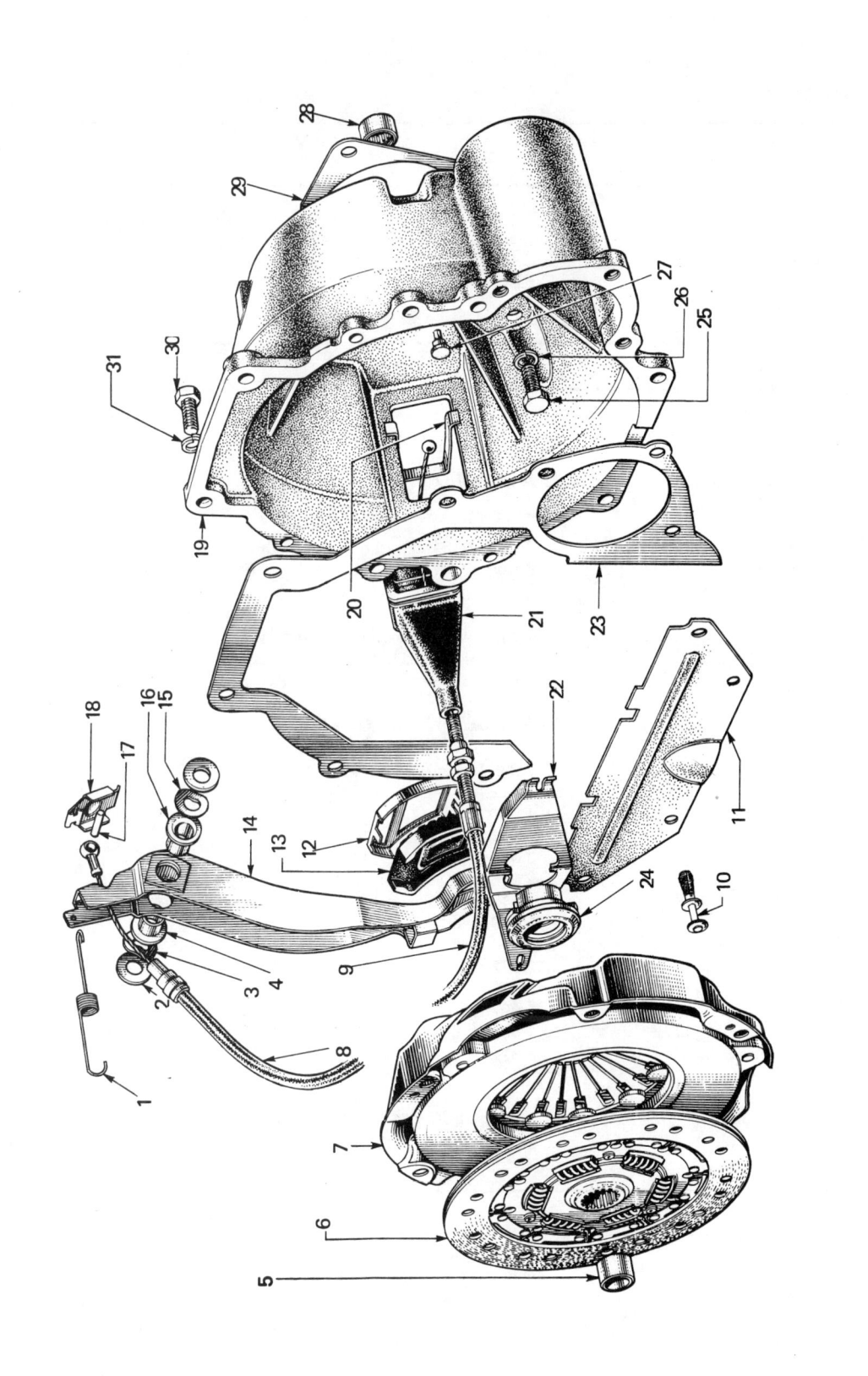

Fig.5.4. EXPLODED VIEW OF THE CLUTCH ASSEMBLY

1. Spring
2. Washer
3. Washer
4. Bush
5. Bearing
6. Friction plate
7. Pressure plate & diaphragm spring assembly
8. Clutch operating cable
9. Inspection plate retainer
10. Inspection plate
11. Inspection plate
12. Cover for pedal rubber
13. Pedal rubber
14. Pedal assembly
15. Washer
16. Bush
17. Pin
18. Clip
19. Bellhousing
20. Retaining spring clip
21. Rubber gaiter
22. Clutch release lever
23. Flywheel housing cover
24. Clutch release bearing assembly
25. Bolt
26. Spring washer
27. Dowel
28. Bearing
29. Gasket
30. Bolt
31. Spring washer

87

Chapter 6/Gearbox

Contents

General Description ... 1	Input Shaft — Dismantling & Reassembly ... 6
Routine Maintenance.. ... 2	Mainshaft — Dismantling & Reassembly ... 7
Gearbox — Removal & Replacement ... 3	Selective Circlip ... 8
Gearbox Dismantling... ... 4	Gearbox Reassembly... ... 9
Gearbox Examination & Renovation ... 5	

Specifications

Gearbox
- Number of gears ... 4 forward, 1 reverse
- Type of gears ... Helical, constant mesh
- Synchromesh ... All forward gears

Selective Circlips
- Mainshaft bearing to extension .. 7 from .0731 in. (1.857 mm) to .0660 in. (1.676 mm)
- Mainshaft bearing to mainshaft.. 8 from .0707 in. (1.796 mm) to .0791 in. (2.009 mm)

Oil Capacity
- Refill ... 1.7 pints (2.1 U.S.pints, .96 litres)
- Initial fill ... 1.97 pints (2.4 U.S.pints, 1.11 litres)
- Grade of oil ... Castrol Hypoy Light (SAE 80 EP)

Ratios

		Gearbox	Overall
1300 and 1300 G.T.	1st gear	3.543 to 1	14.615 to 1
	2nd gear	2.396 to 1	9.883 to 1
	3rd gear	1.412 to 1	5.824 to 1
	Top gear	1.000 to 1	4.125 to 1
	Reverse	3.963 to 1	16.347 to 1
1600	1st gear	3.543 to 1	13.776 to 1
	2nd gear	2.396 to 1	9.318 to 1
	3rd gear	1.412 to 1	5.493 to 1
	Top gear	1.000 to 1	3.889 to 1
	Reverse	3.963 to 1	15.411 to 1
1600 G.T.	1st gear	2.972 to 1	11.225 to 1
	2nd gear	2.010 to 1	7.592 to 1
	3rd gear	1.397 to 1	5.277 to 1
	Top gear	1.000 to 1	3.777 to 1
	Reverse	3.324 to 1	12.555 to 1

Torque Wrench Settings
- Bellhousing to gearbox ... 40 to 45 lb/ft. (5.53 to 6.22 kg.m)
- Gearbox drain and filler plugs ... 25 to 30 lb/ft. (3.46 to 4.15 kg.m)
- Gearbox extension to gearbox ... 30 to 35 lb/ft. (4.15 to 4.84 kg.m)

1. General Description

The gearbox fitted to all models contains four constant mesh helically cut forward gears and one straight cut reverse gear. Synchromesh is fitted between 1st and 2nd, 2nd and 3rd and 3rd and top. The bellhousing can be separated from the gearbox.

Attached to the rear of the gearbox casing is an aluminium alloy extension which supports the rear of the mainshaft and the gearchange shaft cum selector rod arm.

The gearbox is of a simple but clever design, using the minimum of components to facilitate speed of assembly; and the minimum of matched items to simplify fitting. Where close tolerances and limits are required, manufacturing tolerances are compensated for, and excessive endfloat or backlash eliminated by the fitting of selective circlips.

The gear selector mechanism is unusual in that the selector forks are free to slide on the one selector rod which also serves as the gearchange shaft. At the gearbox end of

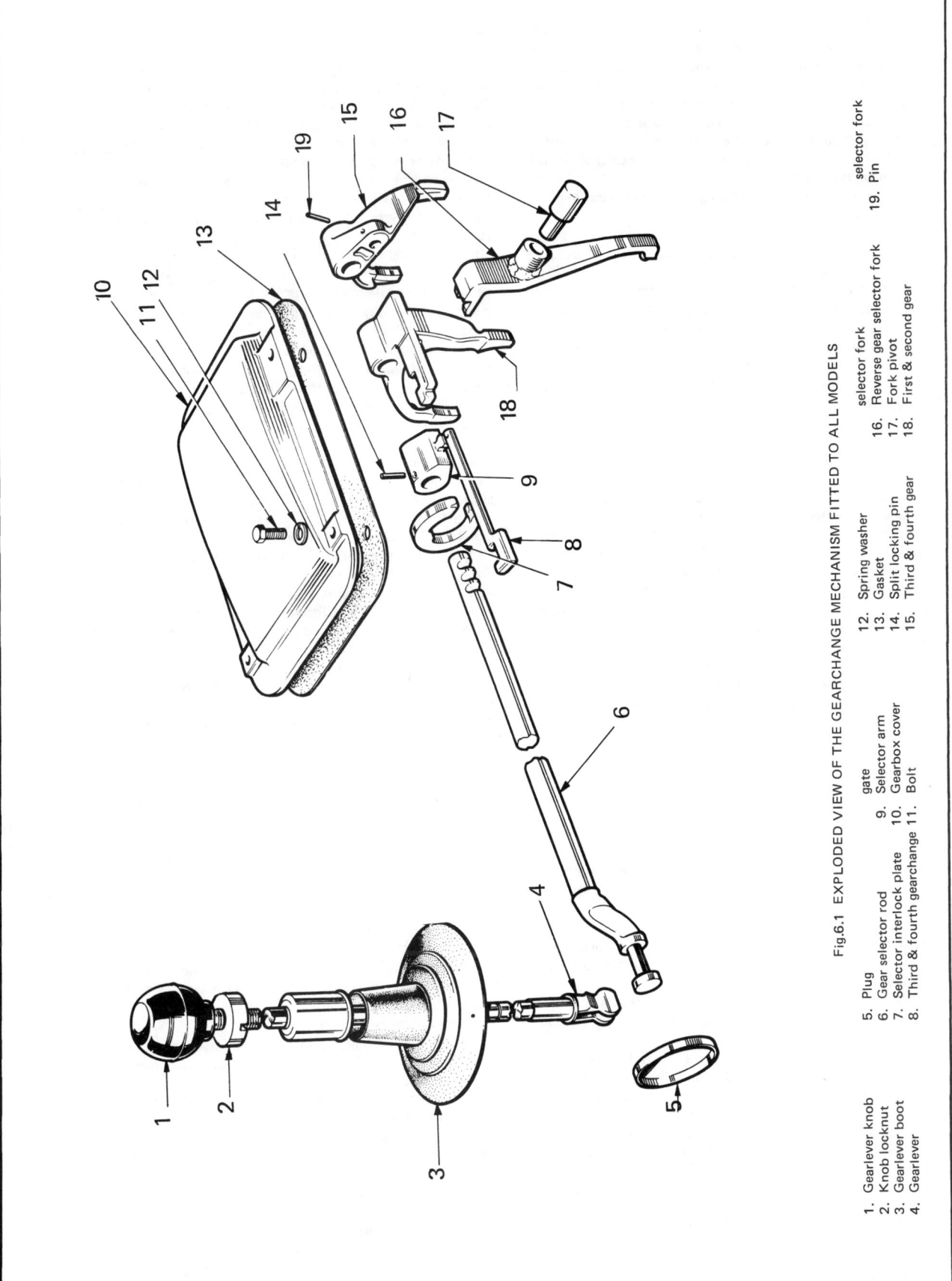

Fig.6.1 EXPLODED VIEW OF THE GEARCHANGE MECHANISM FITTED TO ALL MODELS

1. Gearlever knob
2. Knob locknut
3. Gearlever boot
4. Gearlever
5. Plug
6. Gear selector rod
7. Selector interlock plate
8. Third & fourth gearchange
gate
9. Selector arm
10. Gearbox cover
11. Bolt
12. Spring washer
13. Gasket
14. Split locking pin
15. Third & fourth gear
selector fork
16. Reverse gear selector fork
17. Fork pivot
18. First & second gear
selector fork
19. Pin

Chapter 6/Gearbox

this rod lies the selector arm, which, depending on the position of the gearlever places the appropriate selector fork in the position necessary for the synchroniser sleeve to engage with the dog teeth on the gear selected. Another unusual feature is that some of the bolts are metric sizes. In particular this applies to the top cover bolts and some of the bellhousing bolts. The reverse idler shaft thread is also metric (a bolt is only inserted here when it is wished to remove the shaft).

It is impossible to select two gears at once because of an interlock guard plate.

2. Routine Maintenance

1. The gearbox oil will never require totally draining during use, but a drain plug is provided for use if the gearbox is to be removed.
2. Routine maintenance should be carried out every 6,000 miles. It consists of cleaning the casing in the immediate vicinity of the filler plug on the left-hand side of the gearbox, undoing the filler plug with a square headed key, and topping up the oil in the gearbox with one of the recommended lubricants shown on page 10.

3. Gearbox — Removal & Replacement

1. The gearbox can be removed in unit with the engine through the engine compartment as described in Chapter 1/7 Alternatively the gearbox can be separated from the rear of the engine at the bellhousing and the gearbox lowered from the car. The latter method is easier and quicker than the former. First unscrew the gearlever knob (photo).
2. On G.T. models remove the centre console (photo) by undoing the cross head screws securing it in place.
3. Two of the screws are at the rear by the handbrake cover (photo).
4. Two more screws are placed either side of the console towards the front (photo).
5. Prise out the plastic imitation wood trims to expose two screws under the handbrake (photo A) and a screw in front of the gearlever (photo B).
6. Pull the leads from the back of the electric clock.
7. Then on all models the procedure is the same. At the base of the gear lever, lift off the rubber cover (photo A), knock back the locking tabs (photo B) and unscrew the plastic dome and lift off the gearlever with its washers dome and plastic ball. (photo C).
8. Before jacking the car up, remove the gearbox drain plug and allow all the oil to drain into a container for about ten minutes.
9. Jack up the car and fit stands if these are available as a considerable amount of work has to be carried out under the car.
10. Undo and remove the four bolts (photo) securing the propeller shaft to the rear axle flange having first marked both flanges to ensure correct alignment on reassembly.
11. Remove the two bolts (photo) that hold the centre bearing carrier to its bracket on models fitted with a split propeller shaft, then slide the propeller shaft off the gearbox extension.
12. Disconnect the exhaust pipe where it joins the manifold, by undoing the two brass nuts then remove the two bolts which hold the exhaust pipe to the strengthening bracket on the side of the gearbox. Push the exhaust pipe to one side so it does not get in the way.
13. Slacken off the adjustment on the clutch cable, remove the rubber gaiter and take the end of the clutch cable out of its slot in the release fork (photo). Tuck the cable out of harms way.
14. First disconnect the battery by taking off the earth lead, and remove the starter motor by undoing the two or three retaining bolts depending on the type of motor fitted.
15. Undo the bolts round the bellhousing periphery, noting that some of them are longer than others.
16. Support the rear of the engine by means of a jack or blocks of wood under the sump.
17. The end of the speedometer cable proved very difficult to get at on the model worked on, and it was necessary to remove the gearbox rear crossmember completely to get at it.
18. This is done by placing a jack under the gearbox to take its weight, then undoing the two bolts found at each end of the rear crossmember and then the recessed centre bolt which attaches the crossmember to the gearbox extension (photo).
19. Now remove the circlip holding the speedometer drive in place, and slide it out of the gearbox extension. Disconnect the reversing light wire at the snap joint (photo).
20. Undo and remove the bolts holding the reinforcing plate in place at the front of the bellhousing adjacent to the sump then the gearbox assembly is free to be removed from the car.
21. The gearbox is heavy and on no account should it be allowed to hang on the first motion shaft when it is in the half off position. The best way to remove it is to slide it rearwards supported on a trolley jack.
22. Replacement is a direct reversal of the removal procedure, but note the following points:
23. Check that the adaptor plate is correctly in place on the rear of the engine before fitting the gearbox.
24. Do not forget than an engine earth strap may be fitted to one of the top bellhousing bolts.
25. Ensure the mating marks on the propeller shaft and rear axle flanges are in line, or vibration may become apparent after reassembly.
26. Refill the gearbox with the correct amount and grade of oil as listed in the specifications at the beginning of this chapter.

4. Gearbox Dismantling

1. Remove the clutch release bearing from the gearbox input shaft (photo).
2. Then lift out the clutch release lever (photo).
3. Undo and remove the four bolts holding the bellhousing to the gearbox (photo).
4. Detach the bellhousing from the gearbox (photo).
5. Slightly loosen the gearbox drain plug and mount the gearbox upright in a vice using the drain plug as a pivot. Make sure the vice is firmly gripping the drain plug so the assembly cannot tilt.
6. Referring to Fig.6.2, undo the four bolts holding the gearbox top cover (1) in place (photo A) and remove the cover (photo B).
7. Prise out the cup shaped oil seal (26) on the side of the gearbox extension (photo).
8. From under this seal pull out the speedometer gear (25) (photo). To start it, it may be necessary to tap it from the other end.
9. From where the gear lever enters the extension housing drive out the rear extension oil seal (22) (photo).
10. From the right-hand side of the gearbox casing remove the plunger screw (5) its spring (6) and the ball (7) (photo).
11. Using a small drift drive out the pin holding the selector boss to the central rod (photo).
12. Now withdraw the selector rod (photo A) at the same time holding onto the selector boss and cam (photo B) to

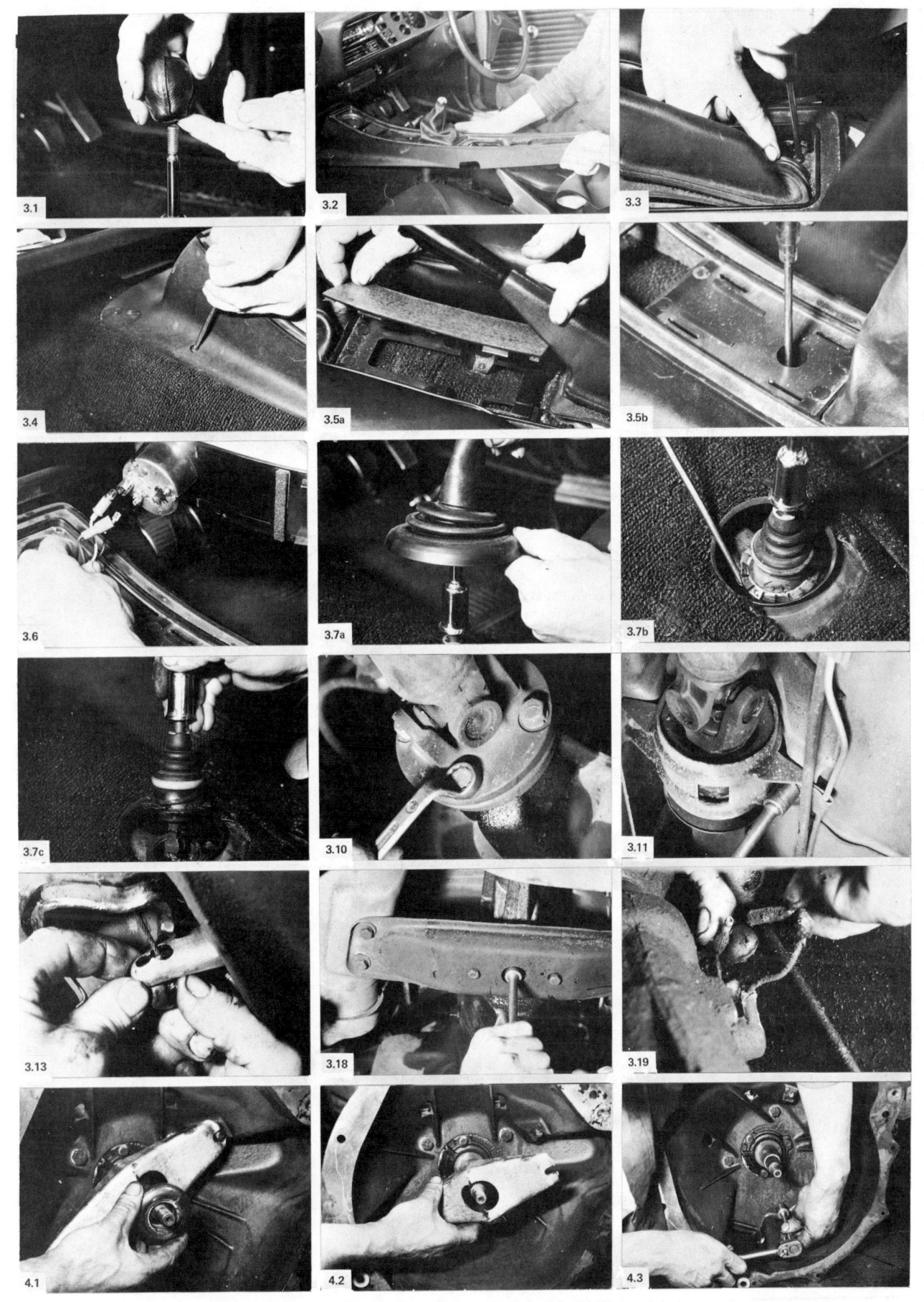

3.1　3.2　3.3
3.4　3.5a　3.5b
3.6　3.7a　3.7b
3.7c　3.10　3.11
3.13　3.18　3.19
4.1　4.2　4.3

91

Fig.6.2. EXPLODED VIEW OF THE GEARBOX EXTERIOR

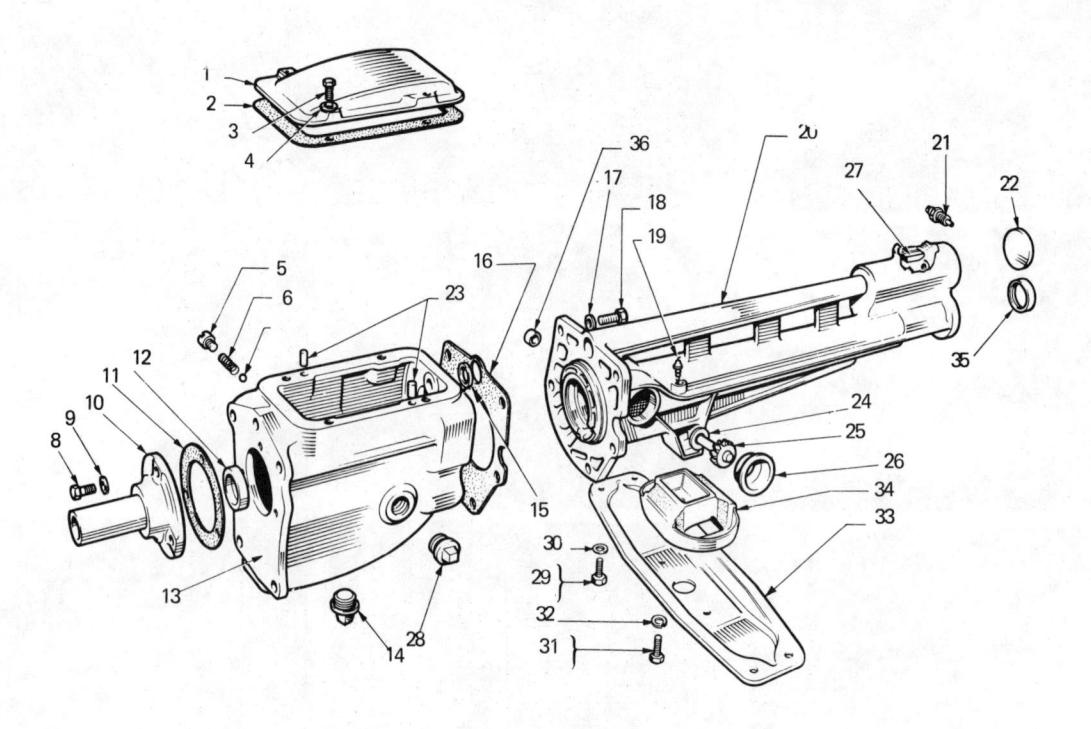

1. Gearbox cover
2. Gasket
3. Bolt
4. Washer
5. Screw
6. Spring
7. Ball
8. Bolt
9. Washer
10. Bearing retainer
11. Gasket
12. Oil seal
13. Gearbox casting
14. Drain plug
15. Selector rod seal
16. Gasket
17. Washer
18. Bolt
19. Breather
20. Gearbox extension
21. Reverse light switch
22. Plug
23. Dowels
24. Circlip
25. Speedometer gear
26. Plug
27. Gearlever orifice
28. Filler/level plug
29. Bolt
30. Washer
31. Bolt
32. Washer
33. Rear crossmember
34. Rubber mounting
35. Oil seal
36. Seal

Fig.6.3. Correct fitting of circlip securing mainshaft bearing to the gearbox extension housing

92

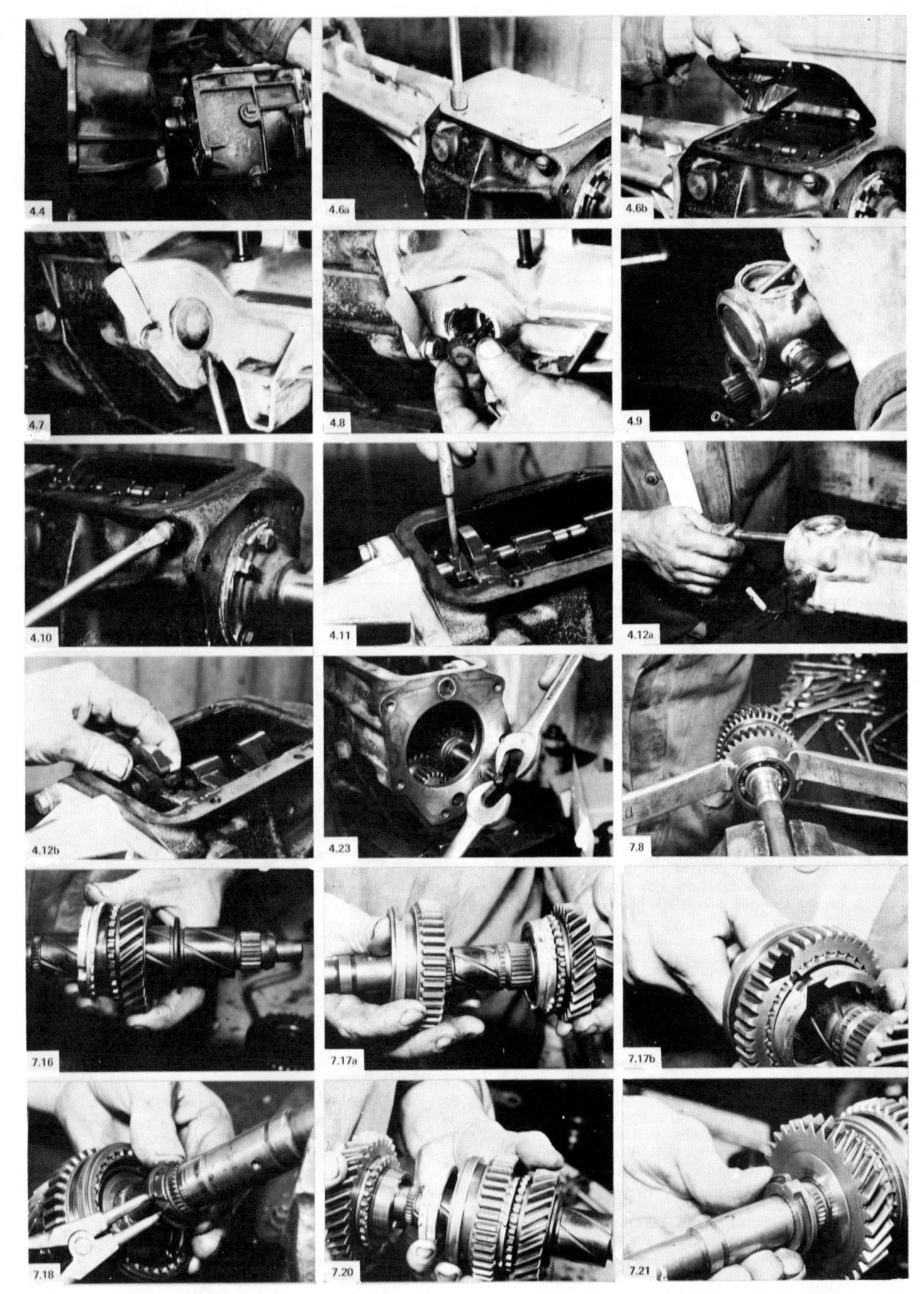

4.4
4.6a
4.6b
4.7
4.8
4.9
4.10
4.11
4.12a
4.12b
4.23
7.8
7.16
7.17a
7.17b
7.18
7.20
7.21

93

Chapter 6/Gearbox

prevent them falling into the gearbox.

13 To remove the selector forks, it is now necessary to knock the two synchro hubs towards the front of the gearbox, this can be done with a small drift or a screwdriver, now lift out the selector forks.

14 Turn now to the gearbox extension (20) and remove the bolts (18) and washers (17) which hold it to the gearbox casing.

15 Knock it slightly rearwards with a soft headed hammer then rotate the whole extension until the cut-out on the extension face coincides with the rear end of the layshaft in the lower half of the gearbox casing.

16 Get hold of a metal rod to act as a dummy layshaft 6 13/16 inches long with a diameter of 5/8 inches.

17 Tap the layshaft rearwards with a drift until it is just clear of the front of the gearbox casing then insert the dummy shaft and drive the layshaft out and allow the laygear duster to drop out of mesh with the mainshaft gears into the bottom of the box.

18 With a pair of circlip pliers release the mainshaft bearing retaining circlip and withdraw the mainshaft and extension assembly from the gearbox casing. A small roller bearing should come away on the nose of the mainshaft, but if it is not there it will be found in its recess in the input shaft and should be removed.

19 Moving to the front of the gearbox remove the bolts (8) retaining the input shaft cover (10) and take it off the shaft.

20 Remove the large circlip now exposed and then with a soft headed hammer tap the input shaft towards the rear and remove it from inside the gearbox.

21 The laygear can now be withdrawn from the rear of the gearbox together with its thrust washers (one at either end).

22 Remove the mainshaft assembly from the gearbox extension, by taking out the large circlip shown in Fig.6.3. Then tapping the rear of the shaft with a soft headed hammer.

23 The reverse idler gear can be removed by screwing a suitable bolt into the end of the shaft and then levering the shaft out with the aid of two large open ended spanners (photo).

24 The gearbox is now stripped right out and must be thoroughly cleaned. If there is any quantity of metal chips and fragments in the bottom of the gearbox casing it is obvious that several items will be found to be badly worn. The component parts of the gearbox should be examined for wear, and the laygear, input shaft and mainshaft assemblies broken down further as described in the following sections.

5. Gearbox Examination & Renovation

1. Carefully clean and then examine all the component parts for general wear, distortion, slackness of fit, and damage to machined faces and threads.

2. Examine the gearwheels for excessive wear and chipping of the teeth. Renew them as necessary.

3. Examine the layshaft for signs of wear, where the laygear needle roller bearings bear. If a small ridge can be felt at either end of the shaft it will be necessary to renew it.

4. The four synchroniser rings (8,12,25,30) (Fig.6.4) are bound to be badly worn and it is false economy not to renew them. New rings will improve the smoothness and speed of the gearchange considerably.

5. The needle roller bearing and cage (2) located between the nose of the mainshaft and the annulus in the rear of the input shaft is also liable to wear, and should be renewed as a matter of course.

6. Examine the condition of the two ball bearing assemblies, one on the input shaft (7) and one on the mainshaft (19). Check them for noisy operation, looseness between the inner and outer races, and for general wear. Normally they should be renewed on a gearbox that is being rebuilt.

7. If either of the synchroniser units (37,38) are worn it will be necessary to buy a complete assembly as the parts are not sold individually.

8. Examine the ends of the selector forks where they rub against the channels in the periphery of the synchroniser units. If possible compare the selector forks with new units to help determine the wear that has occured. Renew them if worn.

9. If the bush bearing in the extension is badly worn it is best to take the extension to your local Ford garage to have the bearing pulled out and a new one fitted.

10 The rear oil seal (35 in Fig.6.2) should be renewed as a matter of course. Drive out the old seal with the aid of a drift or broad screwdriver. It will be found that the seal comes out quite easily.

11 With a piece of wood to spread the load evenly, carefully tap a new seal into place ensuring that it enters the bore in the extension squarely.

12 The only point on the mainshaft that is likely to be worn is the nose where it enters the input shaft. However examine it thoroughly for any signs of scoring, picking up, or flats and if damage is apparent renew it.

6. Input Shaft — Dismantling & Reassembly

1. The only reason for dismantling the input shaft is to fit a new ball bearing assembly, or, if the input shaft is being renewed and the old bearing is in excellent condition, then the fitting of a new shaft to an old bearing.

2. With a pair of expanding circlip pliers remove the circlip (5), (Fig.6.4) from the input shaft.

3. With a soft headed hammer gently tap the bearing forward and then remove it from the shaft.

4. When fitting the new bearing ensure that the groove cut in the outer periphery faces away from the gear. If the bearing is fitted the wrong way round it will not be possible to fit the large circlip which retains the bearing in the housing.

5. Using the jaws of a vice as a support behind the bearing tap the bearing squarely into place by hitting the rear of the input shaft with a plastic or hide faced hammer.

6. Then refit the circlip (5) which holds the bearing to the input shaft.

7. Mainshaft — Dismantling & Reassembly

1. The mainshaft has to be dismantled before some of the synchroniser rings can be inspected. For dismantling it is best to mount the plain portion of the shaft between two pieces of wood in a vice.

2. From the forward end of the mainshaft pull off the caged roller bearing (2) and the synchro ring (8). Fig.6.4.

3. With a pair of circlip pliers remove the circlip (3) which holds the third/fourth gear synchroniser hub in place.

4. Ease the hub (38) and third gear (13) forward by gentle leverage with a pair of long nosed pliers.

5. The hub (38) and synchro ring (12) are then removed from the mainshaft.

6. Then slide off third gear. Nothing else can be removed from this end of the mainshaft because of the raised lip on the shaft.

7. Move to the other end of the mainshaft and remove the small circlip then slide off the speedometer drive taking care not to loose the ball which locates in a groove in the

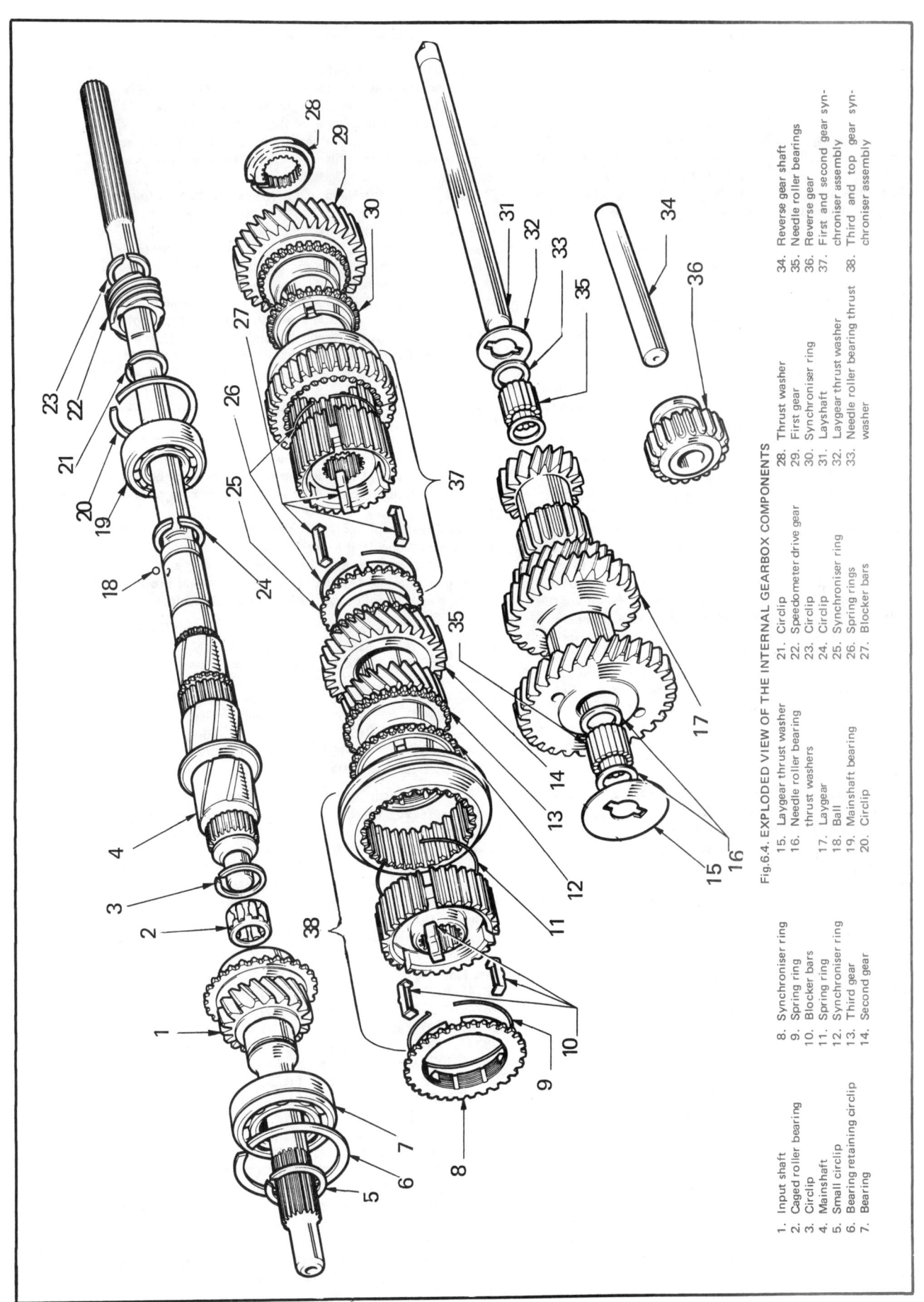

Fig.6.4. EXPLODED VIEW OF THE INTERNAL GEARBOX COMPONENTS

1. Input shaft
2. Caged roller bearing
3. Circlip
4. Mainshaft
5. Small circlip
6. Bearing retaining circlip
7. Bearing
8. Synchroniser ring
9. Spring ring
10. Blocker bars
11. Spring ring
12. Synchroniser ring
13. Third gear
14. Second gear
15. Laygear thrust washer
16. Needle roller bearing thrust washers
17. Laygear
18. Ball
19. Mainshaft bearing
20. Circlip
21. Circlip
22. Speedometer drive gear
23. Circlip
24. Circlip
25. Synchroniser ring
26. Spring rings
27. Blocker bars
28. Thrust washer
29. First gear
30. Synchroniser ring
31. Layshaft
32. Laygear thrust washer
33. Needle roller bearing thrust washer
34. Reverse gear shaft
35. Needle roller bearings
36. Reverse gear
37. First and second gear synchroniser assembly
38. Third and top gear synchroniser assembly

Chapter 6/Gearbox

gear and a small recess in the mainshaft.

8. Remove the circlip (21), and then gently lever off the large bearing with the aid of two tyre levers as shown in the photo.

9. The bearing followed by the large thrust washer (28) can then be pulled off. Follow these items by pulling off first gear (29) and the synchroniser ring (30).

10 With a pair of circlip pliers remove the circlip (24) which retains the first and second gear synchroniser assembly in place.

11 Thr first and second gear synchroniser followed by second gear (14) are then simply slid off the mainshaft The mainshaft is now completely dismantled.

12 If a new sycnrhoniser assembly is being fitted it is necessary to take it to pieces first to clean off all the preservative. These instructions are also pertinent in instances where the outer sleeve has come off the hub accidently during dismantling.

13 To dismantle an assembly for cleaning slide the synchroniser sleeve off the splined hub and clean all the preservative from the blocker bars (27), spring rings (26), the hub itself (A), and the sleeve (B).

14 Oil the components lightly and then fit the sleeve (B) to the hub (A) so the lines marked on them (see Fig.6.5) are in line. Note the three slots in the hub and fit a blocker bar in each.

15 Fit the two springs (26) one on the front and one on the rear face of the inside of the synchroniser sleeve under the blocker bars with the tagged end of each spring locating in the 'U' section of the same bar. One spring must be put on anti-clockwise, and one clockwise when viewed from the side (see Fig.6.6). When either side of the assembly is viewed face on the direction of rotation of the springs should then appear the same.

16 Prior to reassembling the mainshaft read Section 8 of this chapter to ensure that the correct thickness of selective circlips are used. Reassembly commences by replacing second gear (14), gear teeth facing the raised lip and its synchroniser ring (25) on the rear portion of the mainshaft (photo).

17 Next slide on the first and second gear synchroniser assembly (37) (photo A) AND MAKE CERTAIN that the cut-outs in the synchroniser ring fit over the blocker bars in the synchroniser hub (photo B); that the marks on the mainshaft and hub are in line (where made); and that the reverse gear teeth cut on the synchroniser sleeve periphery are adjacent to second gear.

18 Replace the circlip (24) which holds the synchroniser hub in place (photo).

19 Then fit another synchroniser ring (30) again ensuring that the cut-outs in the ring fit over the blocker bars in the synchroniser hub.

20 Next slide on first gear (29) so the synchronising cone portion lies inside the synchronising ring just fitted (photo).

21 Fit the splined thrust washer (28) to the front of first gear (photo).

22 The mainshaft bearing is then slid on as far as it will go (photo).

23 To press the bearing fully home, close the jaws of the vice until they are not quite touching the mainshaft, and with the bearing resting squarely against the side of the vice jaws draw the bearing on by tapping the end of the shaft with a hide or plastic hammer (photo).

24 Replace the small circlip retaining the main bearing in place (photo).

25 At this time it is wise to slide over the main bearing the large circlip which retains the mainshaft assembly to the gearbox extension as it will be needed in this position later (photo).

26 Replace the small ball that retains the speedometer drive in its recess in the mainshaft (photo).

27 Slide on the speedometer drive noting that it can only be fitted one way round as the groove in which the ball fits does not run the whole length of the drive (photo).

28 Now fit the circlip to retain the speedometer drive, (photo). Assembly of this end of the mainshaft is now complete.

29 Moving to the short end of the mainshaft slide on third gear (13) so that the machined gear teeth lie adjacent to second gear, then slide on the synchroniser ring (photo).

30 Fit the third and fourth gear synchroniser assembly (38) (photo) again ensuring that the cut-outs on the ring line up with the blocker bars.

31 With a suitable piece of metal tube over the mainshaft, tap the synchroniser fully home onto the mainshaft (photo).

32 Then fit the securing circlip (3) in place (photo). Apart from the needle roller bearing race which rests on the nose of the mainshaft this completes mainshaft reassembly.

8. Selective Circlips

1. Two of the circlips fitted in the gearbox are available in various thicknesses. This is to ensure that any wear on the mainshaft assembly is taken up and the minimum of end float allowed.

2. During reassembly of the mainshaft the first circlip that is a selective one is the bearing retaining circlip (21 in (Fig.6.4). It is essential that the thickest circlip that will fit in the groove is used so that as much endfloat as possible is eliminated. The following thicknesses are available:—

Part No.	Size.	Colour Code.
2824E-7669-A	.0707 in. (1.795 mm)	Plain
2824E-7669-B	.0719 in. (1.825 mm)	Pink
2824E-7669-C	.0731 in. (1.860 mm)	Magenta
2824E-7669-D	.0743 in. (1.890 mm)	Violet
2824E-7669-E	.0755 in. (1.920 mm)	Green
2824E-7669-F	.0767 in. (1.950 mm)	Blue
2824E-7669-G	.0779 in. (1.980 mm)	Red
2824E-7669-H	.0791 in. (2.010 mm)	Yellow

3. The other circlip which is fitted after selection is the large circlip (20) which holds the bearing in place in the extension housing. Once again it is essential that the thickest circlip that will fit the groove in the housing is used. Although in the mainshaft reassembly it is advised to place this circlip loosely behind the main bearing in the early stages it can in fact be changed when the mainshaft is fitted to the extension housing without any trouble. The following sizes are available:—

Part No.	Size.	Colour Code.
2824E-7030-A	.0731 in. (1.860 mm)	Yellow
2824E-7030-B	.0720 in. (1.830 mm)	Red
2824E-7030-C	.0708 in. (1.800 mm)	Blue
2824E-7030-D	.0696 in. (1.770 mm)	Violet
2824E-7030-E	.0684 in. (1.737 mm)	Green
2824E-7030-F	.0682 in. (1.732 mm)	Magenta
2824E-7030-C	.0670 in. (1.702 mm)	Plain

9. Gearbox Reassembly

1. If removed replace the reverse idler gear and selector lever in the gearbox, by tapping in the shaft (34). Once it is through the casing fit the gear wheel (36) so that 1st gear teeth are facing in towards the main gearbox area.

2. Fit the reverse selector lever in the groove in the idler gear then drive the shaft home with a soft headed hammer until it is flush with the gearbox casing.

Fig.6.5. The synchroniser assembly alignment marks

Fig.6.6. The synchroniser hub springs must be put on as shown in the illustration

97

9.4

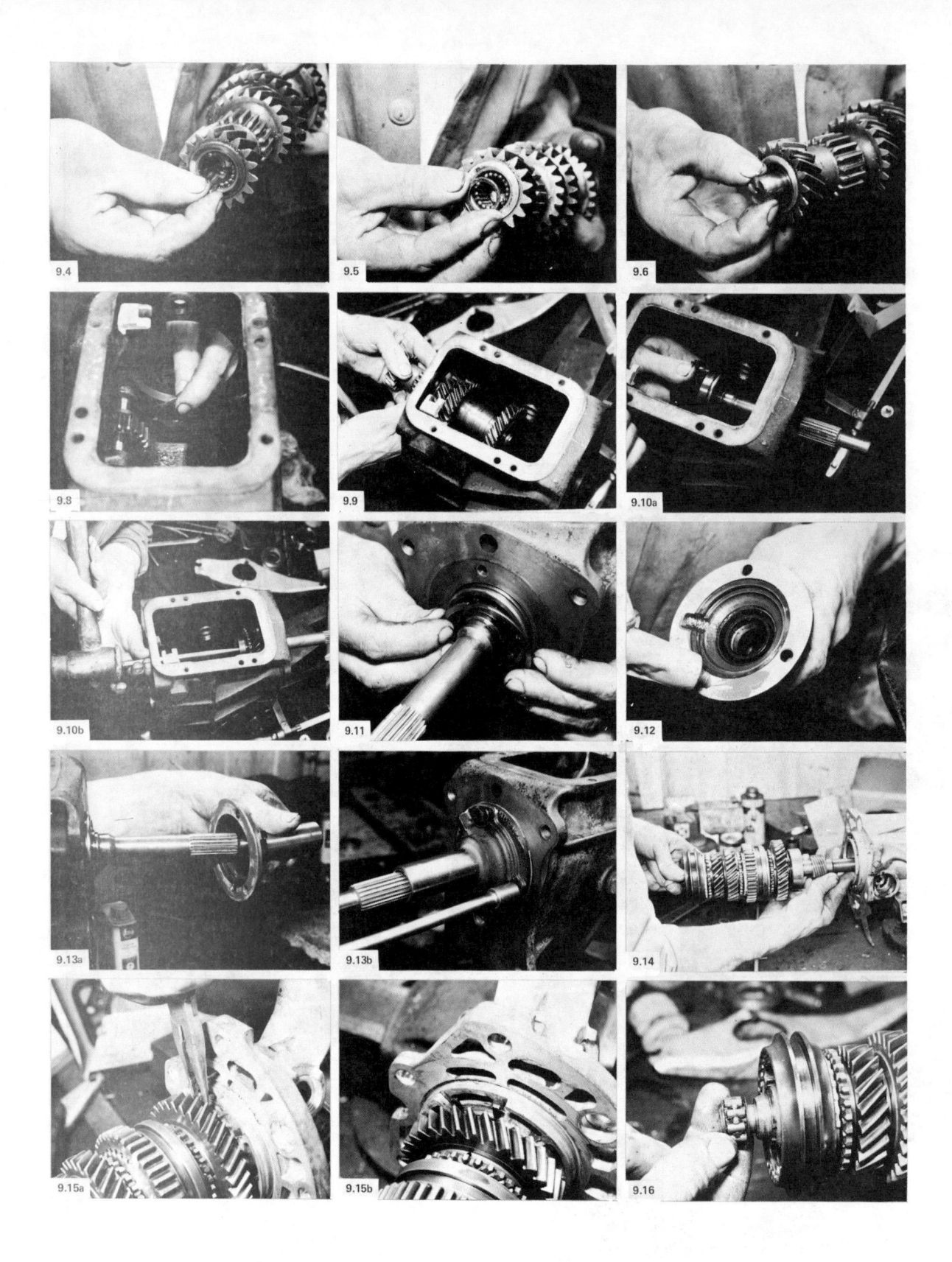

9.5

9.6

9.8

9.9

9.10a

9.10b

9.11

9.12

9.13a

9.13b

9.14

9.15a

9.15b

9.16

9.17 9.19 9.20
9.22 9.23a
9.23b 9.24a 9.24b

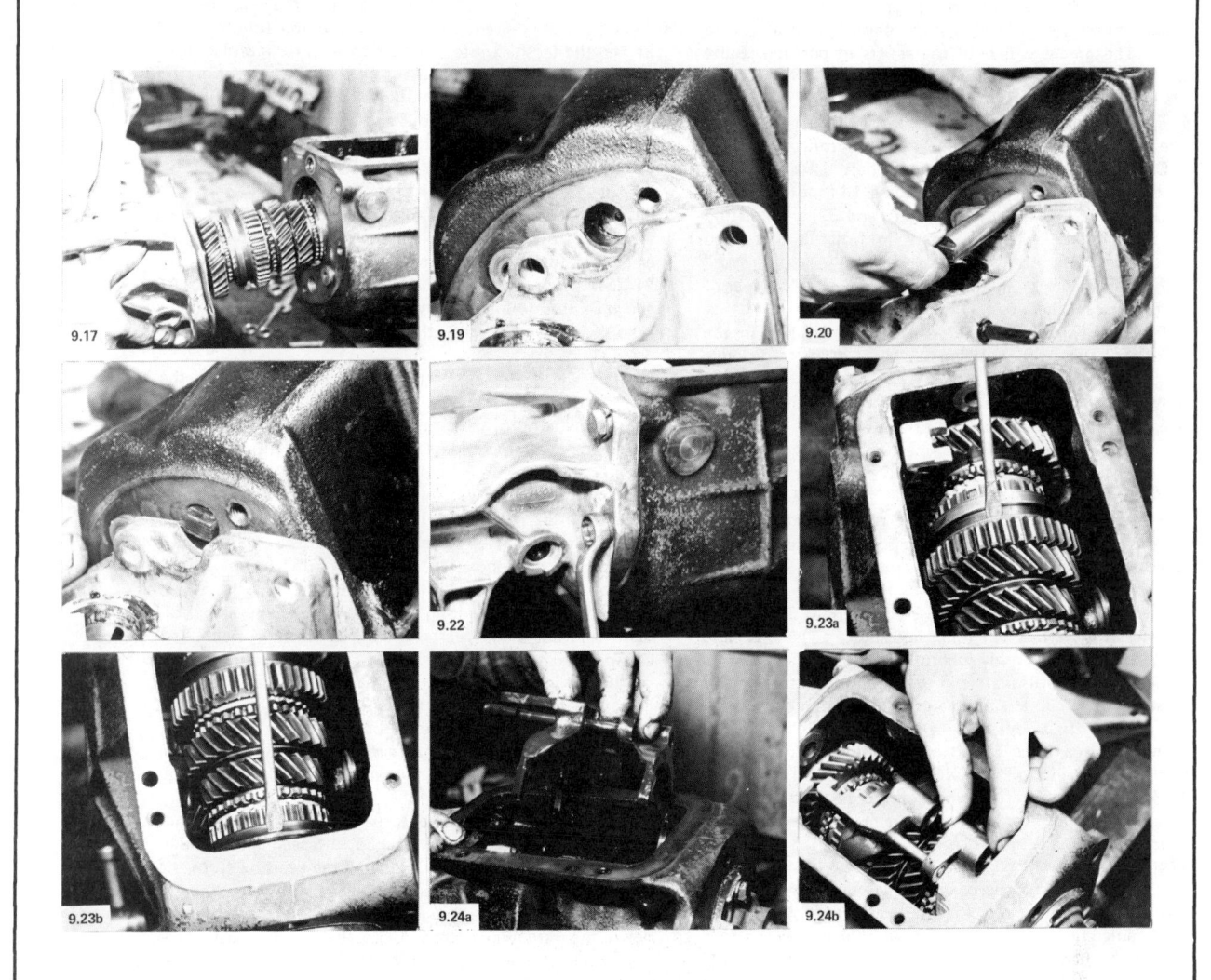

Fig.6.7. Replacing the selector ball, spring and retaining screw

99

Chapter 6/Gearbox

3. Slide a retaining washer (16) into either end of the laygear (17) so that they abut the internal machined shoulders.

4. Smear thick grease on the laygear orifice and fit the needle rollers (35) one at a time (photo) until all are in place. The grease will hold the rollers in position. Build up the needle roller bearings in the other end of the laygear in a similar fashion.

5. Fit the external washer to each end of the laygear, taking care not to dislodge the roller bearings (photo).

6. Carefully slide in the dummy layshaft used previously for driving out the layshaft in Section 4/16 (photo).

7. Grease the two thrust washers (15 and 32) and position the larger of the two (15) in the front of the gearbox so the tongues fit into the machined recesses.

8. Fit the smaller of the thrust washers (32) to the rear of the gearbox in the same way (photo).

9. Fit the laygear complete with dummy layshaft in the bottom of the gearbox casing taking care not to dislodge the thrust washers (photo).

10 Now from inside the gearbox slide in the input shaft assembly (1) (photo A) and drive the bearing into place with a suitable drift (photo B).

11 Secure the bearing in position by replacing the circlip (6) (photo).

12 Fit a new gasket to the bearing retainer and smear on some Wellseal or similar sealing compound (photo).

13 Replace the retainer on the input shaft (photo A) ensuring that the oil drain hole is towards the bottom of the gearbox, and tighten down the bolts (photo B).

14 Place the gearbox extension housing in a vice and slide in the mainshaft assembly (photo).

15 Secure the mainshaft to the gearbox extension by locating the circlip already placed loosely behind the main bearing into its groove in the extension (photo A). If it is found to be a loose fit refer to Section 8 and select a thicker circlip. Photo B shows the circlip correctly located.

16 Fit a new gasket to the extension housing and then replace the small roller bearing on the nose of the mainshaft (photo).

17 Slide the combined mainshaft and housing assembly into the rear of the gearbox and mate up the nose of the mainshaft with the rear of the input shaft (photo).

18 Completely invert the gearbox so that the laygear falls into mesh with the mainshaft gears.

19 Turn the extension housing round until the cut-out on it coincides with the hole for the layshaft (photo). It may be necessary to trim the gasket.

20 Push the layshaft into its hole from the rear thereby driving out the dummy shaft at the same time (photo).

21 Tap the layshaft into position until its front end is flush with the gearbox casing and ensure that the cut-out on the rear end is in the horizontal position so it will fit into its recess in the extension housing flange (photo).

22 Turn the gearbox the right way up again correctly line up the extension housing, and secure it to the gearbox housing by replacing the bolts (photo).

23 The selector forks cannot be replaced until the two synchroniser hubs are pushed by means of a screwdriver or drift to their most forward positions (photos A and B).

24 Now lower the selector forks into position (photo A) and it will be found that they will now drop in quite easily (photo B). Now return the synchroniser hubs to their original positions.

25 Slide the gearchange selector rod into place from the rear of the extension and as it comes into the gearbox housing slide onto it the selector boss and 'C' cam, having just made sure that the cam locates in the cut-outs in the selector fork extension arms.

26 Push the selector rod through the boss and the selector forks until the pin holes on the boss and rail align. Tap the pin into place thereby securing the boss to the selector rod. During this operation ensure that the cut-out on the gearbox end of the selector rail faces to the right.

27 Replace the ball, spring and retaining screw in the top right-hand side of the gearbox casing as shown in Fig.6.7.

28 Apply a small amount of sealer to the blanking plug and gently tap it into position in the rear of the extension hosuing behind the selector rail.

29 Place a new gasket on the gearbox top cover plate, having applied a layer of Loctite or similar sealer to it and then replace the top cover and tighten down its four retaining bolts.

30 Replace the speedometer drive gear in the extension, smear the edges of its retaining cup with sealing compound and tap the cup into place. Remove the gearbox from the vice and tighten down the drain plug.

31 Replace the bellhousing onto the gearbox and tighten down the retaining bolts, replace the clutch release fork and the clutch release bearing. Reassembly is now complete.

Fault Finding Chart — Gearbox

Symptom	Reason/s	Remedy
Ineffective synchromesh	Worn baulk rings or synchro hubs.	Dismantle and renew.
Jumps out of one or more gears (on drive or over-run)	Weak detent springs or worn selector forks or worn gears.	Dismantle and renew
Noisy, rough, whining and vibration.	Worn bearings and/or laygear thrust washers (initially) resulting in extended wear generally due to play and backlash	Dismantle and renew.
Noisy and difficult engagement of gears	Clutch fault.	Examine clutch operation.

NOTE: It is sometimes difficult to decide whether it is worthwhile removing and dismantling the gearbox for a fault which may be nothing more than a minor irritant. Gearboxes which howl, or where the synchromesh can be 'beaten' by a quick gear change, may continue to perform for a long time in this state. A worn gearbox usually needs a complete rebuild to eliminate noise because the various gears, if re-aligned on new bearings will continue to howl when different wearing surfaces are presented to each other.

The decision to overhaul therefore, must be considered with regard to time and money available, relative to the degree of noise or malfunction that the driver has to suffer.

Chapter 7/Propeller Shaft and Universal Joints

Contents

General Description ... 1	One Piece Propeller Shaft - Universal Joints — Reassembly ... 5
One Piece Propeller Shaft - Removal & Replacement ... 2	Two Piece Propeller Shaft - Removal & Replacement ... 6
One Piece Propeller Shaft - Universal Joints - Inspection & Repair ... 3	Two Piece Propeller Shaft, Centre Bearing — Removal & Replacement.. ... 7
One Piece Propeller Shaft - Universal Joints - Dismantling 4	

1. General Description

As a rule all Capri 1300 models with the exception of the 1300 G.T. are fitted with a one piece tubular propeller shaft. The 1300 G.T. and all 1600 c.c. models are normally fitted with a split, two piece propeller shaft. However, due to availability difficulties on Fords' production line either type of propeller shaft may be found to be fitted to any of the models covered by this manual.

At each end of the one piece propeller shaft is a universal joint which allows for vertical movement of the rear axle. Each universal joint comprises a four legged centre spider, four needle roller bearings and two yokes.

The two piece propeller shaft is supported in the centre by a rubber insulated bearing which is bolted to the underframe. The three universal joints on this type of drive shaft have their running clearance set during manufacture and are not replaceable.

The universal joints at either end of the one piece drive shaft are replaceable as a kit. All universal joints are of the sealed type and require no maintenance.

On all models fore and aft movement of the rear axle is absorbed by a sliding spline in the front of the propeller shaft which slides over a mating spline on the rear of the gearbox mainshaft. A supply of oil through very small oil holes from the gearbox lubricates the splines.

2. One Piece Propeller Shaft - Removal & Replacement

1. Jack up the rear of the car, or position the rear of the car over a pit or on a ramp.
2. If the rear of the car is jacked up supplement the jack with support blocks so that danger is minimised, should the jack collapse.
3. If the rear wheels are off the ground place the car in gear or put the handbrake on to ensure that the propeller shaft does not turn when an attempt is made to loosen the four nuts securing the propeller shaft to the rear axle.
4. Unscrew and remove the four self-locking nuts, bolts and securing washers which hold the flange on the propeller shaft to the flange on the rear axle.
5. The propeller shaft is carefully balanced to fine limits and it is important that it is replaced in exactly the same position it was in prior to its removal. Scratch a mark on the propeller shaft and rear axle flanges to ensure accurate mating when the time comes for reassembly.
6. Slightly push the shaft forward to separate the two flanges, and then lower the end of the shaft and pull it rearwards to disengage the gearbox mainshaft splines.
7. Place a large can or a tray under the rear of the gearbox extension to catch any oil which is likely to leak through the spline lubricating holes, when the propeller shaft is removed.
8. Replacement of the propeller shaft is a reversal of the above procedure. Ensure that the mating marks scratched on the propeller shaft and rear axle flanges line up.

3. One Piece Propeller Shaft - Universal Joints - Inspection & Repair

1. Wear in the needle roller bearings is characterised by vibration in the transmission, 'clonks' on taking up the drive, and in extreme cases of lack of lubrication, metallic squeaking, and ultimately grating and shrieking sounds as the bearings break up.
2. It is easy to check if the needle roller bearings are worn with the propeller shaft in position, by trying to turn the shaft with one hand, the other hand holding the rear axle flange when the rear universal is being checked, and the front half coupling when the front universal is being checked. Any movement between the propeller shaft and the front and the rear half couplings is indicative of considerable wear. If worn, the old bearings and spiders will have to be discarded and a repair kit, comprising new universal joint spiders, bearings, oil seals, and retainers purchased. Check also by trying to lift the shaft and noticing any movement in the joints.
3. Examine the propeller shaft splines for wear. If worn it will be necessary to purchase a new front half coupling, or if the yokes are badly worn, an exchange propeller shaft. It is not possible to fit oversize bearings and journals to the trunnion bearing holes.

4. One Piece Propeller Shaft - Universal Joints - Dismantling

1. Clean away all traces of dirt and grease from the circlips located on the ends of the bearing cups, and remove the clips by pressing their open ends together with a pair of pliers (photo), and lever them out with a screwdriver.
NOTE: If they are difficult to remove tap the bearing cup face resting on top of the spider with a mallet which will ease the pressure on the circlip.
2. Take off the bearing cups on the propeller shaft yoke. To do this select two sockets from a socket spanner set, one large enough to fit completely over the bearing cup and the other smaller than the bearing cup (photo).

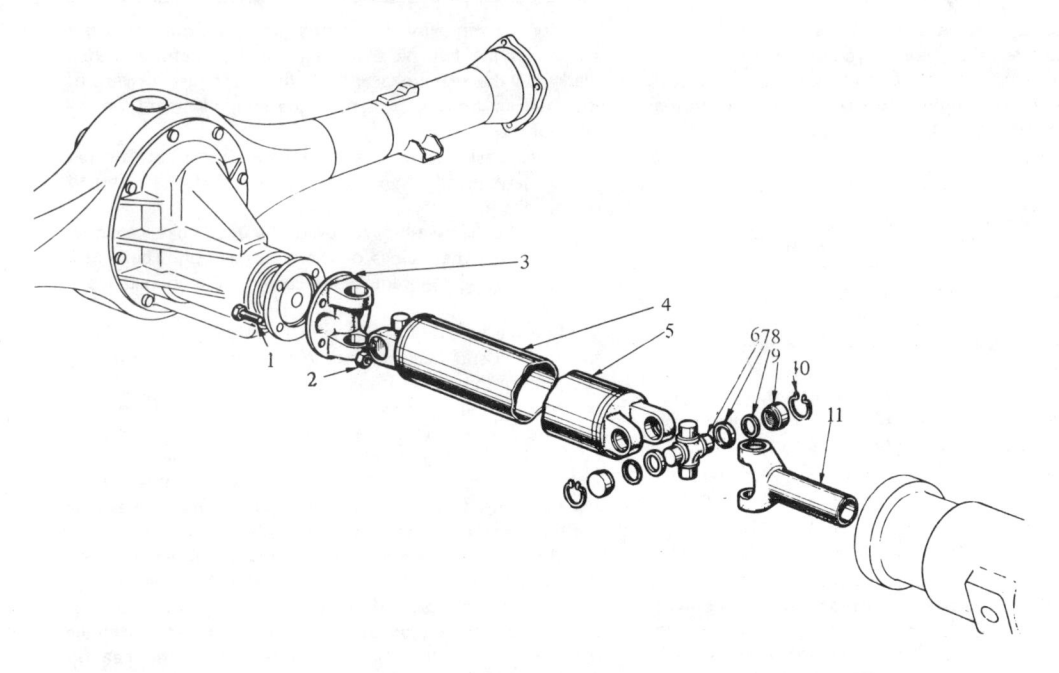

Fig.7.1. EXPLODED VIEW OF THE ONE PIECE PROPELLER SHAFT

1. Bolt
2. Nut
3. Drive shaft flange yoke
4. Propeller shaft
5. Propeller shaft
6. Spider
7. Oil seal retainer
8. Oil seal
9. Needle roller bearings & cap
10. Circlip
11. Splined universal joint knuckle

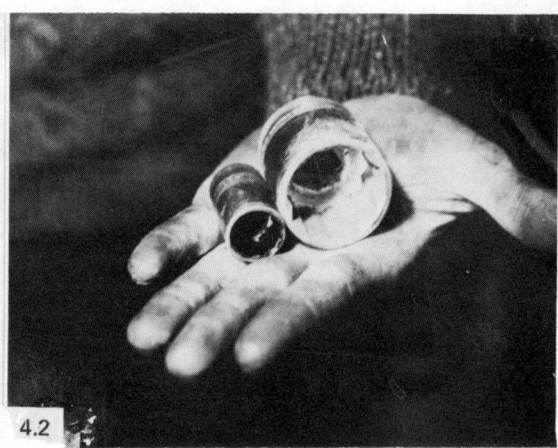

4.1

4.2

103

Chapter 7/Propeller Shaft & Universal Joints

3. Open the jaws of the vice and with the sockets opposite each other and the U.J. in between tighten the vice and so force the narrower socket to move the opposite cup partially out of the yoke (photo) into the larger socket.

4. Remove the cup with a pair of pliers (photo). Remove the opposite cup, and then free the yoke from the propeller shaft.

5. To remove the remaining two cups now repeat the instructions in paragraph 3, or use a socket and hammer as illustrated.

5. One Piece Propeller Shaft - Universal Joints - Reassembly

1. Thoroughly clean out the yokes and journals.
2. Fit new oil seals and retainers on the spider journals, place the spider on the propeller shaft yoke, and assemble the needle rollers in the bearing races with the assistance of some thin grease. Fill each bearing about a third full with Castrolease LM or similar, and fill the grease holes in the journal spider making sure all air bubbles are eliminated.
3. Refit the bearing cups on the spider and tap the bearings home so they lie squarely in position. Replace the circlips.

6. Two Piece Propeller Shaft - Removal & Replacement

1. Follow the instructions given in Section 2, paragraphs 1 to 5 inclusive.
2. Undo and remove the two bolts holding the centre bearing housing to the underframe.
2. Slightly push the shaft forward to separate the two flanges at the rear, then lower the end of shaft and pull it rearwards to disengage it from the gearbox mainshaft splines.
4. Place a large can or tray under the rear of the gearbox extension to catch any oil which is likely to leak through the spline lubricating holes when the propeller shaft is removed.
5. Replacement of the two piece propeller shaft is a reversal of the above procedure. Ensure that the mating marks scratched on the propeller shaft and rear axle flanges line up.

7. Two Piece Propeller Shaft, Centre Bearing - Removal & Replacement

1. Prior to removing the centre bearing from the front section of the two piece propeller shaft, carefully scratch marks on the rear yoke and on the shaft just forward of the bearing housing to ensure correct alignment on re-assembly.
2. Knock back the tab washer on the centre bolt located in the jaws of the rear yoke. Slacken off the nut and remove the 'U' washer from under it.
3. With the 'U' washer removed the rear yoke can now be drawn off the splines of the front section. The centre bolt and its washer remain attached to the splined front section.
4. Slide the bearing housing with its rubber insulator from the shaft. Bend back the six metal tabs on the housing and remove the rubber insulator.
5. The bearing and its protective caps should now be withdrawn from the splined section of the propeller shaft by careful levering with two large screwdrivers or tyre levers. If a suitable puller tool is available this should always be used in preference to any other method as it is less likely to cause damage to the bearing.
6. To replace the bearing, select a piece of piping or tubing that is just a fraction smaller in diameter than the bearing, place the splined part of the drive shaft upright in a vice, position the bearing on the shaft and using a soft hammer on the end of the piece of tubing drive the bearing firmly and squarely onto the shaft.
7. Replace the rubber insulator in the bearing housing ensuring that the boss on the insulator is at the top of the housing and will be adjacent to the underframe when the propeller shafts are replaced.
8. When the insulator is correctly positioned bend back the six metal tabs and slide the housing and insulator assembly over the bearing.
9. Slide the splined end of the shaft into the rear yoke ensuring that the previously scribed mating marks are correctly aligned.
10 Replace the 'U' washer under the centre bolt with its smooth surface facing the front section of the propeller shaft. Tighten down the centre bolt to a torque of 28 lb/ft. and bend up its tab washer to secure it.

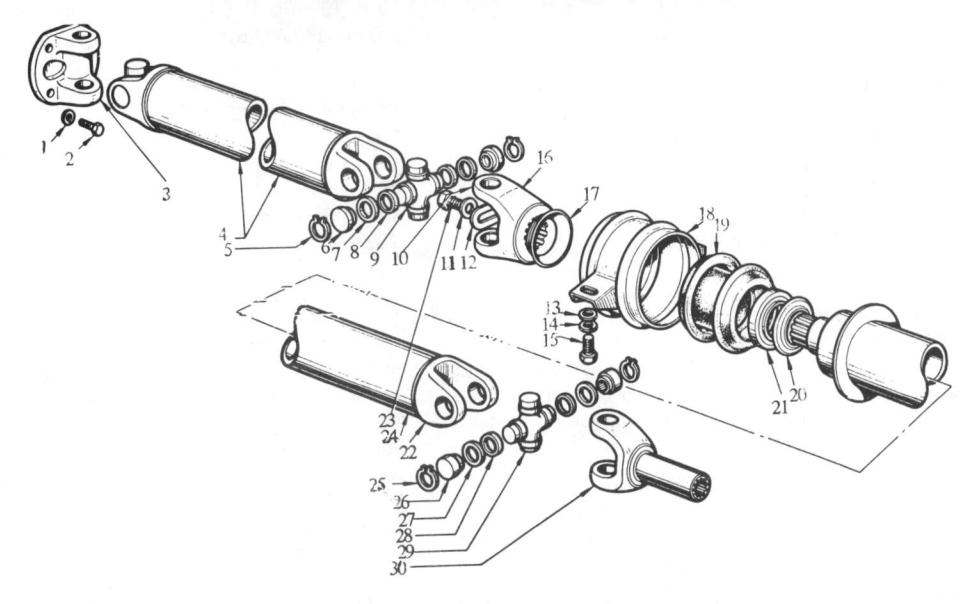

Fig.7.2. EXPLODED VIEW OF THE TWO PIECE PROPELLER SHAFT

1. Lock washer
2. Bolt
3. Drive shaft flange yoke
4. Rear section propeller shaft
5. Circlip
6. Needle roller bearing & cap
7. Oil seal
8. Oil seal retainer
9. Spider
10. Splined centre yoke
11. Washer
12. 'U' washer
13. Washer
14. Lock washer
15. Bolt
16. Yoke
17. Bearing cup
18. Bearing housing
19. Rubber insulator
20. Bearing cup
21. Bearing
22. Front section yoke
23. Bolt
24. Front section propeller shaft
25. Circlip
26. Needle roller bearing & cap
27. Oil seal
28. Oil seal retainer
29. Spider
30. Splined universal joint knuckle

105

Chapter 8/Rear Axle

Contents

General Description	1	Half Shaft Combined Bearing & Oil Seal - Removal & Replacement	5
Rear Axle - Routine Maintenance	2	Differential Carrier - Removal & Replacement	6
Rear Axle - Removal & Replacement	3		
Half Shafts - Removal & Replacement	4		

Specifications

Type	Semi-floating hypoid	
Ratios	Standard	Optional
1300 c.c.	4.125 to 1	4.444 to 1
1300 G.T	4.125 to 1	—
1600 c.c.	3.900 to 1	4.125 to 1
1600 G.T	3.778 to 1	—

Pinion/Crownwheel Number of Teeth

4.125 to 1 ratio	8/33
4.444 to 1 ratio	9/40
3.900 to 1 ratio	9/35
3.778 to 1 ratio	9/34
Pinion/Crownwheel backlash	.005 to .007 inch (.13 to .17 mm)
Pinion bearing pre-load	20 to 26 lb/in. (.23 to .29 kg.m) new bearing
	13 to 19 lb/in. (.15 to .21 kg.m) used bearing
Rear axle oil capacity	2.0 pints (2.4 U.S. pints, 1.1 litres)

Torque Wrench Settings

Crownwheel to differential case bolts	50 to 55 lb/ft. (7.0 to 7.6 kg.m)
Differential carrier to axle housing nuts	25 to 30 lb/ft. (3.45 to 4.41 kg.m)
Differential bearing locking plate bolts	12 to 15 lb/ft. (1.7 to 2.0 kg.m)
Differential bearing cap bolts	45 to 50 lb/ft. (6.3 to 7.0 kg.m)
Axle shaft bearing retainer bolts	15 to 18 lb/ft. (2.1 to 2.4 kg.m)
Universal joint flange to pinion flange	15 to 18 lb/ft. (2.1 to 2.4 kg.m)

1. General Description

The rear axle is of the semi-floating type and is held in place by two semi-elliptic springs and two radius arms. These provide the necessary lateral and longitudinal support for the axle.

The banjo type casing carries the differential assembly which consists of a hypoid crown wheel and pinion and the two star pinion differential bolted in a carrier to the casing nose piece.

All repairs can be carried out to the component parts of the rear axle without removing the axle casing from the car. It will be found simpler in practice to fit a guaranteed second hand axle from a car breakers yard rather than dismantle the differential unit which calls for special tools which very few garages will have.

As an alternative a replacement differential carrier assembly can be fitted which means that the axle can be left in position and dismantling is reduced to a minimum.

2. Rear Axle - Routine Maintenance

1. Every 6,000 miles remove the filler plug in the rear axle casing and top up with an S.A.E.90 E.P. gear oil such as Castrol Hypoy. After topping up do not replace the plug for five minutes to allow any excess to run out. If the axle is overfilled there is a possibility that oil will leak out of the ends of the axle casing and ruin the rear brake linings.

2. Every 36,000 miles drain the oil when hot by removing the drain plug in the bottom of the banjo casing, (if fitted) and refill the axle with 2 pints (2.4 US pints, 1.1 litres) of S.A.E.90 E.P. gear oil. If no drain plug is fitted it will be necessary to half remove the differential carrier as described in Section 6. This is not a factory recommended maintenance task, as there will have been no deterioration in the condition of the oil. However, the oil with time will become contaminated with minute particles of metal and for this reason the author prefers to change the rear axle oil once every three years or 36,000 miles rather than leave it in place for the life of the car.

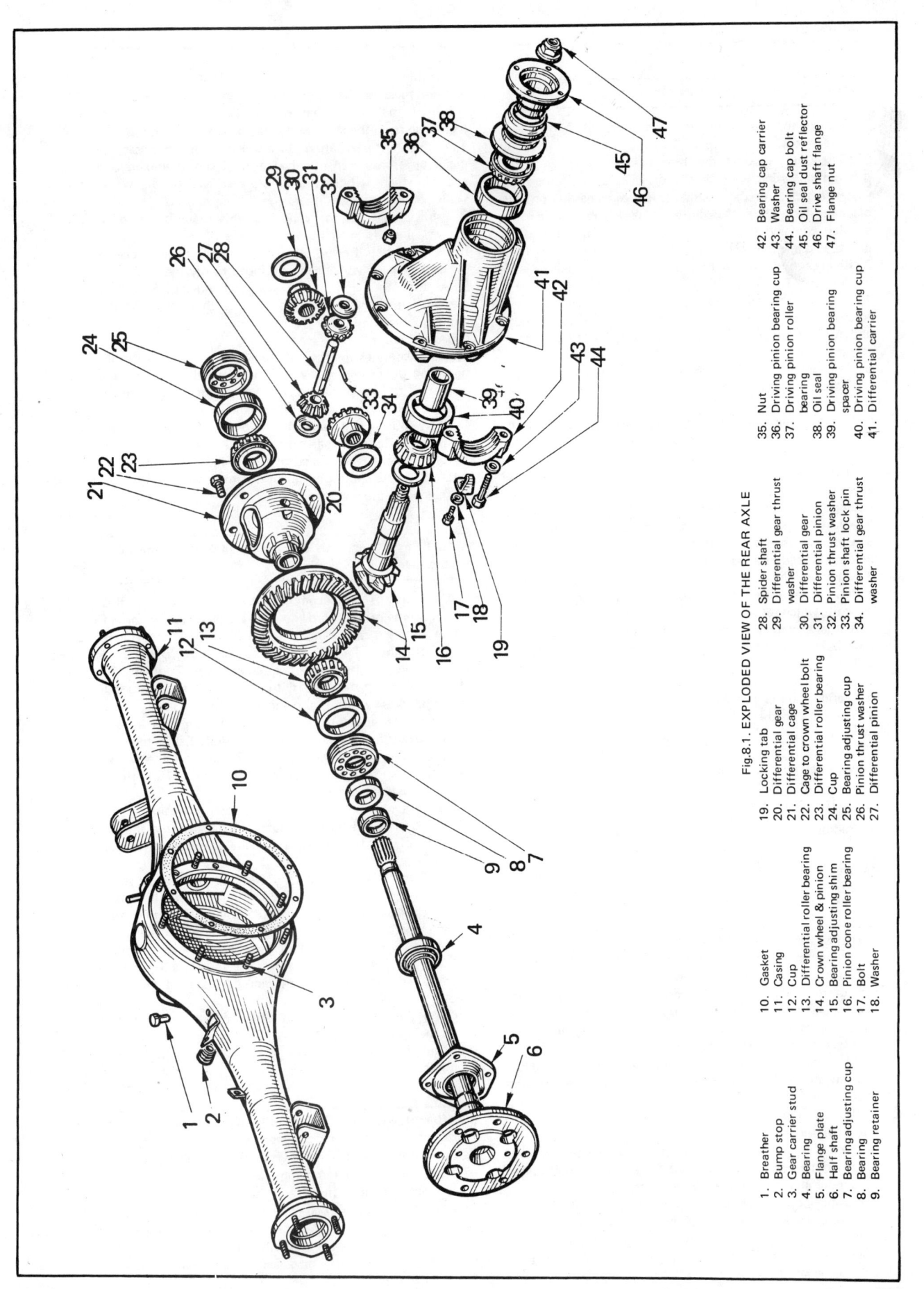

Fig.8.1. EXPLODED VIEW OF THE REAR AXLE

1. Breather
2. Bump stop
3. Gear carrier stud
4. Bearing
5. Flange plate
6. Half shaft
7. Bearing adjusting cup
8. Bearing
9. Bearing retainer
10. Gasket
11. Casing
12. Cup
13. Differential roller bearing
14. Crown wheel & pinion
15. Bearing adjusting shim
16. Pinion cone roller bearing
17. Bolt
18. Washer
19. Locking tab
20. Differential gear
21. Differential cage
22. Cage to crown wheel bolt
23. Differential roller bearing
24. Cup
25. Bearing adjusting cup
26. Pinion thrust washer
27. Differential pinion
28. Spider shaft
29. Differential gear thrust washer
30. Differential gear
31. Differential pinion
32. Pinion thrust washer
33. Pinion shaft lock pin
34. Differential gear thrust washer
35. Nut
36. Driving pinion bearing cup
37. Driving pinion roller bearing
38. Oil seal
39. Driving pinion bearing spacer
40. Driving pinion bearing cup
41. Differential carrier
42. Bearing cap carrier
43. Washer
44. Bearing cap bolt
45. Oil seal dust reflector
46. Drive shaft flange
47. Flange nut

Chapter 8/Rear Axle

3. Rear Axle - Removal & Replacement

1. Remove the rear wheel hub caps (if fitted) then loosen the wheel nuts.
2. Raise and support the rear of the body and the differential casing with chocks or jacks so that the rear wheels are clear of the ground. This is most easily done by placing a jack under the centre of the differential, jacking up the axle and then fitting chocks under the mounting points at the front of the rear springs to support the body.
3. Remove both rear wheels and place the wheel nuts in the hub caps for safe keeping.
4. Mark the propeller shaft and differential drive flanges to ensure replacement in the same relative positions. Undo and remove the nuts and bolts holding the two flanges together.
5. Release the handbrake and by undoing the adjusting nut, disconnect the cable at the pivot point at the rear of the axle casing.
6. Unscrew the union on the brake pipe at the junction on the rear axle and have handy either a jar to catch the hydraulic fluid or a plug to block the end of the pipe.
7. Undo the nuts and bolts holding the shock absorber attachments to the spring seats and remove the bolts thus freeing the shock absorbers. It will probably be necessary to adjust the jack under the axle casing to free the bolts.
8. Unscrew the nuts and withdraw the through bolts holding the radius arms to the rear axle casing.
9. Unscrew the nuts from under the spring retaining plates. These nuts screw onto the ends of the inverted 'U' bolts which retain the axle to the spring.
10 The axle will now be resting free on the jack and can now be removed by lifting it through one of the wheel arches.
11 Reassembly is a direct reversal of the removal procedure, but various points must be carefully noted.
12 The nuts on the 'U' bolts must be tightened to a torque of 18 to 26 lb/ft. (2.49 to 3.60 kg.m).
13 The radius arm nuts on the axle casing must not be fully tightened down until the car is resting on its wheels. This also applies to the shock absorber lower mounting bolts. The torque settings are:-

    Radius arms   25 to 30 lb/ft. (3.46 to 4.15 kg.m).
    Shock absorbers   40 to 45 lb/ft. (5.54 to 6.22 kg.m).

14 Bleed the brakes after reassembly as described in Chapter 9, Section 3.

4. Half Shafts - Removal & Replacement

1. The method described below is normally a very easy way of removing a half shaft together with its combined bearing and oil seal, but should the half shaft fail to move using the method described it will be necessary to make up a special tool to ensure success.
2. After jacking up the car and removing the road wheel unscrew the brake drum retaining screw and take off the brake drum.
3. Remove the four self locking nuts retaining the half shaft bearing housing to the axle casing. These nuts can be reached through the large hole in the half shaft flange.
4. It may be possible at this stage to remove the half shaft by simply pulling on the flange. If this fails replace the road wheel on the studs and tighten the nuts down just enough to prevent movement of the wheel on the studs.
5. Sitting on the ground, with one leg either side of the wheel and braced on the spring, get a firm hold on the outer edge of the tyre and pull straight outwards as hard as possible.
6. Care must be taken not to damage the splines on the end of the half shaft when withdrawing by this method as its release from the axle casing may be a bit sudden.
7. If the shaft still refuses to move it will be necessary to make up from scrap metal a form of slide hammer, one end of which is bolted onto at least two of the wheel studs opposite to each other.
8. Protruding from the centre of this plate bolted onto the wheel studs must be approximately two feet of steel rod on which is free to slide a reasonably heavy piece of cylindrical metal which can be gripped firmly by hand.
9. At the other end of the steel rod must be bolted or welded a further robust plate of metal that will stand the impact of the sliding block hitting it repeatedly with considerable force.
10 The plate designed to fit the wheel studs is firmly tightened down with the wheel nuts, and the sliding piece of metal firmly gripped and repeatedly struck with as much force as possible against the other plate.
11 This action will have the effect of loosening and eventually withdrawing an obstinate half shaft.
12 Replacement is a reversal of the removal procedure, but once again care should be taken not to damage the splines on the end of the half shaft.

5. Half Shaft Combined Bearing & Oil Seal - Removal & Replacement

1. The owner is not recommended to attempt to do this job unless the proper Ford tools are available, as the correct fitting of the bearing and oil seal is of vital importance to its efficiency. The tools required are Tool No.P.4090-2 and 6, which is a half shaft bearing remover; Tool No.370 which is a universal taper base to fit an hydraulic press, and Tool No.P.4084 which is a spring indicator.
2. Locate the adaptors of Tool No.P.4090-6 and a slave ring between the bearing and the half shaft flange then by using the universal taper base No.370 support the whole assembly in an hydraulic press and push the half shaft out of the combined bearing and oil seal.
3. To fit a new bearing locate the bearing retainer plate and the bearing on the half shaft making sure that the oil seal side of the bearing is facing the splined end of the half shaft.
4. Using the adaptors on Tool No.P.4090-2 and a slave ring support the assembly in the bed of an hydraulic press. Fit the spring indicator, Tool No.P.4084 to the arm of the hydraulic press and press the bearing onto the half shaft.
5. The spring indicator should show a minimum pressure of 1,200 lbs. (544 kg.); if the pressure shown is lower this indicates an incorrect fit and another bearing must be tried.
6. Using the same tools as in paragraphs 4 and 5 above, press the bearing collar to abut the bearing. A minimum pressure of 2,400 lb. (1088 kg.) should be required to do the job correctly.

6. Differential Carrier - Removal & Replacement

1. To remove the differential carrier assembly, drain the oil from the axle by removing the drain plug in the base of the banjo casing, (if fitted), jack up the rear of the vehicle, remove both road wheels and brake drums and then withdraw both half shafts as described in Section 4.
2. Disconnect the propeller shaft at the rear end as described in Chapter 7, Sections 2 or 6, according to which type of propeller shaft is fitted.

Chapter 8 /Rear Axle

3. Undo the eight self locking nuts holding the differential carrier assembly to the axle casing. If an oil drain plug has not been fitted, pull the assembly slightly forward and allow the oil to drain in a suitable tray or bowl. The carrier complete with the crown wheel can now be lifted clear with the gasket.

4. Before replacement, carefully clean the mating surfaces of the carrier and the axle casing and always fit a new gasket. Replacement is then a direct reversal of the above instructions. The eight nuts retaining the differential carrier assembly to the axle casing should be tightened to a torque of 25 to 30 lb/ft. (3.45 to 4.41 kg.m).

Chapter 9/Braking System

Contents

Disc/Drum Brakes - General Description...	1
Brakes - Maintenance	2
Bleeding the Hydraulic System..	3
Rear Brake Shoes - Inspection, Removal & Replacement	4
Flexible Hoses - Inspection, Removal & Replacement..	5
Rear Brake Seals - Inspection & Overhaul	6
Rear Wheel Cylinders - Removal & Replacement	7
Brake Master Cylinder - Removal & Replacement	8
Brake Master Cylinder - Dismantling & Reassembly ...	9
Handbrake Linkage - Adjustment...	10
Pedals - Removal & Replacement	11
Disc Brake Friction Pads - Inspection, Removal & Replacement	12
Brake Calliper - Removal, Dismantling & Reassembly...	13
Brake Disc - Removal & Replacement..	14
Dual Braking System - General Description	15
Pressure Differential Warning Actuator - Centralisation	16
Pressure Differential Warning Actuator - Dismantling, Examination & Reassembly...	17
Tandem Master Cylinder - Dismantling, Examination & Reassembly...	18
Vacuum Servo Unit - Removal & Replacement	19
Vacuum Servo Unit - Dismantling, Examination & Reassembly	20

Specifications

Type	Disc at front, drum at rear
Footbrake	Hydraulic on all 4 wheels
Handbrake	Mechanical to rear wheels only
Front brake layout	Trailing callipers

Brake Dimensions
1300
Disc diameter	9.59 inch (24.13 cm)
Disc thickness	.376 inch (.95 cm)
Maximum disc run-out..	.0035 inch (.089 cm)
Cylinder diameter	1.892 inch (4.80 cm)
Total pad swept area	171.9 sq.in. (1,109 sq.cm)
Pad colour coding	Green, Red, Red, Red
Rear drum dimensions	8 x 1.5 inch (20.3 x 3.81 cm)
Total shoe swept area...	75.5 sq.inch (487 sq.cm)
Rear wheel cylinder diameter	.75 inch (1.87 cm)
Master cylinder diameter:-	
Single line without servo	.625 inch (1.59 cm)
Dual line without servo	.70 inch (1.77 cm)
With servo	.813 inch (2.06 cm)

1300 G.T., 1600 and 1600 G.T.
Disc diameter	9.625 inch (24.45 cm)
Disc thickness	.500 inch (1.26 cm)
Maximum disc run-out..	.0035 inch (.089 cm)
Cylinder diameter	2.125 inch (5.39 cm)
Total pad swept area	189.5 sq.in. (1,220 sq.cm)
Pad colour coding	Green, Red, Red, Red
Rear drum dimensions..	9 x 1.75 inch (22.9 x 4.45 cm)
Total shoe swept area	99.0 sq.in. (639 sq.cm)
Rear wheel cylinder diameter..	.75 inch (1.87 cm)

Master Cylinder Diameter
1300 G.T., 1600 without servo	.70 inch (1.77 cm)
1300 G.T., 1600 with servo	.813 inch (2.06 cm)
1600 G.T..	.813 inch (2.06 cm)

Chapter 9/Braking System

Some early models fitted with servo assisted braking systems may have front disc brake pads colour coded Green with a .70 inch (1.77 cm) diameter rear wheel cylinder. Also some models without a servo assisted braking system may have rear wheel cylinders with a diameter of .875 inch (2.22 cm)

It may also be found that certain 1300 G.T., and 1600 models have 9.59 inch (24.13 cm) front disc brakes and 8 inch (20.3 cm) diameter rear brake drums. These cars can be identified by a red paint band on the right-hand side of the handbrake transverse cable. Certain models fitted with 9.59 inch (24.13 cm) front disc brakes may have disc pads coded Yellow, Red, Red, Yellow

Servo boost ratio	2.2 to 1
Diaphragm area	38 sq.in.

Torque Wrench Settings

Brake calliper to suspension	45 to 50 lb/ft. (6.22 to 6.91 kg.m)
Disc to hub	30 to 34 lb/ft. (4.15 to 4.70 kg.m)
Rear backplate to axle housing	15 to 18 lb/ft. (2.07 to 2.49 kg.m)
Bleed valves	5 to 7 lb/ft. (0.7 to 1.0 kg.m)
Brake hose-to-brake tube connections	9 to 11 lb/ft. (1.2 to 1.5 kg.m)
Brake tube-to-brake hose locknuts	10 to 12 lb/ft. (1.3 to 1.6 kg.m)

1. Disc/Drum Brakes - General Description

Disc brakes are fitted to the front wheels of all models together with single leading shoe drum brakes at the rear. The mechanically operated handbrake works on the rear wheels only.

The brakes fitted to the front wheels are of the rotating disc and static calliper type, with one calliper per disc, each calliper containing two piston operated friction pads, which on application of the footbrake pinch the disc rotating between them. The front brakes are of the trailing calliper type to minimise the entry of water.

Application of the footbrake creates hydraulic pressure in the master cylinder and fluid from the cylinder travels via steel and flexible pipes to the cylinders in each half of the callipers, thus pushing the pistons, to which are attached the friction pads, into contact with either side of the disc.

Two seals are fitted to the operating cylinders, the outer seal prevents moisture and dirt entering the cylinder, while the inner seal which is retained in a groove inside the cylinder, prevents fluid leakage.

As the friction pads wear so the pistons move further out of the cylinders and the level of the fluid in the hydraulic reservoir drops. Disc pad wear is therefore taken up automatically and eliminates the need for periodic adjustment by the owner.

All Capri models use a floor mounted handbrake located between the front seats.

A single cable runs from the lever to a compensator mechanism on the back of the rear axle casing. From the compensator a single cable runs to the rear brake drums. As the rear brake shoes wear the handbrake cables operate a self adjusting mechanism in the rear brake drums thus doing away with the necessity for the owner to adjust the brakes on each rear wheel individually. The only adjustment required is on the handbrake compensator mechanism, due to wear in the linkage.

On 1600 G.T. models and all models with dual line braking systems except the 1300 a mechanical servo of the suspended vacuum type is fitted as standard. A servo is also available as an optional extra on all models.

On certain models, in particular those cars for export to the U.S.A. a dual braking system is fitted providing separate hydraulic circuits for the front and rear brakes. Should one circuit fail the other circuit is unaffected and the car can still be stopped. A warning light is fitted on the fascia which illuminates, should either circuit fail. The bulb in the light can also be tested by means of the switch provided.

2. Brakes - Maintenance

1. Every 3,000 miles or more frequently if necessary, carefully clean the top of the brake master cylinder reservoir, remove the cap, and inspect the level of the fluid which should be ¼ inch below the bottom of the filler neck. Check that the breathing holes in the cap are clear.
2. If the fluid is below this level, top up the reservoir with any hydraulic fluid conforming to specification S.A.E.70 R3. It is vital that no other type of brake fluid is used. Use of a non-standard fluid will result in brake failure caused by the perishing of special seals in the master and brake cylinders. If topping up becomes frequent then check the metal piping and flexible hoses for leaks, and check for worn brake or master cylinders which will also cause loss of fluid.
3. Every 6,000 miles check the front brake disc pads and the rear brake shoes for wear and renew them if necessary. Also check the adjustment on the handbrake cable and adjust if necessary. Due to the self adjusting rear brakes it should not be necessary to adjust the handbrake cable unless wear has taken place in the linkage.
4. Every 36,000 miles or three years whichever comes sooner it is advisable to change the fluid in the braking system and at the same time renew all hydraulic seals and flexible hoses.

3. Bleeding the Hydraulic System

1. Removal of all the air from the hydraulic system is essential to the correct working of the braking system, and before undertaking this, examine the fluid reservoir cap to ensure that both vent holes, one on top and the second underneath but not in line, are clear; check the level of fluid and top up if required.
2. Check all brake line unions and connections for possible seepage, and at the same time check the condition of the rubber hoses, which may be perished.
3. If the condition of the wheel cylinders is in doubt, check for possible signs of fluid leakage.
4. If there is any possibility of incorrect fluid having been put into the system, drain all the fluid out and flush through with methylated spirits. Renew all piston seals and cups since these will be affected and could possibly fail under pressure.
5. Gather together a clean jam jar, a 9 inch length of tubing which fits tightly over the bleed nipples, and a tin of the correct brake fluid.
6. To bleed the system, clean the areas around the bleed

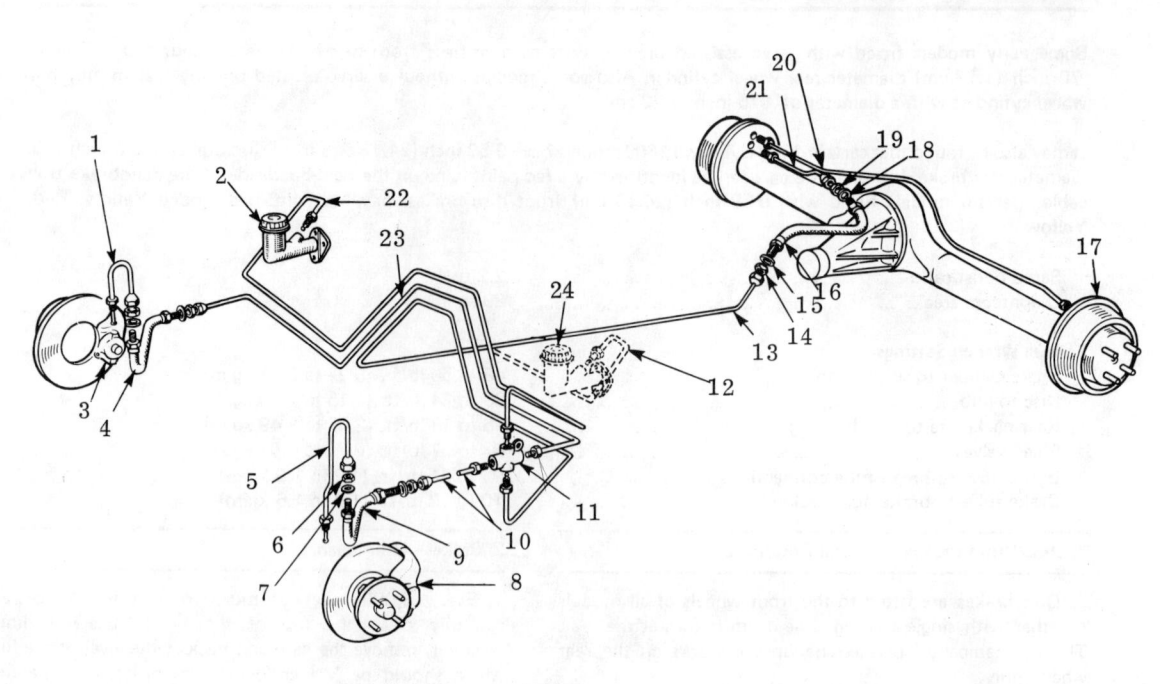

Fig.9.1. SINGLE LINE BRAKE PIPE LAYOUT – WITHOUT SERVO

1. Pipe
2. Master cylinder
3. Brake calliper
4. Flexible hose
5. Pipe
6. Nut
7. Washer
8. Brake calliper
9. Flexible hose
10. Pipe
11. Four-way connector
12. L.H.D. pipe
13. Pipe
14. Nut
15. Washer
16. Flexible hose
17. Brake drum
18. Washer
19. Nut
20. Pipe
21. Pipe
22. Pipe
23. Pipe
24. L.H.D. master cylinder

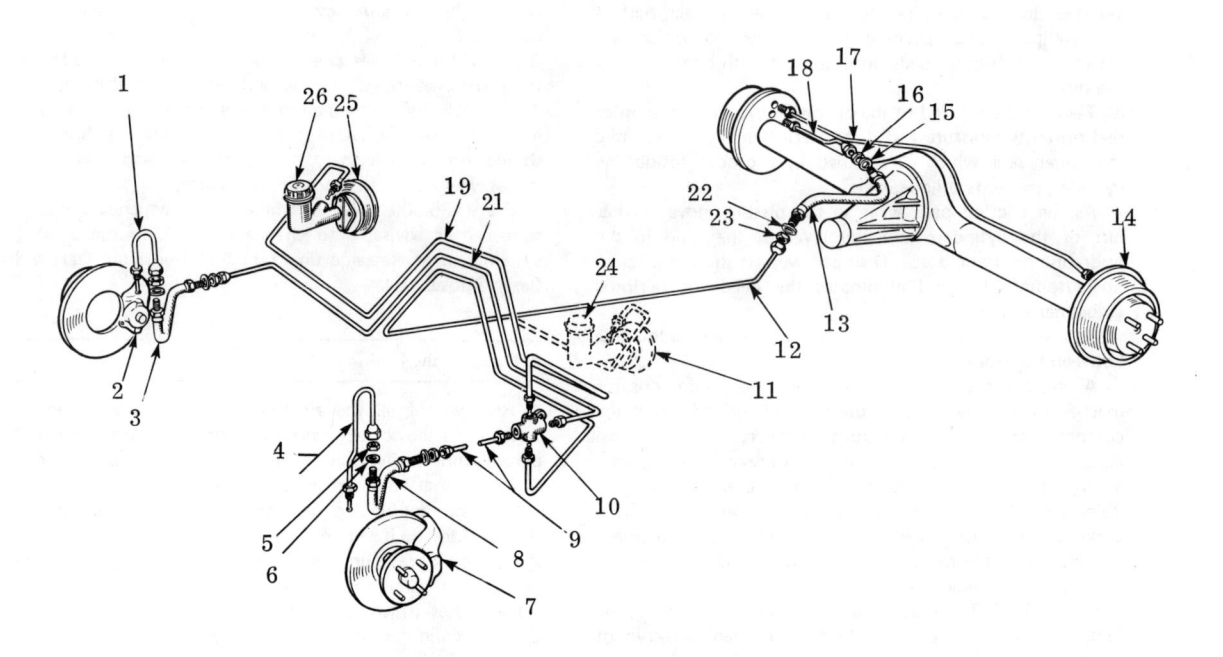

Fig.9.2. SINGLE LINE BRAKE PIPE LAYOUT – WITH SERVO

1. Pipe
2. Brake calliper
3. Flexible hose
4. Pipe
5. Nut
6. Washer
7. Brake calliper
8. Flexible hose
9. Pipe
10. Four-way connector
11. L.H.D. servo
12. Pipe
13. Flexible hose
14. Brake drum
15. Washer
16. Nut
17. Pipe
18. Pipe
19. Pipe
20.
21. Pipe
22. Washer
23. Nut
24. L.H.D. master cylinder
25. Servo
26. Master cylinder

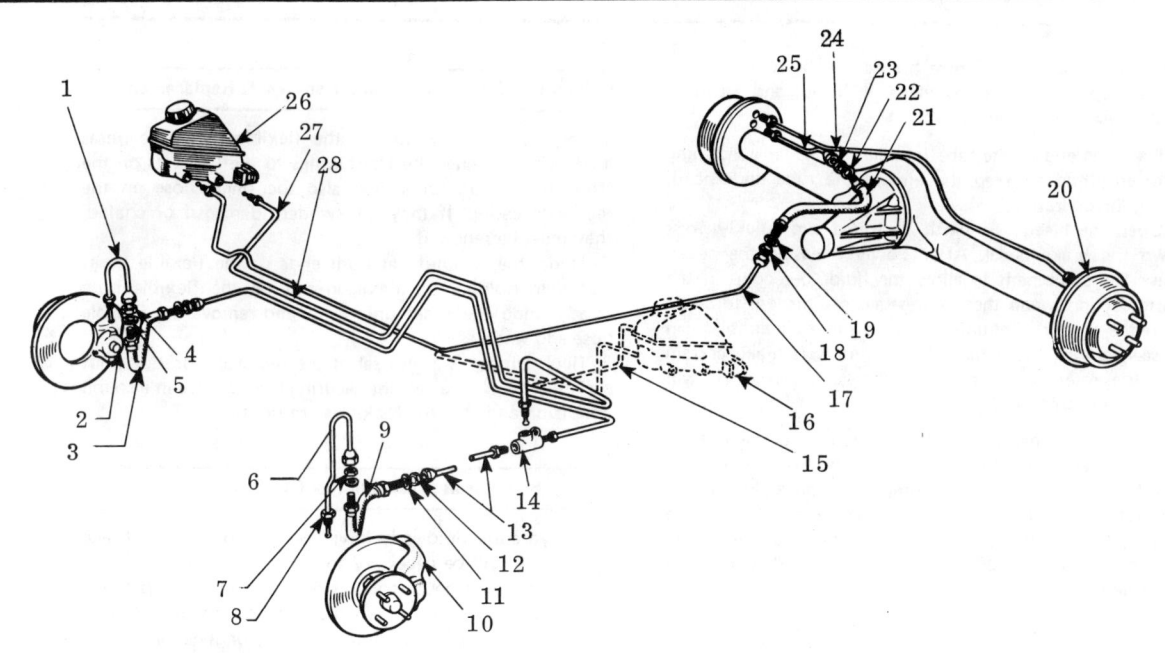

Fig.9.3. DUAL LINE BRAKE PIPE LAYOUT – WITHOUT SERVO

1. Pipe	8. Nut	15. L.H.D. pipe	22. Washer
2. Brake calliper	9. Flexible hose	16. L.H.D. master cylinder	23. Nut
3. Flexible hose	10. Brake calliper	17. Pipe	24. Pipe
4. Nut	11. Washer	18. Nut	25. Pipe
5. Washer	12. Nut	19. Washer	26. Master cylinder
6. Pipe	13. Pipe	20. Brake drum	27. Pipe
7. Nut	14. Three-way connector	21. Flexible hose	28. Pipe

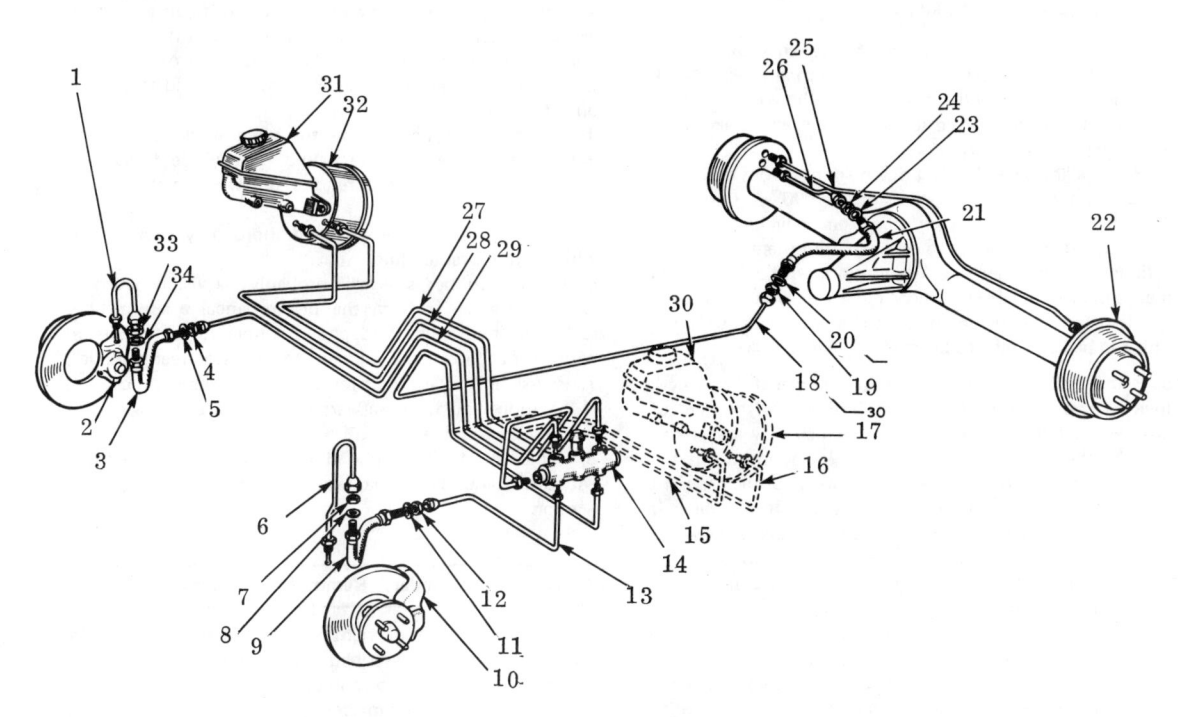

Fig.9.4. DUAL LINE BRAKE PIPE LAYOUT – WITH SERVO

1. Pipe	10. Brake calliper	19. Nut	28. Pipe
2. Calliper	11. Washer	20. Washer	29. Pipe
3. Flexible hose	12. Nut	21. Flexible hose	30. L.H.D. master cylinder
4. Nut	13. Pipe	22. Brake drum	31. Master cylinder
5. Washer	14. Pressure differential valve	23. Washer	32. Servo
6. Pipe	15. L.H.D. pipe	24. Nut	33. Nut
7. Nut	16. L.H.D. pipe	25. Pipe	34. Washer
8. Washer	17. L.H.D. servo	26. Pipe	
9. Flexible hose	18. Pipe	27. Pipe	

113

Chapter 9/Braking System

valves, and start on the front brakes first by removing the rubber cup over the bleed valve, if fitted, and fitting a rubber tube in position.

7. Place the end of the tube in a clean glass jar containing sufficient fluid to keep the end of the tube underneath during the operation.

8. Open the bleed valve with a spanner and quickly press down the brake pedal. After slowly releasing the pedal, pause for a moment to allow the fluid to recoup in the master cylinder and then depress again. This will force air from the system. Continue until no more air bubbles can be seen coming from the tube. At intervals make certain that the reservoir is kept topped up, otherwise air will enter at this point again.

9. Repeat this operation on the other front brake and the left-hand rear brake, there being no bleed valve on the right-hand rear brake. When completed, check the level of the fluid in the reservoir and then check the feel of the brake pedal, which should be firm and free from any 'spongy' action, which is normally associated with air in the system.

4. Rear Brake Shoes - Inspection, Removal & Replacement

After high mileages it will be necessary to fit replacement brake shoes with new linings. Refitting new brake linings to old shoes is not always satisfactory, but if the services of a local garage or workshop with brake lining equipment is available, then there is no reason why your own shoes should not be successfully relined.

1. Remove the hub cap, loosen off the wheel nuts, then securely jack up the car, and remove the road wheel. Chock the front wheels and fully release the handbrake.
2. Undo the single domed screw retaining the brake drum and then pull off the drum.
3. Remove the small holding down springs from each shoe by turning two small top washers through 90°.
4. Pull out the ends of each shoe from their locating slots in the fixed pivot on one side of the drum and the wheel cylinder on the other side. When removing the shoes from their slots in the wheel cylinder great care should be taken not to allow the piston to fall out of the wheel cylinder. This can be kept in place by an elastic band.
5. Remove the shoes with the return springs still attached; then take off the return springs noting that they are of different lengths and the positions in which they are fitted.
6. Take the self adjusting ratchet wheel assembly off the wheel cylinder and turn the ratchet wheel until it is right up against the end of the slot headed bolt on which it rotates. This has the effect of adjusting the rear brake to the fully off position. If this is not done it may be found difficult to get the brake drum to fit over the new shoes when reassembling.
7. The brake linings should be examined and must be renewed if they are so worn that the rivet heads are flush with the surface of the lining. If bonded linings are fitted these must be renewed when the material has worn down to 1/32nd inch at its thinnest point.
8. Replacement of the shoes is a direct reversal of the removal procedure but great care must be taken to ensure that the return springs are correctly fitted.
9. When replacement of the shoes is complete, operate the handbrake several times to allow the rear brake self-adjusting mechanism to bring the shoes into the correct position, then road test the car to ensure the brakes are operating correctly.

5. Flexible Hoses - Inspection, Removal & Replacement

1. Inspect the condition of the flexible hydraulic hoses leading from under the front wings to the brackets on the front suspension units, and also the single hose on the rear axle casing. If they are swollen, damaged or chafed, they must be renewed.
2. Undo the locknuts at both ends of the flexible hoses and then holding the hexagon nut on the flexible hose steady undo the other union nut and remove the flexible hose and washer.
3. Replacement is a reversal of the removal procedure, but carefully check that all the securing brackets are in a sound condition and that the locknuts are tight.

6. Rear Brake Seals - Inspection & Overhaul

If hydraulic fluid is leaking from one of the rear brake cylinders it will be necessary to dismantle the cylinder and replace the dust cover and piston sealing rubber. If brake fluid is found running down the side of the wheel, or it is noticed that a pool of liquid forms alongside one wheel and the level in the master cylinder has dropped, and the hoses are in good order proceed as follows:-

1. Remove the offending brake drum and shoes as described in Section 4.
2. Remove the small metal clip holding the rubber dust cap in place then prise off the dust cap.
3. Take the piston complete with its seal out of the cylinder bore and then withdraw the spring from the bore as well. Should the piston and seal prove difficult to remove gentle pressure on the brake pedal will push it out of the bore. If this method is used, place a quantity of rag under the brake backplate to catch the hydraulic fluid as it pours out of the cylinder.
4. Inspect the cylinder bore for score marks caused by impurities in the hydraulic fluid. If any are found the cylinder and piston will require renewal together as an exchange unit.
5. If the cylinder bore is sound thoroughly clean it out with fresh hydraulic fluid.
6. The old rubber seal will probably be visibly worn or swollen. Detach it from the piston, smear a new rubber seal with hydraulic fluid and assemble it to the piston with the flat face of the seal next to the piston rear shoulder.
7. Reassembly is a direct reversal of the above procedure. If the rubber dust cap appears to be worn or damaged this should also be replaced.
8. Replenish the hydraulic fluid, replace the brake shoes and drum and bleed the braking system as described in Section 3.

7. Rear Wheel Cylinders - Removal & Replacement

1. Remove the left or right-hand brake drum and brake shoes as required, as described in Section 4.
2. To avoid having to completely drain the hydraulic system screw down the master cylinder reservoir cap tightly over a piece of polythene.
3. Free the hydraulic pipe from the wheel cylinder at the union, (there are two unions on the right-hand brakeplate).
4. Working on the inside of the brake backplate remove the spring clip and clevis pin from the handbrake link.
5. From the back of the brake backplate prise off and remove the rubber boot on the back of the wheel cylinder.
6. Pull off the two 'U' shaped retainers holding the wheel cylinder to the backplate noting that the spring retainer

Fig.9.5. EXPLODED VIEW OF THE REAR BRAKE ASSEMBLY

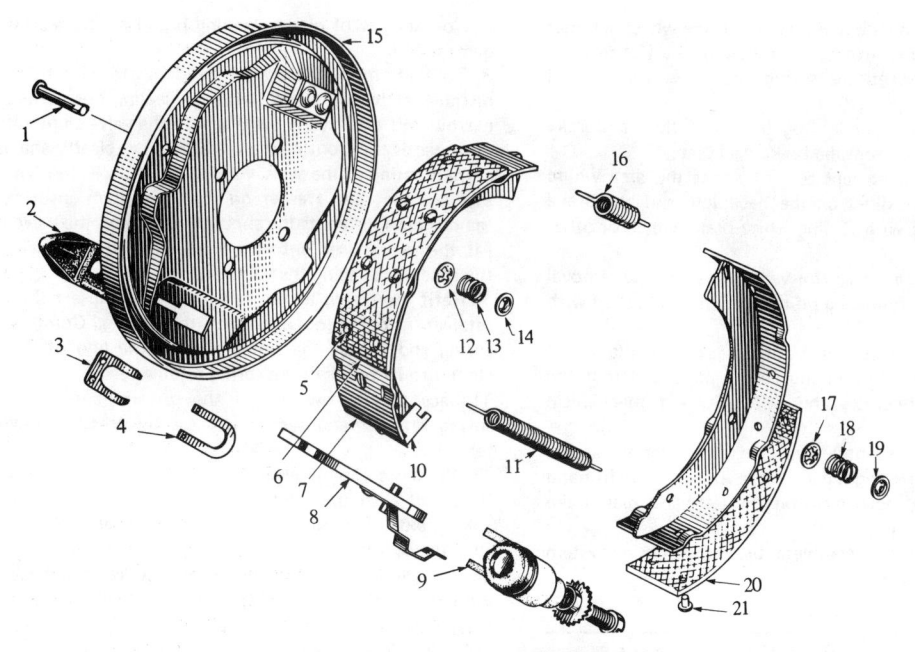

1. Pin
2. Dust cover
3. Cylinder retaining clip
4. Cylinder retaining clip
5. Rivet
6. Lining material
7. Shoe
8. Handbrake lever
9. Wheel cylinder
10. Shoe support plate
11. Return spring
12. Spring seating washer
13. Spring
14. Pin retainer
15. Backplate
16. Return spring
17. Spring seating washer
18. Spring
19. Pin retainer
20. Lining material
21. Rivet

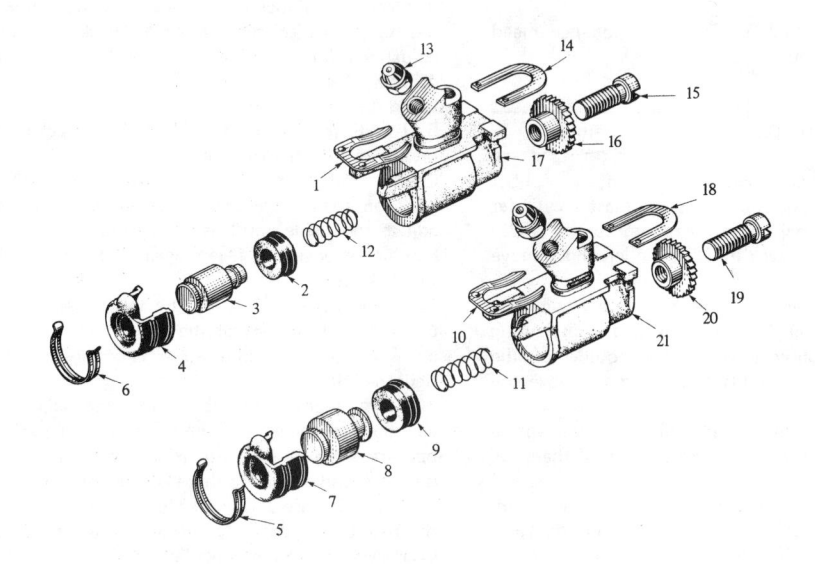

Fig.9.6. EXPLODED VIEW OF THE REAR WHEEL BRAKE CYLINDER

1. Retaining clip
2. Seal
3. Piston
4. Dust cover
5. Retaining clip
6. Retaining clip
7. Dust cover
8. Piston
9. Seal
10. Retaining clip
11. Spring
12. Spring
13. Bleed nipple
14. Retaining clip
15. Screw
16. Adjusting wheel
17. Body
18. Retaining clip
19. Screw
20. Adjusting wheel
21. Body

115

Chapter 9/Braking System

is fitted from the handbrake link end of the wheel cylinder and the flat retainer from the other end, the flat retainer being located between the spring retainer and the wheel cylinder.

7. Now the wheel cylinder together with the handbrake link can be removed from the brake backplate.

8. Before commencing replacement smear the area where the wheel cylinder slides on the backplate and the brake shoe support pads with Girling white brake grease or other approved brake grease.

9. Replacement is a straightforward reversal of the removal sequence, but the following points should be checked with extra care.

10 After fitting the rubber boot, check that the wheel cylinder can slide freely in the carrier plate and that the handbrake link operates the self adjusting mechanism correctly.

11 It is important to note that the self adjusting ratchet mechanism on the right-hand rear brake is right-hand threaded and the mechanism on the left-hand rear brake is left-hand threaded.

12 When replacement is complete, bleed the braking system as described in Section 3.

8. Brake Master Cylinder - Removal & Replacement

1. To remove the master cylinder start by disconnecting the pushrod from the brake pedal inside the car by undoing the single nut and withdrawing the through bolt.

2. Then working under the bonnet disconnect the single hydraulic pipe leading to the master cylinder by undoing the union. Plug the end of the pipe to prevent any dirt entering.

3. Undo the two nuts and spring washers holding the master cylinder to the bulkhead and then remove the master cylinder.

4. Replacement is a reversal of the removal sequence; bleed the brakes after replacement.

9. Brake Master Cylinder - Dismantling & Reassembly

1. To dismantle the master cylinder, pull off the rubber dust cover where the pushrod enters the master cylinder then with a pair of long nosed pliers remove the circlip holding the pushrod in place in the cylinder and remove the pushrod.

2. Now withdraw the piston and valve assembly complete from the master cylinder. The piston is held in the spring retainer by a tab which engages under a shoulder on the front of the piston. Gently lift this tab and remove the piston.

3. Carefully compress the spring and move the spring retainer to one side. This will release the end of the valve stem from the retainer.

4. Slide the valve spacer and shim off the valve stem. Remove the rubber seal from the piston and the valve seal off the other end of the valve stem.

5. Examine the bore of the cylinder carefully for any scores or ridges, and if this is found to be smooth all over, new seals can be fitted. If there is any doubt as to the condition of the bore, then a new cylinder must be fitted.

6. If examination of the seals shows them to be apparently oversize, or very loose on their seats, suspect oil contamination in the system. Oil will swell these rubber seals, and if one is found to be swollen, it is reasonable to assume that all seals in the braking system will need attention.

7. Before reassembly wash all parts in methylated spirit, commercial alcohol or approved brake fluid. Do not use any other type of oil or cleaning liquid or the seals will be damaged.

8. To reassemble the master cylinder start by fitting the piston seal to the piston with the sealing lips towards the narrow end and fit the valve seal to the valve stem with the lip towards the front of the valve, Fig.9.7. clearly shows the correct fitting of the seals.

9. Place the shim washer on the valve stem ensuring that the convex face abuts the shoulder flange on the valve stem. Fit the seal spacer onto the valve stem so that the legs of the spacer are facing the valve seal.

10 Refit the spring to the valve stem then insert the spring retainer into the open end of the spring. Compress the spring and engage the small boss on the end of the valve stem into its recess in the spring retainer.

11 Place the narrow end of the piston in its slot in the spring retainer and secure it there by pressing down the tab.

12 Dip the complete assembly in clean approved hydraulic fluid and with the valve leading slide it into the cylinder taking extra care not to damage the piston seal as it goes into the cylinder.

13 Replace the piston in the master cylinder and secure it with the circlip. Finally replace the rubber dust cap. The master cylinder can now be refitted to the car as described in Section 8.

10. Handbrake Linkage - Adjustment

1. Fit chocks under front wheels to prevent the car moving then release the handbrake and jack up the rear of the car.

2. Before making any adjustments check that the cable from the handbrake and that the transverse cable are correctly located in their guides and that the guides are well greased.

3. Slacken the locknut on the main handbrake cable on the relay lever on the rear of the back axle, and turn the adjusting nut until the main cable is reasonably taut.

4. The relay lever should be just clear of the stop on the banjo rear axle casing.

5. To adjust the single transverse cable, slacken the locknut on the end of the cable next to the right-hand rear brake. Check carefully that both handbrake operating levers are back on their stops and in the fully 'off' position then adjust the cable until it is reasonably taut. Check the handbrake operating levers again and finally tighten down the locknut.

6. The effect of adjusting the transverse cable may have upset the adjustment of the main cable so this should be checked again and adjusted as necessary and the locknut tightened down.

7. At frequent intervals during the adjustments it is advisable to check that the handbrake operating levers on both rear brakes have not moved off their stops. If they do move and are left in that position any adjustments made will be of no use and in fact the car will be motoring with the rear brakes partially applied all the time thus causing excessive wear to the brake linings.

11. Pedals - Removal & Replacement

1. Disconnect the brake master cylinder pushrod from the brake pedal as described in Section 8 of this chapter.

2. Take off the spring clip holding the clutch cable to the top of its pedal and withdraw the short pivot pin.

3. Remove the circlip from the groove on the pedal pivot pin between the brake pedal and the right-hand side of the pedal mounting bracket.

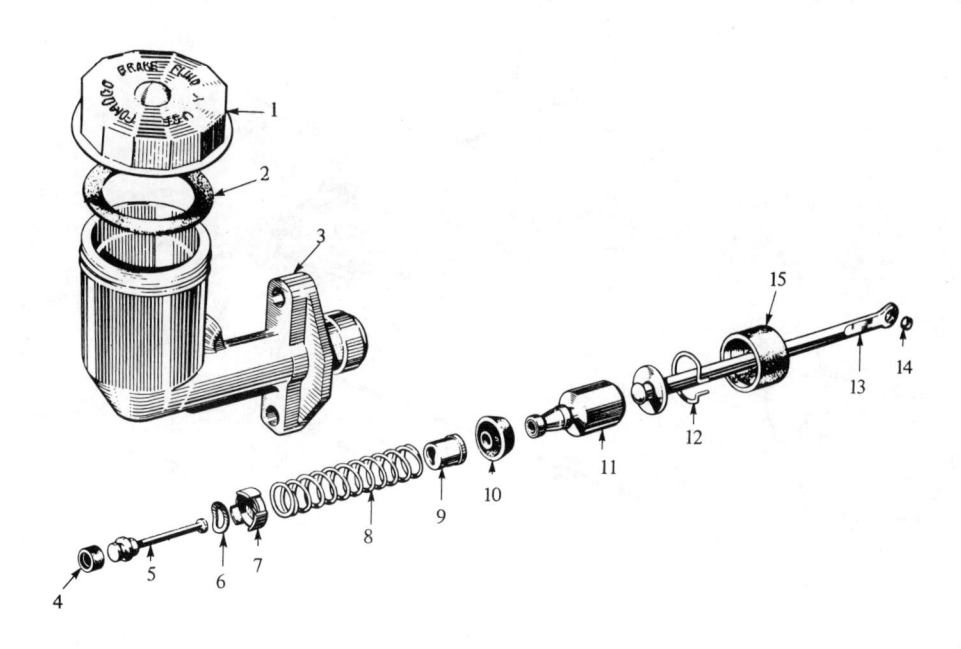

Fig.9.7. EXPLODED VIEW OF THE STANDARD BRAKE MASTER CYLINDER

1. Cap
2. Sealing ring
3. Body
4. Valve seal
5. Valve stem
6. Spring washer
7. Valve spacer
8. Spring
9. Spring retainer
10. Seal
11. Piston
12. Circlip
13. Pushrod
14. Bush
15. Dust cover

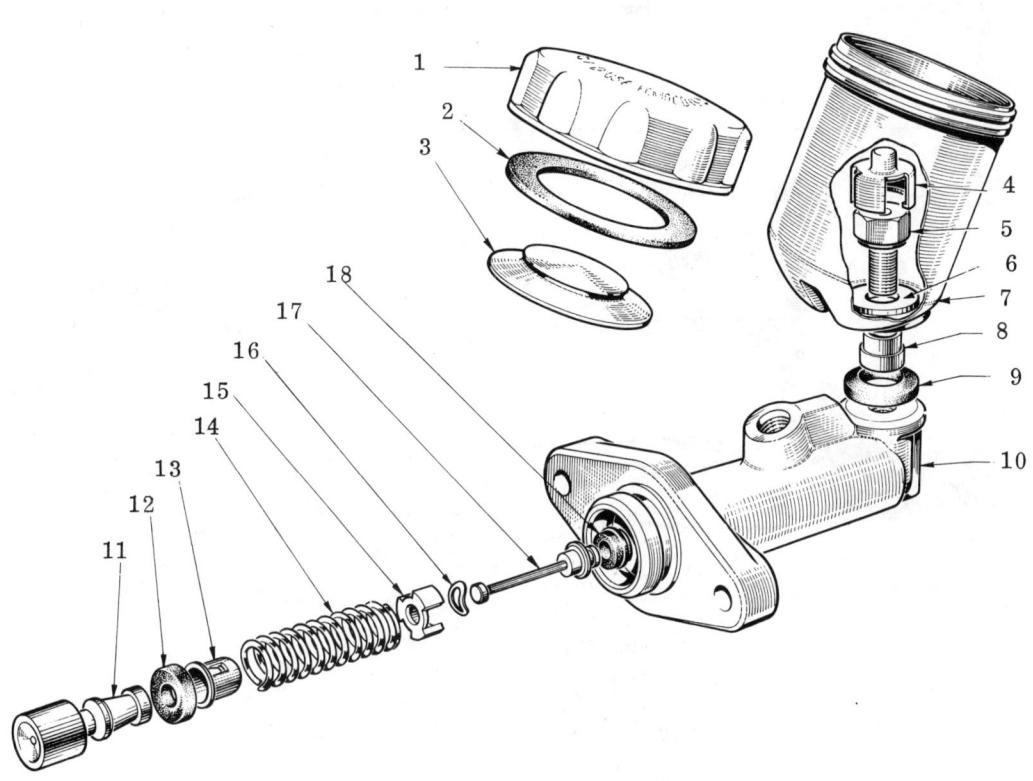

Fig.9.8. EXPLODED VIEW OF THE SINGLE LINE SERVO ASSISTED BRAKE MASTER CYLINDER

1. Reservoir cap
2. Cap seal
3. Seal retainer
4. Baffle
5. Filler opening adaptor
6. Washer
7. Reservoir body
8. Sleeve
9. Seal
10. Master cylinder body
11. Piston
12. Piston seal
13. Spring retainer
14. Spring
15. Valve spacer
16. Spring washer
17. Valve stem
18. Valve seal

117

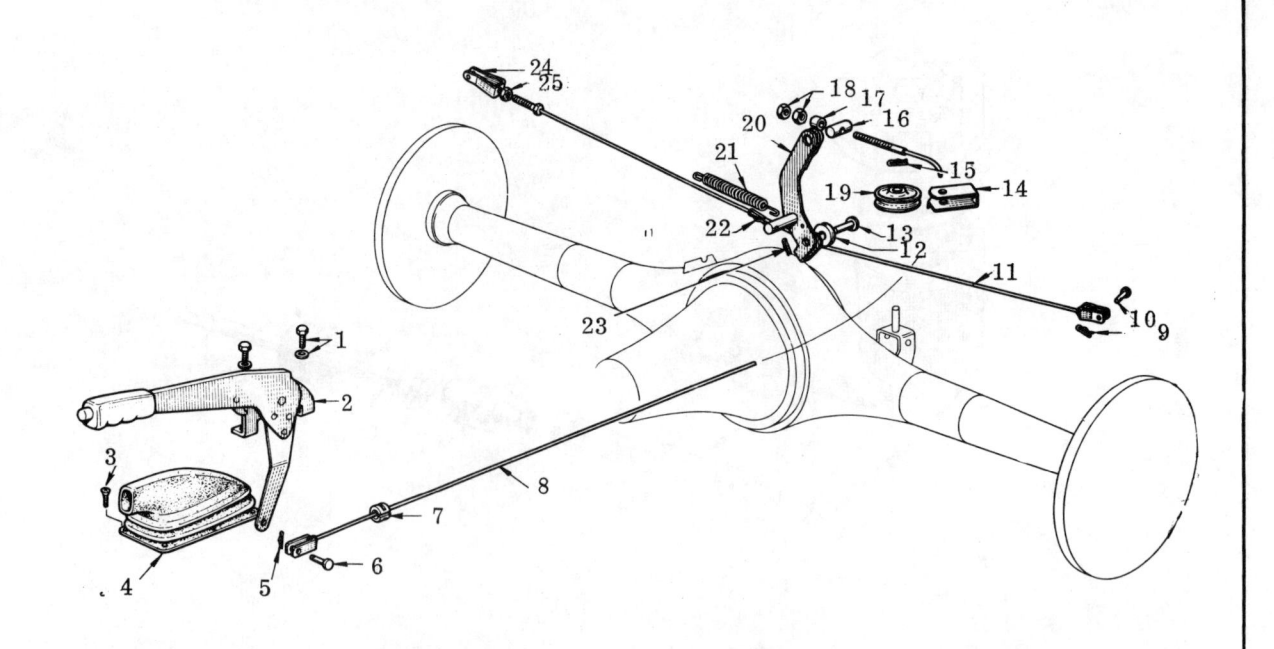

Fig.9.9. EXPLODED VIEW OF THE HANDBRAKE MECHANISM

1. Bolt and washer
2. Handbrake lever
3. Screw
4. Dust cover
5. Retaining pin
6. Clevis pin
7. Cable guide
8. Cable
9. Retaining pin
10. Clevis pin
11. Transverse cable
12. Cable pulley
13. Clevis pin
14. Pulley retainer
15. Retaining pin
16. Pin
17. Spacer
18. Adjusting & locknuts
19. Pulley
20. Compensator
21. Spring
22. Retaining pin
23. Retaining pin
24. Clevis
25. Adjusting nut

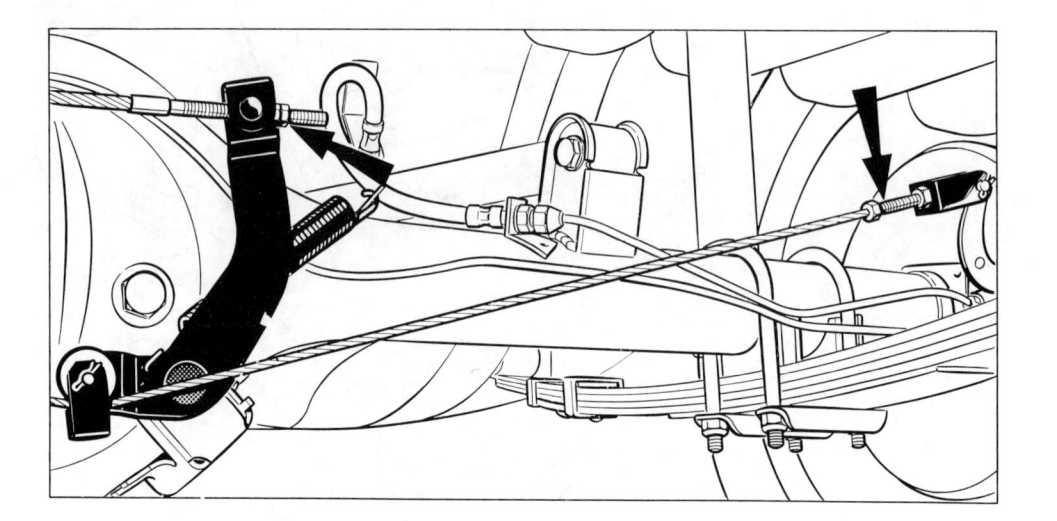

Fig.9.10. The handbrake linkage adjustment points

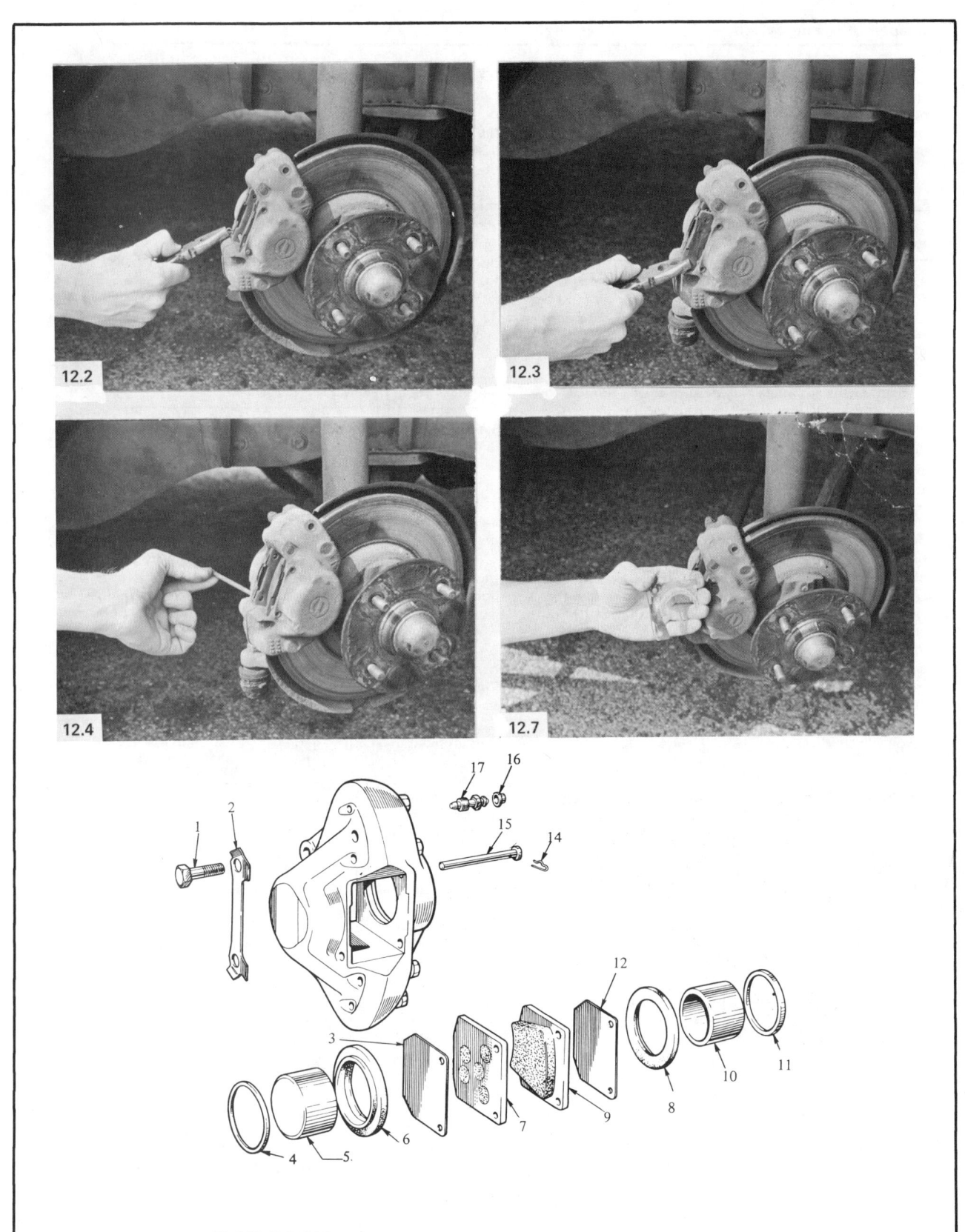

Fig.9.11. EXPLODED VIEW OF THE FRONT BRAKE CALLIPER UNIT – 1300 G.T., 1600 & 1600 G.T.

1. Bolt
2. Tab washer
3. Shim
4. Ring seal
5. Piston
6. Ring seal
7. Brake pad
8. Ring seal
9. Brake pad
10. Piston
11. Ring seal
12. Shim
14. Clip
15. Pin
16. Dust cap
17. Bleed nipple

119

Chapter 9/Braking System

4. Withdraw the pedal pivot pin from the clutch pedal end, then remove the two pedals from the car carefully noting the position of the bushes at either end and the single spacer washer.
5. Replacement is a direct reversal of the removal procedure detailed above.

12. Disc Brake Friction Pads - Inspection, Removal & Replacement

1. Remove the front wheels and inspect the amount of friction material left on the friction pads. The pads must be renewed when the thickness of the material has worn down to 1/16th inch.
2. With a pair of pliers pull out the two small wire clips that hold the main retaining pins in place. (See photo).
3. Remove the main retaining pins which run through the calliper the metal backing of the pads and the shims. (See photo).
4. The friction pads and shims can now be removed from the calliper. If they prove difficult to move by hand a pair of long nosed pliers can be used (see photo).
5. Carefully clean the recesses in the calliper in which the friction pads and shims lie, and the exposed faces of each piston from all traces of dirt and rust.
6. Remove the cap from the hydraulic fluid reservoir and place a large rag underneath the unit. Press the pistons in each half of the calliper, right in - this will cause the fluid level in the reservoir to rise and possibly spill over the brim onto the protective rag.
7. Fit new friction pads and shims ensuring if working on a 1300 calliper that the arrow on the shim is pointing in the direction of forward rotation of the wheel (see photo). On other models the shims can be fitted either way up.
8. Insert the main pad retaining pins and secure them with the small wire clips.

13. Brake Calliper - Removal, Dismantling & Reassembly

1. Jack up the car and remove the road wheel, remove the friction pads and shims as described in the previous section and disconnect the hydraulic fluid pipe at either the back of the calliper or at the bracket on the suspension unit.
2. If it is intended to dismantle the calliper after removal; before disconnecting the hydraulic pipe depress the brake pedal to bring the calliper pistons into contact with the disc. This will make it much easier to remove the pistons when the calliper is removed.
3. Knock back the locking tabs on the calliper mounting bolts (see Fig.9.13), undo the bolts and remove the calliper from the disc.
4. On 1300 models remove the circlips securing the dust covers to the calliper and pull off the dust covers.
5. The pistons can now be removed from their bores. If they prove difficult to move a small amount of air pressure applied at the hydraulic pipe union will effectively push them out of their bores.
6. Withdraw the piston sealing rings from their locations in the cylinder bores.
7. On all other models, which do not have a circlip and dust cover as such on each side of the calliper, partially remove one piston from its bore then remove the sealing bellows from its location in the lower part of the piston skirt. The piston can now be removed.
8. Pull the sealing bellows out of their machined location in the cylinder bore and withdraw the piston sealing ring from the cylinder bore. The operation can now be repeated on the other piston and cylinder.

9. On all models the pistons and piston bores should be carefully cleaned with brake fluid and examined for signs or wear, score marks or damage. All rubber seals should be replaced as a matter of course.
10 Reassembly is a direct reversal of the removal sequence on the various models. On the 1300 GT, 1600 and 1600 GT models great care should be taken when passing the piston through the rubber bellows into the cylinder bore as it is very easy at this stage to damage the bellows.
11 Once the calliper has been reassembled, fit it over the disc and tighten down the securing bolts, using a new locking tab, to a torque of 45 to 50 lb/ft. (6.22 to 6.91 kg.m).
12 Reconnect the hydraulic pipe and bleed the brake system as described in Section 3.

14. Brake Disc - Removal & Replacement

1. The brake disc is not normally removed from the hub unless it is to be replaced with a new disc.
2. Remove the hub and disc assembly complete as described in Chapter 11, Section 4.
3. Separate the hub from the disc by knocking back the locking tabs and undoing the four bolts. Discard the disc, bolts, and locking tabs.
4. Before fitting a new disc to the hub, thoroughly clean the mating surfaces of both components. If this is not done properly and dirt is allowed to get between the hub and the disc this will seriously affect disc brake run-out when it is checked after reassembly.
5. Align the mating marks on the new disc and the hub and fit the two together using new locking tabs and nuts. Tighten the nuts down to a torque of 30 to 34 lb/ft. (4.15 to 4.70 kg.m) and bend up the locking tabs.
6. Replace the disc and hub assembly and check the disc brake run-out as described in Chapter 11, Section 4.

15. Dual Braking System - General Description

1. Certain models of the Capri, in particular those built for the U.S.A. market, are fitted with separate front and rear braking systems. In this way hydraulic failure when it occurs is never complete, only the front or rear brakes going out of action.
2. A tandem master cylinder is used and both the front and rear systems are connected to the opposite sides of a pressure differential warning actuator. Should either the front or the rear brakes fail the pressure drop on one side of the warning actuator causes a shuttle valve to move from its normal mid position so actuating an electrical switch which brings on a warning light on the fascia.
3. It is possible to check the bulb in the warning light by operating a switch on the fascia.

16. Pressure Differential Warning Actuator - Centralisation

1. If the shuttle in the pressure differential actuator has moved, either because air has got into one of the braking circuits or because one of the circuits has failed it will be necessary to centralise the shuttle.
2. This can be done by getting hold of an old screwdriver and cutting it down or grinding it into a tool of the dimensions shown in Fig.9.14.
3. The rubber cover should be removed from the bottom of the pressure differential warning actuator and the tool inserted through the hole where it will engage in a slot in the larger piston thus drawing it into a central position.

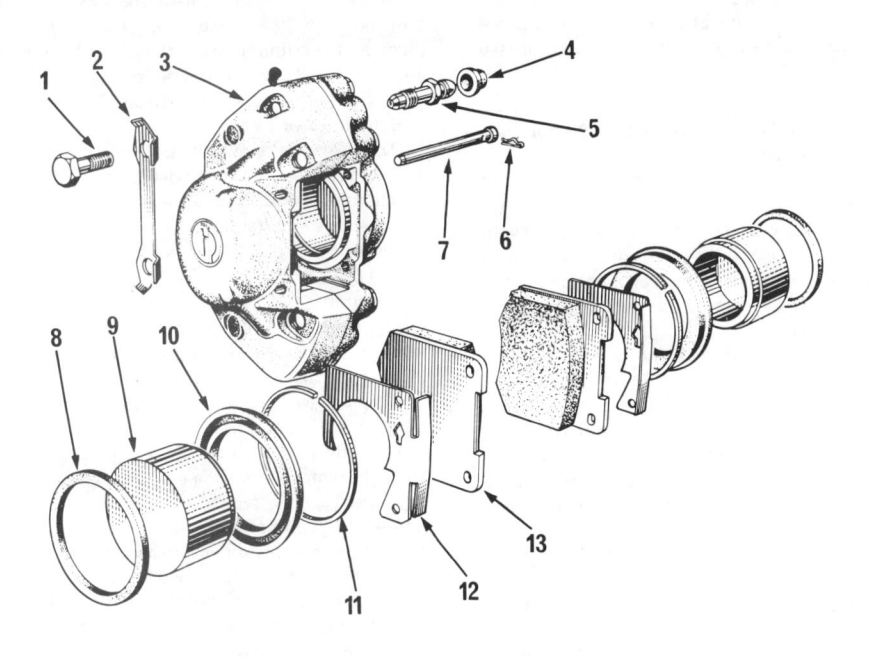

Fig.9.12. EXPLODED VIEW OF THE 1300 FRONT BRAKE CALLIPER UNIT

1. Bolt
2. Locking tab
3. Calliper
4. Dust cap
5. Bleed nipple
6. Clip
7. Pin
8. Seal
9. Piston
10. Seal
11. Circlip
12. Shim
13. Brake pad

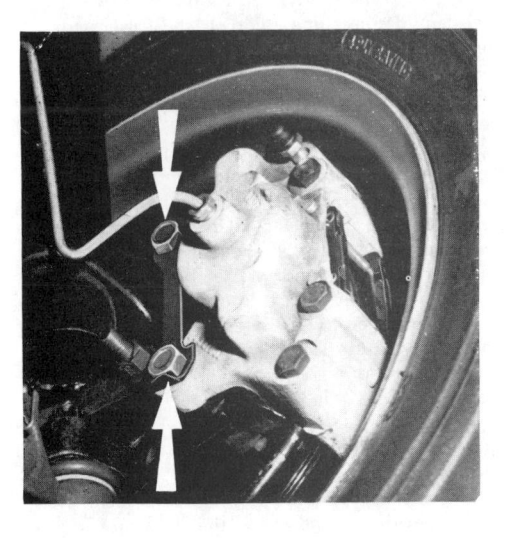

Fig.9.13. View of the brake calliper mounting bolts

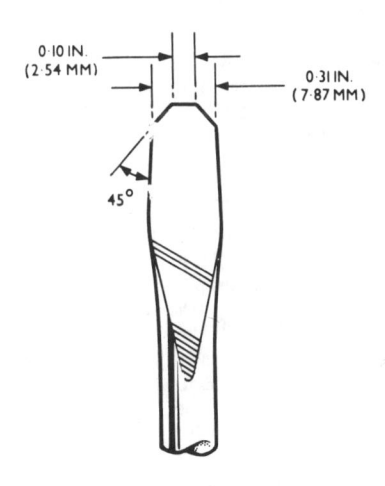

Fig.9.14. Screwdriver special tool dimensions

121

Chapter 9/Braking System

4. During bleeding of the brakes the piston must be held in this position throughout the operation or it will prove very difficult to get the warning light to go out and stay out.

17. Pressure Differential Warning Actuator - Dismantling, Examination & Reassembly

1. Disconnect the five hydraulic pipes at their unions on the pressure differential warning actuator and to prevent too much loss of hydraulic fluid either place a piece of polythene under the cap of the master cylinder and screw it down tightly or plug the ends of the two pipes leading from the master cylinder.
2. Referring to Fig.9.15, disconnect the wiring from the switch assembly (2).
3. Undo the single bolt holding the assembly to the rear of the engine compartment and remove it from the car.
4. To dismantle the assembly start by undoing the end plug (4) and discarding the copper gasket (5). Then undo the adaptor (8) and also discard its copper gasket as they must be replaced.
5. Unscrew the switch assembly (2) from the top of the unit then push the small and large pistons (7) out of their bores taking extreme care not to damage the bores during this operation.
6. Take the small seals (1 & 3) from their pistons making a careful note that the seals are slightly tapered and that the large diameter on each seal is fitted to the slotted end of the pistons. Discard the seals as they must not be reused.
7. Pull the dust cover (6) off the bottom of the unit and also discard this component for the same reasons as above.
8. Carefully examine the pistons (7) and the bore of the actuator for score marks scratches or damage; if any are found the complete unit must be exchanged.
9. To test if the switch assembly (2) is working correctly reconnect the wiring and press the plunger against any part of the bare metal of the engine or the bodywork when the warning light should come on. If it does not come on check the switch by substitution and also check the warning lamp bulb.
10. To reassemble the unit, start by fitting new seals (1 and 3) to the pistons (7) making sure that they are correctly fitted as detailed in paragraph 6 of this section.
11. With the slotted end outwards, gently push the larger piston into the bore until the groove in the other end of the piston is opposite the hole in which the switch assembly (2) is fitted.
12. Screw the switch assembly (2) into position and tighten it down to a torque of 2 to 2.5 lb/ft. (0.28 to 0.34 kg.m). Then gently push the shorter piston, with the slotted end outwards into the other end of the actuator.
13. Fit new copper washers (5) to the adaptor (8) and the end plug (4) and replace them in the assembly tightening them down to a torque of 16 to 20 lb/ft. (2.22 to 2.80 kg.m). Fit a new dust cover (6) over the bottom aperture.
14. Replacement of the pressure differential warning actuator on the car is a direct reversal of the removal sequence. The brakes must be bled after replacement.

18. Tandem Master Cylinder - Dismantling, Examination & Reassembly

1. The tandem master cylinder comprises two piston assemblies, one behind the other operating in a common bore. There are two outlets from the master cylinder, one to the front brakes and one to the rear brakes, both going via the pressure differential warning actuator.
2. To remove the tandem master cylinder, disconnect the pushrod from the brake pedal, detach the two hydraulic pipes at their unions with the side of the master cylinder and undo the two nuts and spring washers holding the master cylinder to the bulkhead. Plug the loose pipes to prevent entry of dirt.
3. To dismantle the unit, pull off the rubber dust cover and remove the circlip and washer under the dust cover which holds the pushrod in place. Remove the pushrod.
4. Take the hydraulic fluid reservoir off the cylinder assembly by undoing the two screws on either side of the cylinder.
5. From the top of the cylinder remove the circlip and spring from the primary recuperating valve and with a suitable hexagon headed key take out the plug which holds this valve in place, then remove the valve assembly.
6. Fit plugs to the two outlet holes and also to the primary recuperating valve aperture, then using a suitable air line blow gently into the other hole on the top of the cylinder. This will remove from the cylinder bore the primary piston and spring, the secondary piston and the secondary recuperating valve assemblies.
7. Remove the piston seal from the primary piston. Lift the tab on the secondary piston spring retainer and remove the piston. Compress the secondary piston spring, move the retainer to one side and remove the secondary recuperating valve stem from the retainer. Then slide the valve spacer and shim from the valve stem, noting the way in which the shim is fitted.
8. Remove the small rubber valve seal and also the secondary piston seal. Examine all the rubber seals for signs of loose fitting or swelling and renew as necessary. Also examine the state of the cylinder bore for signs of scoring or corrosion. If this is damaged in any way a replacement master cylinder must be fitted. It is also advisable to replace all rubber seals as a matter of course whether they are damaged or not.
9. Clean all parts with approved hydraulic fluid prior to reassembly in the cylinder bore.
10. Fit a new seal onto the secondary piston and a new seal to the valve stem. Replace the shim on the valve stem making sure that the convex side faces towards the seal spacer which is fitted next, with its legs towards the valve seal.
11. Refit the secondary piston spring over the valve stem, insert the spring retainer, compress the spring and fit the boss in the valve stem into its location in the spring retainer.
12. Place the narrow end of the secondary piston into the spring retainer and secure it in place by pressing down the tab. Dip the now complete secondary assembly in approved hydraulic fluid and carefully slide it into the cylinder bore with the secondary recuperating valve leading.
13. Place the primary piston spring into the cylinder, fit a new rubber seal to the primary piston, dip it in approved fluid and carefully slide it into the cylinder, drilled end first.
14. Fit the pushrod into the end of the primary piston and retain it with the washer and circlip.
15. Place the primary recuperating valve into its location in the top of the cylinder and check that it is properly located by moving the pushrod up and down a small amount. Screw the retaining plug into position and refit the spring and circlip to the valve plunger.
16. Move the pushrod in and out of the cylinder and check that the recuperating valve opens when the rod is fully withdrawn and closes again when it is pushed in.
17. Check the condition of the front and rear reservoir gaskets and if there is any doubt as to their condition they must be replaced. Refit the reservoir to the cylinder

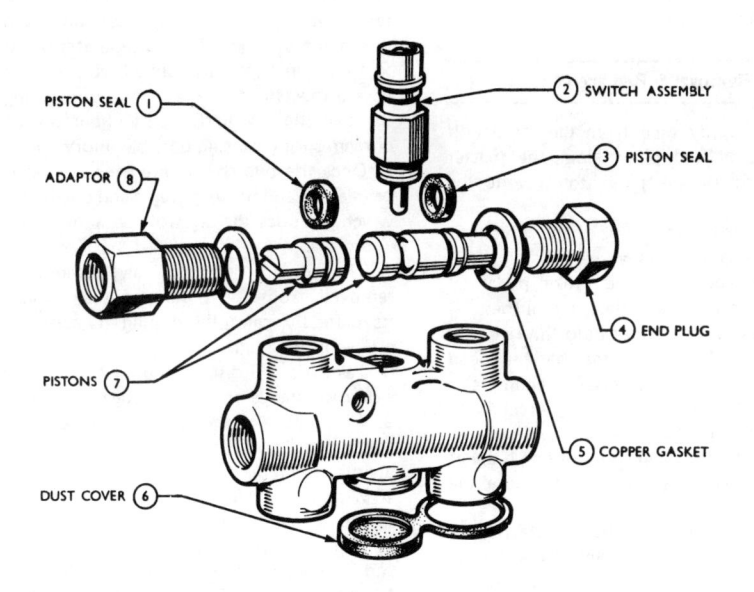

Fig.9.15. Exploded view of the valve and switch unit assembly

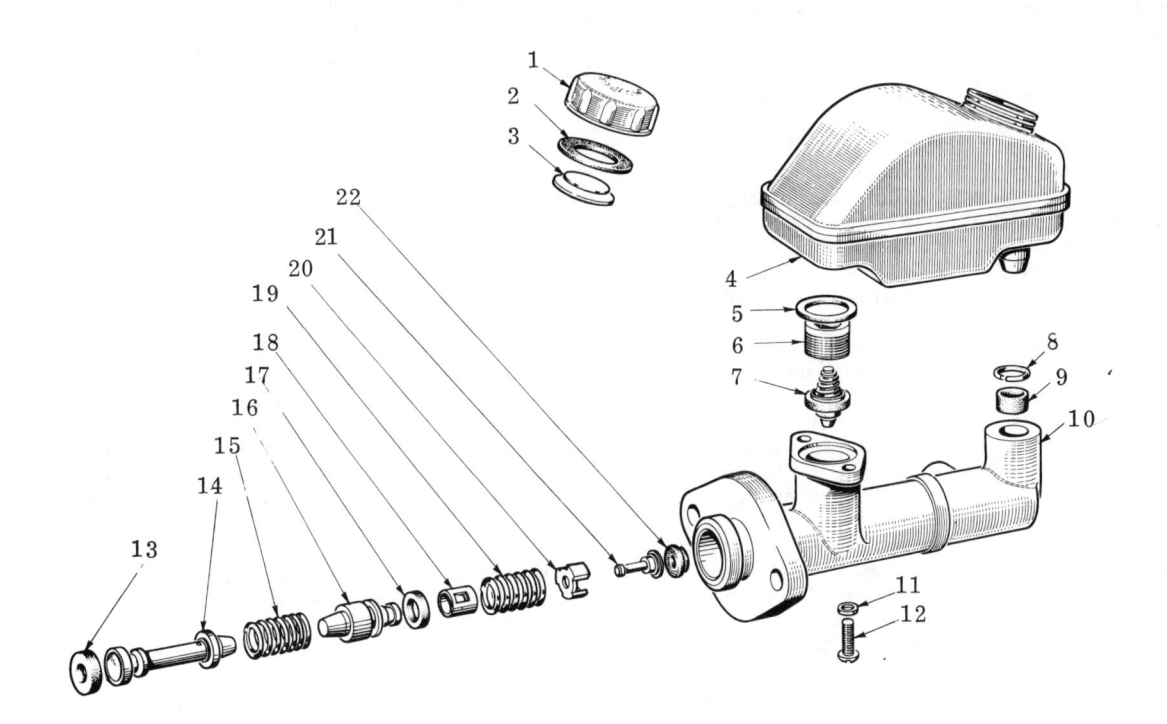

Fig.9.16. EXPLODED VIEW OF THE DUAL LINE BRAKE MASTER CYLINDER

1. Reservoir cap
2. Cap seal
3. Seal retainer
4. Reservoir
5. Sealing ring
6. Tipping valve retainer
7. Tipping valve
8. Circlip
9. Gasket
10. Master cylinder body
11. Washer
12. Screw
13. Seal
14. Primary piston
15. Spring
16. Secondary piston
17. Seal
18. Spring retainer
19. Spring
20. Spring retainer
21. Valve
22. Seal

123

Chapter 9/Braking System

with its two retaining screws.
18 Refitting the master cylinder to the car is a reversal of the removal instructions. When replacement is complete bleed the brakes and road test the car.

19. Vacuum Servo Unit - Removal & Replacement

1. Remove the vacuum supply pipe from the servo unit and then undo the brake fluid pipes from the master cylinder. Block the ends of the pipes to prevent the entry of dirt.
2. Take the master cylinder off the front of the servo unit by undoing the two retaining nuts and washers.
3. Detach the servo pushrod from the brake pedal by removing the spring clip, clevis pin and clevis pin bushes.
4. Undo the four nuts and washers that hold the rear end of the servo unit mounting bracket to the rear bulkhead and lift away the mounting bracket and servo unit complete.
5. Remove the servo unit from its mounting bracket by undoing the four retaining nuts and washers.
6. Replacement of the servo unit and its mounting bracket is a direct reversal of the above procedure, but note the following points:
7. When fitted correctly the pushrod that is attached to the brake pedal must have the yellow paint mark on the clevis yoke facing towards the centre of the car.
8. As shown in Fig.9.18, measure the distance between the centre of the brake pushrod hole and the face of the servo mounting bracket. This dimension should be between 6.16 to 6.28 inch (156.5 to 159.5 mm). If found to be incorrect the length of the pushrod can be adjusted at the clevis yoke 'A'.
9. After replacement, bleed the hydraulic system as described in Section 3.

20. Vacuum Servo Unit - Dismantling, Examination & Reassembly

1. Before starting to dismantle the servo unit it will be necessary to make up two pieces of angle iron or similar metal flat rod about three feet long each with holes drilled in them to fit over the four studs on the pushrod side of the servo unit. You will also require another piece of angle iron about one foot long with holes drilled to coincide with the master cylinder attachment bolts.
2. Scribe marks on both halves of the servo unit so that the shells can be refitted in exactly the same position on reassembly.
3. Fit the three pieces of angle iron to the servo unit as shown in Fig.9.19 and clamp the one foot long piece in a vice so that the servo non-return valve is accessible and pointing downwards. Ensure that the nuts on the angle irons are tight.
4. As it is not possible to separate the two shells with the spring pressure still on the diaphragm it is necessary to create a vacuum behind the diaphragm. This is done by connecting a suitable length of hose to the servo non-return valve and the engine manifold and starting up the engine.
5. It will probably be necessary to get two assistants to help with the next operation, one to steady the servo unit in the vice and one on the end of one of the longer angle irons. Using the top angle irons as leverage turn the servo top shell in an anti-clockwise direction until a mark on the top shell aligns with a cut-away on the bottom shell. At this point the shells should separate, but if they fail to do so they can be gently tapped with a soft headed hammer. It is important to keep the vacuum going all the time or the two shells will fly apart under the action of the diaphragm spring causing possible injury and damage.
6. Once the two shells have been separated the vacuum can be released and the diaphragm and diaphragm plate assembly, which includes the control rod and valve assembly, can be withdrawn.
7. The control rod and valve assembly should now be removed from the plate and the diaphragm taken from its plate by carefully pulling its centre from its locating groove in the plate.
8. Take off and discard the air filter which is found in the extension flange on the rear edge of the diaphragm plate.
9. Withdraw the seal from the larger front shell and also the internal pushrod and remove the slotted disc from the diaphragm plate.
10 With a screwdriver, prise off the seal retainer from the smaller rear shell and take out the seal.
11 With a suitable spanner, unscrew the non-return valve and its seal from the larger front shell.
12 Carefully examine and clean all parts of the servo before reassembly, and as a matter of course replace all rubber parts including the diaphragm. The control and valve assembly are replaced as a unit and should not be broken down.
13 Commence reassembly by fitting a new seal to the non-return valve and replacing the valve in the front shell.
14 Place a new seal into its recess in the rear shell and fit the seal retainer which can be forced into place with a socket just smaller than the retainer.
15 Fit a new air filter to the rear of the diaphragm plate then insert the control rod and valve assembly into the centre of the diaphragm plate and apply a suitable lubricant such as Part No.EM-1C-14 to the bearing surfaces of the control rod and valve assembly. Secure the complete assembly in the plate with the stop key, (see photo).
16 Assemble the new diaphragm to its plate making sure that its centre is correctly located in the groove on the plate. It is advisable to lightly grease the areas of the diaphragm that contact the shells with a grease such as Ford Part No.EM-1C-15. This will help during reassembly and also during later dismantling operations. This grease must not be allowed to come into contact with any of the hydraulic brake system seals or damage will result.
17 Refit the lengths of angle iron as in paragraph 3 and replace the unit in the vice. Reconnect the vacuum pipe, check that the two shells are correctly lined up and start the engine.
18 With the help of the vacuum created and by applying further pressure to the rear shell completely engage the two shells together and with the aid of the angle irons turn the rear shell in a clockwise direction until the scribe marks made prior to dismantling are in line.
19 With the vacuum still being applied, check how far the pushrod extends beyond the front shell. This must be from 0.011 to 0.016 inch (0.28 to 0.40 mm.).

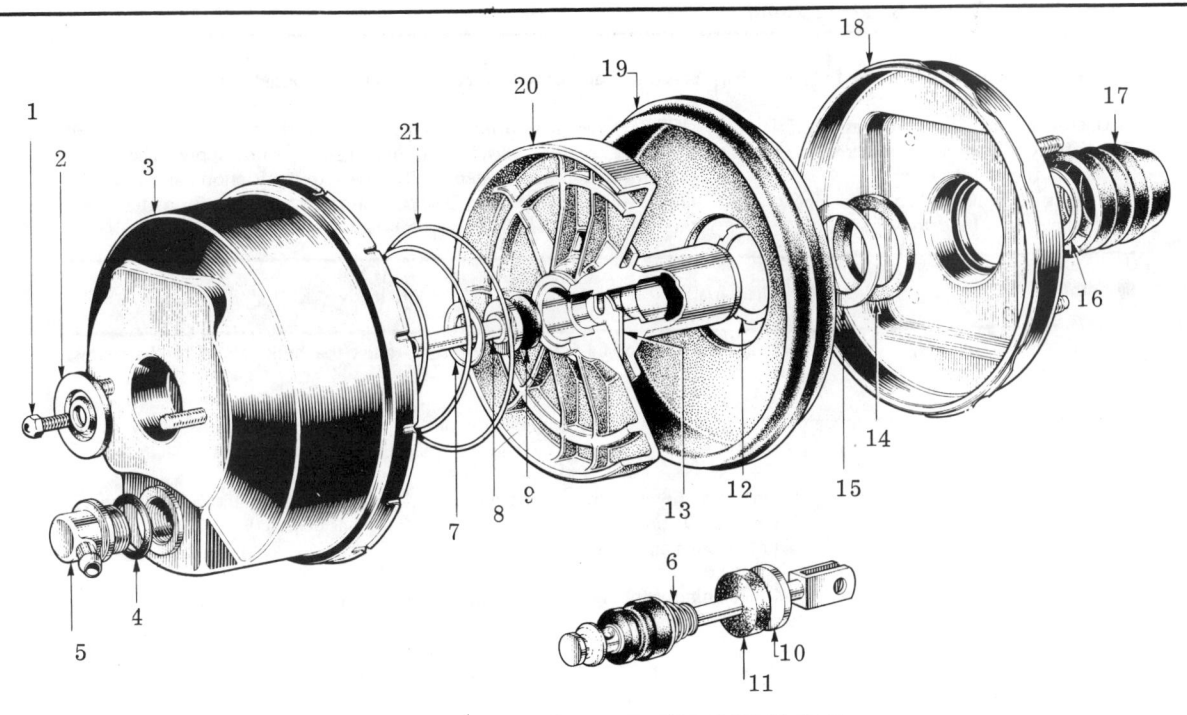

Fig.9.17. EXPLODED VIEW OF THE SERVO UNIT

1. Bolt
2. Seat assembly
3. Front shell
4. Seal
5. Valve assembly
6. Pushrod assembly
7. Dished washer
8. Brake servo pushrod
9. Re-action disc
10. Washer
11. Filter
12. Castellated washer
13. Stop key
14. Seal
15. Piston guide
16. Filter retainer
17. Dust cover
18. Rear shell
19. Diaphragm
20. Diaphragm plate
21. Spring

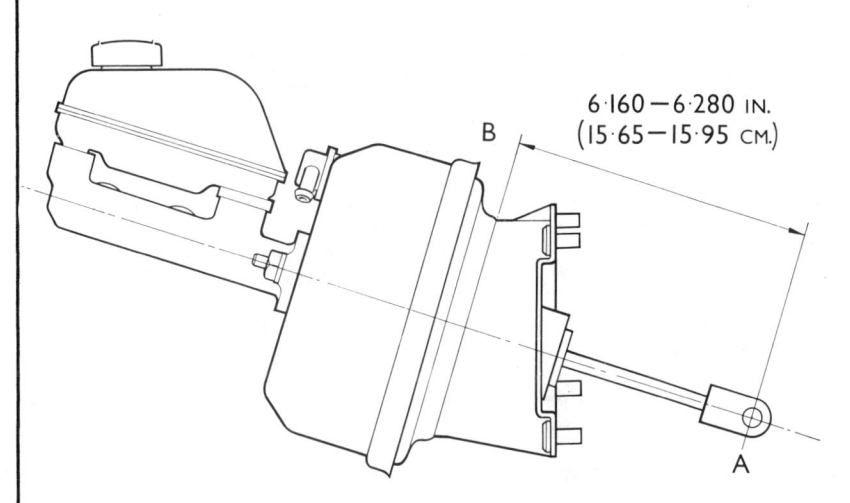

6·160 — 6·280 IN.
(15·65 — 15·95 CM.)

Fig.9.18. Correct fitted dimensions of servo unit. Adjust pushrod at 'A' to give dimension as shown at 'B'

Fig.9.19. Method of separating the front and rear shells of the servo unit

125

Fault Finding Chart — Braking System

Before diagnosing faults from the following chart, check that any braking irregularities are not caused by:—

1. Uneven and incorrect tyre pressures.
2. Incorrect 'mix' of radial and cross-ply tyres.
3. Wear in the steering mechanism.
4. Defects in the suspension and dampers.
5. Misalignment of the body frame.

NOTE: For vehicles fitted with disc brakes at the front the references in the chart to front wheel shoe adjustments do not apply. The causes referring to hydraulic system faults or wear to the friction material of the linings still apply however. Disc pads also come in different material and references to variations are also relevant.

Symptoms	Reason/s	Remedy
Pedal travels a long way before the brakes operate.	Brake shoes set too far from the drums.	Adjust the brake shoes to the drums.
Stopping ability poor, even though pedal pressure is firm.	Linings and/or drums badly worn or scored.	Dismantle, inspect and renew as required.
	One or more wheel hydraulic cylinders seized, resulting in some brake shoes not pressing against the drums (or pads against discs).	Dismantle and inspect wheel cylinders. Renew as necessary.
	Brake linings contaminated with oil.	Renew linings and repair source of oil contamination.
	Wrong type of linings fitted (too hard)	Verify type of material which is correct for the car and fit it.
	Brake shoes wrongly assembled.	Check for correct assembly.
	Servo unit not functioning (disc brakes)	Check and repair as necessary.
Car veers to one side when the brakes are applied.	Brake pads or linings on one side are contaminated with oil.	Renew pads or linings and stop oil leak.
	Hydraulic wheel cylinder(s) on one side partially or fully seized.	Inspect wheel cylinders for correct operation and renew as necessary.
	A mixture of lining materials fitted between sides.	Standardize on types of linings fitted.
	Unequal wear between sides caused by partially seized wheel cylinders.	Check wheel cylinders and renew linings and drums as required.
Pedal feels spongy when the brakes are applied.	Air is present in the hydraulic system.	Bleed the hydraulic system and check for any signs of leakage.
Pedal feels springy when the brakes are applied.	Brake linings not bedded into the drums (after fitting new ones).	Allow time for new linings to bed in after which it will certainly be necessary to adjust the shoes to the drums as pedal travel will have increased.
	Master cylinder or brake backplate mounting bolts loose.	Re-tighten mounting bolts.
	Severe wear in brake drums causing distortion when brakes are applied.	Renew drums and linings.
Pedal travels right down with little or no resistance and brakes are virtually non-operative.	Leak in hydraulic system resulting in lack of pressure for operating wheel cylinders.	Examine the whole of the hydraulic system and locate and repair source of leaks. Test after repairing each and every leak source.
	If no signs of leakage are apparent the master cylinder internal seals are failing to sustain pressure.	Overhaul master cylinder. If indications are that seals have failed for reasons other than wear all the wheel cylinder seals should be checked also and the system completely replenished with the correct fluid.
Binding, juddering overheating.	One or a combination of causes given in the foregoing sections.	Complete and systematic inspection of the whole braking system.

Notes

Chapter 10/Electrical System

Contents

General Description ...	1
Battery - Removal & Replacement.. ...	2
Battery - Maintenance & Inspection ...	3
Electrolyte Replenishment... ...	4
Battery Charging ...	5
Dynamo - Routine Maintenance ...	6
Dynamo - Testing in Position ...	7
Dynamo - Removal & Replacement ...	8
Dynamo - Dismantling & Inspection ...	9
Dynamo - Repair & Reassembly ...	10
Alternator - General Description ...	11
Alternator - Routine Maintenance	12
Alternators - Special Procedures ...	13
Alternator - Removal & Replacement.. ...	14
Alternator - Dismantling & Inspection (brushes only)...	15
Inertia Type Starter Motor - General Description ...	16
Starter Motor - Testing on Engine... ...	17
Starter Motor - Removal & Replacement.. ...	18
Starter Motor - Dismantling & Reassembly ...	19
Starter Motor Drive - General Description ...	20
Starter Motor Drive - Removal & Replacement... ...	21
Pre-Engaged Starter Motors - General Description ...	22
Pre-Engaged Starter Motors - Removal & Replacement	23
Endface Commutator Starter Motor - Dismantling & Reassembly ...	24
Control Box - General Description.. ...	25
Cut-Out & Regulator Contacts - Maintenance ...	26
Voltage Regulator Adjustment.. ...	27
Current Regulator Adjustment.. ...	28
Cut-Out Adjustment ...	29
Fuse Block - Removal & Replacement ...	30
Flasher Circuit - Fault Tracing & Rectification... ...	31
Windscreen Wiper Mechanism — Maintenance ...	32
Windscreen Wiper Blades - Removal & Replacement ...	33
Windscreen Wiper Arms - Removal & Replacement ...	34
Windscreen Wiper Mechanism - Fault Diagnosis & Rectification... ...	35
Windscreen Wiper Motor & Linkage - Removal & Replacement...	36
Windscreen Wiper Motor - Dismantling, Inspection & Reassembly ...	37
Horn - Fault Tracing & Rectification... ...	38
Headlamp & Sidelamp Unit - Removal & Replacement	39
Headlamp Alignment ...	40
Front Indicator Lamp Glass & Bulb - Removal & Replacement...	41
Rear Indicator, Stop & Tail Bulb - Removal & Replacement ...	42
Rear Licence Plate Lamp - Removal & Replacement ...	43
Interior Light - Removal & Replacement. ...	44
Instrument panel & instruments-removal & replacement	45
Instrument Voltage Regulator-Removal & Replacement	46
Direction Indicator, Headlamp Flasher & Horn Switch Assembly - Removal & Replacement... ...	47
Light, Panel Light & Windscreen Wiper Switches - Removal & Replacement ...	48

Specifications

Battery
Type ...	Lead Acid 12 volt
Earthed terminal ...	Negative '—'
Capacity at 20 hr rate ...	3
Standard ...	38 amp/hr
Cold climate ...	57 amp/hr
Plates per cell - standard ...	9
- cold climate ...	13
Specific gravity charged... ...	1.275 to 1.290
Electrolyte capacity - standard.. ...	4.5 pints (5.4 US pints, 2.5 litres)
- cold climate.. ...	6.4 pints (7.7 US pints, 3.6 litres)

Dynamo ... Lucas C40 (C40/L cold start models)
Maximum charge ...	22 amps (25 amp with C40/L)
Number of brushes ...	2
Brush length new ...	.718 inch (18.23 mm)
Brush spring tension ...	18 to 24 ozs.
Field resistance ...	6.0 ohms.

Alternator (Optional)
Type ...	Lucas 15 ACR
Speed (ratio to engine) ...	1.88 to 1
Maximum charge ...	28 amps

Chapter 10/Electrical System

Starter Motor Inertia Type
- Number of brushes ... 4
- Minimum brush length ... 4 in. (10.3 mm)
- Brush spring tension ... 34 ozs. (.96 kg.)
- Gear ratio ... 11 to 1
- Teeth on pinion ... 10
- Teeth on ring gear ... 110

NOTE: A pre-engaged type of starter motor is fitted as standard on cars with 'cold start' equipment and can be fitted as an optional extra on other models

Starter Motor Pre-engaged Type
- Number of brushes ... 4
- Minimum brush length ... .375 in. (9.52 mm)
- Brush spring tension ... 28 ozs. (.805 kg.)
- Gear ratio ... 12 to 1
- Teeth on pinion ... 11
- Teeth on ring gear ... 132

Regulator/Control Box
- Type ... Lucas RB 340 or Autolite
- Cut-in voltage ... 12.6 to 13.4 volts
- Drop off voltage ... 9.25 to 11.25 volts

	Lucas	Autolite
Armature to core air gap	.035 to .045 in. (.9 to 1.1 mm)	.025 to .037 in. (.64 to .94 mm)
Current regulator, on load setting	Max. generator output ∓ 1½ amps.	
Armature to core air gap	.045 to .049 in. (1.14 to 1.24 mm)	.014 to .019 in. (.36 to .48 mm)
Voltage regulator, open circuit setting	14.4 to 15.6 volts at 20°C (68°F)	
Armature to core air gap..	.045 to .049 in. (1.14 to 1.24 mm)	.024 to .028 in. (.61 to .71 mm)
Reverse current	3.0 to 5.0 amps	

- Voltage setting at 2,000 r.p.m ...
  - 10°C (50°F) 14.9 to 15.5 volts
  - 20°C (68°F) 14.7 to 15.3 volts
  - 30°C (86°F) 14.5 to 15.1 volts
  - 40°C (104°F) 14.3 to 14.9 volts

Fuse Unit
- Number of fuses ... 6
- Number of spare fuses in box ... 1

Bulbs
- Headlamps ... 60/45 watt, sealed beam
- Sidelamps ... 5 watt wedge base
- Indicator lamps ... 28 watt
- Flasher unit ... 56 watt
- Tail and stop light ... 7/28 watt
- Licence illumination light ... 5 watt wedge base
- Interior light ... 6 watt festoon
- Warning lights ... 2.2 watt wedge base
- Panel lights ... 2.2 watt wedge base

Torque Wrench Settings
- Starter motor retaining bolts ... 20 to 25 lb/ft. (2.76 to 3.46 kg.m)
- Dynamo pulley ... 14 to 17 lb/ft. (1.93 to 2.35 kg.m)
- Dynamo mounting bolts.. ... 15 to 18 lb/ft. (2.07 to 2.49 kg.m)
- Dynamo mounting bracket ... 20 to 25 lb/ft. (2.76 to 3.46 kg.m)

1. General Description

The electrical system is of the 12 volt type and the major components comprise: a 12 volt battery with the negative terminal earthed; a voltage regulator and cut-out; a Lucas dynamo or alternator both of which are fitted to the left-hand side of the engine and driven by the fan belt from the crankshaft pulley wheel. The 15ACR alternator has its own integral regulator unit but if a dynamo is fitted a three bobbin control box of either Lucas or Autolite manufacture is used. The starter motor which may be either of the inertia or pre-engaged type is mounted to the clutch bellhousing on the left-hand side of the engine.

The 12 volt battery gives a steady supply of current for the ignition, lighting and other electrical circuits, and provides a reserve of electricity when the current consumed by the electrical equipment exceeds that being produced by the dynamo or alternator.

The dynamo is of the two brush type and works in conjunction with the voltage regulator and cut-out. The dynamo is cooled by a multi-bladed fan mounted behind the dynamo pulley, and blows air through cooling holes in the dynamo end brackets. The output from the dynamo is controlled by the voltage regulator which ensures a high output if the battery is in a low state of charge or the

Chapter 10/Electrical System

demands from the electrical equipment high, and a low output if the battery is fully charged and there is little demand from the electrical equipment.

2. Battery - Removal & Replacement

1. The battery is positioned on a tray in the front of the engine compartment forward of the nearside suspension.
2. Disconnect the earthed negative lead and then the positive lead by slackening the retaining nuts and bolts or, by unscrewing the retaining screws if these are fitted.
3. Remove the battery clamp and carefully lift the battery off its tray. Hold the battery vertical to ensure that no electrolyte is spilled.
4. Replacement is a direct reversal of this procedure. NOTE: Replace the positive lead and the earth (negative) lead, smearing the terminals with petroleum jelly (vaseline) to prevent corrosion. NEVER use an ordinary grease as applied to other parts of the car.

3. Battery - Maintenance & Inspection

1. Normal weekly battery maintenance consists of checking the electrolyte level of each cell to ensure that the separators are covered by ¼ inch of electrolyte. If the level has fallen top up the battery using distilled water only. Do not overfill. If a battery is overfilled or any electrolyte spilled, immediately wipe away the excess as electrolyte attacks and corrodes any metal it comes into contact with very rapidly.
2. As well as keeping the terminals clean and covered with petroleum jelly, the top of the battery, and especially the top of the cells, should be kept clean and dry. This helps prevent corrosion and ensures that the battery does not become partially discharged by leakage through dampness and dirt.
3. Once every three months remove the battery and inspect the battery securing bolts, the battery clamp plate, tray, and battery leads for corrosion (white fluffy deposits on the metal which are brittle to touch). If any corrosion is found, clean off the deposits with ammonia and paint over the clean metal with an anti-rust/anti-acid paint.
4. At the same time inspect the battery case for cracks. If a crack is found, clean and plug it with one of the proprietary compounds marketed by firms such as Holts for this purpose. If leakage through the crack has been excessive then it will be necessary to refill the appropriate cell with fresh electrolyte as detailed later. Cracks are frequently caused to the top of the battery cases by pouring in distilled water in the middle of winter AFTER instead of BEFORE a run. This gives the water no chance to mix with the electrolyte and so the former freezes and splits the battery case.
5. If topping up the batteries becomes excessive and the cases have been inspected for cracks that could cause leakage, but none are found, the batteries are being overcharged and the voltage regulator will have to be checked and reset.
6. With the batteries on the bench at the three monthly interval check, measure their specific gravity with a hydrometer to determine the state of charge and condition of the electrolyte. There should be very little variation between the different cells and if a variation in excess of 0.025 is present it will be due to either:-
a) Loss of electrolyte from the battery at sometime caused by spillage or a leak resulting in a drop in the specific gravity of the electrolyte, when the deficiency was replaced with distilled water instead of fresh electrolyte.

b) An internal short circuit caused by buckling of the plates or a similar malady pointing to the likelihood of total battery failure in the near future.
7. The specific gravity of the electrolyte for fully charged conditions at the electrolyte temperature indicated, is listed in Table A. The specific gravity of a fully discharged battery at different temperatures of the electrolyte is given at Table B.

TABLE A
Specific Gravity - Battery Fully Charged
1.268 at 100°F or 38°C electrolyte temperature
1.272 at 90°F or 32°C electrolyte temperature
1.276 at 80°F or 27°C electrolyte temperature
1.280 at 70°F or 21°C electrolyte temperature
1.284 at 60°F or 16°C electrolyte temperature
1.288 at 50°F or 10°C electrolyte temperature
1.292 at 40°F or 4°C electrolyte temperature
1.296 at 30°F or -1.5°C electrolyte temperature

TABLE B
Specific Gravity - Battery Fully Discharged
1.098 at 100°F or 38°C electrolyte temperature
1.102 at 90°F or 32°C electrolyte temperature
1.106 at 80°F or 27°C electrolyte temperature
1.110 at 70°F or 21°C electrolyte temperature
1.114 at 60°F or 16°C electrolyte temperature
1.118 at 50°F or 10°C electrolyte temperature
1.122 at 40°F or 4°C electrolyte temperature
1.126 at 30°F or -1.5°C electrolyte temperature

4. Electrolyte Replenishment

1. If the battery is in a fully charged state and one of the cells maintains a specific gravity reading which is 0.025 or more lower than the others, and a check of each cell has been made with a voltage meter to check for short circuits (a four to seven second test should give a steady reading of between 1.2 to 1.8 volts), then it is likely that electrolyte has been lost from the cell with the low reading at sometime.
2. Top up the cell with a solution of 1 part sulphuric acid to 2.5 parts of water. If the cell is already fully topped up draw some electrolyte out of it with a pipette. The total capacity of each cell is ¾ pint.
3. When mixing the sulphuric acid and water NEVER ADD WATER TO SULPHURIC ACID - always pour the acid slowly onto the water in a glass container. IF WATER IS ADDED TO SULPHURIC ACID IT WILL EXPLODE.
4. Continue to top up the cell with the freshly made electrolyte and then recharge the battery and check the hydrometer readings.

5. Battery Charging

1. In winter time when heavy demand is placed upon the battery, such as when starting from cold, and much electrical equipment is continually in use, it is a good idea to occasionally have the battery fully charged from an external source at the rate of 3.5 to 4 amps.
2. Continue to charge the battery at this rate until no further rise in specific gravity is noted over a four hour period.
3. Alternatively, a trickle charger charging at the rate of 1.5 amps can be safely used overnight.
4 Specially rapid 'boost' charges which are claimed to restore the power of the battery in 1 to 2 hours are most dangerous as they can cause serious damage to the battery

Chapter 10/Electrical System

plates through over-heating.
5. While charging the battery, note that the temperature of the electrolyte should never exceed 100°F.

6. Dynamo - Routine Maintenance

1. Routine maintenance consists of checking the tension of the fan belt, and lubricating the dynamo rear bearing once every 6,000 miles.
2. The fan belt should be tight enough to ensure no slip between the belt and the dynamo pulley. If a shrieking noise comes from the engine when the unit is accelerated rapidly, it is likely that it is the fan belt slipping. On the other hand, the belt must not be too taut or the bearings will wear rapidly and cause dynamo failure or bearing seizure. Ideally ½ inch of total free movement should be available at the fan belt midway between the fan and the dynamo pulley.
3. To adjust the fan belt tension slightly slacken the three dynamo retaining bolts, and swing the dynamo on the upper two bolts outwards to increase the tension, and inwards to lower it.
4. It is best to leave the bolts fairly tight so that considerable effort has to be used to move the dynamo; otherwise it is difficult to get the correct setting. If the dynamo is being moved outwards to increase the tension and the bolts have only been slackened a little, a long spanner acting as a lever placed behind the dynamo with the lower end resting against the block works very well in moving the dynamo outwards. Retighten the dynamo bolts and check that the dynamo pulley is correctly aligned with the fan belt.
5. Lubrication on the dynamo consists of inserting three drops of S.A.E.30 engine oil in the small oil hole in the centre of the commutator end bracket. This lubricates the rear bearing. The front bearing is pre-packed with grease and requires no attention.

7. Dynamo - Testing in Position

1. If, with the engine running, no charge comes from the dynamo, or the charge is very low, first check that the fan belt is in place and is not slipping. Then check that the leads from the control box to the dynamo are firmly attached and that one has not come loose from its terminal.
2. The lead from the 'D' terminal on the dynamo should be connected to the 'D' terminal on the control box, and similarly the 'F' terminals on the dynamo and control box should also be connected together. Check that this is so and that the leads have not been incorrectly fitted.
3. Make sure none of the electrical equipment (such as the lights or radio) is on and then pull the leads off the dynamo terminals marked 'D' and 'F', join the terminals together with a short length of wire.
4. Attach to the centre of this length of wire the positive clip of a 0-20 volts voltmeter and run the other clip to earth on the dynamo yoke. Start the engine and allow it to idle at approximately 750 r.p.m. At this speed the dynamo should give a reading of about 15 volts on the voltmeter. There is no point in raising the engine speed above a fast idle as the reading will then be inaccurate.
5. If no reading is recorded then check the brushes and brush connections. If a very low reading of approximately 1 volt is observed then the field winding may be suspect.
6. If a reading of between 4 to 6 volts is recorded it is likely that the armature winding is at fault.
7. With the Lucas C40-1 windowless yoke dynamo it must be removed and dismantled before the brushes and commutator can be attended to.

8. If the voltmeter shows a good reading, then with the temporary link still in position, connect both leads from the control box to 'D' and 'F' on the dynamo ('D' to 'D' and 'F' to 'F'). Release the lead from the 'D' terminal at the control box and clip one lead from the voltmeter to the end of the cable, and the other lead to a good earth. With the engine running at the same speed as previously, an identical voltage to that recorded at the dynamo should be noted on the voltmeter. If no voltage is recorded then there is a break in the wire. If the voltage is the same as recorded at the dynamo then check the 'F' lead in similar fashion. If both readings are the same as at the dynamo then it will be necessary to test the control box.

8. Dynamo - Removal & Replacement

1. Slacken the two dynamo retaining bolts, and the nut on the sliding link, and move the dynamo in towards the engine so that the fan belt can be removed.
2. Disconnect the two leads from the dynamo terminals.
3. Remove the nut from the sliding link bolt, and remove the two upper bolts. The dynamo is then free to be lifted away from the engine.
4. Replacement is a reversal of the above procedure. Do not finally tighten the retaining bolts and the nut on the sliding link until the fan belt has been tensioned correctly. See 10/6.2 for details.

9. Dynamo - Dismantling & Inspection

1. Mount the dymamo in a vice and unscrew and remove the two through bolts from the commutator end bracket. (See photo).
2. Mark the commutator end bracket and the dynamo casing so the end bracket can be replaced in its original position. Pull the end bracket off the armature shaft. NOTE: Some versions of the dynamo may have a raised pip on the end bracket which locates in a recess on the edge of the casing. If so, marking the end bracket and casing is not necessary. A pip may also be found on the drive end bracket at the opposite end of the casing. (See photo).
3. Lift the two brush springs and draw the brushes out of the brush holders (arrowed in photo).
4. Measure the brushes and, if worn down to 9/32 inch or less, unscrew the screws holding the brush leads to the end bracket. Take off the brushes complete with leads. Old and new brushes are compared in the photo.
5. If no locating pip can be found, mark the drive end bracket and the dynamo casing so the drive end bracket can be replaced in its original position. Then pull the drive end bracket complete with armature out of the casing (see photo)
6. Check the condition of the ball bearing in the drive end plate by firmly holding the plate and noting if there is visible side movement of the armature shaft in relation to the end plate. If play is present the armature assembly must be separated from the end plate. If the bearing is sound there is no need to carry out the work described in the following two paragraphs.
7. Hold the armature in one hand (mount it carefully in a vice if preferred) and undo the nut holding the pulley wheel and fan in place. Pull off the pulley wheel and fan.
8. Next remove the woodruff key (arrowed) from its slot in the armature shaft and also the bearing locating ring.
9. Place the drive end bracket across the open jaws of a vice with the armature downwards and gently tap the armature shaft from the bearing (see photo) in the end plate with the aid of a suitable drift.

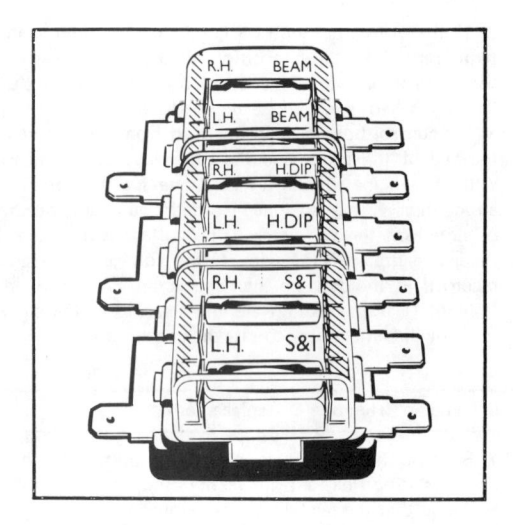

Fig.10.1. View of the fuse block

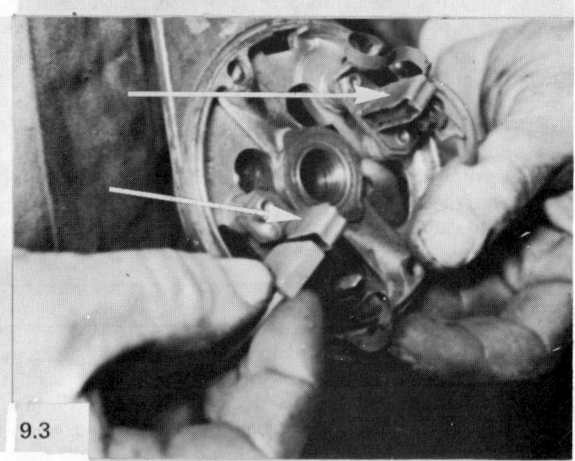

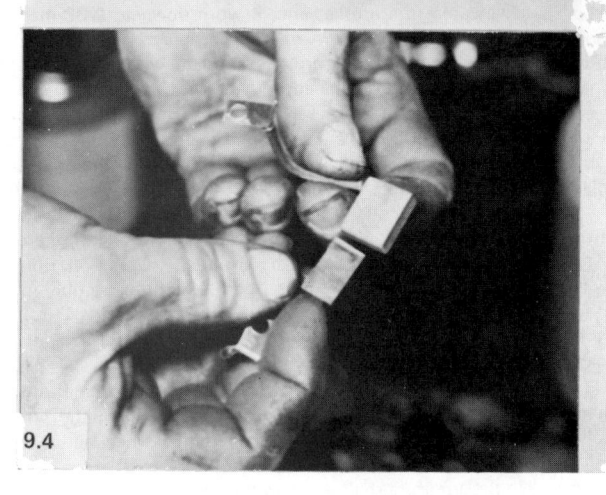

9.1

9.2

9.3

9.4

9.5

132

Fig.10.2. EXPLODED VIEW OF THE LUCAS DYNAMO

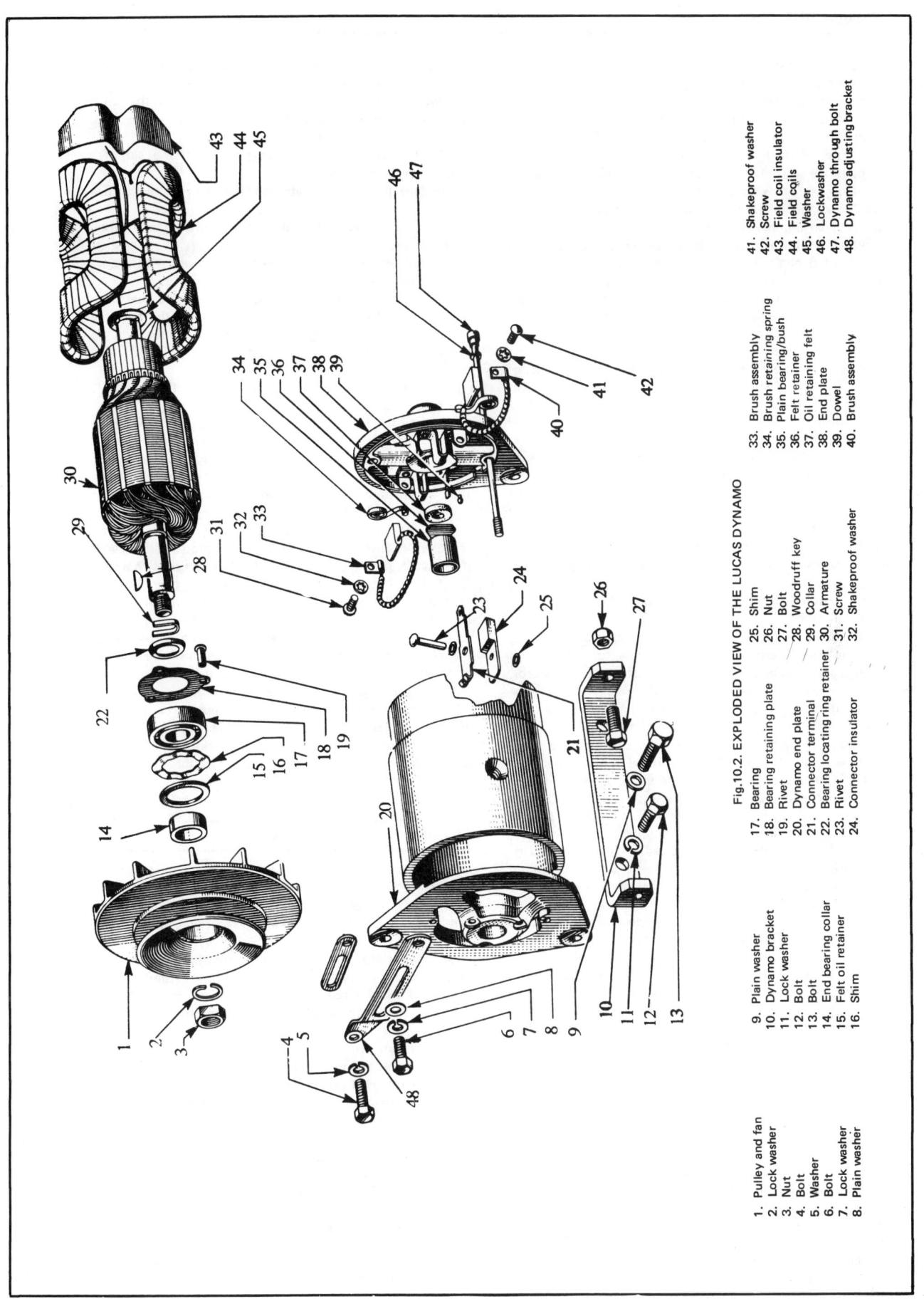

1. Pulley and fan
2. Lock washer
3. Nut
4. Bolt
5. Washer
6. Bolt
7. Lock washer
8. Plain washer
9. Plain washer
10. Dynamo bracket
11. Lock washer
12. Bolt
13. Bolt
14. End bearing collar
15. Felt oil retainer
16. Shim
17. Bearing
18. Bearing retaining plate
19. Rivet
20. Dynamo end plate
21. Connector terminal
22. Bearing locating ring retainer
23. Rivet
24. Connector insulator
25. Shim
26. Nut
27. Bolt
28. Woodruff key
29. Collar
30. Armature
31. Screw
32. Shakeproof washer
33. Brush assembly
34. Brush retaining spring
35. Plain bearing/bush
36. Felt retainer
37. Oil retaining felt
38. End plate
39. Dowel
40. Brush assembly
41. Shakeproof washer
42. Screw
43. Field coil insulator
44. Field coils
45. Washer
46. Lockwasher
47. Dynamo through bolt
48. Dynamo adjusting bracket

Chapter 10/Electrical System

10 Carefully inspect the armature and check it for open or short circuited windings. It is a good indication of an open circuited armature when the commutator segments are burnt. If the armature has short circuited the commutator segments will be very badly burnt, and the overheated armature windings badly discoloured. If open or short circuits are suspected then test by substituting the suspect armature for a new one (see photo).

11 Check the resistance of the field coils. To do this, connect an ohmmeter between the field terminal and the yoke and note the reading on the ohmmeter which should be about 6 ohms. If the ohmmeter reading is infinity this indicates an open circuit in the field winding. If the ohmmeter reading is below 5 ohms this indicates that one of the field coils is faulty and must be replaced.

12 Field coil replacement involves the use of a wheel operated screwdriver, a soldering iron, caulking and riveting and this operation is considered to be beyond the scope of most owners. Therefore, if the field coils are at fault either purchase a rebuilt dynamo, or take the casing to a Ford dealer or electrical engineering works for new field coils to be fitted.

13 Next check the condition of the commutator (arrowed). If it is dirty and blackened as shown clean it with a petrol dampened rag. If the commutator is in good condition the surface will be smooth and quite free from pits or burnt areas, and the insulated segments clearly defined.

14 If, after the commutator has been cleaned, pits and burnt spots are still present, wrap a strip of glass paper round the commutator taking great care to move the commutator ¼ of a turn every ten rubs till it is thoroughly clean. (See photo).

15 In extreme cases of wear the commutator can be mounted in a lathe and with the lathe turning at high speed, a very fine cut may be taken off the commutator. Then polish the commutator with glass paper. If the commutator has worn so that the insulators between the segments are level with the top of the segments, then undercut the insulators to a depth of 1/32 inch (.8 mm). The best tool to use for this purpose is half a hacksaw blade ground to a thickness of the insulator, and with the handle end of the blade covered in insulating tape to make it comfortable to hold. This is the sort of finish the surface of the commutator should have when finished. (photo).

16 Check the bush bearing (arrowed) in the commutator end bracket for wear by noting if the armature spindle rocks when placed in it. If worn it must be renewed.

17 The bush bearing can be removed by a suitable extractor or by screwing a 5/8 inch tap four or five times into the bush. The tap complete with bush is then pulled out of the end bracket.

18 NOTE: Before fitting the new bush bearing that it is of the porous bronze type, and it is essential that it is allowed to stand in S.A.E.30 engine oil for at least 24 hours before fitment. In an emergency the bush can be immersed in hot oil (100°C) for 2 hours.

19 Carefully fit the bush into the end plate, pressing it in until the end of the bearing is flush with the inner side of the end plate. If available, press the bush in with a smooth shouldered mandrel the same diameter as the armature shaft.

10. Dynamo - Repair & Reassembly

1. To renew the ball bearing fitted to the drive end bracket drill out the rivets which hold the bearing retainer plate to the end bracket and lift off the plate.
2. Press out the bearing from the end bracket and remove the corrugated and felt washers from the bearing housing.
3. Thoroughly clean the bearing housing, and the new bearing and pack with high melting-point grease.
4. Place the felt washer and corrugated washer in that order in the end bracket bearing housing (see photo).
5. Then fit the new bearing as shown.
6. Gently tap the bearing into place with the aid of a suitable drift. (See photo).
7. Replace the bearing plate and fit three new rivets. (See photo).
8. Open up the rivets with the aid of a suitable cold chisel. (See photo).
9. Finally peen over the open end of the rivets with the aid of a ball hammer as illustrated.
10. Refit the drive end bracket to the armature shaft. Do not try and force the bracket on but with the aid of a suitable socket abutting the bearing tap the bearing on gently, so pulling the end bracket down with it. (See photo).
11. Slide the spacer up the shaft and refit the woodruff key (See photo).
12. Replace the fan and pulley wheel and then fit the spring washer and nut and tighten the latter. The drive bracket end of the dynamo is now fully assembled as shown.
13. If the brushes are little worn and are to be used again then ensure that they are placed in the same holders from which they were removed. When refitting brushes, either new or old, check that they move freely in their holders. If either brush sticks, clean with a petrol moistened rag and, if still stiff, lightly polish the sides of the brush with a very fine file until the brush moves quite freely in its holders.
14. Tighten the two retaining screws and washers which hold the wire leads to the brushes in place (see photo).
15. It is far easier to slip the end piece with brushes over the commutator if the brushes are raised in their holders as shown and held in this position by the pressure of the springs resting against their flanks (arrowed).
16. Refit the armature to the casing and then the commutator end plate and screw up the two through bolts.
17. Finally, hook the ends of the two springs off the flanks of the brushes and onto their heads so the brushes are forced down into contact with the armature.

11. Alternator - General Description

The Lucas 15 ACR alternator is an optional substitute to the C.40 or C.40L dynamo. The alternators main advantage is its ability to provide a high charge at low revolutions and will ensure a charge reaches the battery with all electrical equipment in use.

An important feature of the alternator is its built-in output control regulator, based on 'thick film' hybrid integrated micro-circuit techniques, which results in the model 15 ACR being a self contained generating and control unit.

The system provides for direct connection of a charge indicator light, and eliminates the need for a field switching relay or warning light control unit, necessary with a dynamo.

The alternator is of rotating field, ventilated design. It comprises principally: A laminated stator on which is wound a star-connected 3-phase output winding: A 12-pole rotor carrying the field windings. Each end of the rotor shaft runs in ball race bearings which are lubricated for life; Natural finish aluminium die cast end brackets, incorporating the mounting lugs: A rectifier pack for converting the a.c. output of the machine to d.c. for battery charging: An output control regulator.

The rotor is belt driven from the engine through a pulley keyed to the rotor shaft. A pressed steel fan adjacent to the pulley draws cooling air through the machine. This

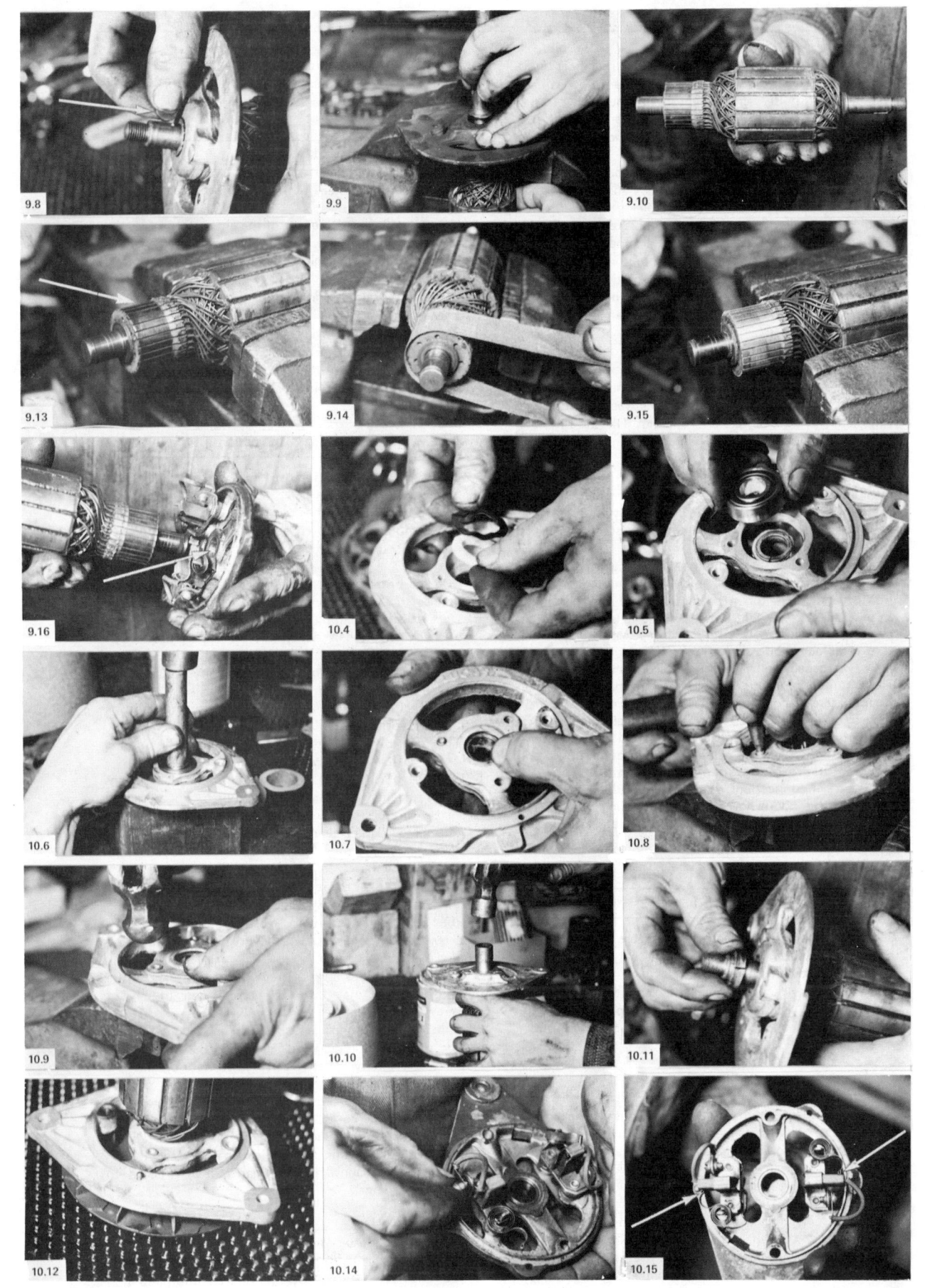

9.8 9.9 9.10
9.13 9.14 9.15
9.16 10.4 10.5
10.6 10.7 10.8
10.9 10.10 10.11
10.12 10.14 10.15

135

Chapter 10/Electrical System

fan forms an integral part of the alternator specification. It has been designed to provide adequate air flow with a minimum of noise, and to withstand the high stresses associated with maximum speed. Rotation is clockwise viewed on the drive end. Maximum continuous rotor speed is 12,500 rev/min.

Rectification of alternator output is achieved by six silicon diodes housed in a rectifier pack and connected as a 3-phase full-wave bridge. The rectifier pack is attached to the outer face of the slip ring end bracket and contains also three 'field' diodes; at normal operating speeds, rectified current from the stator output windings flows through these diodes to provide self-excitation of the rotor field, via brushes bearing on face-type slip rings.

The slip rings are carried on a small diameter moulded drum attached to the rotor shaft outboard of the slip ring end bearing. The inner ring is centred on the rotor shaft axis, while the outer ring has a mean diameter of ¾ inch approximately. By keeping the mean diameter of the slip rings to a minimum, relative speeds between brushes and rings, and hence wear, are also minimal. The slip rings are connected to the rotor field winding by wires carried in grooves in the rotor shaft.

The brushgear is housed in a moulding screwed to the outside of the slip ring end bracket. This moulding thus encloses the slip ring and brushgear assembly, and, together with the shielded bearing, protects the assembly against the entry of dust and moisture.

The regulator is set during manufacture and requires no further attention. Briefly, the 'thick film' regulator comprises resistors and conductors screen printed onto a 1 inch square alumina substrate. Mounted on the substrate are Lucas semiconductor devices comprising of three transistors, a voltage reference diode and a field recirculation diode, and also two capacitors. The internal connections between these components and the substrate are made by special Lucas-patented connectors. The whole assembly is 1/16 inch thick, and is housed in a recess in an aluminium heat sink, which is attached to the slip ring end bracket. Complete hermetic sealing is achieved by a silicone rubber encapsulant to provide environmental protection.

Electrical connections to external circuits are brought out to Lucar connector blades, these being grouped to accept a moulded connector socket which ensures correct connections.

12. Alternator - Routine Maintenance

1. The equipment has been designed for the minimum amount of maintenance in service. The only items subject to wear being the brushes and bearings.
2. Brushes should be examined after about 75,000 miles, and renewed if necessary. The bearings are pre-packed with grease for life, and should not require any further attention.

13. Alternators - Special Procedures

1. A replacement alternator must always be checked to ensure that polarity connections are correct. They are clearly marked and wrong connections can damage the equipment.
2. Never reverse battery connections. The rectifiers could be damaged.
3. Always connect up the battery earth terminal first.
4. Disconnect the alternator/control unit whenever the battery is being charged in position, as a safety precaution.
5. Never disconnect the battery with the engine running, nor run the alternator with the output cable disconnected or any other alternator circuits disconnected.
6. The cable between the battery and alternator is always 'live'. Take care not to short to earth.

14. Alternator - Removal & Replacement

1. Disconnect the battery by removal of the negative earth terminal.
2. Unplug the leads on the rear of the alternator.
3. Slacken the three alternator securing bolts and tilt the alternator towards the engine.
4. Remove the fan belt.
5. Remove the alternator securing bolts and detach the alternator.
6. Replacement is the reversal of the above procedure, but ensure the fan belt has ½ inch (13 mm) free movement at a point midway between the alternator and water pump pulleys after the alternator securing bolts are secured.

15. Alternator - Dismantling & Inspection (Brushes Only)

1. Referring to Fig.10.3. remove the end cover by undoing the screws.
2. To inspect the brushes correctly the brush holder moulding should be removed complete by undoing the two bolts and disconnecting the 'Lucar' connection to the diode plates.
3. With the brush holder moulding removed and the brush assemblies still in position check that they protrude from the face of the moulding by at least 0.2 inches (5 mm). Also check that when depressed, the spring pressure is 7 - 10 ozs. when the end of the brush is flush with the face of the brush moulding. To be done with any accuracy this requires a push type spring gauge.
4. Should either of the foregoing requirements not be fulfilled the spring assemblies should be replaced.
5. This can be done by simply removing the holding screws and fitting a new assembly.
6. With the brush holder moulding removed the slip rings on the face end of the rotor are exposed. These can be cleaned with a petrol soaked cloth and any signs of burning may be removed very carefully with fine glass paper. On no account should any other abrasive be used or any attempt at machining be made.
7. When the brushes are refitted they should slide smoothly in their holders. Any sticking tendency may first be rectified by wiping with a petrol soaked cloth or, if this fails, by carefully polishing with a very fine file where any binding marks may appear.
8. Reassemble in the reverse order of dismantling. Ensure that leads which may have been connected to any of the screws are reconnected correctly. NOTE:-
1. If the charging system is suspect, first check the fan belt tension and condition - refer to Chapter 10/6.2 for details.
2. Check the battery - refer to Chapter 10/3 for details.
3. With an alternator the ignition warning light control feed comes from the centre point of a pair of diodes in the alternator via a control unit similar in appearance to an indicator flasher unit. Should the warning light indicate lack of charge, check this unit and if suspect replace it.
4. Should all the above prove negative then proceed to check the alternator.

16. Inertia Type Starter Motor - General Description

The engine is started by the starter motor pinion engaging with the flywheel ring gear or, on automatic

Fig.10.3. EXPLODED VIEW OF THE LUCAS ALTERNATOR

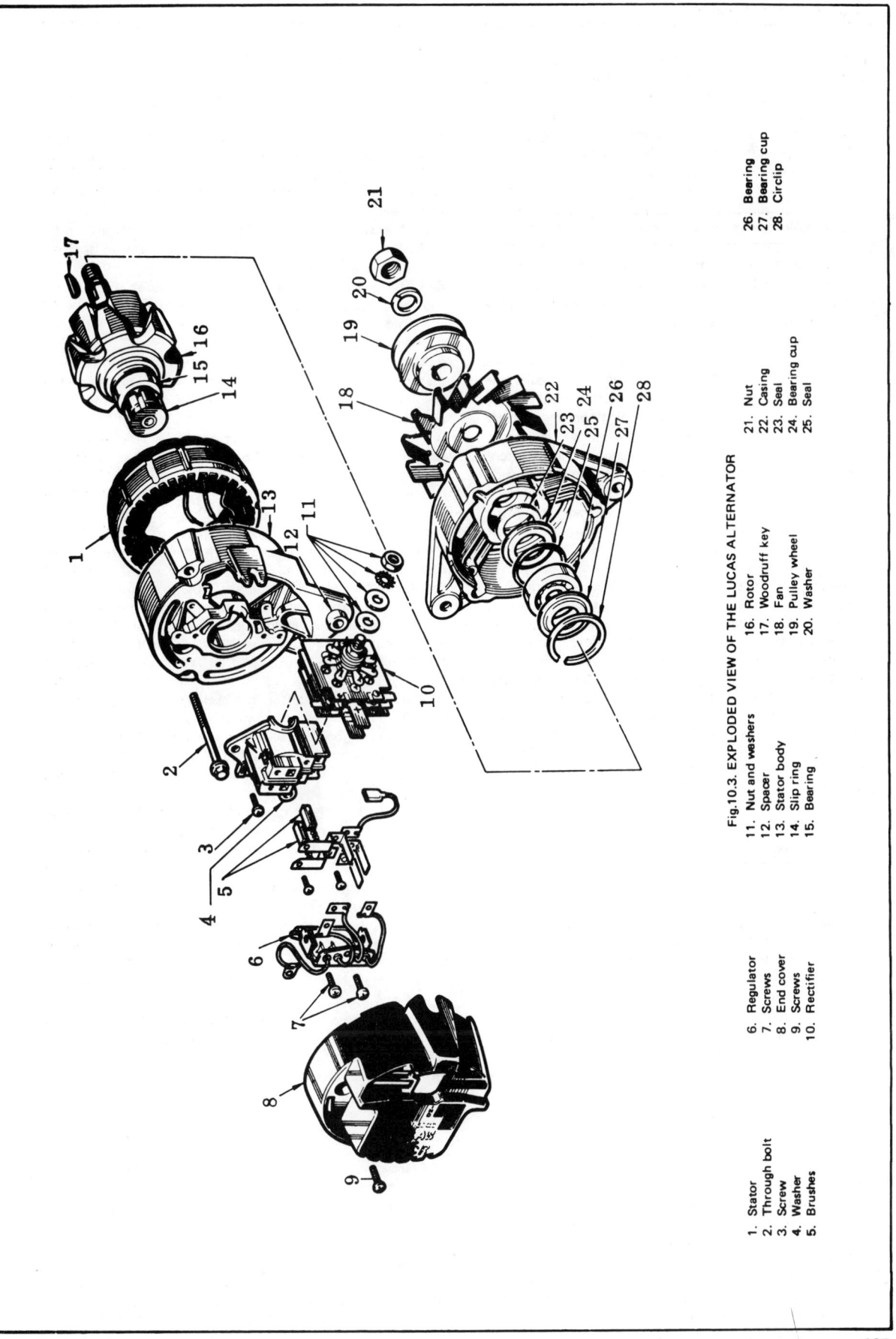

1. Stator
2. Through bolt
3. Screw
4. Washer
5. Brushes
6. Regulator
7. Screws
8. End cover
9. Screws
10. Rectifier
11. Nut and washers
12. Spacer
13. Stator body
14. Slip ring
15. Bearing
16. Rotor
17. Woodruff key
18. Fan
19. Pulley wheel
20. Washer
21. Nut
22. Casing
23. Seal
24. Bearing cup
25. Seal
26. Bearing
27. Bearing cup
28. Circlip

Chapter 10/Electrical System

transmission cars, with the torque converter inertia ring.

The starter motor is held in position by three bolts which also clamp the bellhousing flange.

The motor is of the four field coil, four pole piece type, and utilises four spring-loaded commutator brushes. Two of these brushes are earthed, and the other two are insulated and attached to the field coil ends.

17. Starter Motor - Testing on Engine

1. If the starter motor fails to operate then check the condition of the battery by turning on the headlamps. If they glow brightly for several seconds and then gradually dim, the battery is in an uncharged condition.
2. If the headlamps glow brightly and it is obvious that the battery is in good condition, then check the tightness of the battery wiring connections (and in particular the earth lead from the battery terminal to its connection on the bodyframe). If the positive terminal on the battery becomes hot when an attempt is made to work the starter, this is a sure sign of a poor connection on the battery terminal. To rectify remove the terminal, clean the inside of the cap and the terminal post thoroughly and reconnect. Check the tightness of the connections at the relay switch and at the starter motor. Check the wiring with a voltmeter for breaks or shorts.
3. If the wiring is in order then check that the starter motor is operating. To do this, press the rubber covered button in the centre of the solenoid under the bonnet. If it is working the starter motor will be heard to 'click' as it tries to rotate. Alternatively check it with a voltmeter.

If the battery is fully charged, the wiring in order, and the switch working and the starter motor fails to operate, then it will have to be removed from the car for examination. Before this is done, however, ensure that the starter pinion has not jammed in mesh with the flywheel. Check by turning the square end of the armature shaft with a spanner. This will free the pinion if it is stuck in engagement with the flywheel teeth.

18. Starter Motor - Removal & Replacement

1. Disconnect the battery earth lead from the negative terminal.
2. Disconnect the starter motor cable from the terminal on the starter motor end plate.
3. Remove the upper starter motor securing bolt.
4. Working under the car loosen, and then remove, the two lower starter motor securing bolts taking care to support the motor so as to prevent damage to the drive components.
5. Lift the starter motor out of engagement with the flywheel ring and lower it out of the car.
6. Replacement is a straightforward reversal of the removal procedure.

19. Starter Motor - Dismantling & Reassembly

1. With the starter motor on the bench, loosen the screw on the cover band and slip the cover band off. With a piece of wire bent into the shape of a hook, lift back each of the brush springs in turn and check the movement of the brushes in their holders by pulling on the flexible connectors. If the brushes are so worn that their faces do not rest against the commutator, or if the ends of the brush leads are exposed on their working face, they must be renewed.
2. If any of the brushes tend to stick in their holders then wash them with a petrol moistened cloth and, if necessary, lightly polish the sides of the brush with a very fine file, until the brushes move quite freely in their holders.
3. If the surface of the commutator is dirty or blackened, clean it with a petrol dampened rag. Secure the starter motor in a vice and check it by connecting a heavy gauge cable between the starter motor terminal and a 12V battery.
4. Connect the cable from the other battery terminal to earth in the starter motor body. If the motor turns at high speed it is in good order.
5. If the starter motor still fails to function, or if it is wished to renew the brushes, it is necessary to further dismantle the motor.
6. Lift the brush springs with the wire hook and lift all four brushes out of their holders one at a time.
7. Remove the terminal nuts and washer from the terminal post on the commutator end bracket.
8. Unscrew the two through bolts which hold the end plates together and pull off the commutator end bracket. Also remove the driving end bracket which will come away complete with the armature.
9. At this stage, if the brushes are to be renewed, their flexible connectors must be unsoldered and the connectors of new brushes soldered in their place. Check that the new brushes move freely in their holders as detailed above. If cleaning the commutator with petrol fails to remove all the burnt areas and spots, then wrap a piece of glass paper round the commutator and rotate the armature. If the commutator is very badly worn, remove the drive gear as detailed in the following section. Then mount the armature in a lathe and with the lathe turning at high speed, take a very fine cut-out of the commutator and finish the surface by polishing with glass paper. DO NOT UNDERCUT THE MICA INSULATORS BETWEEN THE COMMUTATOR SEGMENTS.
10 With the starter motor dismantled, test the four field coils for an open circuit. Connect a 12-volt battery with a 12-volt bulb in one of the leads between the field terminal post and the tapping point of the field coils to which the brushes are connected. An open circuit is proved by the bulb not lighting.
11 If the bulb lights, it does not necessarily mean that the field coils are in order, as there is a possibility that one of the coils will be earthing to the starter yoke or pole shoes. To check this, remove the lead from the brush connector and place it against a clean portion of the starter yoke. If tne bulb lights the field coils are earthing. Replacement of the field coils calls for the use of a wheel operated screwdriver, a soldering iron, caulking and riveting operations and is beyond the scope of the majority of owners. The starter yoke should be taken to a reputable electrical engineering works for new field coils to be fitted. Alternatively, purchase an exchange starter motor.
12 If the armature is damaged this will be evident after visual inspection. Look for signs of burning, discolouration, and for conductors that have lifted away from the commutator. Reassembly is a straightforward reversal of the dismantling procedure.

20. Starter Motor Drive - General Description

1. The starter motor drive is of the outboard type. When the starter motor is operated the pinion moves into contact with the flywheel gear ring by moving in towards the starter motor.
2. If the engine kicks back, or the pinion fails to engage with the flywheel gear ring when the starter motor is actuated no undue strain is placed on the armature shaft, as the pinion sleeve disengages from the pinion and turns independently.

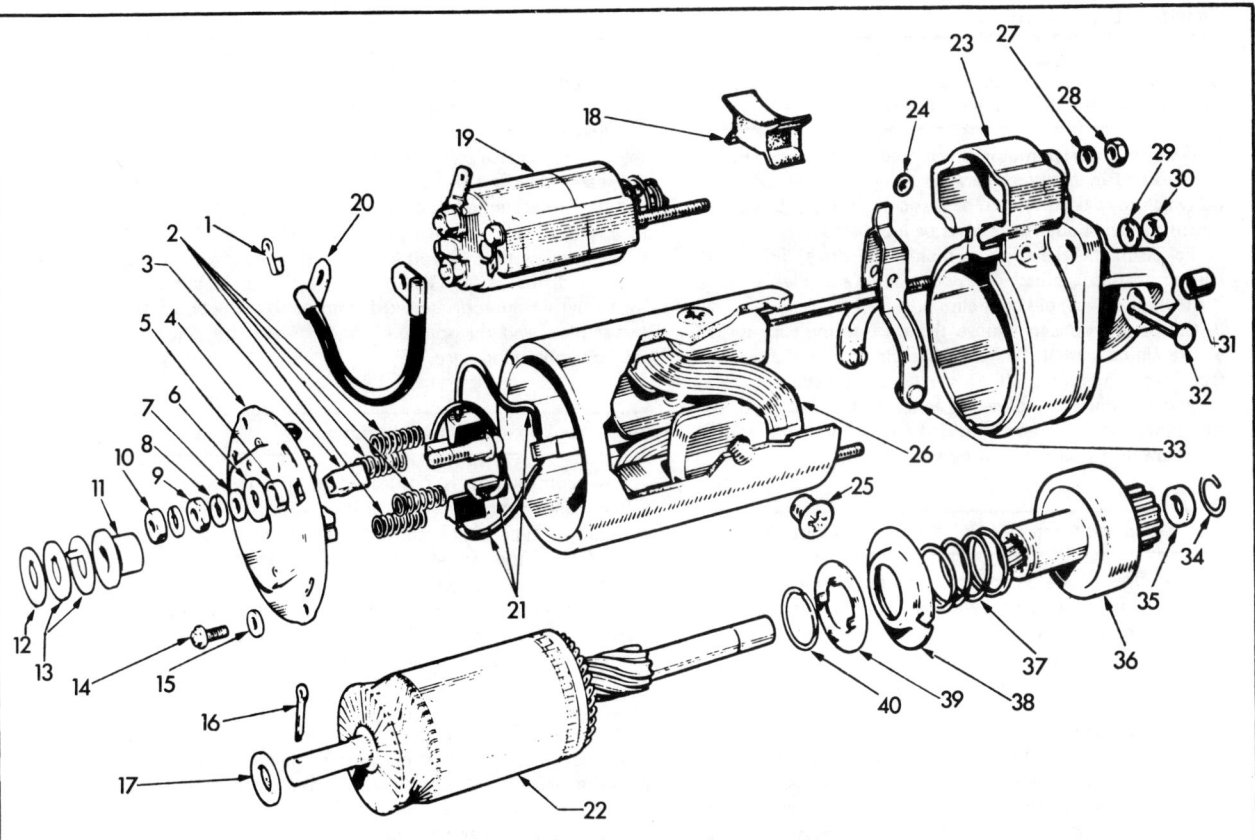

Fig.10.4. EXPLODED VIEW OF THE END FACE COMMUTATOR PRE-ENGAGED TYPE STARTER MOTOR

1. Hook
2. Brush springs
3. Insulator
3. Endplate & brush holder
5. Spacer
6. Washer
7. Washer
8. Lockwasher
9. Nut
10. Nut
11. Bush
12. Washers
13. Tabbed washer
14. Bolt
15. Washer
16. Split pin
17. Washer
18. Grommet
19. Solenoid assembly
20. Cable assembly
21. Brush assembly
22. Armature
23. Starter drive cover and starter motor endplate
24. Pin retaining ring
25. Field coil retaining screw
26. Field coils
27. Washer
28. Nut
29. Lockwasher
30. Nut
31. Bush
32. Lever swivel pin
33. Actuating lever
34. Circlip
35. Spacer
36. Pinion
37. Spring
38. Clutch assembly
39. Clutch assembly
40. Retaining ring

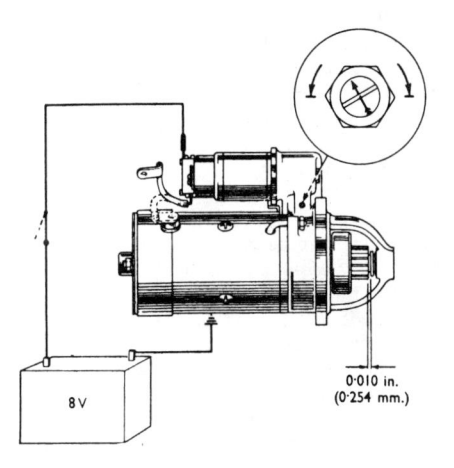

Fig.10.5. Measuring armature endfloat

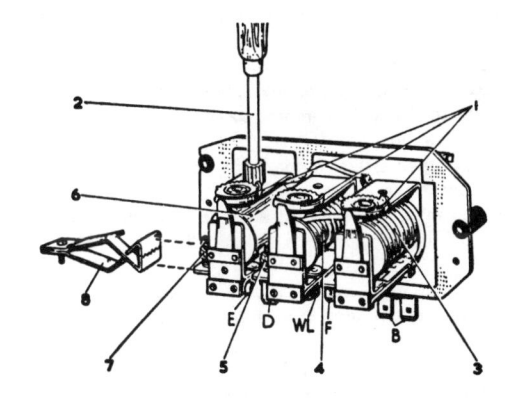

Fig.10.6. THE CONTROL BOX (COVER REMOVED)

1. Adjustment cams
2. Setting tool
3. Cut-out relay
4. Current regulator
5. Current regulator contacts
6. Voltage regulator
7. Voltage regulator contacts
8. Clip

139

21. Starter Motor Drive - Removal & Replacement

1. When the starter motor is removed the drive should be well washed in petrol or paraffin to remove any grease or oil which may be the cause of a sticking pinion. Under no circumstances should these parts be lubricated.
2. To dismantle the drive, compress the drive spring and cup employing a press for this purpose, and then extract the locking device, pin or circlip.
3. Ease the press and remove the drive spring cup, spring and retaining washer. Pull the drive pinion barrel assembly from the armature shaft. If the pinion is badly worn or broken, this must be replaced as an assembly. When refitting the pinion barrel assembly must be fitted with the pinion teeth toward the armature windings.

22. Pre-Engaged Starter Motors - General Description

This type of starter motor is normally only fitted as original equipment to cars with 'cold start' specifications, but it can be fitted as an optional extra on all other models. Two types of motor may be used, the first type being exactly the same as the inertia type described in the previous sections. The second type is a wave wound motor and uses an end-face commutator instead of the normal drum type. On both types, a solenoid is attached to the top of the starter motor which operates a one way clutch when the starter button is pressed, thus engaging the motor to the pinion which is permanently in mesh with the starter ring on the flywheel. The drive to the pinion therefore remains fully engaged until the solenoid is de-activated. The starter motor is attached to the bellhousing by two bolts only and not three as in the inertia type.

23. Pre Engaged Starter Motors - Removal & Replacement

1. Disconnect the battery by removing the earth lead from the negative terminal.
2. Disconnect the starter motor cable from the terminal on the starter motor end plate.
3. Remove the two solenoid retaining nuts and the connecting strap and lift off the solenoid.
4. Remove the upper starter motor retaining bolt.
5. Working under the car, remove the lower retaining bolt taking care to support the motor so as to prevent damage to the drive components.
6. Withdraw the starter motor from the bellhousing and lower it from the car.
7. Replacement is a straightforward reversal of the removal procedure.

24. Endface Commutator Starter Motor - Dismantling & Reassembly

Due to the fact that this type of starter motor uses a face commutator, on which the brushes make contact end on, a certain amount of thrust is created along the armature shaft. A thrust bearing is therefore incorporated in the motor at the commutator end.

1. Remove the split pin from the end of the shaft and slide off the shims, washer and thrust plate.
2. Remove the two screws which retain the end plate and pull off the end plate complete with the brush holders and brushes.
3. Should the brushes have to be renewed follow the instructions given in Section 19, paragraph 9 of this chapter.

4. To remove the armature, unscrew the nuts on the holding studs at the drive end bracket.
5. Withdraw the armature complete with the drive and the one way clutch operating lever.
6. Reassembly is a direct reversal of the above procedure, but the armature end float should be measured as indicated in Fig.10.5. The correct end float should be .010 inch. (.264 mm.) with an 8 volt supply activating the solenoid. If the end float is found to be incorrect it can be corrected by fitting an appropriate sized shim or shims between the thrust plate and the split pin. NOTE: Never use the same split pin more than once.

25. Control Box - General Description

1. The control box is positioned on the left-hand wing valance and comprises three units; two separate vibrating armature - type single contact regulators and a cut-out relay. One of the regulators is sensitive to change in current and the other to changes in voltage.
2. Adjustments can only be made with a special tool which resembles a screwdriver with a multi-toothed blade. This can be obtained through Lucas or Ford agents.
3. The regulators control the output from the dynamo depending on the state of the battery and the demands of the electrical equipment, and ensure that the battery is not overcharged. The cut-out is really an automatic switch and connects the dynamo to the battery when the dynamo is turning fast enough to produce a charge. Similarly it disconnects the battery from the dynamo when the engine is idling or stationary so that the battery does not discharge through the dynamo.

26. Cut-Out & Regulator Contacts - Maintenance

1. Every 12,000 miles check the cut-out and regulator contacts. If they are dirty or rough or burnt place a piece of fine glass paper (DO NOT USE EMERY PAPER OR CARBORUNDUM PAPER) between the cut-out contacts, close them manually and draw the glass paper through several times.
2. Clean the regulator contacts in exactly the same way, but use emery or carborundum paper and not glass paper. Carefully clean both sets of contacts from all traces of dust with a rag moistened in methylated spirits.

27. Voltage Regulator Adjustment

1. The regulator requires very little attention during its service life, and should there be any reason to suspect its correct functioning, tests of all circuits should be made to ensure that they are not the reason for the trouble.
2. These checks include the tension of the fan belt, to make sure that it is not slipping and so providing only a very low charge rate. The battery should be carefully checked for possible low charge rate due to a faulty cell, or corroded battery connections:
3. The leads from the generator may have been crossed during replacement, and if this is the case then the regulator points will have stuck together as soon as the generator starts to charge. Check for loose or broken leads from the generator to the regulator.
4. If after a thorough check it is considered advisable to test the regulator, this should be carried out by an electrician who is well acquainted with the correct method using test bench equipment.
5. Pull off the Lucar connections from the two adjacent

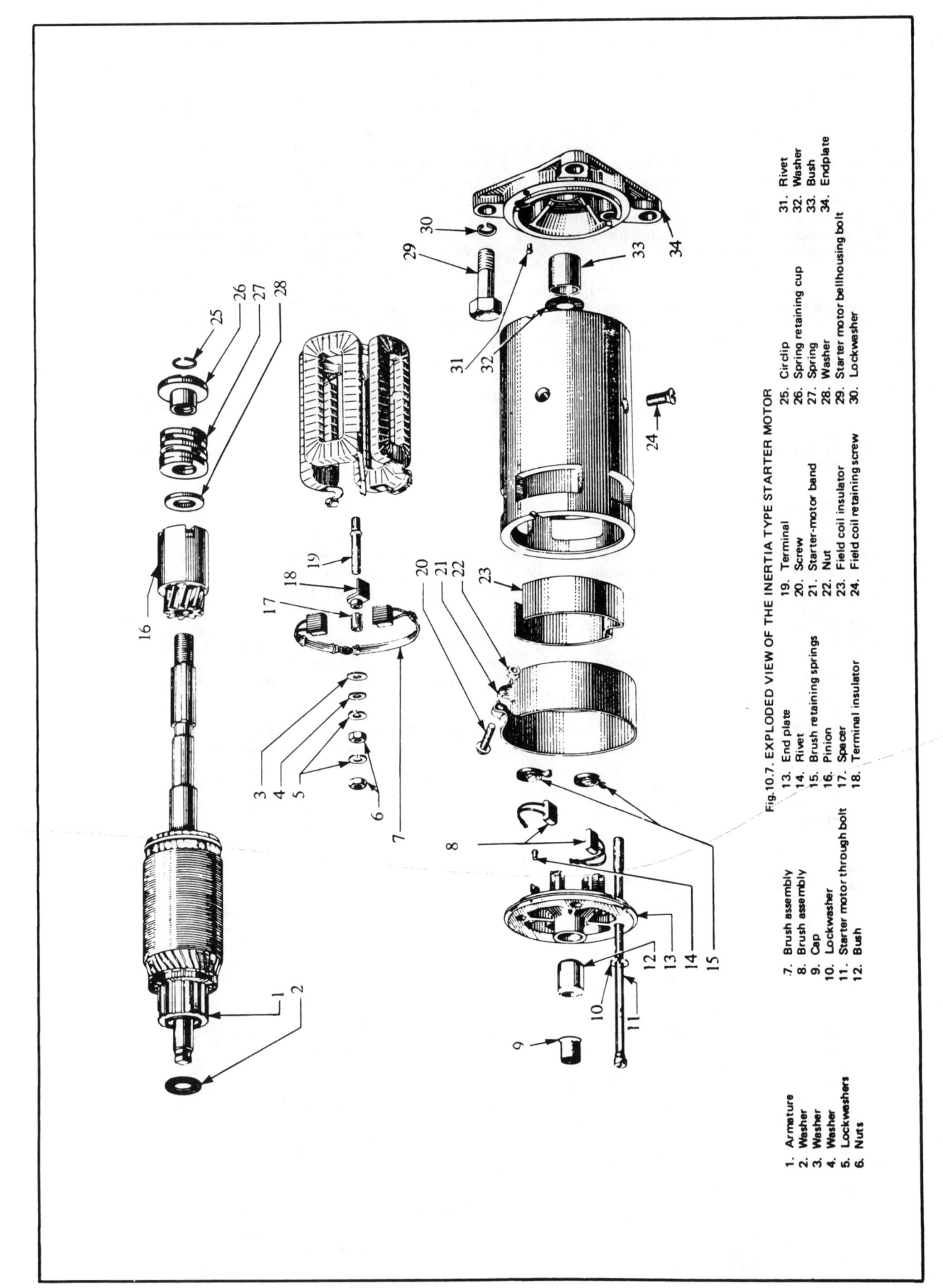

Fig.10.7. EXPLODED VIEW OF THE INERTIA TYPE STARTER MOTOR

1. Armature
2. Washer
3. Washer
4. Washer
5. Lockwashers
6. Nuts
7. Brush assembly
8. Brush assembly
9. Cap
10. Lockwasher
11. Starter motor through bolt
12. Bush
13. End plate
14. Rivet
15. Brush retaining springs
16. Pinion
17. Spacer
18. Terminal insulator
19. Terminal
20. Screw
21. Starter-motor band
22. Nut
23. Field coil insulator
24. Field coil retaining screw
25. Circlip
26. Spring retaining cup
27. Spring
28. Washer
29. Starter motor bellhousing bolt
30. Lockwasher
31. Rivet
32. Washer
33. Bush
34. Endplate

Chapter 10/Electrical System

control box terminals 'B'. To start the engine it will now be necessary to join together the ignition and battery leads with a suitable wire.

6. Connect a 0-30 volt voltmeter between terminal 'D' on the control box and terminal 'WL'. Start the engine and run it at 2,000 r.p.m. The reading on the voltmeter should be steady and lie between the limits detailed in the specification.

7. If the reading is unsteady this may be due to dirty contacts. If the reading is outside the specified limits stop the engine and adjust the voltage regulator in the following manner.

8. Take off the control box cover and start and run the engine at 2,000 r.p.m. Using the correct tool turn the voltage adjustment cam anti-clockwise to raise the setting and clockwise to lower it. To check that the setting is correct, stop the engine, and then start it and run it at 2,000 r.p.m. noting the reading. Refit the cover and the connections to the 'WL' and 'D' terminals.

28. Current Regulator Adjustment

1. The output from the current regulator should equal the maximum output from the dynamo which is 22 amps. To test this it is necessary to by-pass the cut-out by holding the contacts together.

2. Remove the cover from the control box and with a bulldog clip hold the cut-out contacts together. (See Fig.10.6).

3. Pull off the wires from the adjacent terminals 'B' and connect a 0-40 moving coil ammeter to one of the terminals and to the leads.

4. All the other load connections including the ignition must be made to the battery.

5. Start the engine and increase the speed to approximately 3,000 r.p.m. The ammeter should read the rated generator output $\pm$ 1 amp (22 amp standard, 25 amp C40-L dynamo). If the needle flickers it is likely that the points are dirty. If the reading is too low, turn the special Lucas tool clockwise to raise the setting and anti-clockwise to lower it. Decrease and increase engine speed to previous specification and re-check the setting.

29. Cut-Out Adjustment

1. Check the voltage required to operate the cut-out by connecting a voltmeter between the control box terminals 'D' and 'WL'. Remove the control box cover, start the engine and gradually increase its speed until the cut-outs close. This should occur when the reading is between 12.6 to 13.4 volts.

2. If the reading is outside these limits turn the cut-out adjusting cam (1 in the illustration) by means of the adjusting tool, a fraction at a time clockwise to raise the voltage, and anti-clockwise to lower it.

3. To adjust the drop off voltage bend the fixed contact blade carefully. The adjustment to the cut-out should be completed within 30 seconds of starting the engine as otherwise heat build-up from the shunt coil will affect the readings.

4. If the cut-out fails to work, clean the contacts, and if there is still no response, renew the cut-out and regulator unit.

30. Fuse Block - Removal & Replacement

1. Open bonnet and pull off two non-reversible wiring plugs on the fuse block.

2. Pull off the transparent fuse cover, remove the two screws securing the fuse block to the body and remove the fuse block.

3. Replacement is a direct reversal of the above but check operation of lighting circuits after replacement.

31. Flasher Circuit - Fault Tracing & Rectification

1. The flasher unit is a small cylindrical metal container located under the dashboard on top of the steering column brace and is held in place by a clip. The unit is actuated by the direction indicator switch.

2. If the flasher unit fails to operate, or works very slowly or rapidly, check out the flasher indicator circuit as detailed below, before assuming that there is a fault in the unit.

a) Examine the direction indicator bulbs both front and rear for broken filaments.

b) If the external flashers are working but either of the internal flasher warning lights have ceased to function, check the filaments in the warning light bulbs and replace with a new bulb if necessary.

c) If a flasher bulb is sound but does not work check all the flasher circuit connections with the aid of the wiring diagram found at the end of this chapter.

d) With the ignition switched on check that the current is reaching the flasher unit by connecting a voltmeter between the 'plus' terminal and earth. If it is found that current is reaching the unit connect the two flasher unit terminals together and operate the direction indicator switch. If one of the flasher warning lights comes on this proves that the flasher unit itself is at fault and must be replaced as it is not possible to dismantle and repair it.

32. Windscreen Wiper Mechanism - Maintenance

1. Renew the windscreen wiper blades at intervals of approximately 12,000 or more frequently if necessary.

2. The washer round the wheelbox spindle can be lubricated with several drops of glycerine every 6,000 miles. The windscreen wiper links can be lightly oiled at the same time.

33. Windscreen Wiper Blades - Removal & Replacement

1. Lift the wiper arm away from the windscreen and remove the old blade by turning it in towards the arm and then disengage the arm from the slot in the blade.

2. To fit a new blade, slide the end of the wiper arm into the slotted spring fastening in the centre of the blade. Push the blade firmly onto the arm until the raised portion of the arm is fully home in the hole in the blade.

34. Windscreen Wiper Arms - Removal & Replacement

1. Before removing a wiper arm, turn the windscreen wiper switch on and off to ensure the arms are in their normal parked position parallel with the bottom of the windscreen.

2. To remove an arm pivot the arm back and pull the wiper arm head off the splined drive. If the arm proves difficult to remove a screwdriver with a large blade can be used to lever the wiper arm head off the splines. Care must be taken not to damage the splines.

3. When replacing an arm position it so it is in the correct relative parked position and then press the arm head onto

Fig.10.8. Lowering the windscreen wiper motor and linkage out of the car

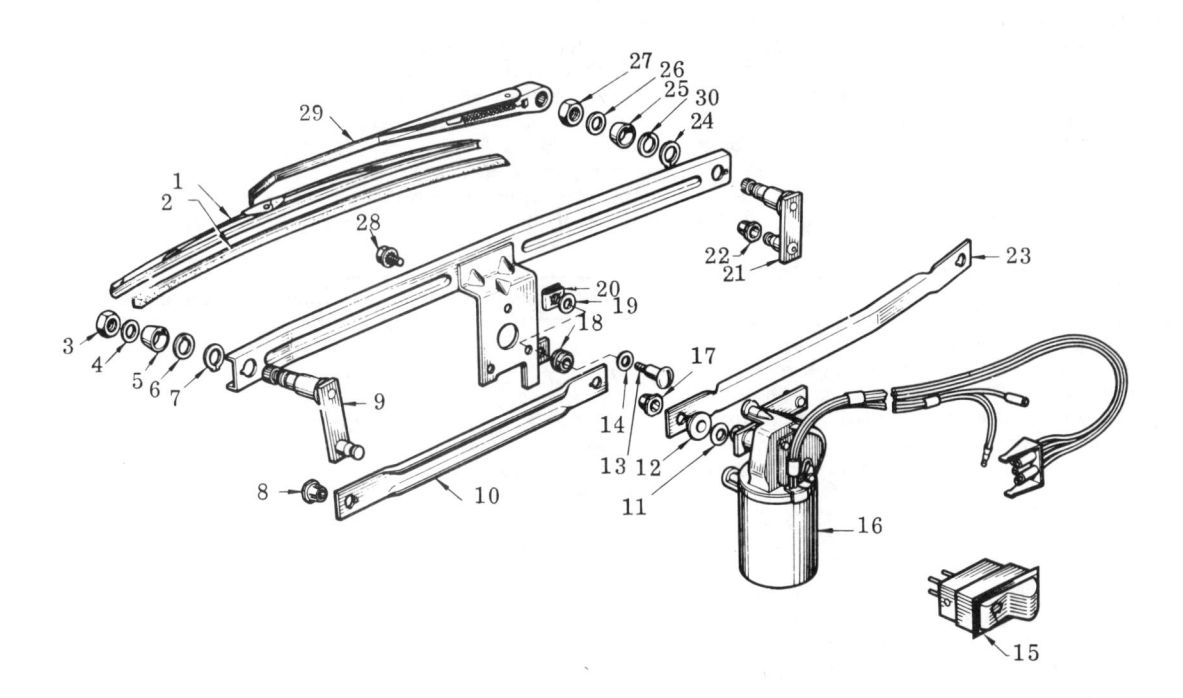

Fig.10.9. EXPLODED VIEW OF THE WINDSCREEN WIPER MECHANISM

1. Blade holder
2. Wiper blade
3. Nut
4. Washer
5. Spacer
6. Seal
7. Ring
8. Bushing
9. Arm and pivot shaft
10. Link arm
11. Spring washer
12. Bushing
13. Screw
14. Washer
15. Switch assembly
16. Wiper motor
17. Bushing
18. Grommet
19. Washer
20. Screw clip
21. Arm and pivot shaft
22. Bushing
23. Link arm
24. Ring
25. Spacer
26. Washer
27. Nut
28. Nut and washer
29. Wiper arm
30. Seal

143

Chapter 10/Electrical System

the splined drive until it is fully home on the splines.

35. Windscreen Wiper Mechanism - Fault Diagnosis & Rectification

1. Should the windscreen wipers fail, or work very slowly, then check the terminals on the motor for loose connections, and make sure the insulation of all the wiring is not cracked or broken thus causing a short circuit. If this is in order then check the current the motor is taking by connecting an ammeter in the circuit and turning on the wiper switch. Consumption should be between 2.3 to 3.1 amps.
2. If no current is passing through the motor, check that the switch is operating correctly.
3. If the wiper motor takes a very high current check the wiper blades for freedom of movement. If this is satisfactory check the gearbox cover and gear assembly for damage.
4. If the motor takes a very low current ensure that the battery is fully charged. Check the brush gear and ensure the brushes are bearing on the commutator. If not, check the brushes for freedom of movement and, if necessary, renew the tension springs. If the brushes are very worn they should be replaced with new ones. Check the armature by substitution if this unit is suspect.

36. Windscreen Wiper Motor & Linkage - Removal & Replacement

1. Disconnect the battery by removing the negative earth lead and then remove the wiper blades and arms as described in Sections 33 and 34.
2. Undo and remove the two nuts holding the wiper spindles to the bodywork in front of the windscreen.
3. Remove the parcel shelf by taking off the two spring clips at either end and by undoing the single screw on the drivers side and the two screws on the passengers side.
4. To gain better access to the wiper motor disconnect the flexible hoses from the heater to the demister vents above the dash and also the aeroflow flexible pipes.
5. Disconnect the two control cables on the heater at the heater end, making a careful note of their correct fitting in relation to the positions of the heater controls on the fascia. Tuck the cables out of the way under the fascia.
6. Remove the single screw holding the wiper motor to its mounting bracket and lower the motor and linkage just enough to be able to see the wires running to the motor.
7. Disconnect the wires at their connectors on the motor making a note of their relative positions for reassembly purposes.
8. Now lower the complete wiper motor and linkage assembly down in front of the heater and remove it from the car.
9. Reassembly is a direct reversal of the removal procedure, but the screw securing the wiper motor to its mounting bracket should not be fully tightened down until the wiper spindle nuts have been replaced thus ensuring correct alignment of the linkage.

37. Windscreen Wiper Motor - Dismantling, Inspection & Reassembly

1. Start by removing the linkage mechanism from the motor. Carefully prise the short wiper link off the motor operating arm and remove the plastic pivot bush.
2. Undo the three screws which hold the linkage to the wiper motor and separate the two.
3. Unscrew the two bolts which hold the motor case to the gearbox housing and withdraw the motor case complete with the armature.
4. Take the brushes out of their holders and remove the brush springs.
5. Undo the three screws which hold the brush mounting plate to the wiper gearbox and withdraw the brush mounting plate.
6. Remove the earth wire on the gearbox cover plate by undoing the screw nearest the motor case. Undo the other screw on the gearbox cover plate and remove the cover plate and switch assembly.
7. Pull the spring steel armature stop out of the gearbox casing. Then remove the spring clip and washer which retain the wiper pinion gear in place and withdraw the gear and washer
8. Undo the nut securing the wiper motor operating arm and remove the lockwasher, arm, wave washer and flat washer in that order.
9. Having removed the operating arm withdraw the output gear, park switch assembly and washer from the gearbox casing.
10 Carefully examine all parts for signs of wear or damage and replace as necessary.
11 Reassembly is a direct reversal of the above procedure.

38. Horn - Fault Tracing & Rectification

1. If the horn works badly or fails completely, check the wiring leading to the horn plug which is located on the body panel next to the horn itself. Also check that the plug is properly pushed home and is in a clean condition free from corrosion etc.
2. Check that the horn is secure on its mounting and that there is nothing lying on the horn body.
3. If the fault is not an external one, remove the horn cover and check the leads inside the horn. If these are sound, check the contact breaker contacts. If these are burnt or dirty clean them with a fine file and wipe all traces of dirt and dust away with a petrol moistened rag.

39. Headlamp & Sidelamp Unit - Removal & Replacement

1. Disconnect the battery by removing the negative earth lead.
2. Open the bonnet and remove the two small screws securing the top of the headlamp bezel to the bodywork.
3. Remove the two lower securing screws from the bezel and lift it away.
4. Remove the four screws holding the sealed beam unit to the body and carefully lift the unit a short distance away from the car.
5. Pull off the wiring plug from the rear of the sealed beam unit and remove the sidelamp bulb which is located just below the plug. Also disconnect the wire leading to the indicator light at its connector. The unit can now be lifted clear of the car.
6. Replacement is a direct reversal of the removal procedure.

40. Headlamp Alignment

1. It is always advisable to have the headlamps aligned on proper optical beam setting equipment but if this is not available the following procedure may be used.
2. Position the car on level ground 10 feet in front of a dark wall or board. The wall or board must be at right angles to the centre line of the car.
3. Draw a vertical line on the board in line with the centre

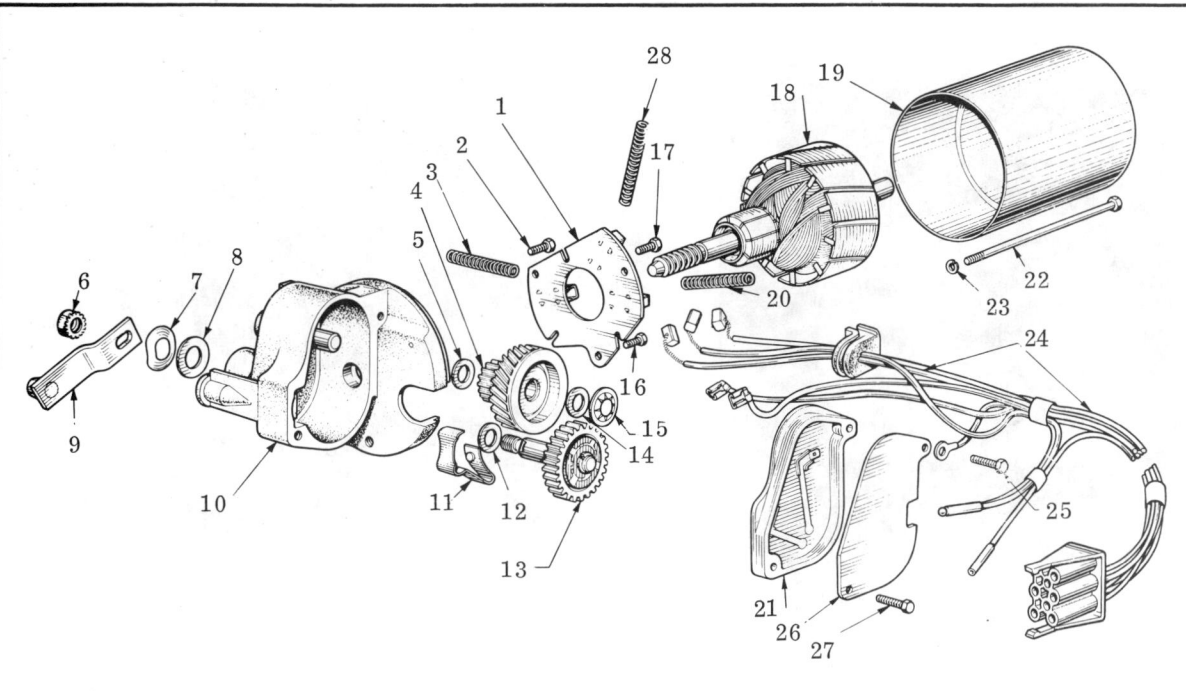

Fig.10.10. EXPLODED VIEW OF THE WINDSCREEN WIPER MOTOR

1. Brush holder plate
2. Screw
3. Spring
4. Wiper gear and pinion
5. Washer
6. Nut
7 & 8 Washers
9. Output arm
10. Housing
11. Stop assembly
12. Washer
13. Shaft & circuit assembly
14. Washer
15. Clip
16. Screw
17. Screw
18. Armature
19. Casing and magnet
20. Spring
21. Switch & cover assembly
22. Through bolt
23. Locking washers
24. Wiring loom and brush assembly
25. Screw
26. Switch wiring cover
27. Screw
28. Spring

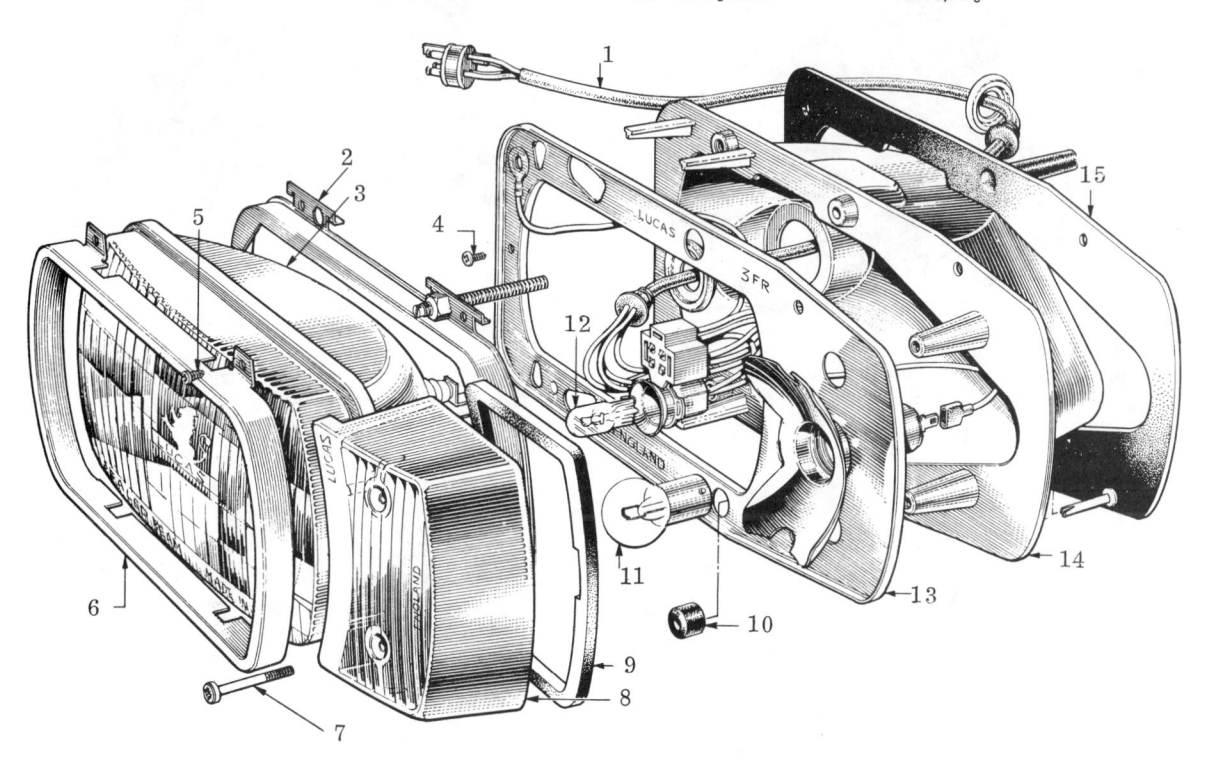

Fig.10.11. EXPLODED VIEW OF THE HEADLAMP ASSEMBLY

1. Wiring
2. Inner bezel
3. Sealed beam unit
4. Screw
5. Screw
6. Outer bezel
7. Screw
8. Flasher lens
9. Gasket
10. Grommet
11. Flasher bulb
12. Sidelamp bulb
13. Frame
14. Lamp body
15. Bracket

145

Fig.10.12. Removing the headlamp unit

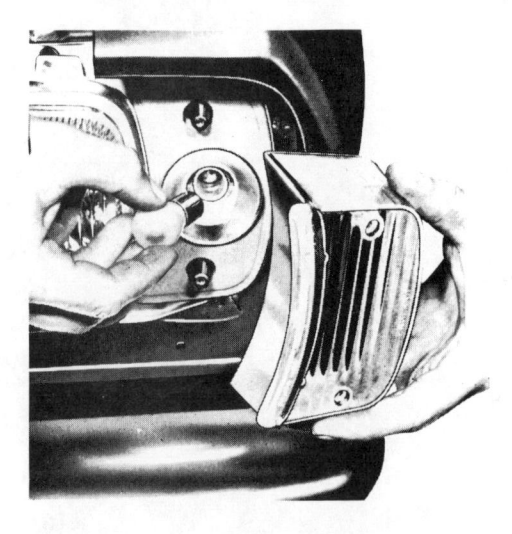

Fig.10.13. Removing the front indicator lens and bulb

Fig.10.14. Removing the rear side, stop and indicator lamp assembly

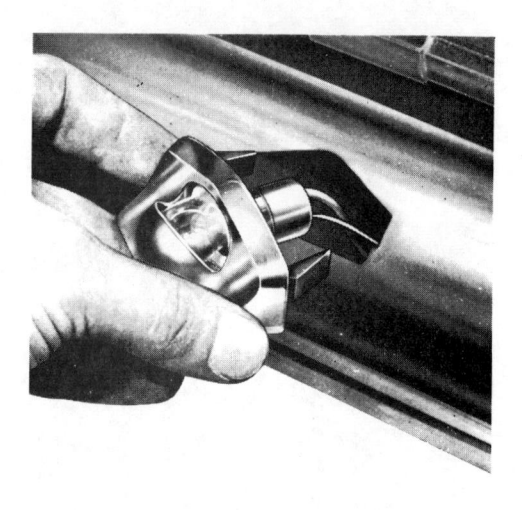

Fig.10.15. Removing the licence plate lamp

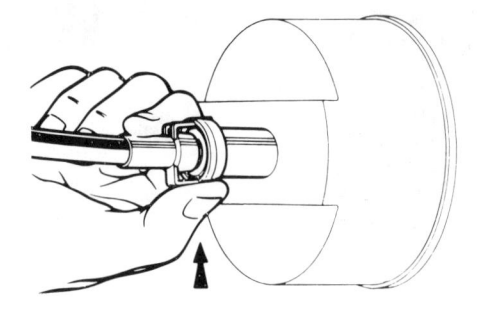

Fig.10.16. Disconnecting the cable from the back of the speedometer

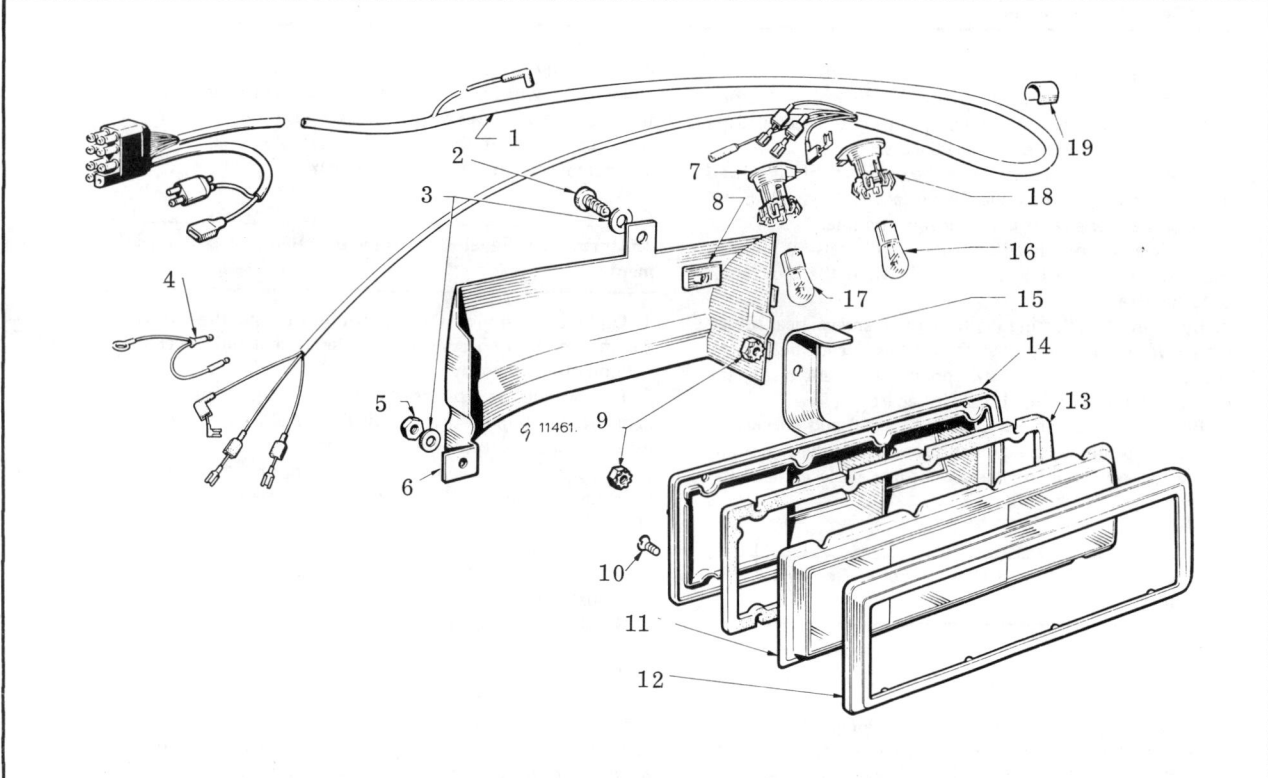

Fig.10.17. EXPLODED VIEW OF THE REAR LAMP ASSEMBLY

1. Wiring
2. Screw
3. Washer
4. Connector
5. Nut
6. Trim cover
7. Bulb holder
8. Screw clip
9. Nuts & washers
10. Screw
11. Lens
12. Bezel
13. Gasket
14. Frame
15. Bracket
16. Bulb
17. Bulb
18. Bulb holder
19. Clip

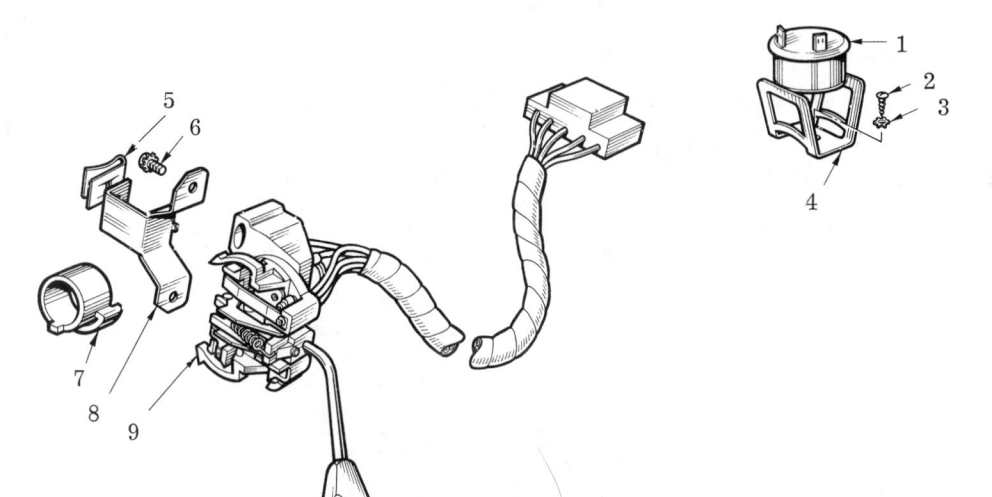

Fig.10.18. EXPLODED VIEW OF THE COMBINED DIRECTION INDICATOR, HEADLAMP FLASHER AND DIPPER SWITCH

1. Flasher unit
2. Screw
3. Shakeproof washer
4. Bracket
5. Screw clip
6. Screw and washer
7. Cancelling cam
8. Bracket
9. Switch assembly

147

Chapter 10/Electrical System

line of the car.

4. Bounce the car on its suspension to ensure correct settlement and then measure the height between the ground and the centre of the headlamps.

5. Draw an horizontal line across the board at this measured height. On this horizontal line mark a cross 21.6 in. (54.8 cm) either side of the vertical centre line.

6. Remove the two head and sidelamp bezels by undoing the four screws on either side and switch the headlamps onto full beam.

7. By carefully adjusting the horizontal and vertical adjusting screws on each lamp, align the centres of each beam onto the crosses which you have previously marked on the horizontal line, 43.2 in. (109.7 cm) apart.

8. Bounce the car on its suspension again and check that the beams return to the correct positions. At the same time check the operation of the dip switch, replace the outer bezels.

41. Front Indicator Lamp Glass & Bulb - Removal & Replacement

1. Disconnect the battery by removing the negative earth lead, then remove the headlamp bezel as described in Section 40.

2. Remove the two screws running through the top and bottom of the lens, lift the lens away and remove the bulb by pushing it in and turning anti-clockwise to release the pins.

3. Replacement is a direct reversal of the removal procedure.

42. Rear Indicator, Stop & Tail Lamps Bulbs - Removal & Replacement

1. Disconnect battery by removal of the negative earth lead.

2. Open the luggage compartment lid and pull off rear lamp trim cover.

3. Pull out the spring-loaded rear and indicator bulb holder and remove the bulbs.

4. Replacement is a direct reversal of the above procedure.

43. Rear Licence Plate Lamp - Removal & Replacement

1. Disconnect battery by removal of negative earth lead.

2. Disconnect the earth and feed wires inside the luggage compartment and pull the wires through the hole in the floor.

3. Press the retaining levers inwards from underneath the bumper and lift off the assembly.

4. Remove the bulb from the assembly.

5. Replacement is a direct reversal of the above procedure, then check the operation of the lamp.

44. Interior Light - Removal & Replacement

1. Disconnect the battery by removal of the negative earth lead.

2. Carefully prise the light assembly from its location above the door.

3. If the bulb is defective it can now be removed by gently pulling it from its spring loaded position.

4. To finally remove the complete assembly simply disconnect the wires from the back of the light taking note of their correct positions for reassembly purposes.

5. Replacement of the complete assembly, or the bulb is a direct reversal of the removal sequence.

45. Instrument Panel & Instruments - Removal & Replacement

1. Undo and remove the two bolts holding the steering column to the underside of the dash panel and lower the column out of the way.

2. Remove the five cross-head screws holding the instrument panel to the bulkhead and pull the panel a short distance into the car so as to expose the wiring.

3. Disconnect the speedometer cable from the speedometer by squeezing the knurled portion of the retaining clip and withdraw the cable.

4. Make a careful note of all the wiring positions then disconnect them at their plugs and connectors and withdraw the panel into the car.

5. Separate the instrument box from the panel by removing the screws at each corner; four in all.

6. The instruments themselves are held to the box by either two small bolts or screws and can easily be removed and replaced as required.

7. Replacement of the instrument and instrument panel is a direct reversal of the removal procedure.

46. Instrument Voltage Regulator - Removal & Replacement

1. Remove the instrument panel from the car as described in Section 45.

2. The voltage regulator is located on the back of the speedometer and is removed by undoing a single retaining bolt and disconnecting the wires running to it.

3. Replacement is a straightforward reversal of the removal procedure.

47. Direction Indicator, Headlamp Flasher & Horn Switch Assembly - Removal & Replacement

1. Disconnect the battery by removing the negative earth lead.

2. Remove the bolts securing the column to the underside of the fascia panel and lower the column.

3. Remove two securing screws on the column shrouds and remove the shrouds.

4. Remove two screws securing the switch to the column.

5. Disconnect the multi pin plug and remove the switch.

6. Replacement is a direct reversal of the removal procedure.

48. Light, Panel Light & Windscreen Wiper Switches - Removal & Replacement

1. Disconnect the battery by removing the negative earth lead.

2. Working under the dash pull off the multi pin plug from whichever switch is being removed.

3. By applying gentle pressure to the back of the switch on one side, carefully ease it into the car.

4. Replacement is a direct reversal of the removal procedure.

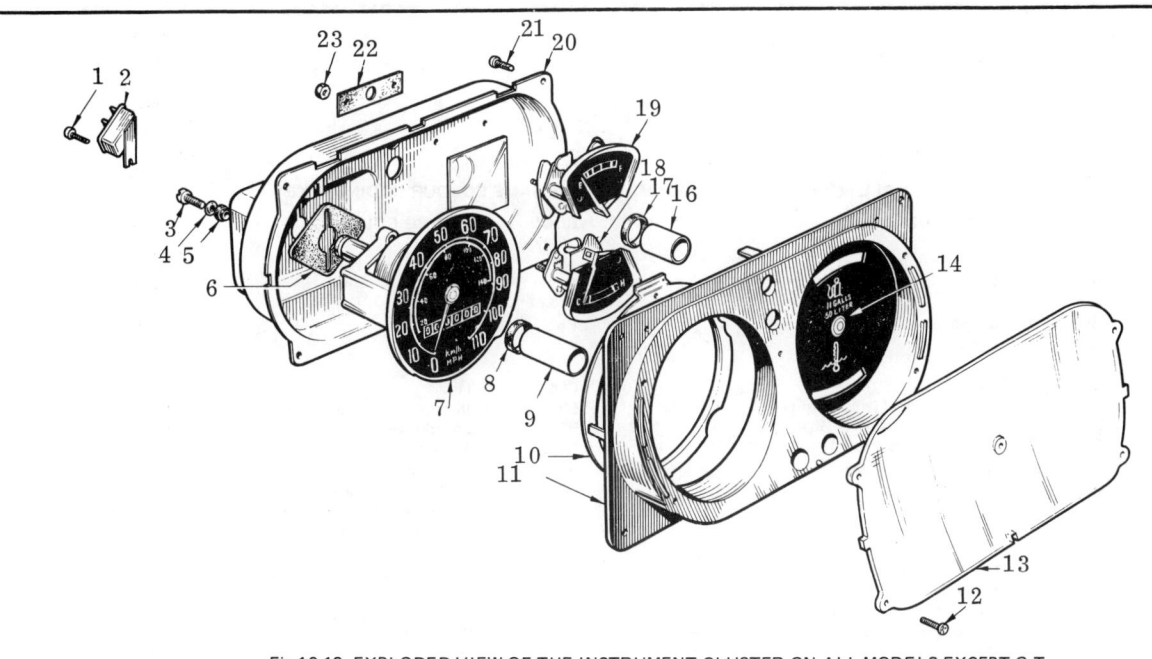

Fig.10.19. EXPLODED VIEW OF THE INSTRUMENT CLUSTER ON ALL MODELS EXCEPT G.T.

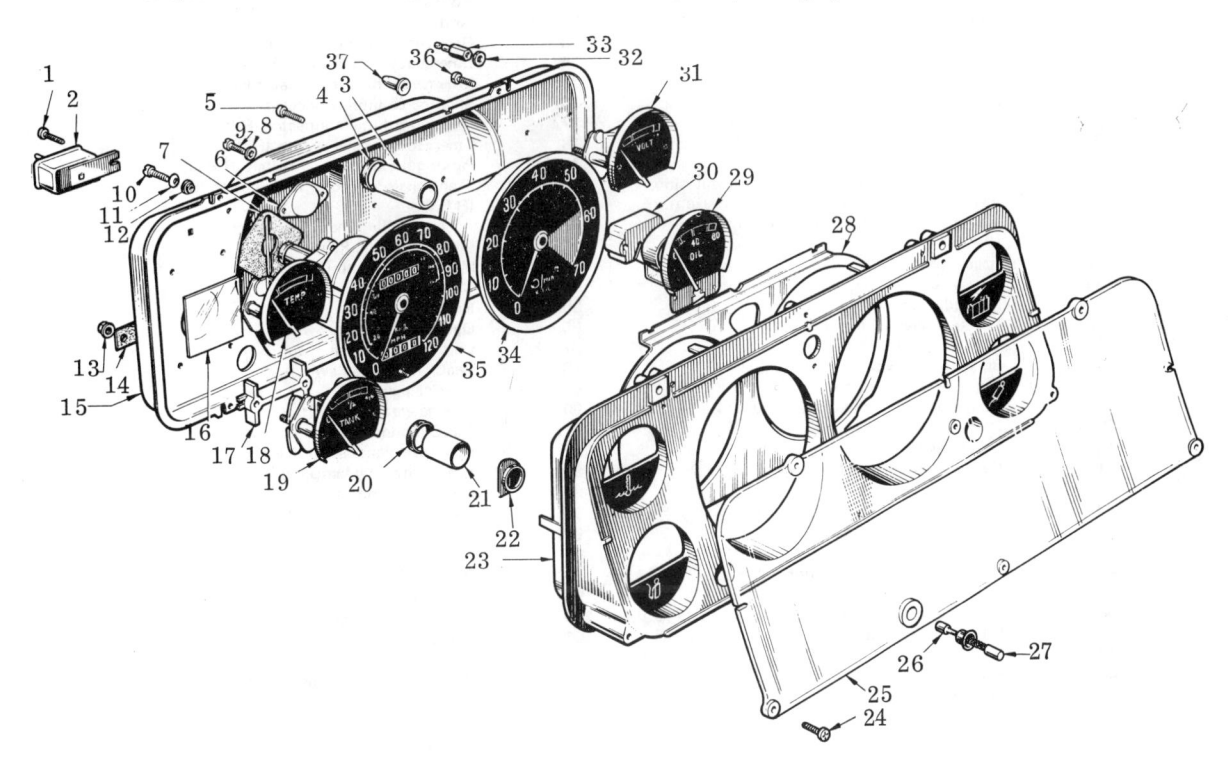

1. Screw	7. Speedometer	13. Glass	19. Fuel gauge
2. Voltage regulator	8. Gasket	14. Dial backing	20. Instrument box
3. Screw	9. Lamp baffle	15. Lamp baffle	21. Screw
4. Washer	10. Frame	16. Lamp baffle	22. Light shield
5. Grommet	11. Panel	17. Gasket	23. Nut
6. Spacer	12. Screw	18. Temperature gauge	

Fig.10.20. EXPLODED VIEW OF THE G.T. INSTRUMENT CLUSTER

1. Screw	11. Washer	21. Lamp baffle	31. Battery condition indicator
2. Voltage regulator	12. Grommet	22. Lens	32. Washer
3. Lamp baffle	13. Nut	23. Panel	33. Terminal
4. Gasket	14. Shield	24. Screw	34. Tachometer
5. Screw	15. Instrument box	25. Glass	35. Speedometer
6. Blue light filter	16. Light filter	26. Shaft	36. Screw
7. Gasket	17. Bracket	27. Odometer reset knob	37. Terminal inhibitor
8. Washer	18. Temperature gauge	28. Frame	
9. Screw	19. Fuel gauge	29. Oil pressure gauge	
10. Screw	20. Gasket	30. Spacer	

ALL FOUR WIRING DIAGRAMS USE THE SAME COLOUR CODING & KEY

CODE	WIRING COLOUR	CODE	WIRING COLOUR
R	Red	Y	Yellow
Bk	Black	LG	Light Green
Bl	Blue	P	Purple
W	White	O	Orange
Br	Brown	Pk	Pink
G	Green		

CODE	ITEM	CODE	ITEM
1.	R.H. turn signal lamp (front)	52.	Instrument illumination lamp
2.	L.H. turn signal lamp (front)	53.	Speedometer
3.	R.H. side lamp (front)	54.	Tachometer
4.	L.H. side lamp (front)	55.	Speedometer illumination lamp
5.	R.H. headlamp	56.	Tachometer illumination lamp
6.	L.H. headlamp	57.	Battery condition indicator
7.	R.H. front loom connector	58.	Oil pressure gauge
8.	L.H. front loom connector	59.	Generator warning lamp
9.	R.H. side flasher (R.P.O.)	60.	Oil pressure warning lamp
10.	L.H. side flasher (R.P.O.)	61.	Main beam warning lamp
11.	Engine compartment loom connector	62.	Turn signal flasher unit
12.	Engine compartment loom connector (R.P.O.)	63.	Fog lamp switch (R.P.O.)
13.	Horn	64.	Road lamp switch (R.P.O.)
14.	Dual horn (R.P.O.)	65.	Interior lamp & panel illumination switch
15.	Road lamp (R.P.O.)	66.	Windscreen wiper switch
16.	Fog lamp (R.P.O.)	67.	Heater switch
17.	Battery (L.H.D.)	68.	Windscreen wiper switch – 2 speed (R.P.O.)
18.	Battery (R.H.D.)	69.	Radio (R.P.O.)
19.	Ignition coil	70.	Radio aerial (R.P.O.)
20.	Distributor	71.	Accessory connector
21.	Oil pressure switch	72.	Ignition switch
22.	Temperature sender unit	73.	Rear wiring loom connector
23.	Generator	74.	Emergency flasher unit (R.P.O.)
24.	Alternator (R.P.O.)	75.	Emergency flasher indicator lamp (R.P.O.)
25.	Starter solenoid (automatic transmission)	76.	Steering column connector
26.	Starter solenoid (manual transmission)	77.	Steering column connector (R.P.O.)
27.	Pre-engaged starter motor-automatic transmission (R.P.O.)	78.	Emergency flasher switch (R.P.O.)
28.	Inertia starter motor—automatic transmission	79.	Parking brake warning switch (R.P.O.)
29.	Inertia starter motor—manual transmission	80.	Transmission selector illumination lamp (R.P.O.)
30.	Pre-engaged starter motor—manual transmission (R.P.O.)	81.	Accessory illumination connector
31.	Regulator	82.	Cigar lighter (R.P.O)
32.	Fuse block	83.	Map-reading lamp (R.P.O.)
33.	R.H. bulkhead wiring connector	84.	Clock (R.P.O.)
34.	L.H. bulkhead wiring connector	85.	Horn switch
35.	Stop lamp switch	86.	Direction indicator switch
36.	Brake fluid low pressure switch (R.P.O.)	87.	Column dip switch
37.	Winscreen wiper motor	88.	Headlamp flasher switch
38.	Windscreen wiper motor—2 speed (R.P.O.)	89.	Interior light
39.	Heater motor	90.	Fuel gauge sender unit
40.	Heater resistance	91.	R.P.O. connectors
41.	Reversing lamp switch – manual transmission (R.P.O.)	92.	R.H. turn signal lamp (Rear)
42.	Reversing lamp and park inhibitor switch—automatic transmission (R.P.O.)	93.	L.H. turn signal lamp (Rear)
43.	Turn signal warning lamp	94.	R.H. stop lamp
44.	Instrument voltage regulator	95.	L.H. stop lamp
45.	Instrument panel earth	96.	R.H. side lamp (Rear)
46.	Brake fluid low pressure warning lamp (R.P.O.)	97	L.H. side lamp (Rear)
47	R.H. courtesy switch	98.	R.H. reversing lamp
48.	L.H. courtesy switch	99.	L.H. reversing lamp
49.	Side/Head lamp switch	100.	Licence plate lamp
50.	Fuel gauge	101.	Clock
51.	Temperature gauge	102.	Cigar lighter
		103.	Headlamp flasher relay (R.P.O.)

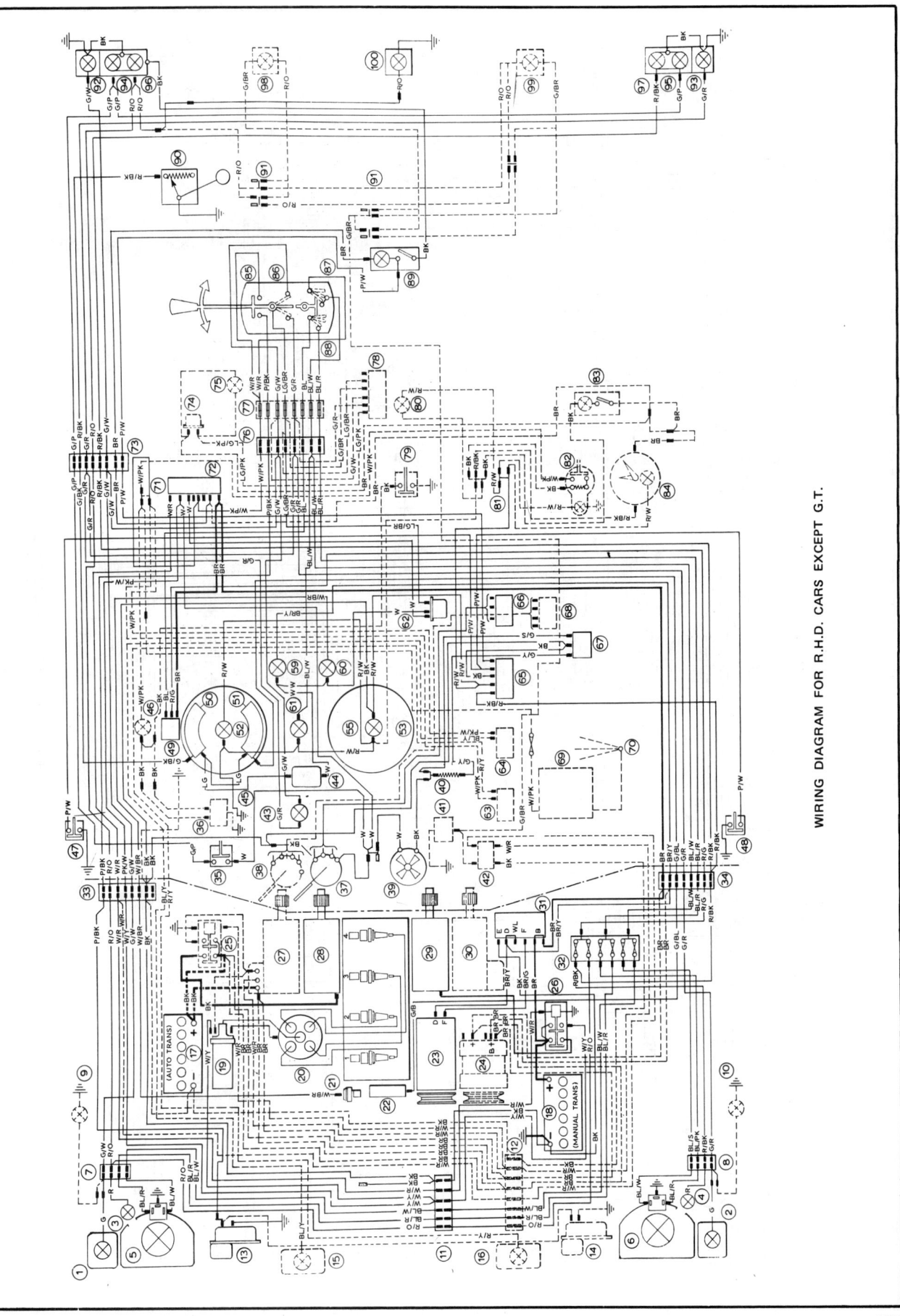

WIRING DIAGRAM FOR R.H.D. CARS EXCEPT G.T.

WIRING DIAGRAM FOR L.H.D. CARS EXCEPT G.T.

WIRING DIAGRAM FOR R.H.D. G.T. CARS

WIRING DIAGRAM FOR L.H.D. G.T. CARS

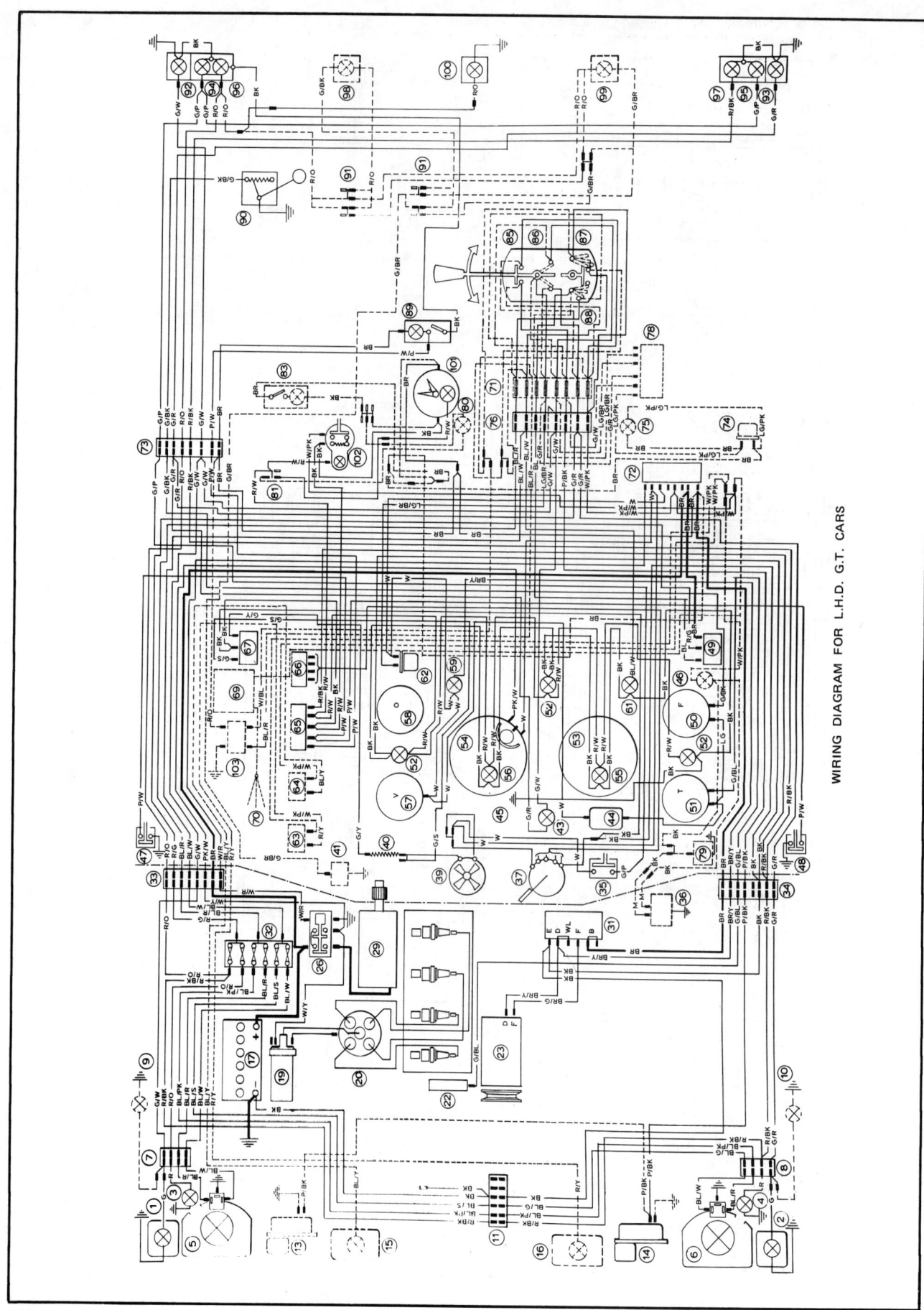

Fault Finding Chart — Electrical System

Sympton	Reason/s	Remedy
No electricity at starter motor	Battery discharged.	Charge battery.
	Battery defective internally.	Fit new battery.
	Battery terminal leads loose or earth lead not securely attached to body.	Check and tighten leads.
	Loose or broken connections in starter motor circuit.	Check all connections and tighten any that are loose.
	Starter motor switch or solenoid faulty	Test and replace faulty components with new.
Electricity at starter motor: faulty motor	Starter motor pinion jammed in mesh with flywheel gear ring.	Disengage pinion by turning squared end of armature shaft.
	Starter brushes badly worn, sticking, or brush wires loose.	Examine brushes, replace as necessary, tighten down brush wires.
	Commutator dirty, worn or burnt	Clean commutator, recut if badly burnt
	Starter motor armature faulty.	Overhaul starter motor, fit new armature.
	Field coils earthed.	Overhaul starter motor.
Electrical defects	Battery in discharged condition.	Charge battery.
	Starter brushes badly worn, sticking, or brush wires loose.	Examine brushes, replace as necessary, tighten down brush wires.
	Loose wires in starter motor circuit.	Check wiring and tighten as necessary.
Dirt or oil on drive gear	Starter motor pinion sticking on the screwed sleeve.	Remove starter motor, clean starter motor drive.
Mechanical damage	Pinion or flywheel gear teeth broken or worn.	Fit new gear ring to flywheel, and new pinion to starter motor drive.
Lack of attention or mechanical damage.	Pinion or flywheel gear teeth broken or worn.	Fit new gear teeth to flywheel, or new pinion to starter motor drive.
	Starter drive main spring broken.	Dismantle and fit new main spring.
	Starter motor retaining bolts loose.	Tighten starter motor securing bolts. Fit new spring washer if necessary.
Wear or damage.	Battery defective internally.	Remove and fit new battery.
	Electrolyte level too low or electrolyte too weak due to leakage.	Top up electrolyte level to just above plates.
	Plate separators no longer fully effective.	Remove and fit new battery.
	Battery plates severely sulphated.	Remove and fit new battery.
Insufficient current flow to keep battery charged.	Fan/dynamo belt slipping.	Check belt for wear, replace if necessary, and tighten.
	Battery terminal connections loose or corroded.	Check terminals for tightness, and remove all corrosion.
	Dynamo not charging properly.	Remove and overhaul dynamo.
	Short in lighting circuit causing continual battery drain.	Trace and rectify.
	Regulator unit not working correctly.	Check setting, clean, and replace if defective.
Dynamo not charging	Fan belt loose and slipping, or broken.	Check, replace, and tighten as necessary.
	Brushes worn, sticking, broken or dirty.	Examine, clean, or replace brushes as necessary.
	Brush springs weak or broken.	Examine and test. Replace as necessary.
	Commutator dirty, greasy, worn, or burnt.	Clean commutator and undercut segment separators.
	Armature badly worn or armature shaft bent.	Fit new or reconditioned armature.
	Commutator bars shorting.	Undercut segment separations.
	Dynamo bearings badly worn.	Overhaul dynamo, fit new bearings.
	Dynamo field coils burnt, open, or shorted.	Remove and fit rebuilt dynamo.

Fault Finding Chart — Electrical System

Symptom	Reason/s	Remedy
Dynamo not charging	Commutator no longer circular.	Recut commutator and undercut segment separators.
	Pole pieces very loose.	Strip and overhaul dynamo. Tighten pole pieces.
Regulator or cut-out fails to work correctly.	Regulator incorrectly set.	Adjust regulator correctly.
	Cut-out incorrectly set.	Adjust cut-out correctly.
	Open circuit in wiring of cut-out and regulator unit.	Remove, examine, and renew as necessary.
Fuel gauge gives no reading	Fuel tank empty!	Fill fuel tank.
	Electric cable between tank sender unit and gauge earthed or loose.	Check cable for earthing and joints for tightness.
	Fuel gauge case not earthed.	Ensure case is well earthed.
	Fuel gauge supply cable interrupted.	Check and replace cable if necessary.
	Fuel gauge unit broken.	Replace fuel gauge.
Fuel gauge registers full all the time	Electric cable between tank unit and gauge broken or disconnected.	Check over cable and repair as necessary.
Horn operates all the time	Horn push either earthed or stuck down.	Disconnect battery earth. Check and rectify source of trouble.
	Horn cable to horn push earthed.	Disconnect battery earth. Check and rectify source of trouble.
Horn fails to operate	Blown fuse.	Check and renew if broken. Ascertain cause.
	Cable or cable connection loose, broken or disconnected.	Check all connections for tightness and cables for breaks.
	Horn has an internal fault.	Remove and overhaul horn.
Horn emits intermittent or unsatisfactory noise	Horn incorrectly adjusted.	Adjust horn until best note obtained.
Lights do not come on	If engine not running, battery discharged.	Push-start car, charge battery.
	Light bulb filament burnt out or bulbs broken.	Test bulbs in live bulb holder.
	Wire connections loose, disconnected or broken.	Check all connections for tightness and wire cable for breaks.
	Light switch shorting or otherwise faulty.	By-pass light switch to ascertain if fault is in switch and fit new switch as appropriate.
Lights come on but fade out	If engine not running battery discharged.	Push-start car, and charge battery.
Lights give very poor illumination	Lamp glasses dirty.	Clean glasses.
	Reflector tarnished or dirty.	Fit new reflectors.
	Lamps badly out of adjustment.	Adjust lamps correctly.
	Incorrect bulb with too low wattage fitted	Remove bulb and replace with correct grade.
	Existing bulbs old and badly discoloured.	Renew bulb units.
	Electrical wiring too thin not allowing full current to pass.	Re-wire lighting system.
Lights work erratically - flashing on and off, especially over bumps	Battery terminals or earth connection loose.	Tighten battery terminals and earth connection.
	Lights not earthing properly.	Examine and rectify.
	Contacts in light switch faulty.	By-pass light switch to ascertain if fault is in switch and fit new switch as appropriate.
Wiper motor fails to work	Blown fuse.	Check and replace fuse if necessary.
	Wire connections loose, disconnected, or broken	Check wiper wiring. Tighten loose connections.

Fault Finding Chart — Electrical System

Symptoms	Reason/s	Remedy
	Brushes badly worn.	Remove and fit new brushes.
	Armature worn or faulty.	If electricity at wiper motor remove and overhaul and fit replacement armature.
	Field coils faulty.	Purchase reconditioned wiper motor.
Wiper motor works very slowly and takes excessive current	Commutator dirty, greasy or burnt.	Clean commutator thoroughly.
	Drive to wheelboxes too bent or unlubricated.	Examine drive and straighten out severe curvature. Lubricate.
	Wheelbox spindle binding or damaged.	Remove, overhaul, or fit replacement.
	Armature bearings dry or unaligned.	Replace with new bearings correctly aligned.
	Armature badly worn or faulty.	Remove, overhaul, or fit replacement armature.
Wiper motor works slowly and takes little current	Brushes badly worn.	Remove and fit new brushes.
	Commutator dirty, greasy or burnt.	Clean commutator thoroughly.
	Armature badly worn or faulty.	Remove and overhaul armature or fit replacement.
Wiper motor works but wiper blades remain static	Driving cable rack disengaged or faulty.	Examine and if faulty, replace.
	Wheelbox gear and spindle damaged or worn.	Examine and if faulty, replace.
	Wiper motor gearbox parts badly worn.	Overhaul or fit new gearbox.

Chapter 11/Suspension - Dampers - Steering

Contents

General Description ... 1	Torsion Bar - Removal & Replacement ... 9
Rear Springs - Routine Maintenance ... 2	Rack & Pinion Steering Gear - Removal & Replacement .. 10
Steering Gear - Routine Maintenance 3	Rack & Pinion Steering Gear - Adjustments.. ... 11
Front Hub Bearings - Maintenance, Removal & Replacement ... 4	Rack & Pinion Steering Gear - Dismantling & Reassembly ... 12
Front Hub Bearings - Adjustment... ... 5	Steering Wheel & Column - Removal & Replacement... .. 13
Front Hub - Removal & Replacement ... 6	Rear Shock Absorbers - Removal & Replacement... ... 14
Front Suspension Units - Removal & Replacement ... 7	Rear Springs - Removal & Replacement... ... 15
Front Coil Spring - Removal & Replacement ... 8	Radius Arms - Removal & Replacement... ... 16

Specifications

Front Suspension ... Independent MacPherson Strut

Coil Springs	Standard	Heavy Duty
Identification ...	Green	Yellow
Part Number ...	3038E-5310-E	3038E-5310-F
Mean load ...	570 lb. (258.7 kg.)	570 lb. (258.7 kg.)
Mean rate ...	100 lb/in. (17.86 kg/cm)	100 lb/in. (17.86 kg/cm)
Diameter of coils...	5.31 in. (134.9 mm)	5.30 in. (134.6 mm)
Wire diameter ...	.426 in. (10.8 mm)	.447 in. (11.36 mm)

Suspension Units | |
---|---|---
Part No - R.H ... | 69EB-3KO33-A-A | 69EB-3K033-B-A
    - L.H ... | 69EB-3KO34-A-A | 69EB-3KO34-B-A
Colour ... | Green | Yellow
Camber angle ... | -0° 30' to + 0° 30' | -0° 10' to + 0° 50'
Castor angle ... | 0° 30' to 1° 30' | 0° 30' to 1° 30'
King pin inclination ... | 7° 30' to 8° 30' | 7° 10' to 8° 10'
Toe-in ... | .06 to .25 in. (1.5 to 6.4 mm) | .06 to .25 in. (1.5 to 6.4 mm)

Rear Suspension ... Semi elliptical leaf spring
    Colour - standard... Orange
          - heavy duty ... Green
    Number of leaves... 3
    Spring length between eye centres.. 47 in. (1144 mm)
    Width of leaves ... 2˙ in. (51 mm)
    Length between radius arm centres ... 9.91 in. (251.7 mm)

Rear Shock Absorbers ... Double acting : hydraulic telescopic
    Colour - standard... Orange
          - heavy duty ... Green

Steering gear type ... Rack and pinion
    Rack travel lock to lock... 5.62 in. (14.27 cm)
    Teeth on pinion ... 6
    Lubricant capacity ... .25 pints (.30 US pints, .15 litres)
    Lubricant type ... Castrol Hypoy 90
    No. turns lock to lock ... 3½ approx.
    Pinion bearing pre-load adjustment ... Shims
    Rack damper adjustment ... Shims

Wheels & Tyres
    Wheels - standard... 4.50 J x 13
          - R or XLR package... 5.00 J x 13
          - Optional on all models .. 5.00 J x 13

Chapter 11/Suspension - Dampers - Steering

Tyres - 1300 and 1600	6.00 x 13
- 1300 G.T. and 1600 G.T	165 x 13
- Optional on all models	165 x 13

Tyre Inflation	Normal		Full Load	
	Front	Rear	Front	Rear
600 x 13 Cross Ply	24 (1.7)	24 (1.7)	24 (1.7)	27 (1.9)
165 x 13 Radial Ply	24 (1.7)	27 (1.9)	27 (1.9)	31 (2.2)

NOTE: The foregoing tyre pressures are quoted in lb/sq.in. and in brackets kg/sq.cm. The recommended pressures should be taken when the tyre is cold, as a hot tyre normally shows a higher pressure.

Torque Wrench Settings

Wheel nuts	50 to 55 lb/ft. (7.0 to 7.7 kg.m)
Suspension unit upper mounting bolts	15 to 18 lb/ft. (2.07 to 2.49 kg.m)
Track control arm ball stud	30 to 35 lb/ft. (4.15 to 4.85 kg.m)
Torsion bar front clamps	15 to 18 lb/ft. (2.07 to 2.49 kg.m)
Torsion bar to track control arm	25 to 30 lb/ft. (3.46 to 4.15 kg.m)
Track control arm inner bushing	22 to 27 lb/ft. (3.04 to 3.73 kg.m)
Radius arms to axle housing	25 to 30 lb/ft. (3.46 to 4.15 kg.m)
Radius arms to body	25 to 30 lb/ft. (3.46 to 4.15 kg.m)
Shock absorber to axle	45 to 45 lb/ft. (5.54 to 6.22 kg.m)
Shock absorber to body	15 to 20 lb/ft. (2.07 to 2.76 kg.m)
Rear spring 'U' bolts	25 to 30 lb/ft. (3.46 to 4.15 kg.m)
Rear spring front hanger	27 to 32 lb/ft. (3.73 to 4.42 kg.m)
Rear spring rear shackle nuts	8 to 10 lb/ft. (1.11 to 1.38 kg.m)
Steering arm to suspension unit	30 to 34 lb/ft. (4.2 to 4.7 kg.m)
Steering gear to crossmember	15 to 18 lb/ft. (2.1 to 2.4 kg.m)
Track rod end to steering arm	18 to 22 lb/ft. (2.5 to 3.0 kg.m)
Flexible coupling to pinion spline	12 to 15 lb/ft. (1.7 to 2.1 kg.m)
Universal joint to steering shaft	12 to 15 lb/ft. (1.7 to 2.1 kg.m)
Steering wheel nut	20 to 25 lb/ft. (2.8 to 3.4 kg.m)

1. General Description

Each of the independent front suspension Macpherson strut units consists of a vertical strut enclosing a double acting damper surrounded by a coil spring.

The upper end of each strut is secured to the top of the wing valance under the bonnet by rubber mountings.

The wheel spindle carrying the brake assembly and wheel hub is forged integrally with the suspension unit foot.

The steering arms are connected to each unit which are in turn connected to track rods and thence to the rack and pinion steering gear.

The lower end of each suspension unit is located by a track control arm. A stabilising torsion bar is fitted between the outer ends of each track control arm and secured at the front to mountings on the body front member.

A rubber rebound stop is fitted inside each suspension unit thus preventing the spring becoming over-extended and jumping out of its mounting plates. Upward movement of the wheel is limited by the spring becoming fully compressed but this is damped by the addition of a rubber bump stop fitted around the suspension unit piston rod which comes into operation before the spring is fully compressed.

Whenever repairs have been carried out on a suspension unit it is essential to check the wheel alignment as the linkage could be altered which will affect the correct front wheel settings.

Every time the car goes over a bump vertical movement of a front wheel pushes the damper body upwards against the combined resistance of the coil spring and the damper piston.

Hydraulic fluid in the damper is displaced and it is then forced through the compression valve into the space between the inner and outer cylinder. On the downward movement of the suspension, the road spring forces the damper body downward against the pressure of the hydraulic fluid which is forced back again through the rebound valve. In this way the natural oscillations of the spring are damped out and a comfortable ride is obtained.

On the front uprights it is worth noting that there is a shroud inside the coil spring which protects the machined surface of the piston rod from road dirt.

The steering gear is of the rack and pinion type and is located on the front crossmember by two 'U' shaped clamps. The pinion is connected to the steering column by a flexible coupling. Above the flexible coupling the steering column is split by a universal joint that is designed to collapse on impact thus minimising injury to the driver in the event of an accident.

Turning the steering wheel causes the rack to move in a lateral direction and the track rods attached to either end of the rack pass this movement to the steering arms on the suspension/axle units thereby moving the road wheels.

Two adjustments are possible on the steering gear, namely rack damper adjustment and pinion bearing pre-load adjustment, but the steering gear must be removed from the car to carry out these adjustments. Both adjustments are made by varying the thickness of shim-packs.

At the rear the axle is located by two inverted 'U' bolts at each end of the casing to underslung semi-elliptical leaf springs which provide both lateral and longitudinal location. Lateral movement of the rear axle is further controlled by the fitting of radius arms which are angled inwards to the axle casing from their body mounting points.

Double acting telescopic shock absorbers are fitted between the spring plates on the rear axles and reinforced mountings in the boot of the car. These shock absorbers work on the same principle as the front shock absorbers.

In the interests of lessening noise and vibration the springs and dampers are mounted on rubber bushes. A rubber spacer is also incorporated between the axle and the springs.

Chapter 11/Suspension - Dampers - Steering

2. Rear Springs - Routine Maintenance

Every 6,000 miles or sooner if the springs start to squeak, clean the dirt off the rear springs and spray them with penetrating oil. With a spanner check the inverted 'U' bolts for tightness. At the same time check the condition of the rubber bushes at either end of each spring.

3. Steering Gear - Routine Maintenance

Every 6,000 miles check the condition of the bellows at either end of the steering gear and the gaiters on the track rod ball joints. If any splits are found it will be necessary to renew the bellows or gaiters.

4. Front Hub Bearings - Maintenance, Removal & Replacement

1. After jacking up the car and removing the front road wheel, disconnect the hydraulic brake pipe at the union on the suspension unit and either plug the open ends of the pipes, or have a jar handy to catch the escaping fluid.
2. Bend back the locking tabs on the two bolts holding the brake calliper to the suspension unit, undo the bolts and remove the calliper.
3. By judicious tapping and levering remove the dust cap from the centre of the hub.
4. Remove the split pin from the nut retainer and undo the larger adjusting nut from the stub axle.
5. Withdraw the thrust washer and the outer tapered bearing.
6. Pull off the complete hub and disc assembly from the stub axle.
7. From the back of the hub assembly carefully prise out the grease seal and remove the inner tapered bearing.
8. Carefully clean out the hub and wash the bearings with petrol making sure that no grease or oil is allowed to get onto the brake disc.
9. Working the grease well into the bearings fully pack the bearing cages and rollers with Castrolease LM, NOTE: Leave the hub and grease seal empty to allow for subsequent expansion of the grease.
10 To reassemble the hub assembly first fit the inner bearing and then gently tap the grease seal back into the hub. If the seal was at all damaged during removal a new one must be fitted.
11 Replace the hub and disc assembly on the stub axle and slide on the outer bearing and the thrust washer.
12 Tighten down the centre adjusting nut to a torque of 27 lb/ft. (3.73 kg.m) whilst rotating the hub and disc to ensure free movement then slacken the nut off 90° and fit the nut retainer and new split pin but at this stage do not bend back the split pin.
13 At this stage it is advisable, if a dial gauge is available to check the disc for run-out. The measurement should be taken as near to the edge of the worn, smooth part of the disc as possible and must not exceed .0035 in. (.089 mm). If this figure is found to be excessive check the mating surfaces of the disc and hub for dirt or damage and also check the bearings and cups for excessive wear or damage.
14 If a dial gauge is not available refit the calliper to the suspension unit, using new locking tabs, and tighten the securing bolts to a torque of 45 to 50 lb/ft. (6.22 to 6.94 kg.m).
15 The brake disc run-out can now be checked by means of a feeler gauge or gauges between the casting of the calliper and the disc. Establish a reasonably tight fit with the gauges between the top of the casting and the disc (on the author's car it was found to be .041 in.) and rotate the disc and hub. Any high or low spot will immediately become obvious by the extra tightness or looseness of the fit of the gauges, and the amount of run-out can be checked by adding or subtracting gauges as necessary. It is only fair to point out that this method is not as accurate as when using a dial gauge owing to the rough nature of the calliper casting.
16 Once the disc run-out has been checked and found to be correct, bend the ends of the split pin back and replace the dust cap.
17 Reconnect the brake hydraulic pipe and bleed the brakes as described in Chapter 9, Section 3.

5. Front Hub Bearings - Adjustment

1. To check the conditions of the hub bearings, jack up the front end of the car and grasp the road wheel at two opposite points to check for any rocking movement in the wheel hub. Watch carefully for any movement in the steering gear, which can easily be mistaken for hub movement.
2. If a front wheel hub has excessive movement, this is adjusted by removing the hub cap and then levering off the small dust cap. Remove the split pin through the stub axle and take off the adjusting nut retainer.
3. If a torque wrench is available tighten the centre adjusting nut down to a torque of 27 lb/ft. (3.73 kg.m) and then slacken it off 90° and replace the nut retainer and a new split pin.
4. Assuming a torque wrench is not available however, tighten up the centre nut until a slight drag is felt on rotating the wheel. Then loosen the nut very slowly until the wheel turns freely again and there is just a perceptible end float.
5. Now replace the nut retainer, a new split pin and the dust cap.

6. Front Hub - Removal & Replacement

1. Follow the instructions given in Section 4 of this chapter up to, and including paragraph 7.
2. Bend back the locking tabs and undo the four bolts holding the hub to the brake disc.
3. If a new hub assembly is being fitted it is supplied complete with new bearing cups and bearings. The bearing cups will already be fitted in the hub. It is essential to check that the cups and bearings are of the same manufacture; this can be done by reading the name on the bearings and by looking at the initial letter stamped on the hub. 'T' stands for Timken and 'S' for Skefco.
4. Clean with scrupulous care the mating surfaces of the hub and check for blemishes or damage. Any dirt or blemishes will almost certainly give rise to disc run-out. Using new locking tabs bolt the disc and the hub together and tighten the bolts to a torque of 30 to 34 lb/ft. (4.15 to 4.70 kg.m).
5. To grease and reassemble the hub assembly follow the instructions given in Section 4, paragraphs 9 on.

7. Front Suspension Units - Removal & Replacement

1. It is difficult to work on the front suspension of the Capri without one or two special tools, the most important of which is a set of adjustable spring clips which is Ford tool No.P.5045. This tool, or similar clips are vital and any attempt to dismantle the units without them may result in

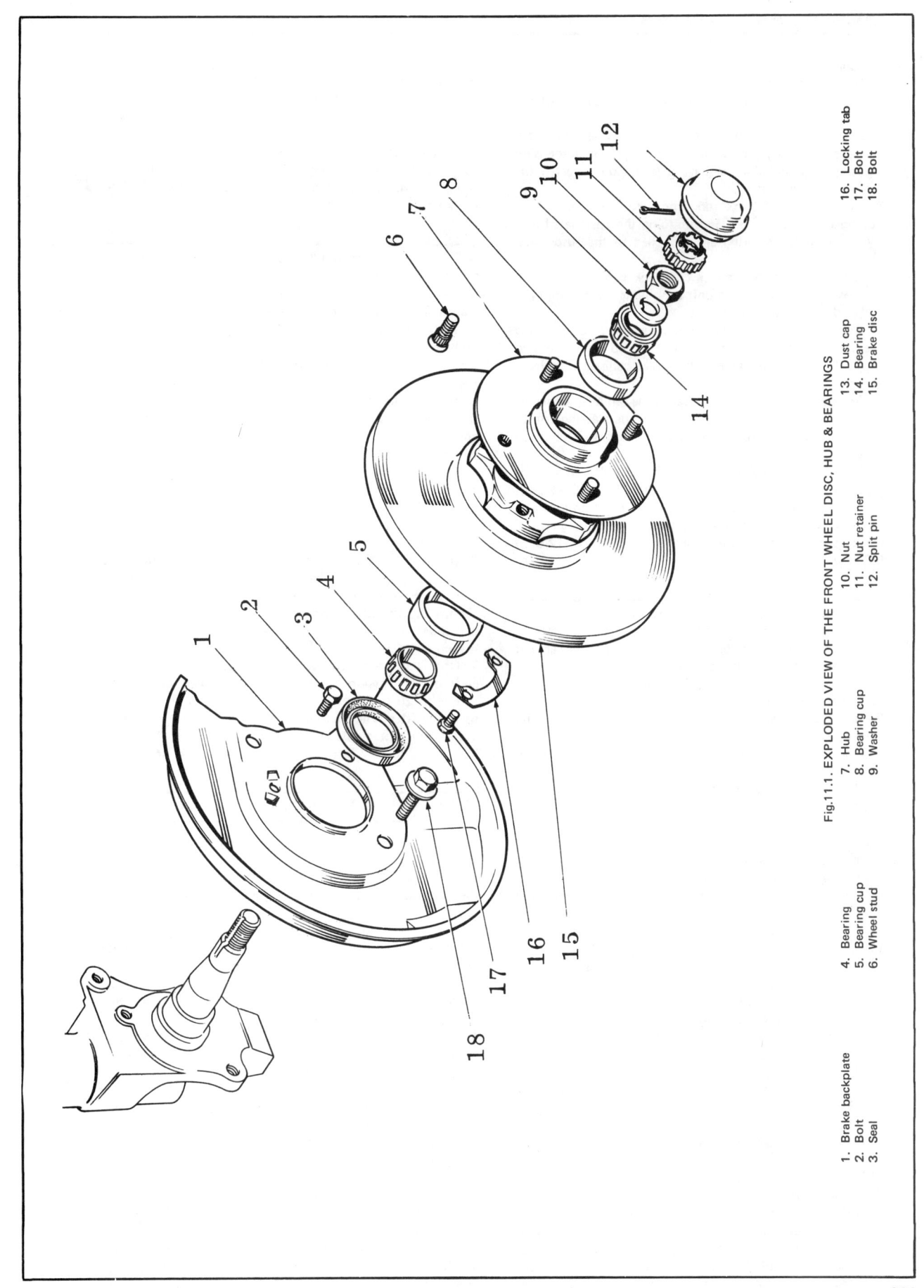

Fig.11.1. EXPLODED VIEW OF THE FRONT WHEEL DISC, HUB & BEARINGS

1. Brake backplate
2. Bolt
3. Seal
4. Bearing
5. Bearing cup
6. Wheel stud
7. Hub
8. Bearing cup
9. Washer
10. Nut
11. Nut retainer
12. Split pin
13. Dust cap
14. Bearing
15. Brake disc
16. Locking tab
17. Bolt
18. Bolt

161

Chapter 11/Suspension - Dampers - Steering

personal injury.

2. Get someone to sit on the wing of the car and with the spring partially compressed in this way, securely fit the spring clips.

3. Jack up the car and remove the road wheel, then disconnect the brake pipe at the bracket on the suspension leg and plug the pipes or have a jar handy to catch the escaping hydraulic fluid.

4. Disconnect the track rod from the steering arm by pulling out the split pin and undoing the castellated nut, thus leaving the steering arm attached to the suspension unit.

5. Remove the outer end of the track control arm from the base of the suspension unit by pulling out the split pin and undoing the castellated nut.

6. Working under the bonnet undo the three bolts holding the top end of the suspension unit to the side panel and lower the unit complete with the brake calliper away from the car.

7. Replacement is a direct reversal of the removal sequence, but remember to use new split pins on the steering arm to track rod nut and also on the track control arm to suspension unit nut.

8. The top suspension unit mounting bolts should be tightened to a torque of 15 to 18 lb/ft. (2.1 to 2.5 kg.m), the track control arm to suspension unit nut to a torque of 30 to 35 lb/ft. (4.2 to 4.8 kg.m) and the steering arm to track rod nut to a torque of 18 to 22 lb/ft. (2.5 to 3.0 kg.m).

8. Front Coil Spring - Removal & Replacement

1. Get someone to sit on the front wing of the car and with the spring partially compressed in this way securely fit spring clips or if available Fords adjustable spring restrainer tool No.P.5045.

2. Jack up the front of the car, fit stands and remove the road wheel.

3. Working under the bonnet, remove the nut and the angled retainer.

4. Undo and remove the three bolts securing the top of the suspension unit to the side panel.

5. Push the piston rod downwards as far as it will go. It should now be possible to remove the top mounting assembly, the dished washer and the upper spring seat from the top of the spring.

6. The spring can now be lifted off its bottom seat and removed over the piston assembly.

7. If a new spring is being fitted check extremely carefully that it is of the same rating as the spring on the other side of the car. The colour coding of the springs can be found in the specifications at the beginning of this chapter.

8. Before fitting a new spring it must be compressed with the adjustable restrainers and make sure that the clips are placed on the same number of coils, and in the same position as on the spring that has been removed.

9. Place the new spring over the piston and locate it on its bottom seat, then pull the piston upwards and fit the upper spring seat so that it locates correctly on the flats cut on the piston rod.

10 Fit the dished washer to the piston rod ensuring that the convex side faces upwards.

11 Now fit the top mount assembly. With the steering in the straight ahead position fit the angled retainer facing inwards at 90° to the wheel angles and the piston rod nut having previously applied Loctite or similar compound to the thread. Do not fully tighten down the nut at this stage.

12 If necessary pull the top end of the unit upwards until it is possible to locate correctly the top mount bracket and fit the three retaining bolts from under the bonnet. These nuts must be tightened down to a torque of 15 to 18 lb/ft. (2.1 to 2.5 kg.m).

13 Remove the spring clips, fit the road wheel and lower the car to the ground.

14 Finally, slacken off the piston rod nut, get an assistant to hold the upper spring seat to prevent it turning, and retighten the nut to a torque of 28 to 30 lb/ft. (3.9 to 4.4 kg.m).

9. Torsion Bar - Removal & Replacement

1. Jack up the front of the car, support the car on suitable stands and remove both front road wheels.

2. Working under the car at the front, knock back the locking tabs on the four bolts securing the two front clamps that hold the torsion bar to the frame and then undo the four bolts and remove the clamps and rubber insulators.

3. Remove the split pins from the castellated nuts retaining the torsion bar to the track control arms then undo the nuts and pull off the large washers, carefully noting the way in which they are fitted.

4. Pull the torsion bar forwards out of the two track control arms and remove it from the car.

5. With the torsion bar out of the car remove the sleeve and large washer from each end of the bar again noting the correct fitting positions.

6. Reassembly is a reversal of the above procedure, but new locking tabs must be used on the front clamp bolts and new split pins on the castellated nuts. The nuts on the clamps and the castellated nuts on each end of the torsion bar must not be fully tightened down until the car is resting on its wheels.

7. Once the car is on its wheels the castellated nuts on the ends of the torsion bar should be tightened down to a torque of 25 to 30 lb/ft. (3.46 to 4.15 kg.m) and the new split pins fitted. The four clamp bolts on the front mounting points must be tightened down to a torque of 15 to 18 lb/ft. (2.07 to 2.47 kg.m) and the locking tabs knocked up.

10. Rack & Pinion Steering Gear - Removal & Replacement

1. Before starting this job, set the front wheels in the straight ahead position. Then jack up the front of the car and place blocks under the wheels; lower the car slightly on the jack so that the track rods are in a near horizontal position.

2. Remove the nut and bolt from the clamp at the front of the flexible coupling on the steering column. This clamp holds the coupling to the pinion splines.

3. Working on the front crossmember, knock back the locking tabs on the two nuts on each 'U' clamp, undo the nut and remove the locking tabs and clamps.

4. Remove the split pins and castellated nuts from the ends of each track rod where they join the steering arms. Separate the track rods from the steering arms and lower the steering gear downwards out of the car.

5. Before replacing the steering gear make sure that the wheels have remained in the straight ahead position. Also check the condition of the mounting rubbers round the housing and if they appear worn or damaged renew them.

6. Check that the steering gear is also in the straight ahead position. This can be done by ensuring that the distances between the ends of both track rods and the steering gear housing on both sides are the same.

7. Place the steering gear in its location on the crossmember and at the same time mate up the splines on the pinion with the splines in the clamp on the steering column

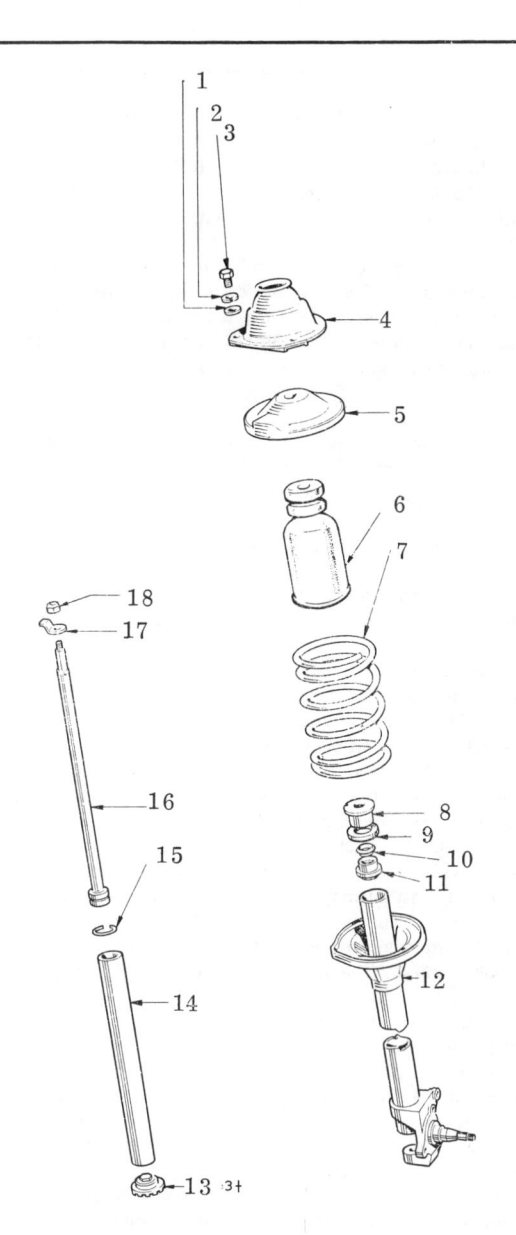

Fig.11.2. EXPLODED VIEW OF THE FRONT SUSPENSION UNIT

1. Washer
2. Spring washer
3. Bolt
4. Upper mounting
5. Upper spring seat
6. Bump stop
7. Coil spring
8. Piston rod gland cap
9. Oil seal ring
10. Rod gland
11. Rod bush & guide
12. Tube & spindle assembly
13. Compression valve
14. Cylinder
15. Ring
16. Piston
17. Cranked retainer
18. Nut

Fig.11.3. View of the front suspension upper mounting points showing the cranked retainers correctly fitted pointing inwards at 90°

163

Chapter 11/Suspension - Dampers - Steering

flexible coupling.

8. Replace the two 'U' clamps using new locking tabs under the bolts, tighten down the bolts to a torque of 12 to 15 lb/ft. (1.7 to 2.0 kg.m) and bend up the locking tabs.

9. Refit the track rod ends into the steering arms, replace the castellated nuts and tighten them to a torque of 18 to 22 lb/ft. (2.5 to 3.0 kg.m). Use new split pins to retain the nuts.

10 Tighten the clamp bolt on the steering column flexible coupling to a torque of 12 to 15 lb/ft. (1.7 to 2.1 kg.m) having first made sure that the pinion is correctly located in the splines.

11 Jack up the car, remove the blocks from under the wheels and lower the car to the ground. It is advisable at this stage to take your car to your local Ford dealer and have the toe-in checked.

11. Rack & Pinion Steering Gear - Adjustments

1. For the steering gear to function correctly, two adjustments are necessary. These are pinion bearing pre-load and rack damper adjustment.

2. To carry out these adjustments, remove the steering gear from the car as described in the previous section, then mount the steering gear in a soft jawed vice so that the pinion is in a horizontal position and the rack damper cover plate to the top.

3. Remove the rack damper cover plate by undoing the two retaining bolts, then take off the gasket and shims from under the plate. Also remove the small spring and the recessed yoke which bears on the rack.

4. Now remove the pinion bearing pre-load cover plate from the base of the pinion, by undoing the two bolts. Then take off the gasket and shim pack.

5. To correctly set the pinion bearing pre-load, replace the cover plate without the gasket and shims and tighten down the bolts evenly until the cover plate is just touching the pinion bearing.

6. Using feeler gauges, measure the gap between the cover plate and the steering gear casing. To be sure that the cover plate has been evenly tightened, take a reading adjacent to each bolt. These readings should be the same. If they are not, loosen the cover plate and retighten it more evenly.

7. Assemble a shim pack including a gasket, which must be fitted next to the cover plate on refitting, which is .002 to .004 in. (.05 to .10 mm) less than the measured gap. Shim thicknesses available are listed below:-

Part No.	Material	Thickness
3038E-3N597-C	Steel	.010 in. (.254 mm)
3038E-3N597-B	Steel	.005 in. (.127 mm)
3038E-3N597-A	Steel	.002 in. (.051 mm)
3038E-3N598-A	Paper	.005 in. (.127 mm)

8. Remove the cover plate again, fit the assembled shim pack and gasket, with the gasket next to the cover plate, refit the cover plate and having applied Loctite or similar sealer on the threads of the bolts, tighten them down to a torque of 6 to 8 lb/ft. (0.9 to 1.1 kg.m).

9. To set the rack damper adjustment, replace the yoke in its location on the rack and make sure it is fully home. Then measure the distance between the bottom of the recess in the yoke and the top of the steering gear casing.

10 Assemble a shim pack with a gasket on either side of the shims which is between .0005 to .0035 in. greater than the dimension measured in the previous paragraph. Shim thicknesses available are as listed in next column.

Part No.	Material	Thickness
3024E-3K544-C	Steel	.010 in. (.254 mm)
3024E-3K544-B	Steel	.005 in. (.127 mm)
3024E-3K544-A	Steel	.002 in. (.051 mm)
3024E-3581-A	Paper	.005 in. (.127 mm)

11 Refit the spring into its recess in the yoke and fit the shim pack and gaskets. Replace the cover plate having first applied Loctite or similar sealing compound to the bolt threads. Then tighten down the bolts to a torque of 6 to 8 lb/ft. (0.9 to 1.1 kg.m).

12. Rack & Pinion Steering Gear - Dismantling & Reassembly

1. Remove the steering gear from the car as described in Section 10.

2. Unscrew the ball joints and locknuts from the end of each track rod, having previously marked the threads to ensure correct positioning on reassembly. Alternatively the number of turns required to undo the ball joint can be counted and noted.

3. Slacken off the clips securing the rubber bellows to each track rod and the steering gear housing then pull off the bellows. Have a quantity of rag handy to catch the oil which will escape when the bellows are removed.

4. To dismantle the steering gear, it is only necessary to remove the track rod which is furthest away from the pinion on either right or left-hand drive cars.

5. To remove the track rod place the steering gear in a soft jawed vice. Working on the track rod ball joint carefully drill out the pin that locks the ball housing to the locknut. Great care must be taken not to drill too deeply or you will drill into the threads on the rack thus causing irrepairable damage. The hole should be about 3/8th inch deep.

6. Hold the locknut with a spanner, then grip the ball housing with a mole wrench and undo it from the threads on the rack.

7. Take out the spring and ball seat from the recess in the end of the rack and then unscrew the locknut from the threads on the rack. The spring and ball seat must be replaced by new components on reassembly.

8. Carefully prise out the pinion dust seal then withdraw the pinion together with the bearing assembly nearest the flexible coupling. As the bearings utilise bearing tracks and loose balls (14 in each bearing) care must be taken not to lose any of the balls or drop them into the steering gear on reassembly.

9. With the pinion removed, withdraw the complete rack assembly with one track rod still attached from the pinion end of the casing, having first removed the rack damper cover, gasket, shims, springs and yoke as described in Section 11, paragraph 3.

10 Now remove the remaining pinion bearing assembly from the rack casing.

11 It is always advisable to withdraw the rack from the pinion end of the casing. This avoids passing the rack teeth through the bush at the other end of the casing and causing possible damage.

12 Carefully examine all parts for signs of wear or damage. Check the condition of the rack support bush at the opposite end of the casing from the pinion. If this is worn renew it. If the rack or pinion teeth are in any way damaged a completely new steering gear will have to be fitted.

13 Take the pinion oil seal off the top of the casing and replace it with a new seal.

14 To commence reassembly fit the lower pinion bearing and thrust washer into their recess in the casing. The loose balls can be held in place by a small amount of grease.

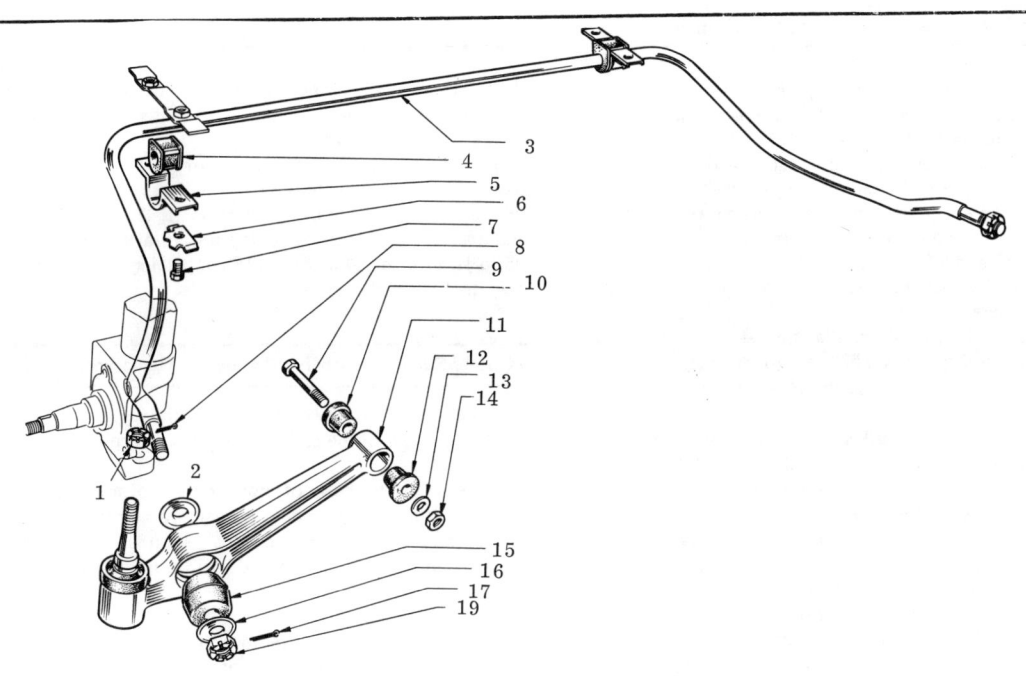

Fig.11.4. EXPLODED VIEW OF THE TORSION BAR & TRACK CONTROL ARM

1. Castellated nut
2. Dished washer
3. Torsion bar
4. Rubber bush
5. 'U' clamp
6. Locking tab
7. Bolt
8. Split pin
9. Bolt
10. Bush
11. Track control arm
12. Bush
13. Washer
14. Nut
15. Bush
16. Dished washer
17. Split pin
18. Castellated nut

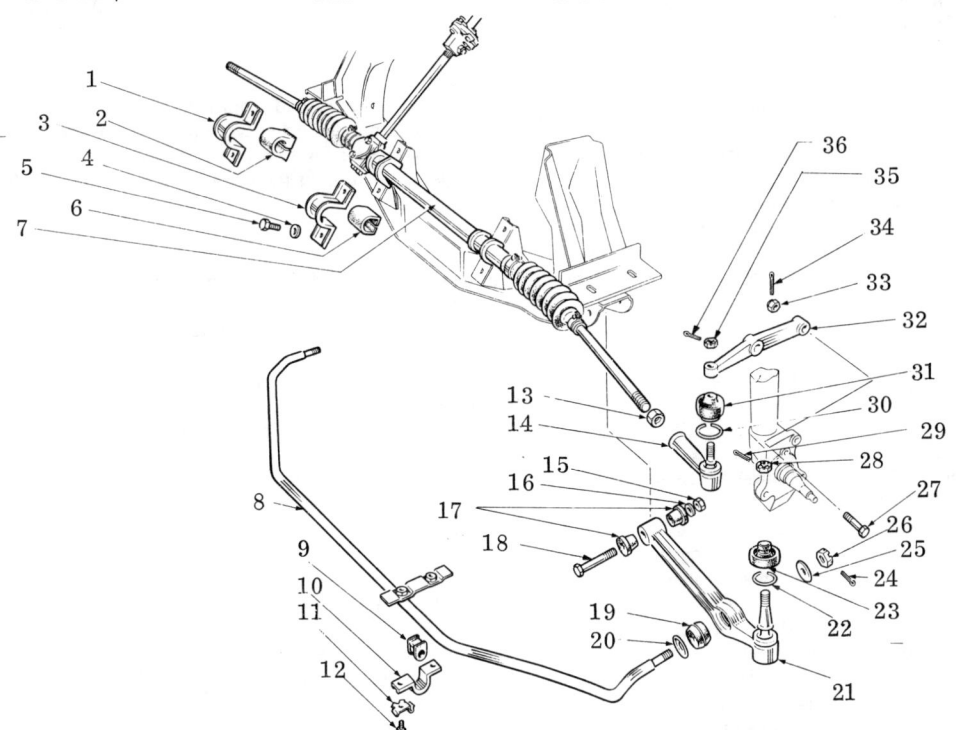

Fig.11.5. EXPLODED VIEW OF THE RACK & PINION & TRACK CONTROL ASSEMBLIES

1. 'U' clamp
2. Rubber bush
3. 'U' clamp
4. Washer
5. Bolt
6. Bush
7. Rack housing
8. Torsion bar
9. Rubber bush
10. Clamp
11. Locking tab
12. Bolt
13. Locknut
14. Track rod end
15. Nut
16. Washer
17. Bush
18. Bolt
19. Bush
20. Washer
21. Track control arm
22. Ring
23. Seal
24. Split pin
25. Washer
26. Castellated nut
27. Bolt
28. Castellated nut
29. Split pin
30. Ring
31. Bush
32. Steering arm
33. Nut
34. Split pin
35. Castellated nut
36. Split pin

165

Chapter 11/Suspension - Dampers - Steering

15 Replace the rack in the casing from the pinion end and position it in the straight ahead position by equalising the amount it protrudes at either end of the casing.

16 Replace the remaining pinion bearing and thrust washer onto the pinion and fit the pinion into the casing so that the larger master spline on the pinion shaft is parallel to the rack and on the right-hand side of the pinion. This applies to both right and left-hand drive cars.

17 Replace the rack damper yoke, springs, shims, gasket and cover plate.

16 To replace the track rod that has been removed, start by fitting a new spring and ball seat to the recess in the end of the rack shaft and replace the locknut onto the threads of the rack.

18 Lubricate the ball, ball seat and ball housing with a small amount of SAE 90 EP oil. Then slide the ball housing over the track rod and screw the housing onto the rack threads keeping the track rod in the horizontal position until the track rod starts to become stiff to move.

19 Using a normal spring balance hook it round the track rod half an inch from the end and check the effort required to move it from the horizontal position.

20 By adjusting the tightness of the ball housing on the rack threads the effort required to move the track rod must be set at 5 lbs. (2.8 kg.).

21 Tighten the locknut up to the housing and then recheck that the effort required to move the track rod is still correct at 5 lb. (2.8 kg.).

22 On the line where the locknut and ball housing meet, drill a 1/8th inch, (3.18 mm) diameter hole which must be 3/8th inch, (9.52 mm) deep. Even if the two halves of the old hole previously drilled out align a new hole must be drilled.

23 Tap a new retaining pin into the hole and peen the end over to secure it.

24 Replace the rubber bellows and the track rod ends ensuring that they are replaced in exactly the same position from which they were removed.

25 Remove the rack damper cover plate and pour in 0.25 pint (0.3 US pints, 0.15 litre) of SAE 90 EP oil. Then carry out both steering gear adjustments as detailed in the previous section.

26 After replacing the steering gear on the car as described in Section 10, it is strongly recommended that you take the car to your nearest Ford dealer and have the toe-in correctly adjusted.

13. Steering Wheel & Column - Removal & Replacement

1. Place the car with its wheels in the straight ahead position, disconnect the battery by removing the negative earth lead and disconnect the choke cable from the carburetter.
2. Working under the bonnet undo the clamp bolt on the top of the steering column universal joint.
3. Moving inside the car, prise out the centre emblem on the steering wheel, knock back the locking tab on the centre nut and undo the nut. Remove the locking tab and pull the steering wheel off its splines.
4. Undo the two screws securing the steering column shrouds to the column as shown in Fig.11.9. Then remove the two bolts securing the bottom of the shroud and the column to the underside of the fascia. Lift the indicator cancelling cam and its spring off the shaft, noting the position in which they are fitted in relation to the switch.
5. Pull off the multi-pin connectors to the indicator switch and ignition switch, then remove the indicator switch assembly from the top of the column by undoing the two small retaining screws.
6. Withdraw the steering column into the car taking care not to damage the grommet where the column passes through the floor of the car.
7. Replacement is a direct reversal of the above procedure. Note that the clamp bolt on the universal joint must be tightened to a torque of 12 to 15 lb/ft. (1.7 to 2.1 kg.m) and the steering wheel retaining nut to a torque of 20 to 25 lb/ft. (2.8 to 3.4 kg.m). Before replacing this nut ensure that the indicators cancel correctly.

14. Rear Shock Absorbers - Removal & Replacement

1. Chock the front wheels to prevent the car moving, then jack up the rear of the car and for convenience sake remove the road wheels.
2. Working inside the boot, hold the top of the piston and prevent it turning by holding a small spanner (¼ inch A/F) across the flats provided and then with an open ended spanner remove the locknut and main nut from the piston rod.
3. Lift off the large steel washer and the rubber bush.
4. Working under the car, remove the nut, lock washer and bolt that retain the lower end of the damper to the axle casing.
5. Lower the damper from the car, then remove the further rubber bush and steel washer from the top of the piston rod.
6. Replacement is a reversal of the above procedure.
7. The nut on the bolt securing the lower end of the damper must be tightened down to a torque of 40 to 45 lb/ft. (5.54 to 6.22 kg.m).
8. The main nut on the top mounting must be tightened to a torque of 20 to 25 lb/ft. (2.76 to 3.46 kg.m) but the piston must be prevented from rotating during this operation. Most torque wrenches will not allow the flats on the piston rod to be held to prevent turning so it is better to get an assistant to hold the upper half of the damper from under the car.

15. Rear Springs - Removal & Replacement

1. Chock the front wheels to prevent the car moving, then jack up the rear of the car and support it on suitable stands. To make the springs more accessible remove the road wheels.
2. Then place a trolley jack underneath the differential housing to support the rear axle assembly when the springs are removed. Do not raise the jack under the differential housing so that the springs are flattened, but raise it just enough to take the full weight of the axle with the springs fully extended.
3. Undo the rear shackle nuts and remove the combined shackle bolt and plate assemblies. Then remove the rubber bushes.
4. Undo the nut from the front mounting and take out the bolt running through the mounting.
5. Undo the nuts on the ends of the four 'U' bolts and remove the 'U' bolts together with the attachment plate and rubber spring insulators.
6. Replacement is a direct reversal of the above procedure. The nuts on the 'U' bolts, spring front mounting and rear shackles must be torqued down to the figures given in the specifications at the beginning of this chapter only AFTER the car has been lowered onto its wheels.

16. Radius Arms - Removal & Replacement

1. Chock the front wheels to prevent the car moving, then

Fig.11.6. View of the steering column universal joint and flexible coupling

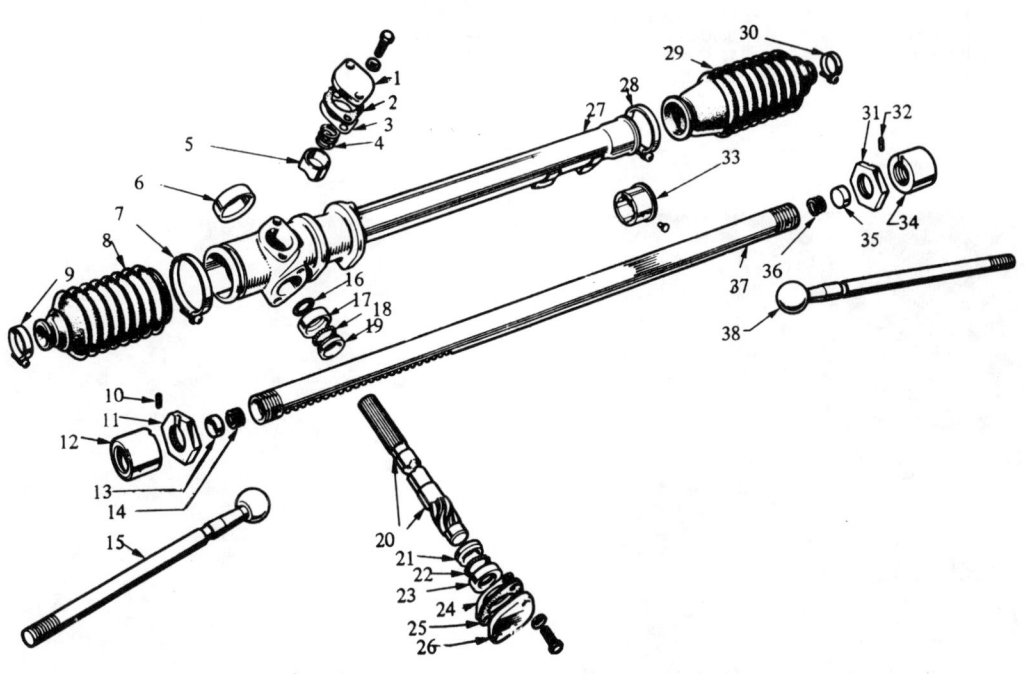

Fig.11.7. EXPLODED VIEW OF THE RACK & PINION ASSEMBLY

1. Cover
2. Gasket
3. Shim
4. Spring
5. Rack adjusting slipper
6. Seal
7. Clip
8. Rubber bellows
9. Clip
10. Locking pin
11. Nut
12. Ball joint housing
13. Ball joint housing
14. Spring
15. Track rod
16. Oil seal
17. Pinion adjustment bearing
18. Ball bearing
19. Race
20. Pinion
21. Race
22. Ball bearing
23. Pinion adjustment bearing
24. Shim
25. Gasket
26. Cover
27. Rack housing
28. Clip
29. Rubber bellows
30. Clip
31. Nut
32. Locking pin
33. Bush
34. Ball joint housing
35. Ball joint housing
36. Spring
37. Rack
38. Track rod

167

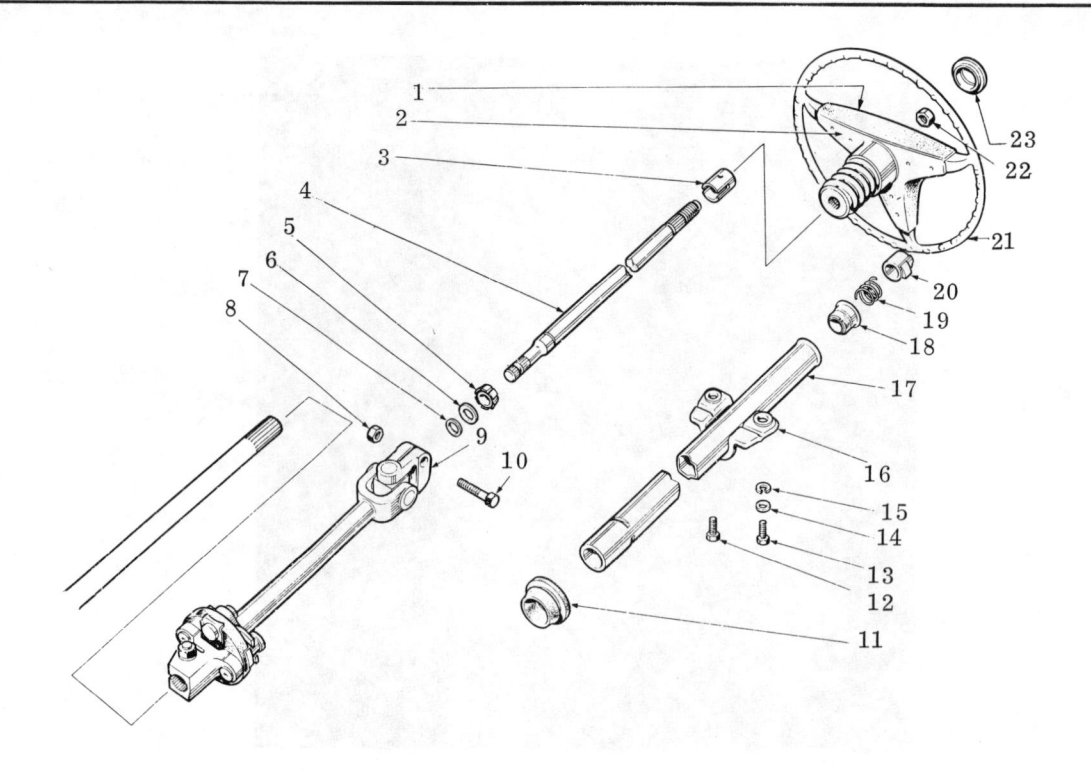

Fig.11.8. EXPLODED VIEW OF THE STEERING COLUMN ASSEMBLY

1. Steering wheel
2. Padding
3. Flange
4. Steering shaft
5. Bearing
6. Washer
7. Seal
8. Nut
9. Universal joint
10. Clamp bolt
11. Grommet
12. Bolt
13. Bolt
14. Washer
15. Spring washer
16. 'U' clamp
17. Outer column
18. Bearing
19. Spring
20. Indicator cancelling cam
21. Wheel rim
22. Steering wheel nut
23. Centre emblem

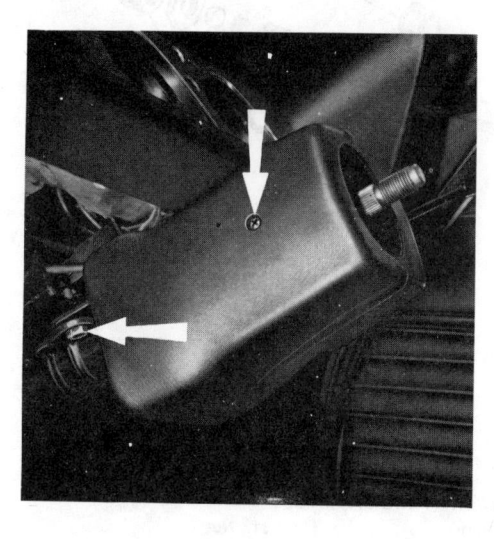

Fig.11.9. View of the left and right-hand screws and bolts to be removed to release the shroud and steering column

168

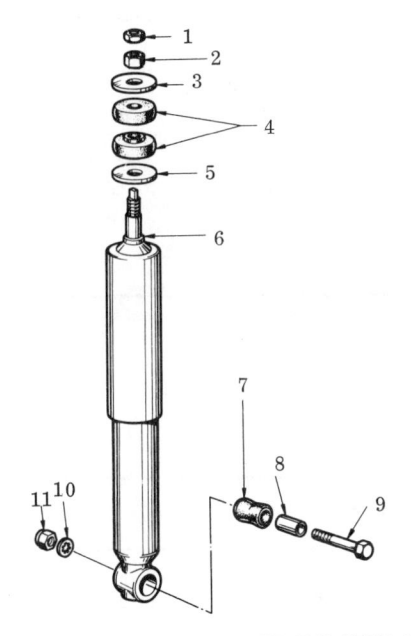

Fig.11.10. EXPLODED VIEW OF THE REAR SHOCK ABSORBER

1. Locknut
2. Nut
3. Washer
4. Rubber bushes
5. Washer
6. Shock absorber
7. Bush
8. Insert
9. Bolt
10. Shakeproof washer
11. Nut

Fig.11.11. View of the rear spring 'U' bolts and lower shock absorber mounting

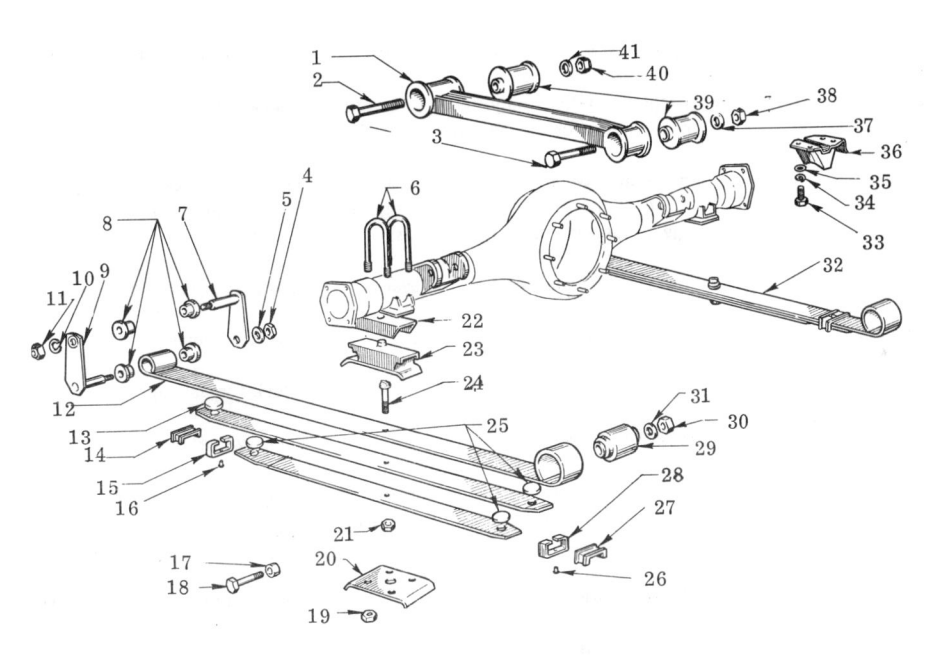

Fig.11.12. EXPLODED VIEW OF THE REAR SPRING & RADIUS ARM ASSEMBLIES

1. Radius arm
2. Bolt
3. Bolt
4. Nut
5. Washer
6. 'U' bolts
7. Shackle bar & stud
8. Bushes
9. Shackle bar & stud
10. Spring washer
11. Nut
12. Spring leaf
13. Spacer
14. Clamp insulator
15. Clamp
16. Pin
17. Bush
18. Bolt
19. Nut
20. 'U' bolts plate
21. Bolt
22. Plate
23. Insulator
24. Stud
25. Spacers
26. Pin
27. Clamp insulator
28. Clamp
29. Bush
30. Nut
31. Washer
32. Spring assembly
33. Bolt
34. Spring washer
35. Washer
36. Plate
37. Washer
38. Nut
39. Bush
40. Bolt
41. Washer

169

Chapter 11/Suspension - Dampers - Steering

jack up the rear of the car and support it on suitable stands.

2. Undo the nut and remove the bolt holding the rear end of the radius arm to the axle casing.

3. To take the tension off the radius arm it may be necessary to slightly raise the axle casing with a jack.

4. Repeat this procedure on the front mounting nut and bolt and remove the radius arm from the car.

5. Replacement is a reversal of the above procedure but the nuts should be torqued down to the figures given in the specifications at the beginning of this chapter AFTER the car has been lowered onto its wheels.

Fault Finding Chart — Suspension - Dampers - Steering

Before diagnosing faults from the following chart, check that any irregularities are not caused by:—
1. Binding brakes.
2. Incorrect 'mix' of radial and cross-ply tyres.
3. Incorrect tyre pressures.
4. Misalignment of the body frame.

Symptom	Reason/s	Remedy
Steering wheel can be moved considerably before any sign of movement of the wheels is apparent.	Wear in the steering linkage, gear and column coupling.	Check movement in all joints and steering gear and overhaul and renew as required.
Vehicle difficult to steer in a consistent straight line - wandering.	As above.	As above.
	Wheel alignment incorrect (indicated by excessive or uneven tyre wear).	Check wheel alignment.
	Front wheel hub bearings loose or worn.	Adjust or renew as necessary.
	Worn ball joints or suspension arms.	Renew as necessary.
Steering stiff and heavy.	Incorrect wheel alignment (indicated by excessive or uneven tyre wear).	Check wheel alignment.
	Excessive wear or seizure in one or more of the joints in the steering linkage or suspension arm ball joints.	Renew as necessary or grease the suspension unit ball joints.
	Excessive wear in the steering gear unit.	Adjust if possible or renew.
Wheel wobble and vibration.	Road wheels out of balance.	Balance wheels.
	Road wheels buckled.	Check for damage.
	Wheel alignment incorrect.	Check wheel alignment.
	Wear in the steering linkage, suspension arm ball joints or suspension arm pivot bushes.	Check and renew as necessary.
	Broken front spring.	Check and renew as necessary.
Excessive pitching and rolling on corners and during braking.	Defective dampers and/or broken spring	Check and renew as necessary.

Chapter 12/Bodywork and Underframe

Contents

General Description	1	Door Lock Assembly - Removal & Replacement	13
Maintenance - Bodywork & Underframe	2	Door Lock Interior Remote Control Handle - Removal & Replacement	14
Maintenance - Upholstery & Carpets	3	Door Glasses - Removal & Replacement	15
Minor Body Repairs	4	Door Outer Belt Weatherstrip - Removal & Replacement	16
Major Body Repairs	5		
Maintenance - Hinges & Locks	6	Bonnet - Removal & Replacement	17
Front Bumper - Removal & Replacement	7	Boot Lid - Removal & Replacement	18
Rear Bumper - Removal & Replacement	8	Window Regulator - Removal & Replacement	19
Windscreen Glass - Removal & Replacement	9	Heater Assembly - Removal & Replacement	20
Door Rattles - Tracing & Rectification	10	Heater Motor - Removal & Replacement	21
Door Striker Plate - Removal, Replacement & Adjustment	11	Heater Radiator - Removal & Replacement	22
Door Trim Panel - Removal & Replacement	12	Heater Control Cables - Adjustment	23

1. General Description

The combined body and underframe is of an all steel welded construction. This makes a very strong and torsionally ridged shell.

The Capri is only available in two door form. The door hinges are welded to the doors and securely bolted to the body. To prevent the doors opening too wide and causing damage check straps are fitted. The driver's door is locked from the outside by means of a key, the other door being locked from the inside.

Toughened safety glass is fitted to all windows; as an additional safety precaution the windscreen glass has a specially toughened 'zone' in front of the driver. In the event of the windscreen shattering this 'Zone' breaks into much larger pieces than the rest of the screen thus giving the driver much better vision than would otherwise be possible.

The interior of all models is basically the same except that the G.T. models have a more comprehensive range of instruments including separate ammeter, oil pressure gauge, fuel gauge and water temperature gauge. The normal combined instrument on the fascia being replaced by a tachometer.

The Capri uses the Aeroflow type of ventilation system. Air being drawn in through a grille on the scuttle can either be heated or pass straight into the car. Used air passes out through a grille at the base of the rear window.

All models are fitted with bucket type front seats with seat belts as standard. The rear seats are also fitted with anchor points for belts which can be obtained as an optional extra.

2. Maintenance - Bodywork & Underframe

1. The condition of your car's bodywork is of considerable importance as it is on this that the second-hand value of the car will mainly depend. It is very much more difficult to repair neglected bodywork than to renew mechanical assemblies. The hidden portions of the body, such as the wheels arches and the underframe and the engine compartment are equally important, through obviously not requiring such frequent attention as the immediately visible paintwork.

2. Once a year or every 12,000 miles, it is a sound scheme to visit your local main agent and have the underside of the body steam cleaned. This will take about 1½ hours and cost about £4. All traces of dirt and oil will be removed and the underside can then be inspected carefully for rust, damaged hydraulic pipes, frayed electrical wiring and similar maladies. The car should be greased on completion of this job.

3. At the same time the engine compartment should be cleaned in the same manner. If steam cleaning facilities are not available then brush 'Gunk' or a similar cleanser over the whole engine and engine compartment with a stiff paint brush, working it well in where there is an accumulation of oil and dirt. Do not paint the ignition system but protect it with oily rags when the Gunk is washed off. As the Gunk is washed away it will take with it all traces of oil and dirt, leaving the engine looking clean and bright.

4. The wheel arches should be given particular attention as undersealing can easily come away here and stones and dirt thrown up from the road wheels can soon cause the paint to chip and flake, and so allow rust to set in. If rust is found, clean down to the bare metal with wet and dry paper, paint on an anti-corrosive coating such as Kurust, or if preferred, red lead, and renew the paintwork and undercoating.

5. The bodywork should be washed once a week or when dirty. Thoroughly wet the car to soften the dirt and then wash the car down with a soft sponge and plenty of clean water. If the surplus dirt is not washed off very gently, in time it will wear the paint down as surely as wet and dry paper. It is best to use a hose if this is available. Give the car a final wash down and then dry with a soft chamois leather to prevent the formation of spots.

6. Spots of tar and grease thrown up from the road can be removed with a rag dampened with petrol.

7. Once every six months, or every three months if wished,

Chapter 12/Bodywork & Underframe

give the bodywork and chromium trim a thoroughly good wax polish. If a chromium cleaner is used to remove rust on any of the car's plated parts remember that the cleaner also removes part of the chromium so use sparingly.

3. Maintenance - Upholstery & Carpets

1. Remove the carpets and thoroughly vacuum clean the interior of the car every three months or more frequently if necessary.
2. Beat out the carpets and vacuum clean them if they are very dirty. If the headlining or upholstery is soiled apply an upholstery cleaner with a damp sponge and wipe off with a clean dry cloth.

4. Minor Body Repairs

1. At some time during your ownership of your car it is likely that it will be bumped or scraped in a mild way, causing some slight damage to the body.
2. Major damage must be repaired by your local Ford agent, but there is no reason why you cannot successfully beat out, repair, and respray minor damage yourself. The essential items which the owner should gather together to ensure a really professional job are:-

a) A plastic filler such as Holts 'Cataloy'.
b) Paint whose colour matches exactly that of the bodywork, either in a can for application by a spray gun, or in an aerosol can.
c) Fine cutting paste.
d) Medium and fine grade wet and dry paper.

3. Never use a metal hammer to knock out small dents as the blows tend to scratch and distort the metal. Knock out the dent with a mallet or rawhide hammer and press on the underside of the dented surface a metal dolly or smooth wooden block roughly contoured to the normal shape of the damaged area.
4. After the worst of the damaged area has been knocked out, rub down the dent and surrounding area with medium wet and dry paper and thoroughly clean away all traces of dirt.
5. The plastic filler comprises a paste and a hardener which must be thoroughly mixed together. Mix only a small portion at a time as the paste sets hard within five to fifteen minutes depending on the amount of hardener used.
6. Smooth on the filler with a knife or stiff plastic to the shape of the damaged portion and allow to thoroughly dry - a process which takes about six hours. After the filler has dried it is likely that it will have contracted slightly so spread on a second layer of filler if necessary.
7. Smooth down the filler with fine wet and dry paper wrapped round a suitable block of wood and continue until the whole area is perfectly smooth and it is impossible to feel where the filler joins the rest of the paintwork.
8. Spray on from an aerosol can, or with a spray gun, an anti-rust undercoat, smooth down with wet and dry paper, and then spray on two coats of the final finishing using a circular motion.
9. When thoroughly dry polish the whole area with a fine cutting paste to smooth the resprayed area into the remainder of the wing and to remove the small particles of spray paint which will have settled round the area.
10 This will leave the wing looking perfect with not a trace of the previous unsightly dent.

5. Major Body Repairs

1. Because the body is built on the monocoque principle and is integral with the underframe, major damage must be repaired by competent mechanics with the necessary welding and hydraulic straightening equipment.
2. If the damage has been serious it is vital that the body is checked for correct alignment, as otherwise the handling of the car will suffer and many other faults such as excessive tyre wear and wear in the transmission and steering may occur. Fords produce a special alignment jig and to ensure that all is correct a repaired car should always be checked on this jig.

6. Maintenance - Hinges & Locks

Once every six months or 6,000 miles the door, bonnet and boot hinges should be oiled with a few drops of engine oil from an oil can. The door striker plates can be given a thin smear of grease to reduce wear and ensure free movement.

7. Front Bumper - Removal & Replacement

1. Undo the single retaining bolt on either end of the bumper from inside the front wings.
2. Working at the back of the bumper remove the nuts from the two chrome headed bolts, withdraw the bolts and lift the bumper away.
3. Replacement is a reversal of the above procedure, but before replacing the two bolts from inside the wings ensure that the bumper is correctly located. To make sure this is correct it is advisable not to tighten the centre nuts fully down until the end bolts have been located.

8. Rear Bumper - Removal & Replacement

1. From behind the bumper bar remove the nuts from the four chrome headed bolts, withdraw the bolts and lift the bumper away.
2. Replacement is a direct reversal of the removal procedure, but it is advisable not to fully tighten down the nuts until it is certain that the bumper is perfectly straight and correctly located.

9. Windscreen Glass - Removal & Replacement

1. If you are unfortunate enough to have a windscreen shatter, or should you wish to renew your present windscreen, fitting a replacement is one of the few jobs which the average owner is advised to leave to a professional. For the owner who wishes to attempt the job himself the following instructions are given.
2. Cover the bonnet with a blanket or cloth to prevent accidental damage and remove the windscreen wiper blades and arms as detailed in Chapter 10, Sections 33 and 34.
3. Put on a pair of lightweight shoes and get into one of the front seats. With a piece of soft cloth between the soles of your shoes and the windscreen glass, place both feet in one top corner of the windscreen and push firmly. (See Fig.12.1).
4. When the weatherstrip has freed itself from the body flange in that area repeat the process at frequent intervals

Chapter 12/Bodywork & Underframe

along the top edge of the windscreen until, from outside the car the glass and weatherstrip can be removed together.

5. If you are having to replace your windscreen due to a shattered screen, remove all traces of sealing compound and broken glass from the weatherstrip and body flange.

6. Gently prise out the clip which covers the joint of the chromium finisher strip and pull the finisher strip out of the weatherstrip. Then remove the weatherstrip from the glass or if it is still on the car, as in the case of a shattered screen, remove it from the body flange.

7. To fit a new windscreen start by fitting the weatherstrip around the new windscreen glass.

8. Apply a suitable sealer such as Expandite SR-51-B to the weatherstrip to body groove. In this groove then fit a fine but strong piece of cord right the way round the groove allowing an overlap of about six inches at the joint.

9. From outside the car place the windscreen in its correct position making sure that the loose end of the cord is inside the car.

10 With an assistant pressing firmly on the outside of the windscreen get into the car and slowly pull out the cord thus drawing the weatherstrip over the body flange. (See Fig.12.2).

11 Apply a further layer of sealer to the underside of rubber to glass groove from outside the car.

12 Replace the chromium finisher strip into its groove in the weatherstrip and replace the clip which covers its joint.

13 Carefully clean off any surplus sealer from the windscreen glass before it has a chance to harden and then replace the windscreen wiper arms and blades.

10. Door Rattles - Tracing & Rectification

1. The most common cause of door rattle is a misaligned, loose, or worn striker plate, however other causes may be:-

a) Loose door or window winder handles.
b) Loose, or misaligned door lock components.
c) Loose or worn remote control mechanism.

2. It is quite possible for door rattles to be the result of a combination of the above faults so a careful examination should be made to determine the exact cause of the rattle.

3. If striker plate wear or misalignment is the cause of the rattle the plate should be renewed or adjusted as necessary. The procedures for these tasks are detailed in Section 11.

4. Should the window winder handle rattle, this can be easily rectified by inserting a rubber washer between the escutcheon and door trim panel.

5. If the rattle is found to be emanating from the door lock it will in all probability mean that the lock is worn and therefore should be replaced with a new unit as described in Section 13.

6. Lastly, if it is worn hinge pins causing the rattle they should be renewed. This is not a D.I.Y. job as a special tool is required for their removal and replacement.

11. Door Striker Plate - Removal, Replacement & Adjustment

1. Striker plate removal and adjustment are not really D.I.Y. tasks as a special tool is required to turn the plate retaining screws. However, if the tool (Churchill No.RIBE M6 special screwdriver) can be hired or loaned from your local Ford dealers, proceed as follows.

2. If it is wished to renew a worn striker plate mark its position on the door pillar with a pencil. This will enable the new plate to be fitted in exactly the same position.

3. To remove the plate, simply undo the four special screws which hold the plate and anti-slip shim in position. Replacement is equally straightforward.

4. To adjust the striker plate slacken the retaining screws until the plate can just be moved, gently close the door, with the outside push button depressed, to the fully closed position. Release the button.

5. Move the door in and out until it is flush with the surrounding bodywork. Then fully depress the button and gently open the door.

6. Check that the striker plate is vertical and tighten down the four special screws. Adjustment is now completed.

12. Door Trim Panel - Removal & Replacement

1. Carefully prise the black plastic trim from its recess in the window winder handle. This will expose the handle retaining screws. Remove the screw, handle and escutcheon.

2. Prise the black plastic trim out of the recess in the escutcheon of the interior lock release handle. Unscrew the screw securing the escutcheon in position. Remove the escutcheon.

3. Unscrew and remove the black plastic knob on the interior door lock. Carefully prise the escutcheon beneath it out of the trim.

4. Remove the two screws securing the lower part of the armrest. Move the armrest towards the top front corner of the door. This will release the retaining lug. Remove the armrest complete.

5. Insert a thin strip of metal with all the sharp edges removed (A six inch steel rule is ideal) between the door and the recessed trim panel. This will release one or two of the panel retaining clips without damaging the trim. The panel can now be gently eased off by hand. Removal is now complete.

6. Replacement is generally a reversal of the removal procedure.

NOTE: When replacing the panel ensure that each of the panel retaining clips is firmly located in its hole by sharply striking the panel in the approximate area of each clip with the palm of the hand. This will eliminate the possibility of the trim rattling.

13. Door Lock Assembly - Removal & Replacement

1. Remove the door trim panel as described in Section 12.

2. Temporarily replace the window winder handle and wind the window up. Remove the polythene sheet covering the interior of the door by cutting through the adhesive around its periphery with a sharp blade.

3. Disconnect the remote control rod by freeing it from the clip at the remote handle end.

4. Disconnect the push button rod, exterior operating rod and locking rod from the lock by releasing their clips.

5. Unscrew and remove the two screws securing the window channel.

6. Remove the three screws securing the lock to the door, the lock can now be withdrawn. Remove the four rod connecting clips from the lock. Removal is now complete.

7. Replacement: Replace the four rod connecting clips on the lock.

8. Reposition the lock assembly in the door recess and secure it with the three screws. Replace the two window channel retaining screws.

9. Reconnect all operating rods, and check the operation of the lock.

10 Replace the polythene sheet over the door apertures, a suitable adhesive is Bostik No.3, followed by the door trim panel and fitments.

This sequence of photographs deals with the repair of the dent and paintwork damage shown in this photo. The procedure will be similar for the repair of a hole. It should be noted that the procedures given here are simplified — more explicit instructions will be found in the text

In the case of a dent the first job — after removing surrounding trim — is to hammer out the dent where access is possible. This will minimise filling. Here, the large dent having been hammered out, the damaged area is being made slightly concave

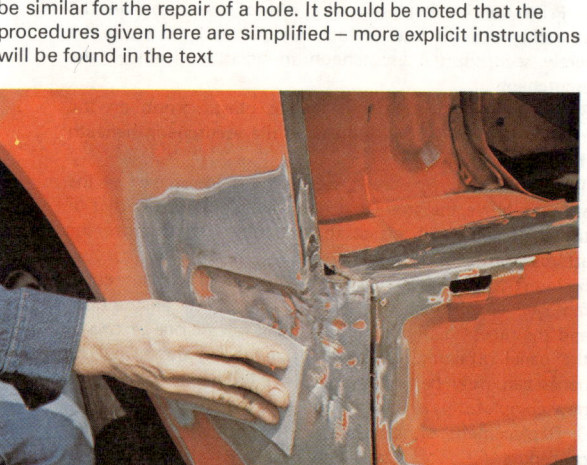

Now all paint must be removed from the damaged area, by rubbing with coarse abrasive paper. Alternatively, a wire brush or abrasive pad can be used in a power drill. Where the repair area meets good paintwork, the edge of the paintwork should be 'feathered', using a finer grade of abrasive paper

In the case of a hole caused by rusting, all damaged sheet-metal should be cut away before proceeding to this stage. Here, the damaged area is being treated with rust remover and inhibitor before being filled

Mix the body filler according to its manufacturer's instructions. In the case of corrosion damage, it will be necessary to block off any large holes before filling — this can be done with aluminium or plastic mesh, or aluminium tape. Make sure the area is absolutely clean before ...

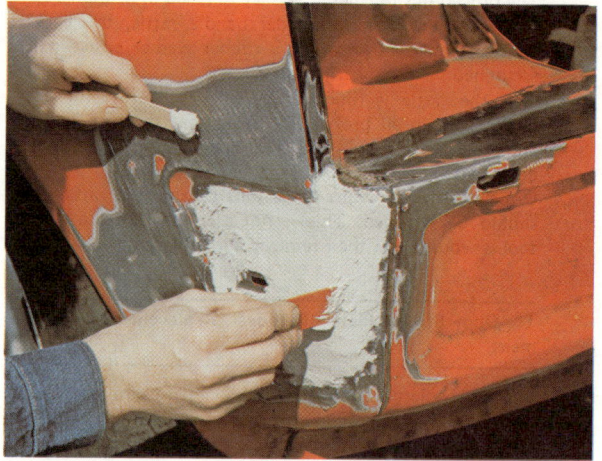

... applying the filler. Filler should be applied with a flexible applicator, as shown, for best results; the wooden spatula being used for confined areas. Apply thin layers of filler at 20-minute intervals, until the surface of the filler is slightly proud of the surrounding bodywork

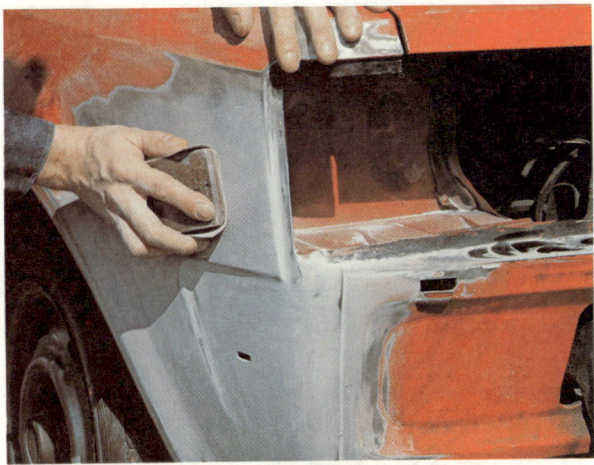

Initial shaping can be done with a Surform plane or Dreadnought file. Then, using progressively finer grades of wet-and-dry paper, wrapped around a sanding block, and copious amounts of clean water, rub down the filler until really smooth and flat. Again, feather the edges of adjoining paintwork

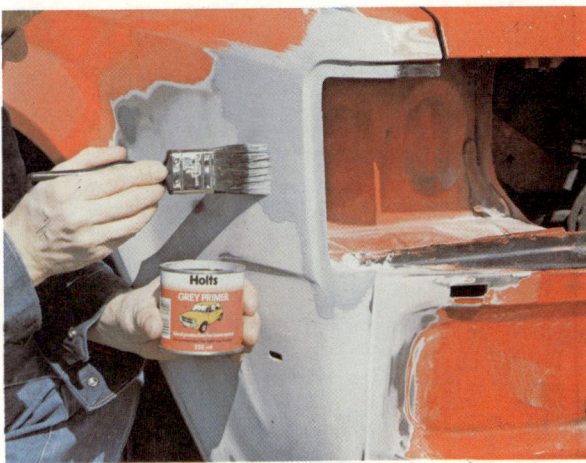

The whole repair area can now be sprayed or brush-painted with primer. If spraying, ensure adjoining areas are protected from over-spray. Note that at least one inch of the surrounding sound paintwork should be coated with primer. Primer has a 'thick' consistency, so will find small imperfections

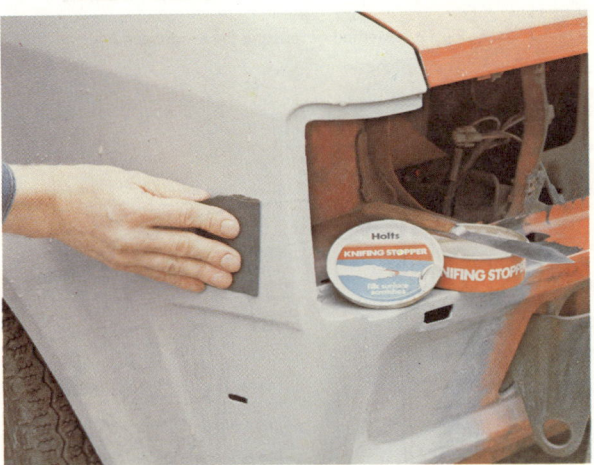

Again, using plenty of water, rub down the primer with a fine grade wet-and-dry paper (400 grade is probably best) until it is really smooth and well blended into the surrounding paintwork. Any remaining imperfections can now be filled by carefully applied knifing stopper paste

When the stopper has hardened, rub down the repair area again before applying the final coat of primer. Before rubbing down this last coat of primer, ensure the repair area is blemish-free – use more stopper if necessary. To ensure that the surface of the primer is really smooth use some finishing compound

The top coat can now be applied. When working out of doors, pick a dry, warm and wind-free day. Ensure surrounding areas are protected from over-spray. Agitate the aerosol thoroughly, then spray the centre of the repair area, working outwards with a circular motion. Apply the paint as several thin coats

After a period of about two weeks, which the paint needs to harden fully, the surface of the repaired area can be 'cut' with a mild cutting compound prior to wax polishing. When carrying out bodywork repairs, remember that the quality of the finished job is proportional to the time and effort expended

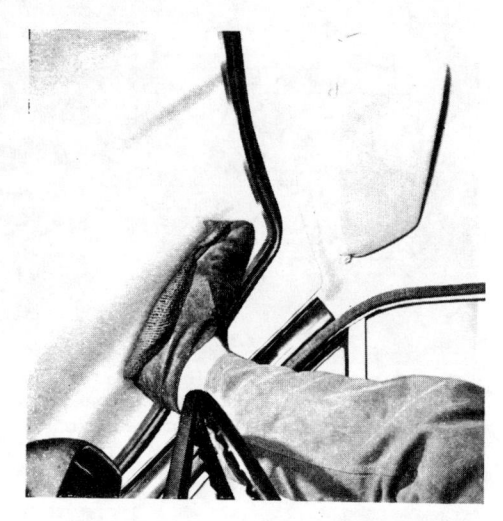

Fig.12.1. Method of removing the windscreen

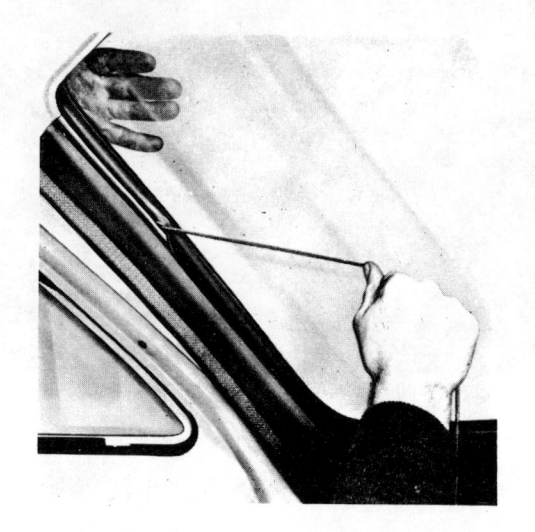

Fig.12.2. Method of refitting the windscreen

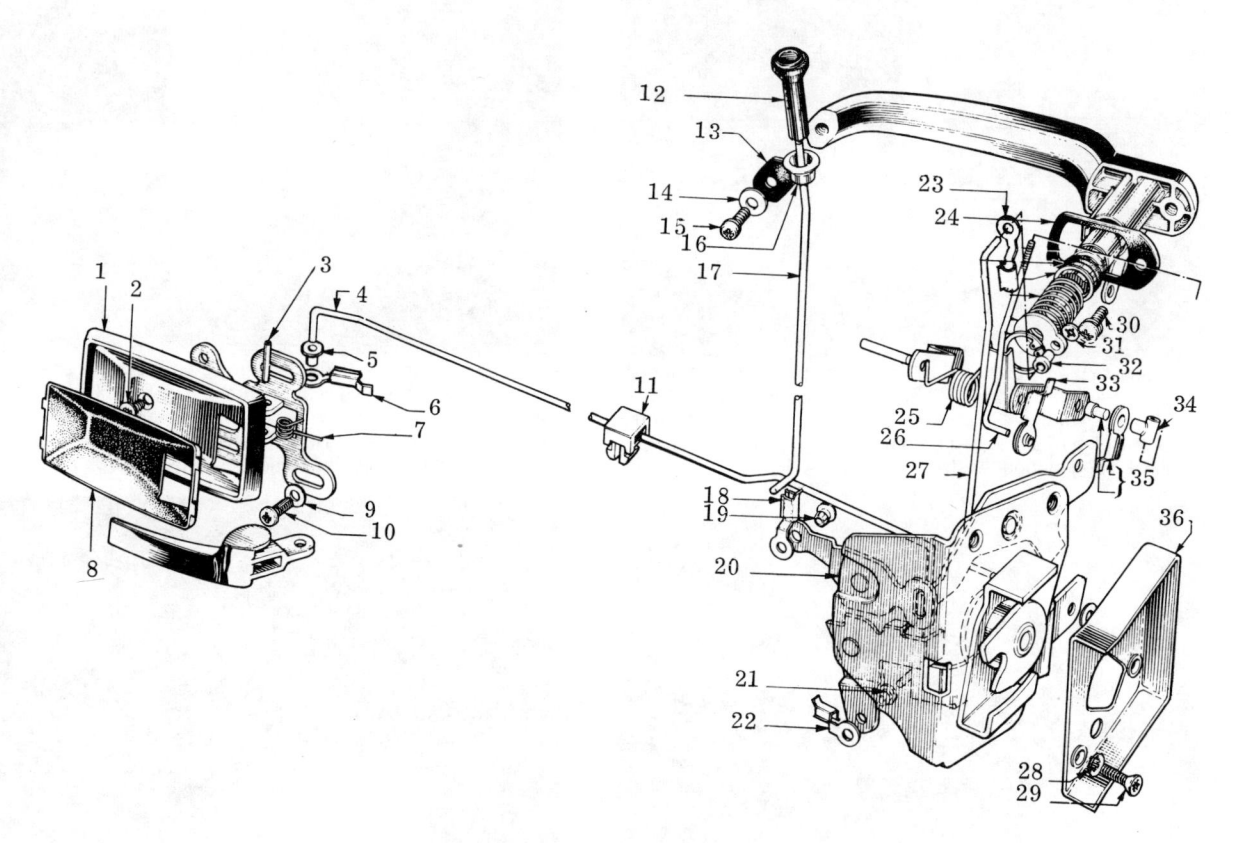

Fig.12.3. EXPLODED VIEW OF THE DOOR CONTROLS

1. Bezel
2. Screw
3. Pivot pin
4. Remote control rod
5. Bush
6. Clip
7. Spring
8. Insert
9. Washer
10. Screw
11. Guide clip
12. Interior lock button
13. Gasket
14. Washer
15. Screw
16. Escutcheon
17. Interior locking rod
18. Clip
19. Bush
20. Door lock assembly
21. Bush
22. Clip
23. Exterior handle
24. Gasket
25. Spring
26. Operating rod
27. Locking rod
28. Washer
29. Screw
30. Screw
31. Lock washer
32. Bush
33. Clip
34. Stud
35. Bush and clip
36. Cover plate

176

Chapter 12/Bodywork & Underframe

Fig.12.4. Removing the remote control handle from the door frame

Fig.12.5. Removing the door window glass

14. Door Lock Interior Remote Control Handle - Removal & Replacement

1. Remove the door trim panel as described in Section 12, followed by the polythene sheet covering the door apertures.
2. Disconnect the spring clip securing the remote control operating rod to the lock mechanism.
3. Remove the three screws securing the remote control assembly to the door inner panel. Push out the anti-rattle clip around the remote control operating rod and remove the remote control assembly through the door access hole. (See Fig.12.4). Removal is now complete.
4. Replacement is a straightforward reversal of the removal procedure.

15. Door Glasses - Removal & Replacement

1. First remove the door trim panel and window regulator assembly as described in Sections 12 and 19 respectively.
2. The window glass can now be rotated through 90° and removed through the top of the door (See Fig.12.5).
3. Replacement is a straightforward reversal of the removal procedure.

16. Door Outer Belt Weatherstrip - Removal & Replacement

1. Wind the window down to its fullest extent. Carefully prise the weatherstrip out of the groove in the door outer bright metal finish moulding.
2. Replacement: Correctly position the weatherstrip over its groove. With the thumbs, carefully press the strip fully into the groove.
3. Wind the window up and check that the weatherstrip is correctly fitted.

17. Bonnet - Removal & Replacement

1. Open the bonnet lid and prop it in the open position with its stay.
2. Using a suitable sharp implement, scribe a line around the exterior of the hinges in the bonnet. (See Fig.12.6). Unscrew and remove the two nuts and washers on each side, followed by the bolt plates. With the help of an assistant the bonnet can now be lifted off, after releasing the stay.
3. Replacement is a reversal of the removal procedure. However, before finally tightening the nuts which secure the bonnet ensure that the hinges are correctly aligned with the scribed lines. This will ensure correct bonnet/body alignment.

18. Boot Lid - Removal & Replacement

1. Open the boot lid to its fullest extent. Using a suitable implement scribe a line around the exterior of the hinges.
2. Remove the two bolts and washers on each side securing the boot lid to its hinges. With assistance the boot lid can now be lifted off.

Fig.12.6. Scribing around the bonnet hinge positions

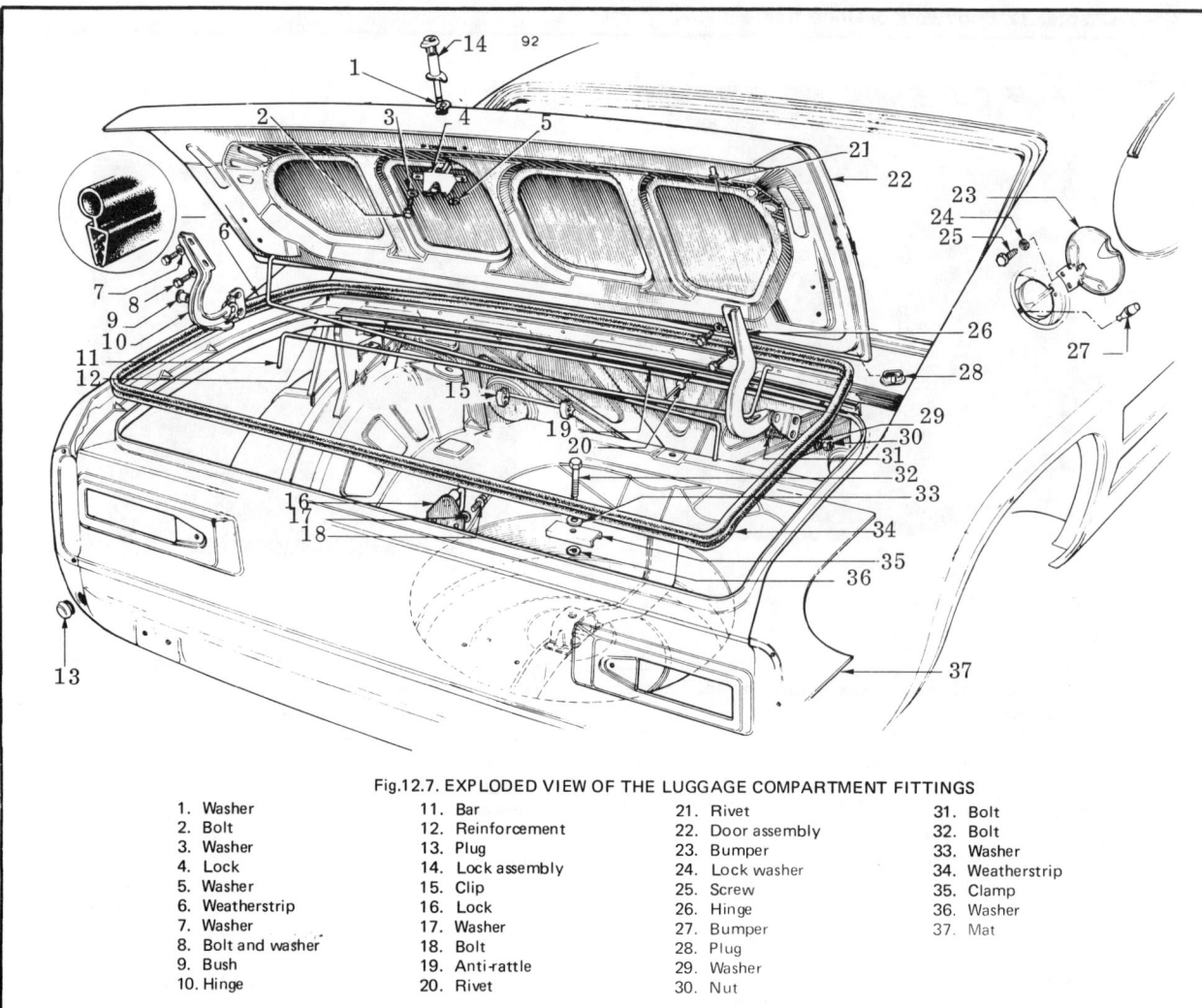

Fig.12.7. EXPLODED VIEW OF THE LUGGAGE COMPARTMENT FITTINGS

1. Washer
2. Bolt
3. Washer
4. Lock
5. Washer
6. Weatherstrip
7. Washer
8. Bolt and washer
9. Bush
10. Hinge
11. Bar
12. Reinforcement
13. Plug
14. Lock assembly
15. Clip
16. Lock
17. Washer
18. Bolt
19. Anti-rattle
20. Rivet
21. Rivet
22. Door assembly
23. Bumper
24. Lock washer
25. Screw
26. Hinge
27. Bumper
28. Plug
29. Washer
30. Nut
31. Bolt
32. Bolt
33. Washer
34. Weatherstrip
35. Clamp
36. Washer
37. Mat

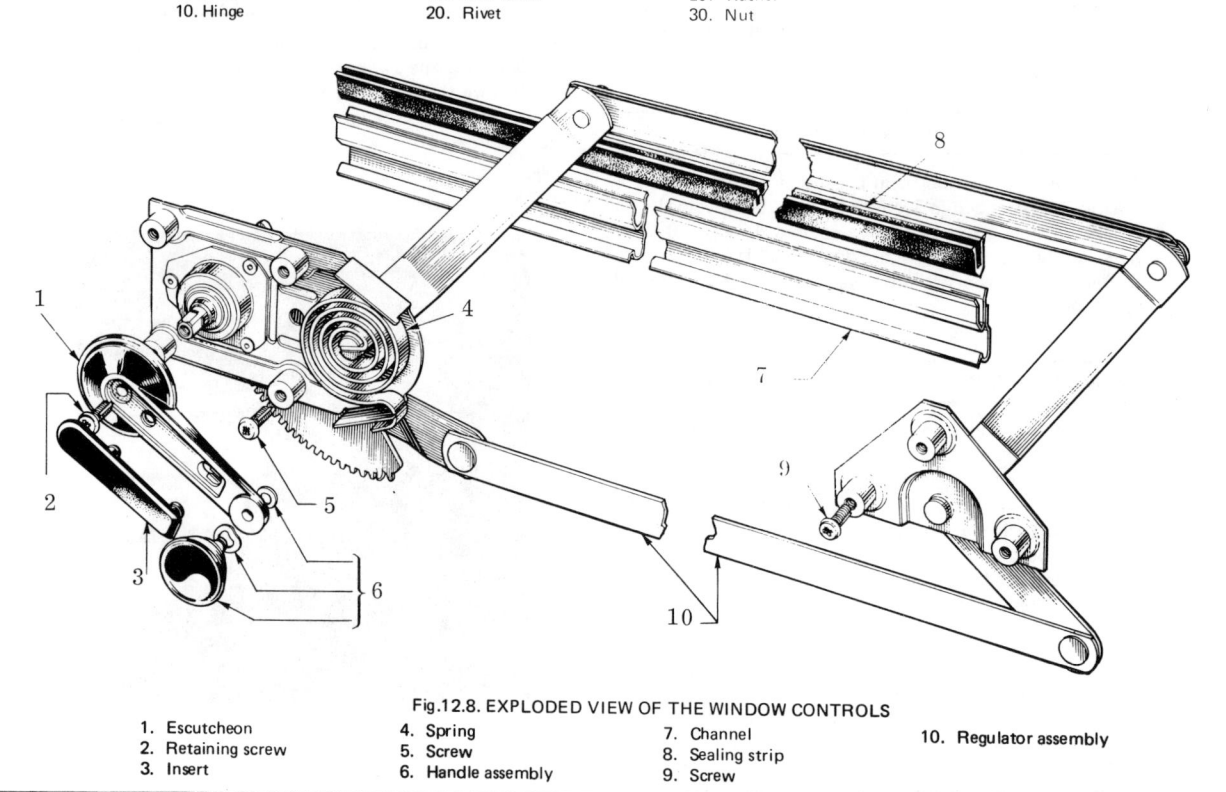

Fig.12.8. EXPLODED VIEW OF THE WINDOW CONTROLS

1. Escutcheon
2. Retaining screw
3. Insert
4. Spring
5. Screw
6. Handle assembly
7. Channel
8. Sealing strip
9. Screw
10. Regulator assembly

Fig.12.9. Removing the window regulator assembly from the aperture in the base of the door

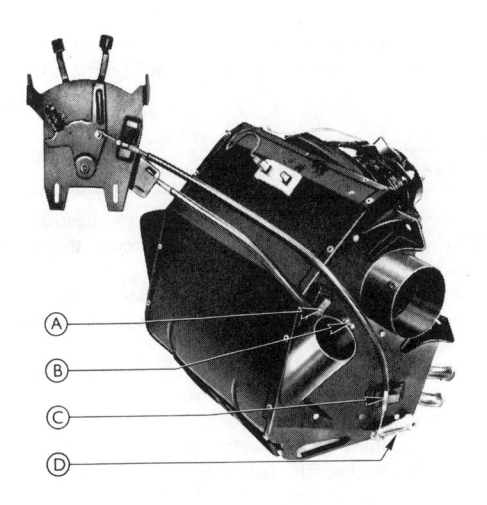

Fig.12.10. Figure shows heater control component positions

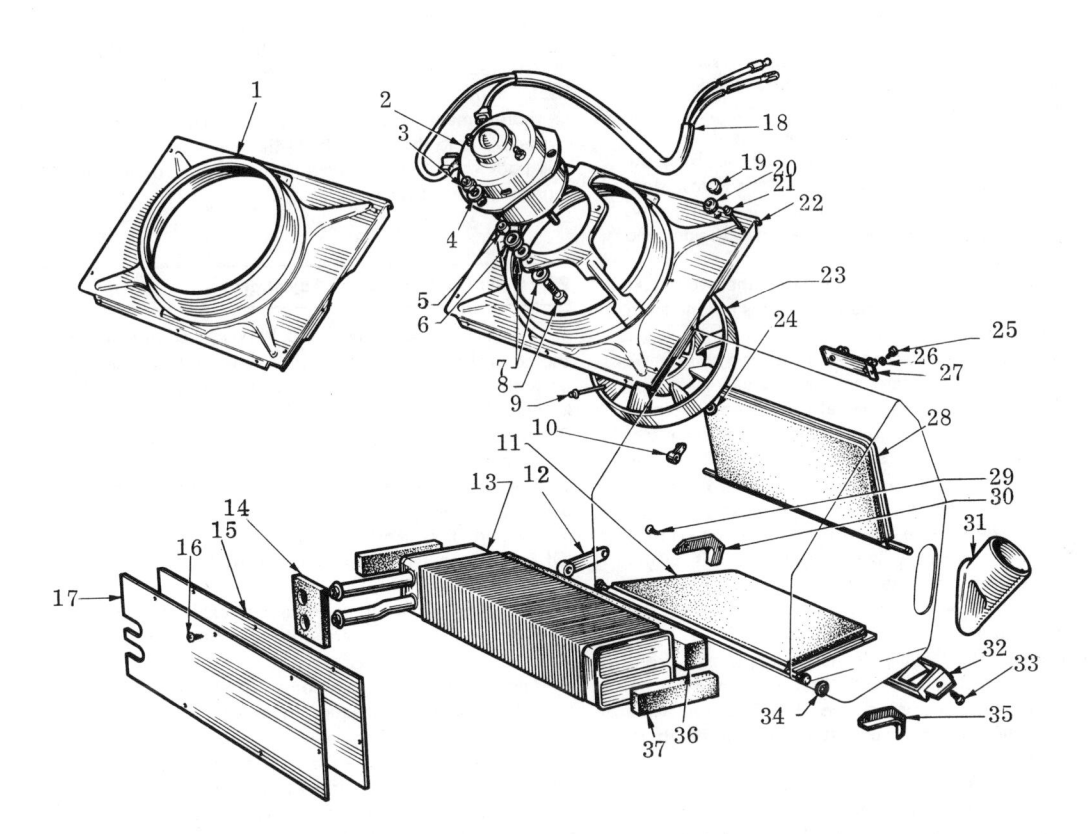

Fig.12.11. EXPLODED VIEW OF THE HEATER & VENTILATOR UNITS

1. Mounting plate
2. Motor
3. Nut
4. Washer
5. Sleeve
6. Grommet
7. Washer
8. Screw
9. Rivet
10. Lever
11. Valve & seal assembly
12. Lever
13. Radiator
14. Front seal
15. Front cover
16. Screw
17. Front cover
18. Heater motor wiring assembly
19. Plug
20. Grommet
21. Rivet
22. Heater motor mounting plate assembly
23. Fan
24. Ring
25. Screw
26. Washer
27. Resistor
28. Valve assembly
29. Screw
30. Deflector
31. Windscreen defroster outlet
32. Deflector
33. Screw
34. Clip spire
35. Deflector
36. Rear seal
37. Side seal

179

Chapter 12/Bodywork & Underframe

3. Replacement is a reversal of the removal procedure, however, before fully tightening the boot lid securing bolts ensure that the hinges are aligned with the scribed marks in the lid. This will ensure correct boot lid/body alignment.

19. Window Regulator - Removal & Replacement

1. Remove the door trim panel as described in Section 12. Carefully peel off the polythene sheet over the door apertures.
2. Temporarily replace the window regulator handle and wind the window down. Remove the seven screws securing the regulator assembly to the door.
3. Carefully draw the regulator assembly towards the rear of the door, this will disengage it from the runner in the base of the window glass.
4. Push the window glass up and support it in the raised position with a wedge. The regulator assembly can now be withdrawn through the access hole in the door. (See Fig. 12.9).

20. Heater Assembly - Removal & Replacement

1. Remove the earth terminal connection from the battery. Remove the radiator cap, open the cooling system drain taps and allow all of the coolant to drain. NOTE: If the coolant contains anti-freeze, drain it into a suitable container, this will allow the coolant to be re-used.
2. Next remove the seven cross-head screws securing the under-dash cowl panel, followed by the four parcel shelf securing trim clips, two each side. Remove the two screws on the passenger side, and one on the driver's side, and withdraw the parcel shelf.
3. Slacken the two wire clips and disconnect the two heater pipes from their unions on the bulkhead. This is done from inside the engine compartment.
4. Still in the engine compartment, remove the two screws holding the heater pipe plate and sealing gasket to the bulkhead. Detach the plate and gasket from the bulkhead.
5. Remove the ashtray and pull off the heater control knobs. Detach the heater control quadrant from the dashboard, by removing its two securing screws. Withdraw the control quadrant from beneath the dashboard.
6. Remove the temperature control and direction control outer cable clips from the quadrant plate and detach the two inner cables from the control levers.
7. Note the wiring positions and detach the wires from the heater blower motor.
8. Working under the fascia pull the air supply pipe from the face level vent. Remove the belt rail finishing strip by unscrewing the three securing screws. The face level vent assembly can then be removed after undoing its three securing screws.
9. If it is a G.T. model being worked on it will now be necessary to remove the centre console.
10 Finally remove the four retaining bolts and withdraw the heater assembly.

11 Replacement is generally a reversal of the removal procedure. Note: when the heater assembly is reinstalled it will probably be necessary to adjust the heater control cables as detailed in Section 23.

21. Heater Motor - Removal & Replacement

1. Remove the heater assembly as described in Section 20, and also the heater radiator as detailed in Section 22.
2. Withdraw the blower motor fan, after releasing its retaining spring clip. Note the wiring positions and disconnect the two wires from their terminals on the motor.
3. Lastly unscrew and remove the three screws securing the motor to the mounting plate and remove the motor.
4. Replacement is a reversal of the removal procedure.

22. Heater Radiator - Removal & Replacement

1. Remove the heater assembly from the car as described in Section 20.
2. Remove the two circlips securing the ends of the control flap pivots.
3. Unscrew and remove the sixteen screws holding the right-hand heater side panel in position. Remove the panel.
4. The radiator can now be carefully drawn out of the heater body.
5. Replacement is a reversal of the removal procedure. However, note that after the radiator has been replaced in the body, the foam packing should be positioned before replacing the side panel.

23. Heater Control Cables - Adjustment

1. Control cable adjustment should be carried out whenever the control cables have been disconnected from the heater, or if the heater cannot be 'shut off'. (Note: all bracketed letters refer to Fig. 12.10).
2. Move the two heater control levers to the 'OFF' and 'HOT' positions.
3. Release the spring clip (C) securing the direction control cable, outer cable to the heater.
4. Position the heater distribution valve firmly in the 'OFF' position by raising the end of the lever (D) to the end of its travel.
5. Any slack in the direction control cable should now be taken up and the cable secured to the heater with a spring clip.
6. Release the temperature control cable, outer cable from its mounting on the heater, by releasing the spring clip (A).
7. Raise the mixing valve (B) lever to the end of its travel. This will ensure that it is firmly in the 'HOT' position.
8. Take up any slack in the temperature control cable and re-secure it to the heater body with a spring clip.
9. Finally check the heater controls for correct operation.

Chapter 13/Supplement

Contents

Introduction ... 1	Selector cable - renewal
Specifications ... 2	Selector inhibitor cable – renewal and adjustment
Engine ... 3	Braking system ... 8
Oversize components	Handbrake – adjustment
Valves	Electrical system ... 9
Timing chain	Fuel level and water temperature gauges – checking
Flywheel and ring gear	Front indicator assembly (later type) – removal and refitting
Oil pump and oil filter	Front indicator assembly (later type) – bulb renewal
Cooling system ... 4	Rear lamp cluster assembly – removal and refitting
Prevention of engine overheating	Glove compartment lamp – bulb renewal
Fuel system ... 5	Heated rear window warning light – bulb renewal
Safety precautions when handling fuel	Clock – removal and refitting
Choke and fast idling adjustment	Cigarette lighter assembly – removal and refitting
Automatic choke adjustment – revised procedure	Suspension and steering ... 10
Ignition system ... 6	Steering coupling – alignment
Engine tuning for low grade fuels	Intermittently stiff steering
Automatic transmission ... 7	Rear anti-roll bar – removal and refitting
Automatic transmission – special precautions	Anti-roll bar rubber bushes – renewal
Automatic transmission – routine maintenance	Bodywork and underframe ... 11
Automatic transmission – removal and refitting	Sliding roof guide rail assembly – removal and refitting
Downshift cable – adjustment	Sliding roof outer panel – removal and refitting
Starter inhibitor switch – renewal and adjustment	Sliding roof winder mechanism – removal, refitting and adjusting
Front brake band – adjustment	Glove compartment lock – removal and refitting
Rear brake band – adjustment	Centre console – removal and refitting
Gear selector assembly – removal and refitting	Door windows – adjustment
Selector cable – adjustment	

2 Specifications

Engine

Lubrication system
Sump capacity (including filter) ... 6·0 Imp pt (7·0 US pt, 3·25 litres)
Oil filter capacity ... 0·85 Imp pt (1·02 US pt, 0·43 litres)

Automatic transmission

Gear ratios
First ... 2·393 : 1
Second ... 1·450 : 1
Third ... 1·000 : 1
Reverse ... 2·094 : 1

Torque converter
Fluid capacity (including converter) ... 11¼ Imp pt (13.5 US pt, 6·39 litres)
Fluid type ... Ford specification M2C–33F, Castrol TQF or equivalent
Normal operating temperature ... 100 to 115°C (212 to 235°F)

Shift speed, to nearest mph (km/h)
1600 (with 3·889 : 1 axle ratio)

	Gear change			
	1–2	2–3	3–2	2–1
Light throttle	6 to 11 (10 to 18)	10 to 15 (16 to 24)	—	—
Part throttle	—	—	23 to 32 (37 to 51)	—
Zero throttle	—	—	—	6 to 9 (10 to 14)

Chapter 13/Supplement

Kickdown	30 to 39 (48 to 63)	54 to 62 (87 to 100)	47 to 59 (76 to 95)	22 to 34 (35 to 55)
1600 (with 4·125 : 1 axle ratio)		*Gear change*		
	1 – 2	2 – 3	3 – 2	2 – 1
Light throttle	6 to 10 (10 to 14)	9 to 14 (14 to 23)	—	—
Part throttle	—	—	22 to 30 (35 to 48)	—
Zero throttle	—	—	—	6 to 9 (10 to 14)
Kickdown	28 to 37 (45 to 60)	50 to 59 (82 to 95)	44 to 56 (71 to 90)	20 to 32 (32 to 51)
1600 GT		*Gear change*		
	1 – 2	2 – 3	3 – 2	2 – 1
Light throttle	7 to 11 (11 to 18)	10 to 15 (16 to 24)	—	—
Part throttle	—	—	24 to 33 (39 to 53)	—
Zero throttle	—	—	—	7 to 10 (11 to 16)
Kickdown	31 to 41 (50 to 66)	56 to 64 (90 to 103)	49 to 61 (79 to 98)	22 to 35 (35 to 56)

Torque wrench settings | lbf ft | kgf m

Engine
Front cover	5 to 7	0·69 to 0·97
Sump	7 to 9	0·97 to 1·24
Tappet adjusting screw locknut	10 to 14	1·38 to 1·93
Chain tensioner-to-cylinder block	5 to 7	0·69 to 0·97
Engine rear insulator-to-extension housing	40 to 45	5·53 to 6·22

Automatic transmission
Transmission case-to-converter housing	8 to 13	1·11 to 1·80
Extension housing-to-transmission case	30 to 55	4·15 to 7·60
Gearbox sump	8 to 13	1·11 to 1·80
Gear support-to-transmission case	10 to 18	1·38 to 2·49
Gearbox drain plug	9 to 12	1·4 to 1·66
Starter inhibitor switch locknut	4 to 6	0·55 to 0·83
Downshift valve control cable adaptor-to-case	8 to 9	1·11 to 1·24
Driveplate-to-torque converter	25 to 30	3·45 to 4·14

1 Introduction

This supplement covers the new features of the 1973 Capri and details the repair operations applicable to them which have not been incorporated in the original manual.

Also included is additional information which was not available previously and details of modifications which have been made in the course of Ford's policy of continuous development.

3 Engine

Oversize components

1 The crankshaft bearing liner parent bore in the cylinder block may be either standard or 0.015 in (0.38 mm) oversize. Where the bore is oversize, the bearing caps and inside the crankcase are marked with *white* spots.
2 The camshaft bearing parent bore may be 0.020 in (0.51 mm) oversize, but in this case the block is unmarked.
3 Tappet bores may also be 0.004 in (0.10 mm) oversize, and the cylinder block in this case is marked with *white* paint adjacent to the tappet bores.
4 A letter 'T' stamped on the engine build code number pad provides additional identification.

Valves

5 The head of the inlet valve has a coating of diffused aluminium, to increase the resistance of the valve to oxidation at high temperatures and to form a hard wear-resistant surface to the seating area of the valve. Removal of the aluminised coating will reduce both the wear resistance and the heat resistance of the valve and aluminised valves must never be ground in. If the valve faces are worn or pitted, they should be re-cut and new valves should be fitted. Alternatively, the valve seats may be lapped using old valves.
6 Exhaust valves are not aluminised and their faces may be ground or lapped as necessary.
7 When adjusting the valve clearances, some models have stiff-nuts incorporated in the rockers and the valves are adjusted without the need to release locknuts.

Timing chain

8 The single-row timing chain is tensioned automatically by means of a spring-loaded snail cam bearing against a pivoted tensioner arm (Fig. 13.1)
9 The timing chain runs against a synthetic rubber pad on the tensioner arm and in use the links wear two grooves in the pad until the pad bears on the chain rollers. This condition is normal and the pad should not be dressed so that the grooves are removed.

Chapter 13/Supplement

Flywheel and ring gear

10 The cast iron flywheel is located concentrically on the crankshaft flange and is retained by six bi-hexagonal bolts fitted without lockwashers.

11 The number of teeth on the ring gear varies with the type of starter motor used; 110 teeth with an inertia starter and 132 teeth with a pre-engaged starter. The 110 tooth ring has chamfered teeth which makes it easily identifiable compared with the 132 tooth ring which has no chamfers.

12 Lighter flywheels are used on GT engines; the correct flywheel weights for the various engines are as follows

```
1300 cc and 1600 cc HC
 and LC engines . . . . . . . . . . . . . . . . .   26 lb (11.8 kg)
1300 cc GT engine . . . . . . . . . . . . . .   16.75 lb (7.60 kg)
1600 cc GT engine . . . . . . . . . . . . . .   18.5 lb (8.39 kg)
```

Oil pump and oil filter

13 On Capri 1 models with Kent engines produced in 1971 and 1972 and on re-conditioned engines of the same type, care is necessary to ensure that the correct oil filter is obtained. Motorcraft oil filter type EFL 89 is available with two designs of oil filter-to-oil pump mating face, one having a raised flange and the other having five flat depressions. The raised flange pattern can be fitted to any model Capri and must be used on the 1971 and 1972 engines with oil pump 2735E – 6600B pump 2735E – 6600 B has two raised segments on its filter mating face (Fig. 13.2) and if the filter with 5 flat depressions (Part No. 741M – 6714 – BA) is used with it inadequate sealing of the filter gasket and consequent oil leakage will occur.

14 To overcome the difficulty of removing stubborn oil filters having restricted access, a special tool is now available. This is Oil Filter Wrench MS 70, and consists of a strap-wrench which

Fig. 13.1 Timing chain tensioner

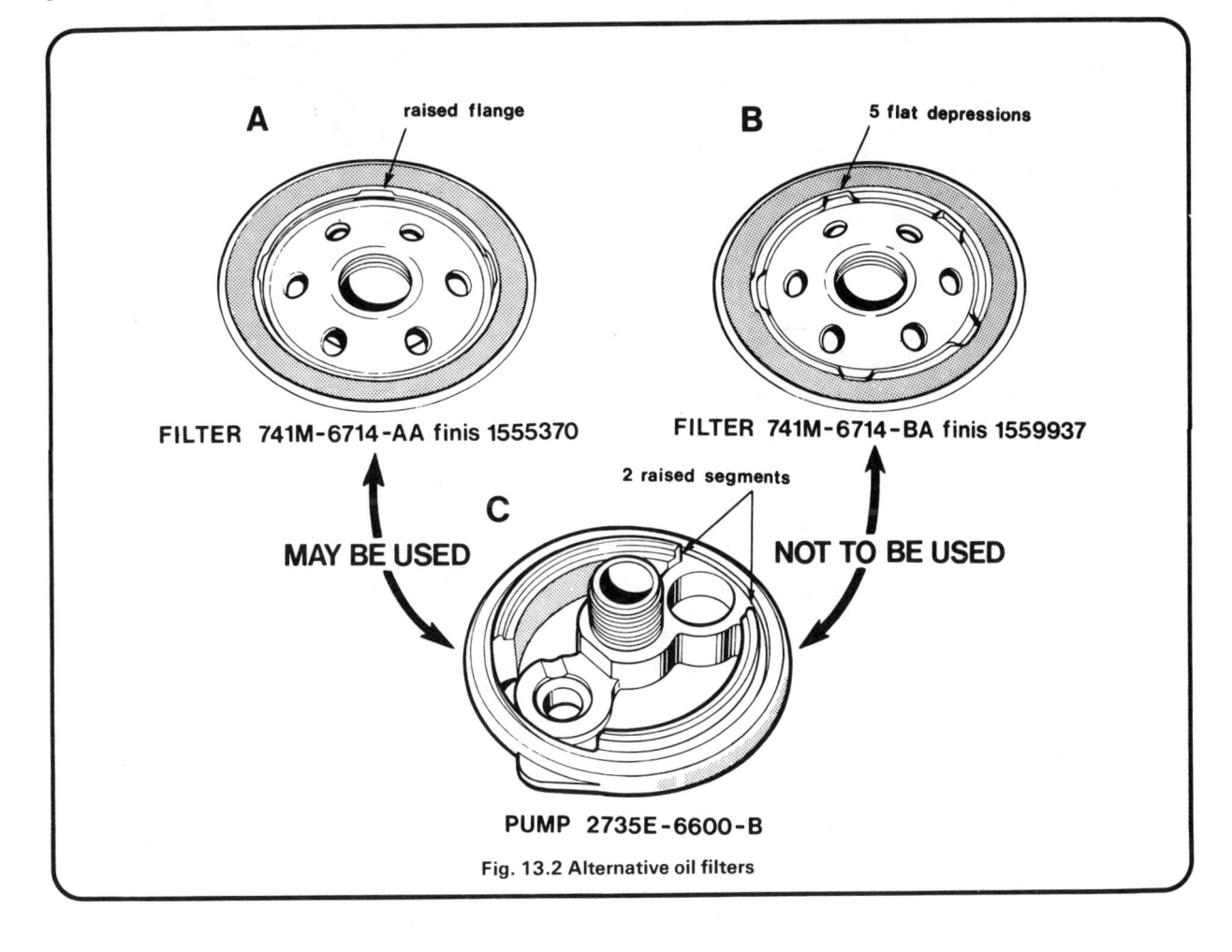

Fig. 13.2 Alternative oil filters

can be used in conjunction with a ½ in square drive socket wrench. (Figs. 13.3 and 13.4)

15 When fitting a new oil filter do not use a strap-wrench or any other tool. Adequate sealing can be obtained by screwing the filter in by hand; *the use of tools can deform the filter case.*

4 Cooling system

Prevention of engine overheating
1 If as a result of retarding the ignition, or for any other reason the engine tends to overheat, the problem may be overcome by fitting a more effective fan, or by fitting a fan shroud if one is not fitted already. A range of fans and shrouds is available and on quoting the part number of the fan already fitted, your Ford dealer will be able to advise on a suitable replacement.

5 Fuel system

Safety precautions when handling fuel
1 The risks associated with handling fuel should not be underestimated, and the following basic precautions should be taken when working on the fuel system:

  a) Always disconnect the battery before doing any work on the fuel system.
  b) Always empty fuel tanks in the open; make sure that there is no smoking by anyone in the area and that there are no naked lights.
  c) Make sure that a fire extinguisher is close at hand.
  d) Drain the fuel into a suitably marked metal container which has a tightly fitting pressure-vented cap, and store the fuel safely. The local fire prevention officer will advise you on the legal requirements for storing fuel.
  e) A drained petrol tank will contain vapour and is potentially more dangerous than a full tank. Precautions with naked lights and other sources of ignition must be very strict and the tank must be steam-cleaned before any work is done on it.
  f) On vehicles where the fuel line is connected to the fuel tank outlet by steel spring band clips, the clips should be released before the fuel line is disconnected, or the tank sender unit is removed. By observing this procedure, any sparks which may be generated when removing the clips cannot ignite residual fuel fumes in the fuel tank.
  g) Never empty a fuel tank over an inspection pit, because fuel vapour is heavier than air and will remain in the pit for several hours. The same applies when removing carburettor bowls and fuel pumps, because even small amounts of fuel can produce enough vapour to give a considerable explosion risk.

Choke and fast idling adjustment
2 The procedure for adjusting the choke fast idling is given in Chapter 3 Section 21, and the speed should be as given below:

		Fast idle speed rpm	
	Carburettor	Manual	Automatic
	Part No.	transmission	transmission
	Prefix and	Manual	Automatic
	Suffix	choke	choke
1300 cc engine	C7AH 691W	1400	1950
	711W 711F	1500	2150
1600 cc engine	C9CH 691W	1000	1950

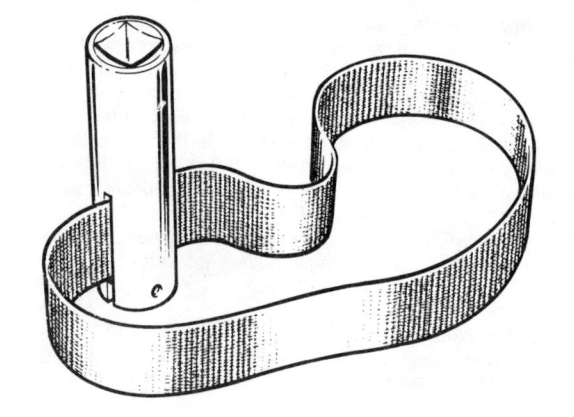

Fig. 13.3 Oil filter wrench MS70

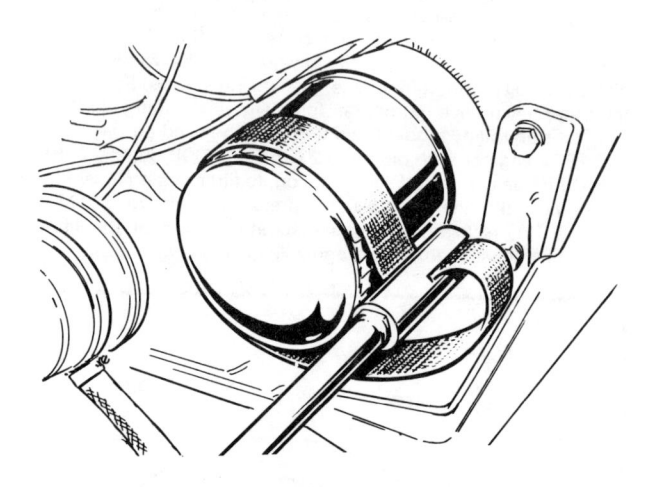

Fig. 13.4 Using wrench MS70

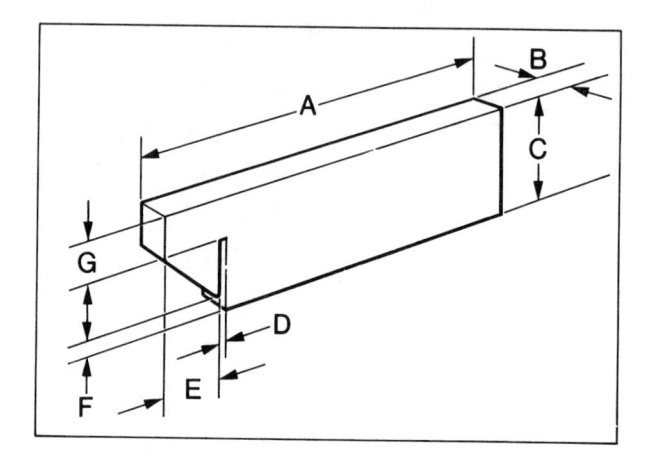

Fig. 13.5 Automatic choke preload tool

A 2.6 in   E 0.375 in
B 0.25 in   F 0.12 in
C 0.75 in   G 0.25 in
D 0.06 in

711W-VA/ ANA/BNA/VB/ ANB/BJB	1000	–
711W-VC/ ANC	1600	–
711W-BNA/ ZA/BFA/BNB/ ZB/BFB	–	2150
711F-KCA/ KDA	–	2150

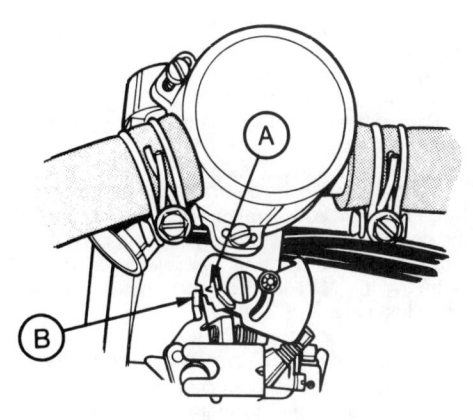

Fig. 13.6 Automatic choke set in fast idle position

A V-mark lined up with fast idle lever
B Adjusting tag

Automatic choke adjustment – revised procedure

3 The vacuum choke plate pull-down is adjusted using a simply-made special preload tool from mild steel to the dimensions shown in Fig. 13.5. The finished weight of the tool must be checked and must be within the range 50 to 65 grams.

4 To check the adjustment, run the engine until it achieves normal operating temperature, then switch off, lift the bonnet and remove the air cleaner. Position the fast idle cam in the fast idle position with the V-mark on the cam in line with the top of the fast idle lever (Fig. 13.6).

5 Start the engine and check that the fast idle speed is 2150 rpm, making any necessary adjustment by bending the adjusting tag after stopping the engine.

6 Position the special tool on the choke adjusting cover as shown in Fig. 13.7, after removing the choke housing and bi-metal spring assembly. Locate the throttle on the high part of the cam (Fig. 13.7), after removing the choke housing and bi-metal spring assembly. Locate the throttle on the high part of the cam (Fig. 13.7), not in the fast idle position (Fig. 13.6), and start the engine.

7 When the engine is at normal operating temperature, ensure that the preload tool is floating and then check that no. 29 ($\frac{1}{8}$ in/0.13 in/3.3 mm) twist drill shank just fits between the choke plate and the wall of the air horn.

8 If it is necessary to make any adjustment, stop the engine and bend the pull-down lever (Fig. 13.7) to achieve the correct setting.

9 Re-check the setting and then refit the choke housing and bi-metal spring assembly. Fit a new gasket if necessary and connect the choke bi-metal spring to the centre slot of the choke operating lever.

10 Place the outer housing in position and fit the three retaining screws loosely. Rotate the housing until the mark on the spring housing lines up with the centre mark on the automatic choke housing (Fig. 13.8) then tighten the fixing screws fully.

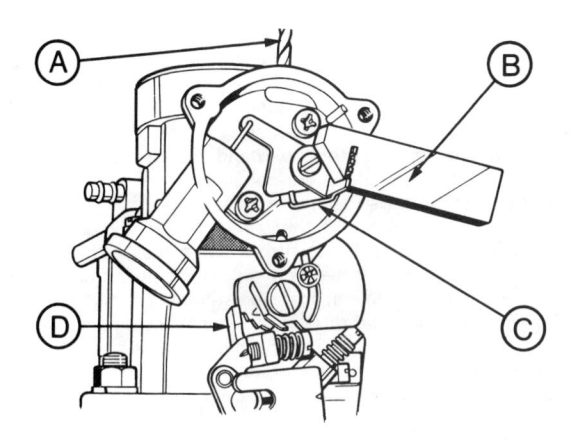

Fig. 13.7 Use of choke pre-load tool

A Twist drill
B Preload tool
C Pull-down lever
D Throttle set on high part of cam

6 Ignition system

Engine tuning for low grade fuels

1 The ignition settings given in the Specifications of Chapter 4 are for the grades of fuel normally used on the different engines. It is usual to use an octane rating of 97 minimum on the high compression engine and 91 minimum on the low compression engine, and problems of detonation may occur if octane ratings lower than these are used with standard ignition settings.

2 If a lower grade of fuel is used, the basic ignition timing must be retarded by 1° for every octane rating below the minimum quoted in paragraph 1 (see below).

High compression engine

96 octane fuel – retard ignition by 1° from basic specification
95 octane fuel – retard ignition by 2° from basic specification
93 octane fuel – retard ignition by 4° from basic specification

Low compression engine

90 octane fuel – retard ignition by 1° from basic specification
89 octane fuel – retard ignition by 2° from basic specification
78 octane fuel – retard ignition by 13° from basic specification

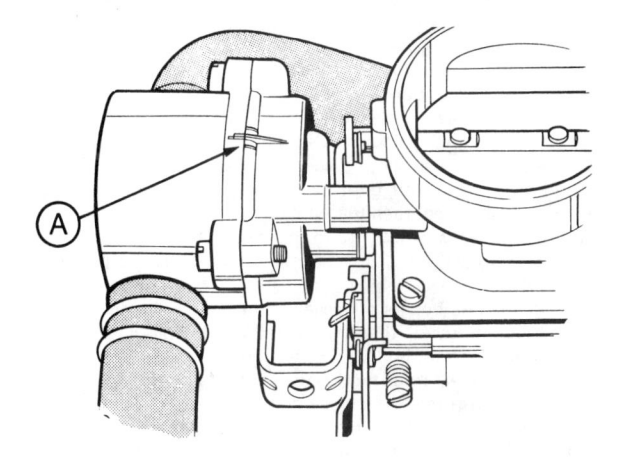

Fig. 13.8 Choke housing alignment

A Mating marks

3 After making the adjustment, the vehicle should be road-tested and checked for detonation by accelerating in third gear from 10 mph (16 km/h) to 50 mph (80 km/h) with the throttle wide open and the engine at normal operating temperature. If detonation is experienced, the ignition should be retarded by 2° and a further road test made.

7 Automatic transmission

General Description

1 The Borg Warner Model 35 automatic transmission is available as an optional extra on 1600 and 1600 GT models. It consists of a torque converter and a hydraulically controlled automatic epicyclic gearbox with three forward and one reverse speeds. In all gears the drive is through the torque converter and this results in maximum flexibility, especially in top gear.
2 The gears are selected automatically by engaging clutches and /or applying brake bands in various combinations, the operation being performed by a hydraulic control system. The hydraulic control system and the torque converter are supplied from a common pump of the gear type.
3 Selection of the desired drive range is by a floor-mounted lever between the front seats; a fixed quadrant adjacent to it indicates which range has been selected.
4 An inhibitor switch, mounted on the gearbox, makes it impossible to start the engine unless the transmission is selected to 'Park' or 'Neutral', and a spring-loaded button on the side of the selector handle prevents the unintentional selection of certain gear selections which could cause damage to the engine and transmission.

The selections available are:

P–Park This position locks the transmission mechanically and should be used to supplement the handbrake. Under no circumstances should this position be selected while the vehicle is moving.

R–Reverse Do not select reverse while the vehicle is moving.

N–Neutral In this position the torque converter is not connected to the drive chain, so there is no drive to the rear wheels.

D–Drive This gives fully automatic drive with upward and downward changes, using all three forward gears.

2–Drive In this position there is automatic upward and downward changing of first and second gear. This position must not be selected when the vehicle is travelling over 55 mph.

1–Lock Selection of this position will cause selection of first gear if the vehicle speed is sufficiently low. Once selected, the transmission will remain in this gear until the selector is moved to another position. The use of the Lock position is beneficial when descending steep hills.

5 Because the repair of automatic transmissions requires specialist knowledge and equipment, it should not be attempted by anyone lacking these essentials. The contents of the following is therefore confined to service information which can be used by the owner.

Automatic transmission – special precautions

6 *Towing:* Capris fitted with automatic transmission which are to be used for caravan or trailer towing, should be fitted with an oil cooler, to prevent the transmission fluid from overheating.
7 *Recovery towing:* If it is necessary to tow the car to recover it, first ensure that the fluid level is correct and that the transmission is operating satisfactorily. Under these conditions the car may be towed at speeds of up to 30 mph (48 km/h) for a distance not exceeding 15 miles. For high speed, or long distance towing, or if the transmission is suspect, the propeller shaft must be removed before towing.
8 *Starting:* Cars with automatic transmission cannot be push- or tow-started.

Automatic transmission – routine maintenance

9 Every 6000 miles (10 000 km) check the transmission fluid level with the engine running at idling speed and normal operating temperature, while the transmission selector is at 'P'. If the fluid level is below the MIN level on the dipstick, top up with fluid of the specified type.

Automatic transmission – removal and installation

10 Lift and prop the bonnet lid, then cover the wings to protect them from scratches during the subsequent operations.
11 Remove the battery connections then detach the downshift cable from the bracket on the rocker cover and from the throttle linkage.
12 Remove the upper four bolts securing the engine to the torque converter housing. One of these bolts holds the dipstick tube in position.
13 Preferably position the car over a pit, then jack it up and place firmly based axle-stands under the front and rear of the vehicle.
14 Remove the clip and bolt, and disconnect the speedometer cable from the transmission assembly.
15 Remove the starter motor cables and then the starter motor securing bolts (two bolts for a pre-engaged starter and three for the inertia type). Remove the starter motor.
16 Rotate the crankshaft so that each of the drive plate-to-converter bolts is accessible in turn through the starter motor aperture. Slacken the bolts evenly and finally remove them.
17 Detach the engine-to-transmission stiffener bracket.
18 Remove the converter dust cover, then place a container of approximately two gallons capacity under the sump. Remove the drain plug and drain the sump, taking care not to come in contact with the oil which may be hot enough to cause severe burns to the skin.
19 Disconnect the selector cable from the operating arm and from the support bracket.
20 Mark the two faces of the drive shaft flange to ensure correct alignment on refitting. Unscrew the four self-adjusting nuts and remove the four bolts from the coupling flange. Gently tap the coupling to separate the two flanges. Remove the two bolts securing the centre bearing carrier to its bracket, then lower the shaft and slide it rearwards to disengage it from the splines of the mainshaft. Plug the rear of the gearbox to prevent loss of oil and the entry of dirt.
21 Support the gearbox on a jack or blocks and remove the supporting crossmember.
22 Label the wires to the gearbox inhibitor switch to ensure their correct refitting, then remove them.
23 If there is an earth wire (black cable) for the reversing lamp attached to one of the gearbox-to-extension housing bolts, remove the bolt and detach the wire.
24 Remove the two nuts from the exhaust manifold clamp; detach the exhaust pipe from the manifold and tie the pipe out of the way.
25 Lower the gearbox as necessary, so that the dipstick and its tube can be removed, then remove the remaining two bolts securing the converter housing to the engine.
26 Position a jack under the front of the engine to support the engine, then lower the transmission and remove it from beneath the car, at the same time removing the converter dust cover which is held between the converter housing and the cylinder block.
27 Clean the transmission case with paraffin then place it on a bench, so that the transmission sump is uppermost.
28 To remove the torque converter, remove the six bolts and spring washers securing the converter housing to the transmission case then remove the converter housing.

29 To re-install the transmission, first refit the converter housing to the transmission case and secure it with the six bolts and spring washers. The bolts should be tightened to a torque of 8 to 13 lbf ft (1.11 to 1.80 kgf m).
30 Align the front pump drive tangs with the slots in the inner gear and carefully refit the torque converter, taking care not to damage the oil seal.
31 Locate the converter dust cover on the dowels at the rear of the cylinder block, then with the gearbox supported on a jack, reposition the gearbox and fit the two lower bolts securing the converter housing to the engine.
32 Using the access provided by the starter motor aperture, align the torque converter and the driveplate until one of the securing bolts can be inserted. Insert all the bolts in turn then tighten them evenly and progressively to a torque of 25 to 30 lbf ft (3.6 to 4.14 kgf m)
33 Reposition the dipstick and tube assembly then fit the upper housing bolt which secures it.
34 Remove the jack from the front of the engine. Jack up the rear of the gearbox and refit the gearbox support crossmember, then remove the jack supporting the gearbox.
35 Remove the plug from the end of the gearbox and insert the splined end of the propeller shaft. Align the mating marks of the two halves of the rear side drive coupling, insert the four bolts, fit new self-locking nuts and tighten to a torque of 15 to 18 lbf ft (2.1 to 2.5 kgf m). Locate the centre bearing carrier in position, insert the two bolts to secure it to its brackets, and tighten them to a torque of 15 to 18 lbf ft (2.1 to 2.5 kgf m).
36 Reconnect the selector cable to the operating arm of the transmission and to the support bracket on the underbody. Put the selector lever in the car to position '1', then pull the operating arm on the transmission fully rearwards and adjust the cable length to suit.
37 Refit the converter housing lower dust cover and locate the engine-to-transmission stiffener bracket.
38 Fit the starter motor in position, insert the two bolts for the pre-engaged starter, or three bolts for the inertia starter, and tighten them to a torque of 20 to 25 lbf ft (2.76 to 3.46 kgf m)
39 Refit the speedometer cable and secure it with a clip and bolts.
40 Refit the remaining three converter housing-to-engine bolts and tighten all six bolts to a torque of 30 to 35 lbf ft (4.15 to 4.84 kgf m).
41 Reconnect the downshift cable to the throttle linkage and the bracket on the rocker cover, and fit the downshift and return spring.
42 Fit the exhaust pipe to the exhaust manifold and tighten the nuts to a torque of 15 to 20 lbf ft (2.1 to 2.8 kgf m) except on GT models for which the correct torque is 6 to 8 lbf ft (0.85 to 1.1 kgf m).
43 Adjust the starter inhibitor switch as described later in this Section.
44 Refill the transmission to within $\frac{3}{8}$ in of the FULL mark on the dipstick using the specified type of fluid. The quantity of fluid will be less than 11.25 Imp pts (13.5 US pints, 6.39 litres), because the system will not have drained completely. Re-check the fluid level as described earlier in this Section after the car has been road-tested for at least five miles and top up if necessary.
45 Start the engine and run it until it is warm, at the same time checking for leaks.
46 Adjust the downshift cable as described in the following sub-section.

Downshift cable-adjustment
Note: *This method of adjustment is only applicable to the refitting of a cable and is only capable of accurate adjustment if there is no wear in the accelerator linkage and the original crimped collar is still on the downshift cable. When a new cable is being fitted, or when there is wear in the linkage, this method will only give an approximate setting and accurate adjustment should then be done by an authorised dealer.*
47 With the accelerator linkage correctly set, run the engine up to normal operating temperature then allow it to run at idle speed.
48 Slacken the downshift valve cable adjuster locknut. (Fig. 13.9). Adjust the outer cable length by turning the outer cable adjuster until the crimped collar on the inner cable is just in contact with the outer cable adjuster when the inner cable is taut. Lock the adjuster in this position.

Starter inhibitor switch – renewal and adjustment
49 Note the position of the starter inhibitor and reversing light wires which are connected to the switch, so that they can be reconnected correctly, then remove the wires.
50 Slacken the switch locknut then unscrew and withdraw the switch, being careful to count the number of turns required to remove it.
51 Refit the switch as a reverse of this procedure, taking care that it is screwed in exactly the same number of turns as were necessary to remove it. Lock the switch in this position with the locknut and reconnect the wires to the appropriate terminals.
52 To adjust the switch, first note the positions of the wires attached to it and then remove them.
53 Slacken the switch locknut. Connect a lamp and battery to

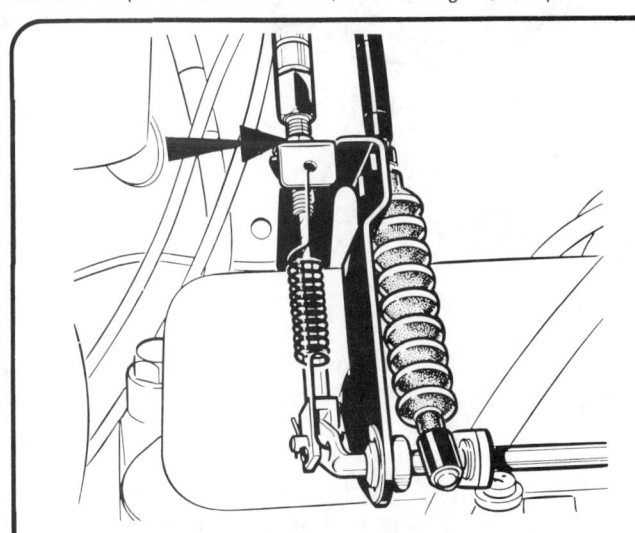

Fig. 13.9 Downshift valve cable adjustment

Fig. 13.10 Front band adjustment

Fig. 13.11 Rear band adjustment

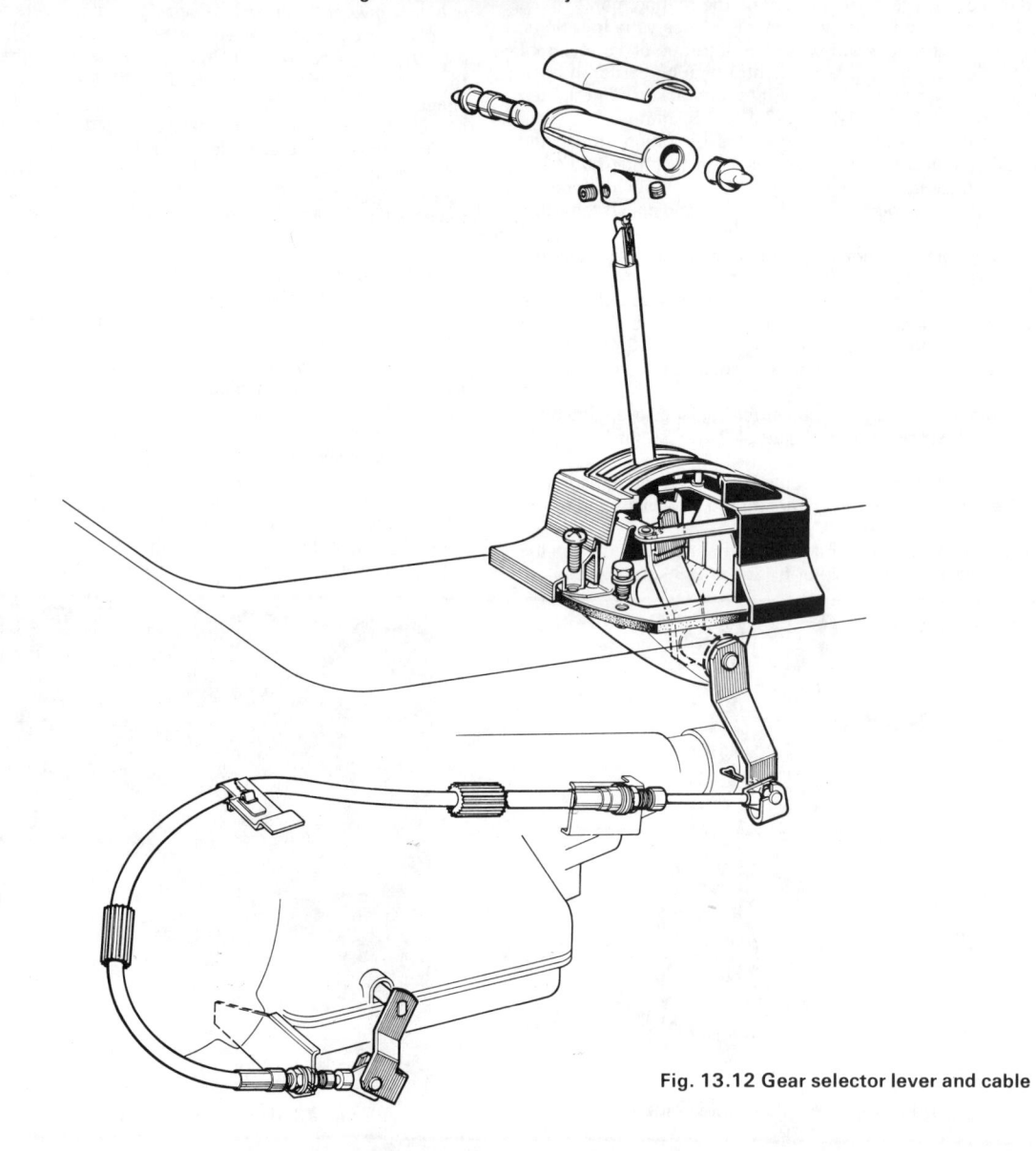

Fig. 13.12 Gear selector lever and cable

the smaller part of switch terminals (the starter inhibitor terminals) and another lamp and battery to the larger pair of switch terminal (the reversing light terminals).

54 Place the gear selector lever in position 'D', '2' or '1', then screw the switch in, or out, as necessary until a point is found where the reversing light goes from ON to OFF. Note this position and count the number of turns which the switch then has to be screwed in before the lamp across the starter inhibitor switch lights. Unscrew the switch half the number of turns which have just been counted and lock the switch in this position.

55 Remove the lamps and batteries, and reconnect the starter circuit and reversing light cables to the terminals from which they were removed.

Front brake band – adjustment

56 Remove the transmission drain plug and drain the fluid into a container of approximately two gallons capacity. If the vehicle is at normal operating temperature, take care to avoid being splashed by the fluid, which may be hot enough to cause skin burns.

57 Remove the fifteen screws and lockwashers securing the sump and remove the sump.

58 Slacken the adjusting screw locknut, move the servo lever outwards and place a 0.25 in gauge block or twist drill between the piston pin and the adjusting screw (Fig. 13.10).

59 Tighten the adjusting screw to 10 lbf in (0.14 kgf m) then tighten the locknut to 15 to 20 lbf ft (2.1 to 2.8 kgf m).

60 Remove the gauge block or twist drill.

61 Clean the mating surfaces of the oil pan and the transmission casing, and refit the pan using a new gasket. Refit the fifteen bolts and lockwashers, and tighten the bolts to a torque of 8 to 10 lbf ft (1.1 to 1.4 kgf m).

62 Refill the transmission to within $\frac{3}{8}$ in of the full mark on the dipstick (refer to filling instructions in paragraph 44).

63 Check for leaks, road-test and top-up the fluid again if necessary.

Rear brake band – adjustment

64 Slacken the adjusting screw locknut on the right-hand side of the gearbox case.

65 Tighten the adjusting screw to 10 lbf ft (1.4 kgf m) (Fig. 13.11) then slacken the adjusting screw one complete turn.

66 Hold the adjuster in this position and tighten the locknut to a torque of 30 to 40 lbf ft (4.2 to 5.5 kgf m).

Gear selector assembly – removal and refitting

67 Remove the socket-head screw from the front of the handle (Fig. 13.12), and pull the handle off.

68 Lift the lever escutcheon up and withdraw it over the selector lever handle.

69 Remove the three crosshead screws and lift off the base-plate.

70 Remove the bulb holder and the four bolts which secure the selector housing to the floor.

71 Jack-up the car and support it securely on stands, or position it over a pit, then remove the clevis pin to disconnect the selector cable from the selector lever.

72 From inside the car, remove the selector housing, lever assembly and attached cable.

73 Refitting the assembly is the reverse of these operations and it is then necessary to check the adjustment of the cable as described in the following paragraphs.

Selector cable – adjustment

74 Remove the clip and clevis pin securing the selector cable to the operating arm.

75 Put the selector lever in position '1' and pull the operating arm fully rearwards.

76 Adjust the cable length at the adjuster on the bracket, so that the clevis pin holes in the operating arm and the end of the cable are aligned. Tighten the locknut.

77 Grease the clevis pin, insert it and retain it with a washer and split cotter.

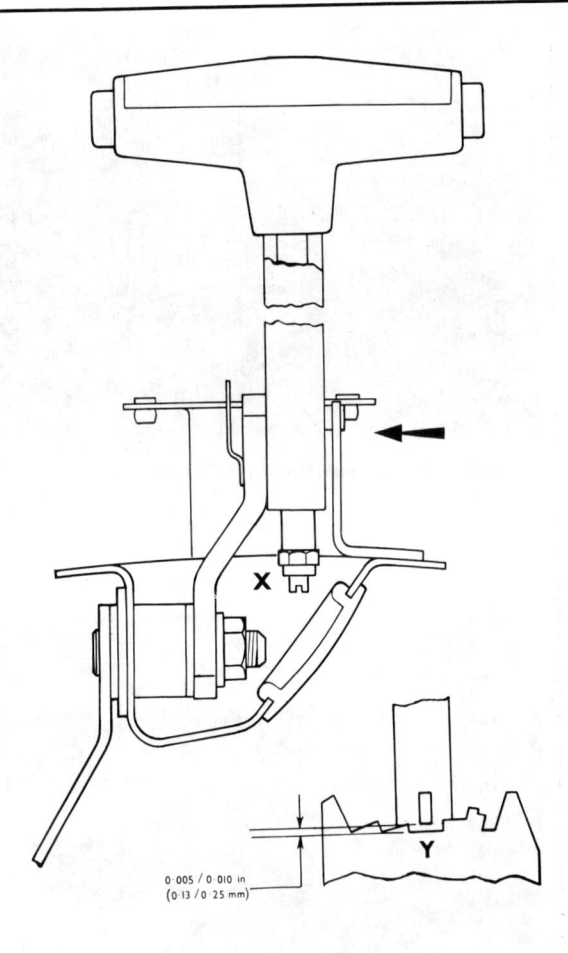

Fig. 13.13 Selector inhibitor cable adjustment

78 Check that the gear selector lever can be set into each gear position.

Selector cable – removal

79 Remove the clip and clevis pin to detach the cable from the base of the selector lever.

80 Free the cable from the abutment brackets (one on the body and one on the transmission), and from the cable clip (Fig. 13.12).

81 Fit the new cable and secure it at the two abutment brackets and the cable clip.

82 Line-up the upper end of the cable with the base of the selector lever, grease the clevis pin and assemble the clevis pin and clip. Ensure that the ends of the cable are symmetrical in the fork ends.

Selector inhibitor cable – renewal and adjustment

83 Remove the rubber grommet and fully release the locknut at the base of the selector lever.

84 Remove the locknut and remove the lever and operating arm from the housing.

85 Push the pivot pin from the top of the lever, remove the nylon bush, pawl and spring, and remove the cable.

86 Engage the top of the new cable in the lever and complete the assembly with the nylon bush, pivot pin, spring and pawl, before securing the locknut to the cable.

87 Position the arm, bushes and lever on the housing and secure with the locknut.

88 Adjust the cable at point X to give the clearance down at Y (See Fig. 13.13), and refit the rubber grommet.

Fig. 13.14 Removing the front indicator fixing screws

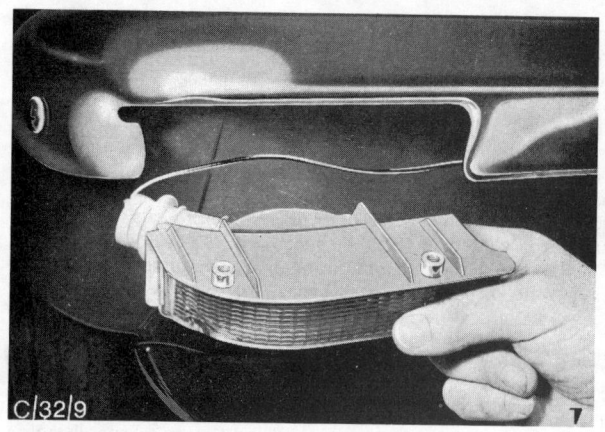

Fig. 13.15 Removing the front indicator

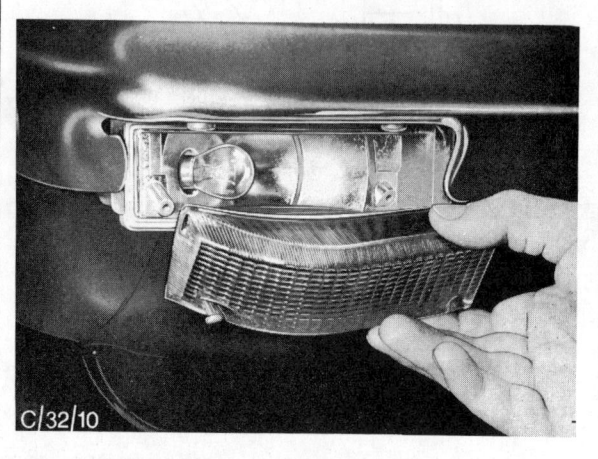

Fig. 13.16 Removing the flasher unit lens

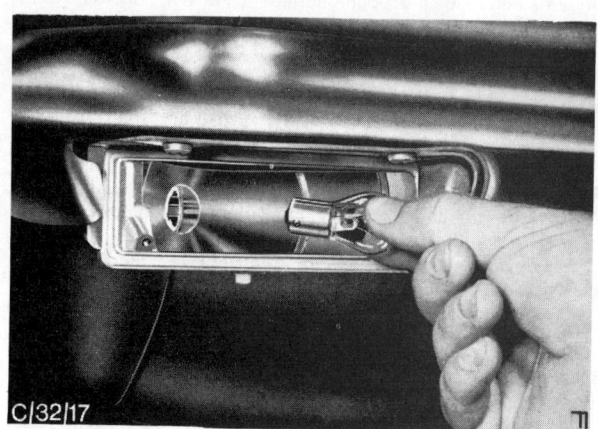

Fig. 13.17 Removing the flasher unit bulb

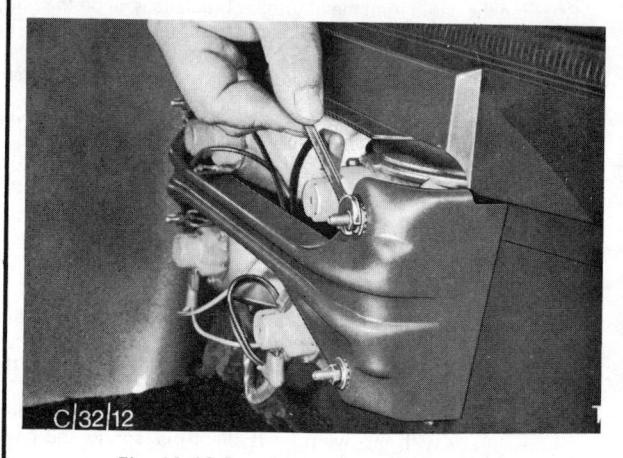

Fig. 13.18 Rear lamp cluster fixing nuts

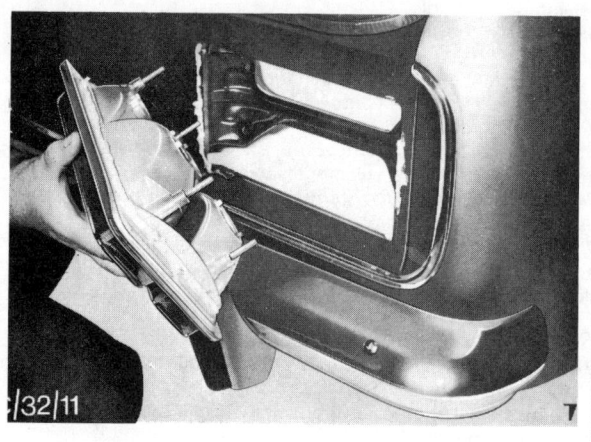

Fig. 13.19 Removing the rear lamp cluster assembly

Chapter 13/Supplement

8 Braking system

Handbrake – adjustment

1 The handbrake systems on all Ford cars have been designed to operate with a lever travel of up to 10 notches and while this amount of travel may seem excessive, it is necessary to achieve optimum performance with the ability of the rear brakes to be self-adjusting. The amount of handbrake travel must not be judged as a measure of handbrake performance and if the handbrake cable is too tight, it may cause the rear brakes to malfunction.

2 If a brake meter is available, check that the handbrake can produce a minimum retardation of 25% when the car with driver only is travelling on a flat dry road at approximately 30 mph (50 km/h). An alternative performance check is to see whether the handbrake will hold the car on a dry surface with a gradient of 1 in 6 with the driver only in the vehicle. If this level of performance cannot be achieved, the handbrake system must be investigated systematically until the fault is found.

9 Electrical system

Fuel level and water temperature gauges – checking

1 If the gauges are either inoperative or erratic first check that the battery-to-body earth connection is clean and tight. Check that the fuel tank sender and temperature unit sender connections are clean and secure, then recheck the gauge operation.

2 If the gauges are not operating, check the continuity of the circuit by removing the wire from the sender unit and connecting a bulb or voltmeter between the sender wire and earth. With the ignition switched on, there should be a 12V supply to the sender unit.

3 If the gauges operate, but their indications are suspect, connect a 10 ohm 5 watt resistor between the sender unit wire and earth. There are two calibration dots towards the upper end of the instrument scale and the pointer should be between these dots when the ignition is switched on. Repeat the test with a 73 ohm 5 watt resistor in place of the 10 ohm one, and check that the pointer is between the calibration dots at the lower end of the instrument scale.

Front indicator assembly (later type) – removal and refitting

4 Open the bonnet and disconnect the battery.
5 Remove the crosshead screw from the retaining clip above the headlamp; depress the clip, pull the headlamp forward gently and lift it out.
6 Disconnect the headlamp multi-plug and remove the rubber grommet.
7 Disengage and remove the bulb retaining spring, remove the side lamp, then remove the headlamp assembly.
8 In a similar manner, remove the second headlamp assembly then remove eight screws and detach the grille assembly.
9 Disconnect the indicator lamp feed wire, remove two screws securing the lamp to the bumper and detach the lamp assembly (Figs. 13.14 and 13.15).

Front indicator assembly (later type) – bulb renewal

10 Remove the two crosshead screws securing the lens, and detach the lens from the indicator assembly (Fig. 13.16)
11 Remove the bulb (Fig. 13.17) by pressing it in and then turning in an anti-clockwise direction to disengage it.
12 Refit a new bulb (28 watt) and check the operation of the flasher.
13 Refit the lens, ensuring that the gasket is properly seated to prevent entry of dirt and water.

Rear lamp cluster assembly – removal and refitting

14 Open the boot lid and remove the four retaining nuts and shroud from the lamp cluster.

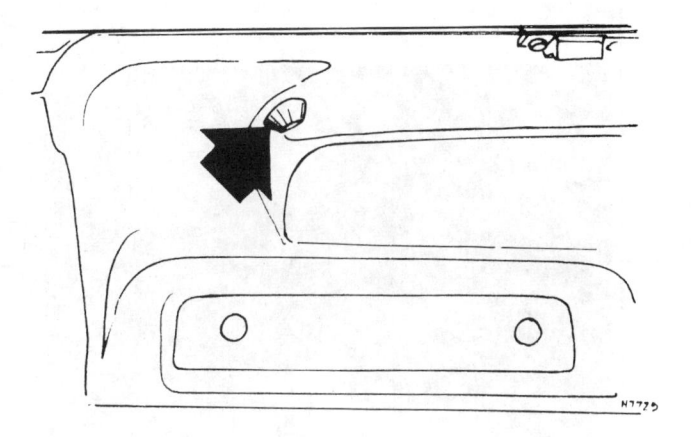

Fig. 13.20 Glove compartment light location

Fig. 13.21 Heated rear window warning light

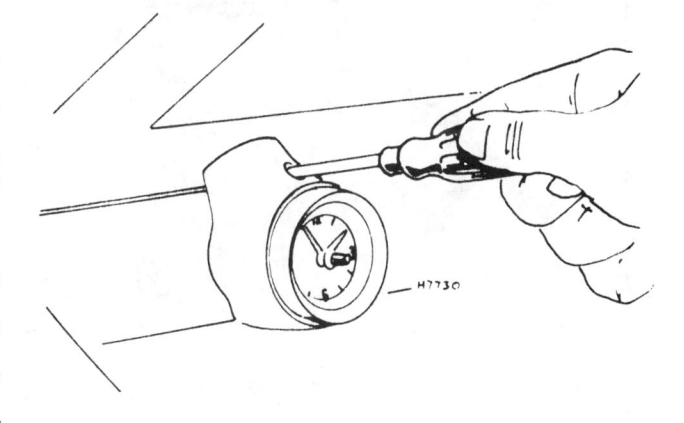

Fig. 13.22 Removing the clock

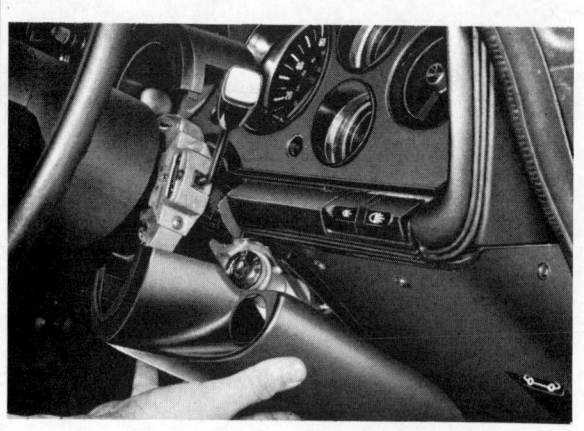

Fig. 13.23 Removing the steering column shroud

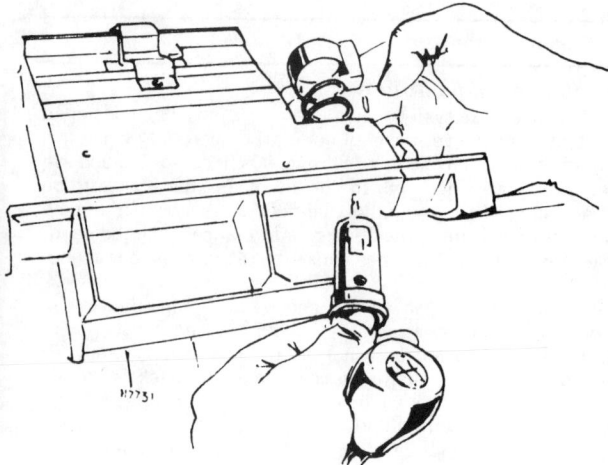

Fig. 13.24 Removing the cigarette lighter

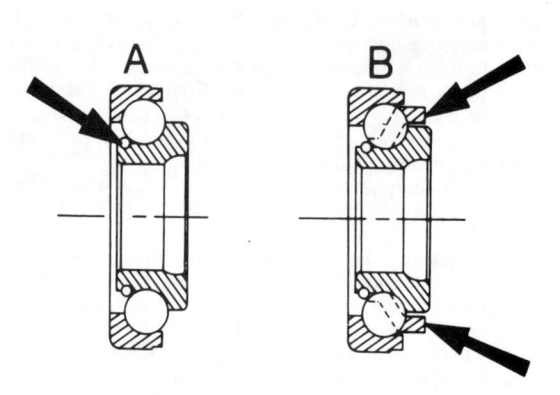

Fig. 13.26 Pinion lower bearing

A Uncaged 14 balls – retaining ring arrowed
B Caged 11 balls – cage arrowed

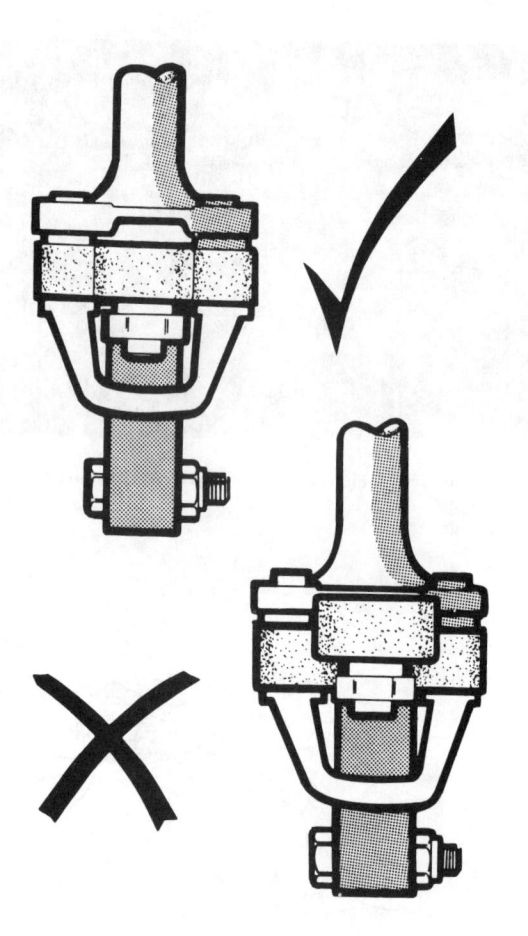

Fig. 13.25 Correct and incorrect fitting of flexible coupling

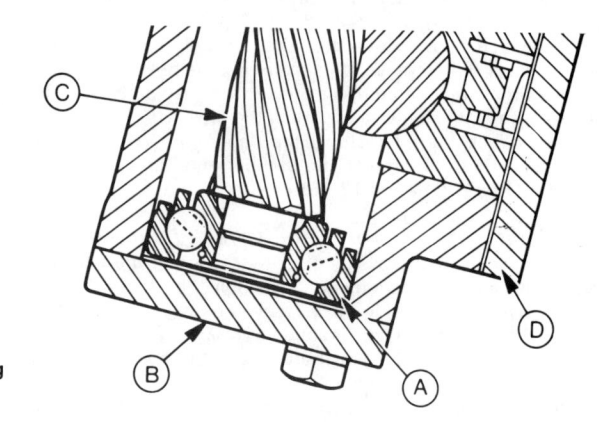

Fig. 13.27 Correct installation of pinion lower bearing

A Pinion lower bearing   C Pinion
B Pinion cover-plate   D Preload cover-plate

Chapter 13/Supplement

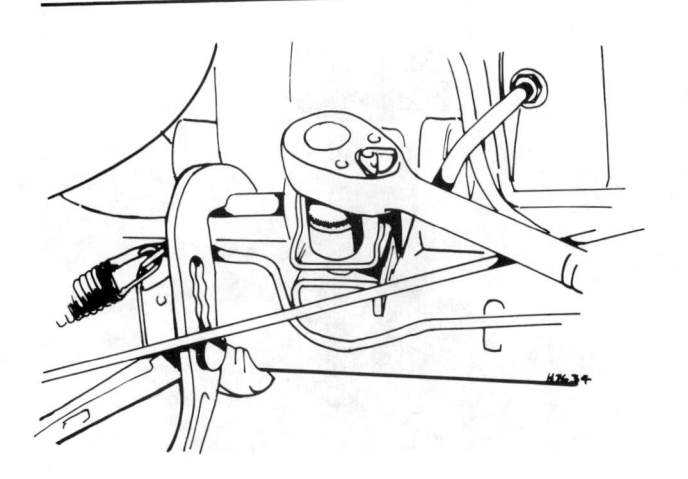

Fig. 13.28 Removing the anti-roll bar pre-load

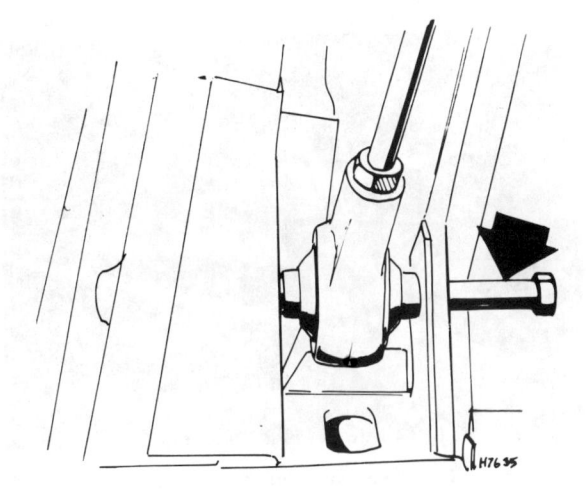

Fig. 13.29 Fitting the end bolts

15 Remove the bulb holders and bulbs.
16 Remove four nuts and washers (Fig. 13.18) and pull the assembly clear of its retaining bracket (Fig. 13.19).
17 Before refitting, apply sealer around the lamp assembly.
18 Locate the assembly so that its screwed fixings engage the holes in the fixing bracket and secure it with the four nuts and washers.
19 Push the four bulb holders into their places in the lens and check the lights to ensure that the various bulbs are in their correct places.
20 Refit the shroud and secure it with four nuts, then close the boot lid.

Glove compartment lamp – bulb renewal
21 Open the bonnet and disconnect the battery.
22 Pull the lens assembly from its location at the top left hand side of the glove box (Fig. 13.20).
23 Disconnect the lead, detach the bulb and holder, and remove the bulb.
24 Insert a new bulb into the holder and locate the holder in the lens.
25 Reconnect the leads and push the assembly back into the aperture.
26 Reconnect the battery and close the bonnet.

Heated rear window warning light – bulb renewal
27 Open the bonnet and disconnect the battery.
28 Pull the switch assembly from its location in the facia panel (Fig. 13.21), disconnect the multiplug and remove the bulb.
29 Fit a new bulb and reverse the previous operations.

Clock – removal and refitting
30 Open the bonnet and disconnect the battery.
31 Remove one screw (Fig. 13.22) and slide the clock from its location below the ashtray.
32 Disconnect three wires from the loom, then remove the clock from its surround.
33 Refitting is a direct reversal of removal operations.

Cigarette lighter assembly – removal and refitting
34 Open the bonnet and disconnect the battery.
35 Remove two screws and detach the lower part of the steering column shroud (Fig. 13.23).
36 Remove eight screws from the lower dash panel and after easing it over the ignition switch, allow it to swing down.
37 Disconnect the wires from the loom
38 Push the cigarette lighter outer collar against the spring, and turn it until the cut-outs in the collar align with the retaining lugs on the lighter body. Allow the collar to slide over and

remove with the spring (Fig. 13.24).
39 Refitting is a direct reversal of the removal operations.

10 Suspension and steering

Steering coupling – alignment
1 If when removing the steering column (Chapter 11, Section 13) the rubber coupling is disturbed, or if new rubbers are fitted, it is important that the segmented rubber couplings are aligned correctly. Fig. 13.25. shows the correct and incorrect fitting of the rubber segments.

Intermittently stiff steering
2 If the above condition is experienced, a check should be made to ensure that the tyres are of the correct specification and inflation pressure, the front suspension ball joints are not worn excessively and that the MachPherson strut upper mountings are in good condition and tightened to the recommended torque.
3 Should none of the foregoing be abnormal, it is possible that the problem may be due to the crowding of the balls in the steering gear. Chapter 11 Section 12 refers to the older type of bearing with tracks and 14 loose balls and these bearings may give intermittently stiff steering through crowding of the balls. If this is the case a bearing cage (Part No. 76EB-3L538-AA) should be purchased and 11 of the original 14 balls fitted to it as described in paragraphs 4 to 7 following.
4 Carefully remove the retaining ring from the uncaged bearing (A in Fig. 13.26), and dismantle the bearing ensuring that the 14 balls are collected in a clean container.
5 Reassemble the pinion lower bearing, using the bearing cage (Part No. 76EB-3L 538-AA) and only 11 balls, as in B of the figure.
6 Refit the bearing in the pinion housing, ensuring that it is fitted correctly (fig. 13.27). Fit the shims, gasket, cover-plate and bolts, then tighten the cover-plate bolts to a torque of 13 to 18 lbf ft (1.7 to 2.4 kgf m).
7 Pour SAE90 EP oil through the rack preload cover-plate aperture, until the rack is full, (total rack capacity is 0.25 pints), then fit the cover-plate and tighten the bolts to a torque of 13 to 18 lbf ft (1.7 to 2.4 kgf m).

Rear anti-roll bar – removal and refitting
8 Later models of Capri I have an anti-roll bar incorporated in the rear suspension in place of radius arms, and this necessitates modification of the instructions given in Chapter 8 Section 3.
9 Remove the parking brake cable from the lever and with-

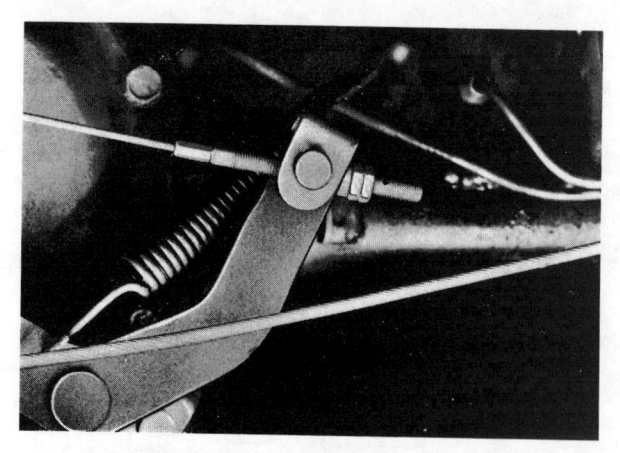

Fig. 13.30 Brake lever adjusted just clear of stop

Fig. 13.31 Removing and inserting the bushes

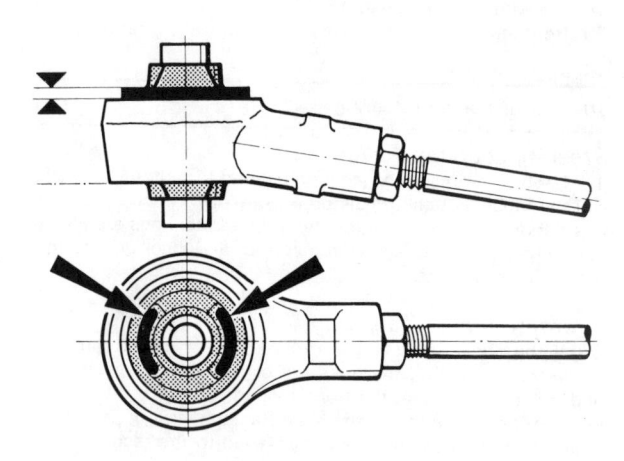

Fig. 13.32 Correct position of bush in end-piece

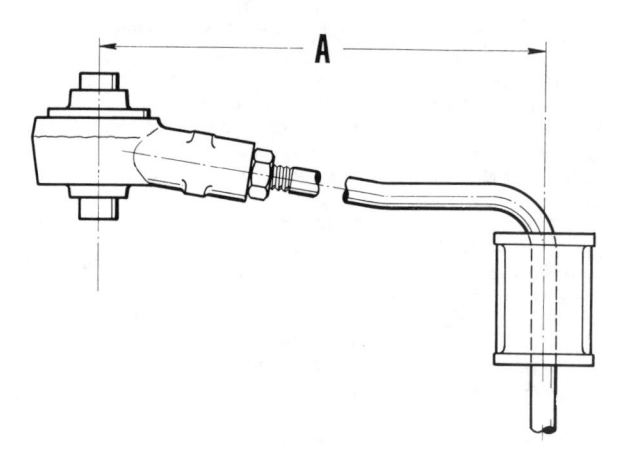

Fig. 13.33 Setting for end-pieces on bar

A = 10.25 in ± 0.1 in (262 mm ± 2.5 mm)

draw it.
10 Pull the anti-roll bar rearwards using a suitable tool (Fig. 13.28) in order to remove the preload from the bolts, then remove both anti-roll bar brackets from the rear axle.
11 Disconnect the anti-roll bar from the floor assembly and lift it clear.
12 When refitting the anti-roll bar, fit the mounting bolts from the inside, towards the outside (Fig. 13.29). Fit the washers and self-locking nuts, but do not tighten them at this stage.
13 Press the anti-roll bar against the bracket supports, using a suitable tool, then fit the brackets and bolt; tighten the bolts to a torque of 30 to 36 lbf ft (4.0 to 5.0 kgf m). If the anti-roll bar end pieces have been loosened, tighten their locknuts to a torque of 25 to 30 lbf ft (3.5 to 4.0 kgf m).
14 Attach the handbrake cable to the lever and adjust the nut so that the lever just clears the stop (Fig. 13.30).
15 Tighten the self-locking nuts of the front mountings of the anti-roll bar with the weight of the vehicle resting on the wheels. The correct torque is 33 to 36 lbf ft (4.5 to 5.0 kgf m).

Anti-roll bar rubber bushes – renewal
16 Remove the anti-roll bar as described in the previous paragraphs. Slacken the locknuts, then unscrew and remove the anti-roll bar end-pieces.
17 Remove the old bushes by pressing them out using suitable sized sockets, or pieces of tubing (Fig. 13.31).
18 Smear the outer surface of the new bushes with glycerine and press them into the anti-roll bar ends, chamfered ends of the bushes first. The two semi-circular recesses in the rubber bush should be positioned as in Fig. 13.32.
19 Screw the ends on to the anti-roll bar, to obtain dimension A in Fig. 13.33 and ensure that the difference in the dimension between the two ends does not exceed 0.1 in (2.5 mm).

11 Bodywork and underframe

Sliding roof guide rail assembly – removal and refitting
1 Open the roof fully and remove the four self-tapping outer screws and the two standard-thread inner screws from the front cable cover section (Fig. 13.34).
2 Prise out the two clips locating the cable in the winder mechanism gear (Fig. 13.35).
3 Remove three guide rail cover screws from each side and prise out the guide rails from both sides.
4 Using the services of an assistant to avoid possible damage to the roof, slide the roof forward along the guide rails until it is almost in the fully closed position, then lift the guide rails up and remove the assembly (Fig. 13.36).

Chapter 13/Supplement

5 When refitting, slide the assembly back into position, ensuring that the rear guide rail pegs locate in the hole in the rear body member. Push the roof into the open position.
6 Position and secure the two side guide rail cover sections.
7 Locate the cables in the front channels and position the two clips which locate the cables into the winder mechanism. Ensure that when positioning the clips, the first clip locates between the cable and the channel, and the second clip goes over the whole assembly.
8 Position and secure the front cable cover section.
9 Check the operation and close the roof. If necessary, adjust the winder mechanism as described later in this Section.

Sliding roof outer panel – removal and refitting

10 Open the sliding roof half-way. Unclip the roof panel from the front and then fully close the roof, leaving the trim panel in the half-closed position. From inside the vehicle, then slide the trim panel into its rearmost position.
11 Detach the two front roof-to-guide rail mounting slides, after removing the two bolts from each side.
12 Swing the spring arms (Fig. 13.37) clear of the rear roof fixings, remove the two bolts securing the rear mounting brackets to the roof panel and pull off the lock-plate. When all the bolts have been removed, lift the roof panel off.
13 When refitting, first place the sliding panel back into position on the roof. Place the rear mounting bracket lock-plates into position and secure the mountings to the roof panel. Reposition the spring arms into their proper positions.
14 Position the front roof-to-guide rail mounting slide and secure it loosely (Fig. 13.38).
15 With the roof panel in the closed position, adjust the front mounting slide to give the correct roof panel height, then tighten the front mountings fully.
16 Loosen the rear adjusting clamps and raise or lower the roof to give the correct adjustment, then fully tighten the clamp bolts of both sides.
17 Open the roof fully and test the operation of the mechanism; then, with clean hands and after opening the roof panel partially, slide the trim panel in from the front, ensuring that the front guide rail does not tear the material. Locate the trim and position it under the front guide rail mounting slide, then clip the trim panel into position.

Sliding roof winder mechanism – removal, refitting and adjusting

18 From inside the vehicle, and with the sliding roof closed, remove one screw and remove the winder handle.
19 Remove two screws and lift out the winder mechanism assembly (Fig. 13.39).
20 When refitting, ensure that the roof is in the fully closed position.
21 Wind back the winder gear mechanism until it abuts the

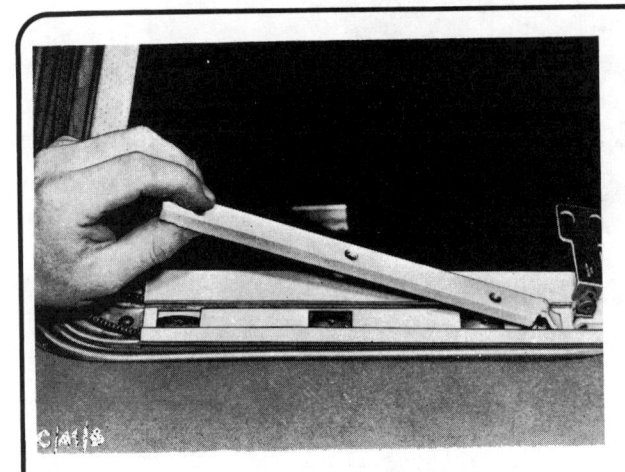

Fig. 13.34 Removing the winder cover

Fig. 13.35 Removing a cable clip

Fig. 13.36 Removing the guide rail assembly

Fig. 13.37 Normal position of the spring arms

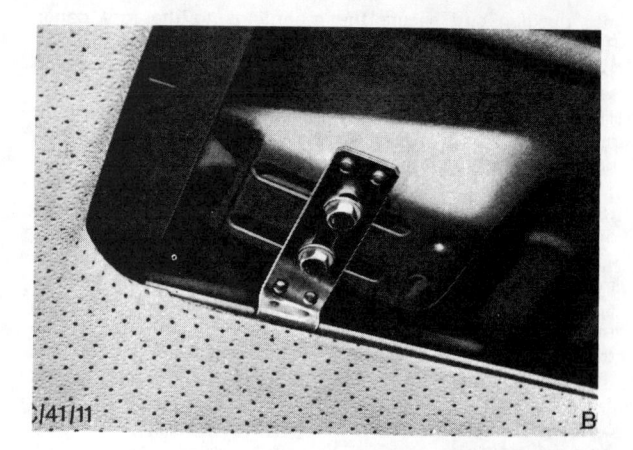

Fig. 13.38 Attachment of roof guide rail

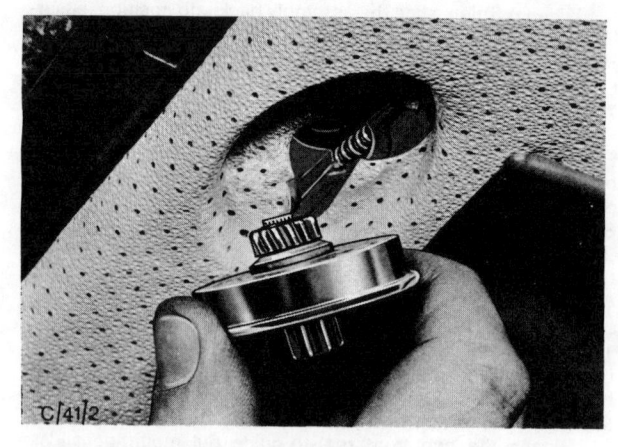

Fig. 13.39 Removing the sliding roof winder mechanism

Fig. 13.40 Removing the glove compartment lock

lock-stop within the mechanism, then refit the mechanism and secure it with two screws.
22 Refit the winder handle and insert the screw to secure the handle.

Glove compartment lock – removal and refitting
23 Open the glove compartment lid. Remove the two crosshead screws from the backplate and withdraw the lock (Fig. 13.40).
24 When refitting, position the two parts of the lock, insert the fixing screws and partially tighten them.
25 Check the operation of the lock, adjusting if necessary, then fully tighten the screws.

Centre console – removal and refitting
26 Remove the clock, as described in Section 9.
27 Lever out the front package tray, centre cover section and handbrake surround, from the console top.
28 Unscrew the gear lever knob and locking nut.
29 Unscrew two screws located under the front package tray, two screws from the console centre, and three screws and washers from the glovebox section; lift out the centre console assembly.
30 Remove six screws retaining the finish panel to the underside of the arm rest. Remove three screws retaining the hinge assembly to the console glove compartment wall, and lift the hinge assembly clear.
31 Turn the assembly over, prise out four clips and detach the gear lever gaiter.
32 Prise out the glovebox lid catch.
33 When refitting, the order of removal operations is reversed.

Door windows – adjustment
34 If the door windows cannot be fully closed, remove the window regulator (Chapter 12, Section 19) and check to see which tooth on the quadrant gear has been bent over to act as a stop.
35 If it is the fourth tooth, as on early models, straighten this tooth and with a small hacksaw make a $\frac{1}{4}$ inch deep cut between the second and third teeth. Bend over the third tooth to act as a stop and reinsert the window regulator.

Index

A

Air cleaners
  removal, replacement and servicing – 54
Alternator
  brushes – dismantling and inspection – 136
  general description – 134
  removal and replacement – 136
  routine maintenance – 136
  special procedures – 136
Anti-freeze mixture – 52
Automatic transmission
  downshift cable – adjustment – 187
  front brake band – adjustment – 189
  gear selector assembly – removal and refitting – 189
  general description – 186
  rear brake band – adjustment – 189
  removal and refitting – 186
  routine maintenance – 186
  selector cable – adjustment – 189
  selector cable – removal – 189
  selector inhibitor cable – renewal and adjustment – 189
  special precautions – 186
  starter inhibitor switch – renewal and adjustment – 187
  specifications – 182

B

Battery
  charging – 130
  electrolyte replenishment – 130
  maintenance and inspection – 130
  removal and replacement – 130
Big-end and main bearings
  examination and renovation – 32
Body repairs
  major – 172
  minor – 172
  repair sequence (colour) – 174/175
Bodywork and underframe
  centre console – removal and refitting – 196
  door windows – adjustment – 196
  general description – 171
  glove compartment lock – removal and refitting – 196
  maintenance – 171
  sliding roof guide rail assembly – 194
  sliding roof outer panel – 195
  sliding roof winder mechanism – 195
Bonnet
  removal and replacement – 177
Boot lid
  removal and replacement – 177
Bumper
  front – removal and replacement – 172
  rear – removal and replacement – 172
Braking system
  bleeding the hydraulic system – 111
  brake caliper – removal, dismantling and reassembly – 120
  brake disc – removal and replacement – 120
  brake master cylinder – dismantling and reassembly – 116
  brake master cylinder – removal and replacement – 116
  disc brake friction pads – inspection, removal and replacement – 120
  dual – general description – 120
  dual – pressure differential warning actuator – centralisation – 120
  dual – pressure differential warning actuator – dismantling, examination and reassembly – 122
  fault finding chart – 126
  flexible hoses – inspection, removal and replacement – 114
  general description – 111
  handbrake – adjustment – 191
  handbrake, linkage – adjustment – 116
  maintenance – 111
  pedals – removal and replacement – 116
  rear brake seals – inspection and overhaul – 114
  rear brake shoes inspection – removal and replacement – 114
  rear wheel cylinders – removal and replacement – 114
  specifications – 110
  tandem master cylinder – dismantling, examination and reassembly – 122
  vacuum servo unit – dismantling, examination and reassembly – 124
  vacuum servo unit – removal and replacement – 124

C

Camshaft
  removal – 26
Camshaft and camshaft bearings
  examination and renovation – 33
Carburettor
  dismantling and reassembly – general – 59
  general description – 58
  routine servicing – 56
Carburettor – Ford single choke
  accelerator pump adjustment – 62
  automatic choke adjustment – 62
  choke and fast idling adjustment – 62
  dismantling and reassembly – 59
  fuel level setting – 62
  idling adjustment – 62
  removal and replacement – 58
Carburettor – Weber twin choke

Index

choke adjustment – 68
dismantling and reassembly – 64
fuel level setting – 68
removal and replacement – 58
slow running adjustment – 68
Clutch and actuating mechanism
general description – 82
routine maintenance – 82
specifications – 82
Clutch
adjustment – 82
cable – removal and replacement – 84
dismantling and replacement – 84
faults – 86
inspection – 84
judder – diagnosis and cure – 86
pedal – removal and replacement – 84
release bearing – removal and replacement – 84
removal – 84
replacement – 84
slip – diagnosis and cure – 86
spin – diagnosis and cure – 86
squeal – diagnosis and cure – 86
Condenser
removal, testing and replacement – 74
Connecting rods
examination and renovation – 34
Contact breaker
adjustment – 74
points – removing and replacing – 74
Control box
general description – 138
Cooling system
draining – 48
fault finding chart – 52
filling – 48
flushing – 48
general description – 46
prevention of engine overheating – 184
routine maintenance – 48
specifications – 46
Crankshaft
examination and renovation – 32
Current regulator
adjustment – 142
Cut-out
adjustment – 142
Cut-out and regulator contacts
maintenance – 138
Cylinder bores
examination and renovation – 33
Cylinder head removal
engine in car – 26
engine on bench – 24

D

Decarbonisation – 34
Distributor
dismantling – 76
inspection and repair – 76
lubrication – 76
reassembly – 76
refitting – 78
removal – 76
Door
glass – removal and replacement – 177
lock assembly – removal and replacement – 173
lock interior remote control handle – removal and replacement – 177
outer belt weatherstrip – removal and replacement – 177
rattles – tracing and rectification – 173

striker plate – removal, replacement and adjustment – 173
trim panel – removal and replacement – 173
window adjustment – 196
Dynamo
dismantling and inspection – 131
removal and replacement – 131
repair and reassembly – 134
routine maintenance – 131
testing in position – 131

E

Electrical system
clock – removal and refitting – 193
cigarette lighter assembly – removal and refitting – 193
direction indicator, headlamp flasher and horn switch assembly – removal and refitting – 148
fault finding chart – 155
front indicator lamp glass and bulb – removal and replacement – 148
front indicator assembly (later type) – removal and refitting – 191
front indicator assembly (later type) – bulb renewal – 191
fuel level and water temperature gauges - checking – 191
general description – 129
glove compartment lamp – bulb renewal – 193
heated rear window warning light – bulb renewal – 193
instrument panel and instruments – removal and replacement – 148
instrument voltage regulator – removal and replacement – 148
interior light – removal and replacement – 148
light panel light and windscreen wiper switches – removal and replacement – 148
rear indicator, stop and tail bulb – removal and replacement – 148
rear lamp cluster assembly – removal and replacement – 191
rear licence plate lamp – removal and replacement – 148
specifications – 128
wiring diagrams – 151—154
Engine
assembling – 36
dismantling – general – 22
examination and renovation – general – 32
flywheel and ring gear – 183
fault finding chart – 45
final assembly – 44
front mounting – removal and replacement – 32
general description – 18
major operations with engine in place – 19
major operations with engine removed – 19
oil pump and oil filter – 183
oversize components – 182
methods of removal – 19
reassembly – general – 36
removal with gearbox – 22
removal without gearbox – 19
removing ancillary components – 24
replacement – general – 44
replacement with gearbox – 44
replacement without gearbox – 19
routine maintenance – 18
specifications – 14, 181
timing chain – 182
valves – 182
Exhaust system
description, removal and replacement – 68

F

Fan belt

Index

adjustment – 50
removal and replacement – 50
Flasher circuit
fault tracing and rectification – 142
Flywheel
removal – 30
starter ring – examination and renovation – 34
Front coil spring
removal and replacement – 162
Front hub
bearings – maintenance , removal and replacement – 160
bearings – adjustment – 160
removal and replacement – 160
Front suspension units
removal and replacement – 160
Fuel gauge and sender unit
fault finding – 70
removal and replacement – 58
Fuel pump (AC)
description – 56
dismantling – 56
examination and reassembly – 56
removal and replacement – 56
routine servicing – 56
testing – 56
Fuel system
automatic choke adjustment – revised procedure – 185
choke and fast idling adjustments – 184
safety precautions when handling fuel – 184
Fuel system and carburation
fault finding – 70, 71
general description – 54
lack of fuel at engine – 70
rich mixture – 70
specifications – 53
weak mixture – 70
Fuel tank
cleaning – 58
removal and replacement – 58
Fuse block
removal and replacement – 142

G

Gearbox
dismantling – 90
examination and renovation – 94
fault finding chart – 101
general description – 88
input shaft – dismantling and reassembly – 94
mainshaft – dismantling and reassembly – 94
reassembly – 96
removal and replacement – 90
routine maintenance – 90
selective circlips – 96
specifications – 88
Gudgeon pin
removal – 30

H

Headlamp
alignment – 144
Headlamp and sidelamp unit
removal and replacement – 144
Heater
assembly – removal and replacement – 180
control cables – adjustment – 180
motor – removal and replacement – 180
radiator – removal and replacement – 180
Hinges and locks

maintenance – 172
Horn
fault tracing and rectification – 144

I

Ignition system
engine tuning for low grade fuels – 185
fault finding – 79
general description – 74
specifications – 72
Ignition timing – 78

L

Lubrication and crankshaft ventilating systems
description – 30

M

Main bearing and crankshaft
removal – 30

O

Oil filter
removal and replacement – 32
Oil pump
overhaul – 32

P

Pistons, connecting rods and big-ends
removal – 30
Pistons and piston rings
examination and renovation – 33
Piston ring
removal – 30
Propeller shaft and universal joints
general description – 102
Propeller shaft – one piece
removal and replacement – 102
universal joints – dismantling – 102
universal joints – inspection and repair – 102
universal joints – reassembly – 104
Propeller shaft – two piece
centre bearing – removal and replacement – 104
removal and replacement – 104

R

Radiator
removal, inspection, cleaning and replacement – 48
Radius arms
removal and replacement – 166
Rear axle
differential carrier – removal and replacement – 108
general description – 106
half shaft combined bearing and oil seal – removal and replacement – 108
half shafts – removal and replacement – 108
removal and replacement – 108
routine maintenance – 106
specifications – 106
Rocker assembly
dismantling – 26
Rockers and rocker shaft

Index

examination and renovation – 34

S

Shock absorbers – rear
removal and replacement – 166
Spark plug chart (colour) – 81
Sparking plugs and leads – 78
Springs – rear
removal and replacement – 166
Starter motor
dismantling and reassembly – 140
drive – general description – 140
drive – removal and replacement – 138
end face commutator – dismantling and reassembly – 138
inertia type – general description – 136
pre-engaged type – general description – 138
pre-engaged type – removal and replacement – 138
removal and replacement – 140
testing on engine – 140
Steering gear (rack and pinion)
adjustments – 164
coupling – alignment – 193
dismantling and reassembly – 164
intermittently stiff steering – 193
removal and replacement – 162
routine maintenance – 160
Steering wheel and column
removal and replacement – 166
Sump
removal – 26
Suspension – dampers – steering
anti-roll bar rubber bushes – removal and refitting – 194
fault finding chart – 170
general description – 159
rear anti-roll bar – removal and refitting – 193
rear springs – removal and refitting – 166
rear springs – routine maintenance – 160
specifications – 158

T

Tappets
examination and renovation – 34
Temperature gauge and sender unit
removal and replacement – 50

Temperature gauge
fault finding – 50
Thermostat
removal, testing and replacement – 48
Timing chain tensioner – 30
Timing cover, gearwheel and chain
removal – 26
Timing gear and chain
examination and renovation – 34
Torsion bar
removal and replacement – 162
Tyre pressures – 159

U

Upholstery and carpets
maintenance – 172

V

Valve
removal – 26
Valve guides
examination and renovation – 36
Valves and valve seats
examination and renovation – 33
Voltage regulator
adjustment – 138

W

Water pump
dismantling and reassembly – 50
removal and replacement – 50
Window regulator
removal and replacement – 180
Windscreen glass
removal and replacement – 172
Windscreen wiper
arms – removal and replacement – 142
blades – removal and replacement – 142
mechanism – fault diagnosis and rectification – 144
mechanism – maintenance – 142
motor and linkage – removal and replacement – 144
motor – dismantling, inspection and reassembly – 144

**Printed by
Haynes Publishing Group
Sparkford Yeovil Somerset
England**